SECOND EDITION

VOICES AND VALUES

A READER FOR WRITERS

SECOND EDITION

VOICES AND VALUES

A READER FOR WRITERS

JANET M. GOLDSTEIN • JOHN LANGAN

Books in the Townsend Press Reading Series
Groundwork for College Reading with Phonics
Groundwork for College Reading
Ten Steps to Building College Reading Skills
Ten Steps to Improving College Reading Skills
Ten Steps to Advancing College Reading Skills
Ten Steps to Advanced Reading

Books in the Townsend Press Vocabulary Series
Vocabulary Basics
Groundwork for a Better Vocabulary
Building Vocabulary Skills
Building Vocabulary Skills, Short Version
Improving Vocabulary Skills
Improving Vocabulary Skills, Short Version
Advancing Vocabulary Skills
Advancing Vocabulary Skills, Short Version
Advanced Word Power

Other Reading and Writing Books
The Reading-Writing Connection
The Advanced Reading-Writing Connection
English Essentials

Supplements Available for Most Books
Instructor's Edition
Instructor's Manual and Test Bank
Online Exercises

Copyright © 2015 by Townsend Press, Inc.
Printed in the United States of America
9 8 7 6 5 4 3 2 1

Cover design: Akisia Grigsby

ISBN-13 (Student Edition): 978-1-59194-443-0
ISBN-13 (Instructor's Edition): 978-1-59194-444-7

Send book orders and requests for desk copies or supplements to:

Townsend Press Book Center
439 Kelley Drive
West Berlin, New Jersey 08091

For even faster service, contact us in any of the following ways:

By telephone: 1-800-772-6410
By fax: 1-800-225-8894
By e-mail: cs@townsendpress.com
Through our website: www.townsendpress.com

Contents

Unit Four: Educating Ourselves   275

Unit Five: Examining Social Issues   355

Unit Six: Writing a Research Paper with Sources   435

Alternate Table of Contents

Narration

Description

Examples

Process

Definition

Division and Classification

Comparison and Contrast

Cause and Effect

Argumentation and Persuasion

Preface: To the Instructor

How often have you, as a reading or writing teacher, asked yourself questions such as these:

- Why must I spend so much time looking for timely selections that students will *want* to read?
- Where can I find a book of essays that also helps me teach the reading and writing skills my students need to know?
- Is there a reader out there devoted to old-fashioned human values—ones that can inspire and motivate even today's students?

If you've asked any of the above questions, *Voices and Values* may be the book for you. Suitable for reading and/or writing classes, the book provides a series of forty lively and thought-provoking essays that will compel student attention. Each selection is accompanied by a set of activities to help students read, understand, and write about the essay. By providing instruction and practice in the skills necessary for close and thoughtful reading, the text will help all those teachers whose students say, "I read it, but I didn't understand it." And by providing a wide number and range of writing assignments, as well as help with getting started on these assignments, the text will help all those teachers whose students say, "I don't know what to write about."

Distinguishing Features of the Book

Readings that celebrate human values. The book contains forty essays chosen for their celebration of significant human values. For example, in the first selection, "The Blind Vet," an author describes the despair and helplessness felt by an injured veteran and the steps he took to regain his independence. The story becomes an argument for the importance of perseverance—never giving up despite the odds—and the need for love and compassion. Other essays—in a style that never preaches—cover such values as gratitude, personal growth, fairness, responsibility, kindness, courage, common sense, and moderation.

Emphasis on clear thinking.   A basic truth that is at the heart of both the reading and the writing process is that any thoughtful communication of ideas has two basic parts: (1) a point is made and (2) that point is supported. As they work their way through this book, students learn to apply this principle of point and support. They are encouraged when *reading* an essay to look for a central idea as well as for the reasons, examples, facts, and details that support that idea. They are reminded when *writing* to follow the same basic principle—to make a point and then provide support for that point. And they discover that clear *thinking* (which they also do when actively reading or writing) involves both recognizing ideas and deciding whether there is solid support for those ideas.

Frequent skills practice.   Accompanying the high-interest selections is a series of high-quality activities that truly help students improve their reading, thinking, and writing. As we have already stated, the book assumes that reading and writing are interrelated skills. Work on reading can improve writing; work on writing can improve reading. Extensive practice in reading, thinking, and writing follows each of the forty selections. Here is the sequence of activities—prepared by two authors who have themselves been teachers—for each essay:

- *First Impressions* Following each reading is a freewriting activity titled "First Impressions" that encourages students to come to terms with what they have read. The activity consists of three questions that permit students to respond on different levels of feeling and opinion. For example, the first question is always "Did you enjoy reading this selection? Why or why not?" The two other questions focus on particular issues raised by the essay—issues about which every student should have something to say. Students can respond to one or all of these questions at the beginning of a class session; or, alternatively, students can record their responses in a "reading journal."

    The "First Impressions" activity provides at least two additional benefits. First, it lays the groundwork for oral participation; many more students can contribute intelligently to classroom discussion after they have collected their thoughts on paper in advance. Second, as an integral step in the writing process, freewriting or journal keeping can supply students with raw material for one or more of the paragraph and essay assignments that follow the selections.

- *Words to Watch* and *Vocabulary Check* Students need to strengthen their vocabularies in order to succeed in school—and they know it. *Voices and Values* builds vocabulary in the most research-proven and interesting way, by providing hundreds of useful words in context. The most challenging words and phrases in each selection are defined in the "Words to Watch" section that precedes each reading, and several additional words from the reading that may be unfamiliar to students are tested in the "Vocabulary Check" activity that follows each reading. Students thus have frequent opportunities to sharpen their skill at deriving meaning from context.

- *Reading Check* Practice in reading skills is provided through an activity titled "Reading Check," a series of comprehension questions that follow the Vocabulary Check. The questions involve four key skills: finding the central point and main ideas, recognizing key supporting details, making inferences, and understanding the writer's craft. The craft questions include such elements as introduction and conclusion strategies; types of support; patterns of organization and the transitions that indicate these patterns; tone; purpose; intended audience; and titles. As students sharpen these crucial reading skills, they will become better, more insightful readers—and they will be ready to use the same techniques in their own writing.

- *Discussion Questions* Four discussion questions follow the Reading Check. These questions provide a final chance for students to deepen their understanding of an essay and the issues and values that it contains. They also function as a helpful intermediate step between reading a selection and writing about it. If the instructor chooses, these discussion questions can serve as additional writing topics.

- *Paragraph Assignments* and *Essay Assignments* Four writing topics—two paragraph assignments and two essay assignments—conclude the activities for each selection. In each pair of assignments, the first one will be a first-person assignment allowing students to write about personal experiences; the second will be a third-person assignment, possibly involving some Internet research. The assignments emphasize the basic principle of clear communication: that a student make a point and support that point. Numerous sample topic sentences and thesis statements, along with specific suggestions for supporting these points, help students to succeed on these assignments. Fifteen additional topics on pages 449–454 invite students to read pairs of essays and write papers inspired by both.

Versatility. Since it is "a reader for writers," *Voices and Values* can be used in a number of teaching and learning situations:
- As a reader in a writing course covering paragraphs, essays, or both
- As an anthology in an English course studying the essay as a *genre*
- As the core text in a reading course employing a whole-language approach
- As a collection of inspiring motivational readings

Ease of use and helpful support. The book is designed to be simple for both instructors and students to use. The activities already listed are easy to present in class and convenient to correct. Answers to the activities appear in two places. First, an annotated *Instructor's Edition* of the book—chances are you are holding it in your hand—includes answers to the Vocabulary Checks and Reading Checks as well as explanations of the answers, making the book very easy for teachers to use. Second, an *Instructor's Manual,* available online at the Townsend Press Learning Center (**www.townsendpress.net**), provides complete answers on letter-sized sheets for these activities. At the instructor's option, these sheets can easily be duplicated and distributed to students so they can check their own answers. The manual also contains teaching suggestions, suggested answers to the "Discussion Questions" that follow each reading, and ten additional guided writing assignments.

In short, *Voices and Values* contains an appealing collection of readings and an exceptional series of activities that will give students extensive guided practice in reading and writing. We believe the book's value lies in the humanistic quality of the selections, the variety of activities that follow each essay, and the integrated approach to reading and writing that is maintained throughout.

Changes in the Second Edition

Changes in this new edition include the following:

- **Twenty new readings.** Half of the readings have been replaced with new selections, many taken from current newspapers and magazines. These new readings speak directly to 21st-century concerns. In addition, several of the readings originally in the first edition have been updated.

- **Added questions on the writer's craft.** These questions, located at the end of each Reading Check, will help students further sharpen both their reading and their writing skills.

- **A full-color design.** Color has been carefully used throughout—not as window dressing, but to add clarity and readability to the different parts of each chapter in the book.

- **Appealing visuals.** Because so many students today are visual learners, a photograph or other illustration has been added to each reading to help engage students' interest.

- **New third-person writing assignments.** Half of the paragraph assignments and half of the essay assignments are first-person; the other half of the assignments are third-person. Many of these include suggestions for Internet research, thereby permitting students to become familiar with using Google and other search engines to gather material for a paper.

- **A new unit on the research paper.** Unit Six contains material on writing a research paper with sources, as well as a sample research paper in MLA format.

Acknowledgments

We appreciate the many helpful suggestions provided by the following reviewers: Marlys Barrett, Wenatchee Valley College; Elizabeth Keefe, Gateway Community College; Deborah and Eric Morrison, Pima Community College; Bonita Rees, Gateway Community College; Carla Young, Community College of Allegheny County; and Patrick Wall, San Joaquin Delta College.

At Townsend Press, we thank Kathryn Bernstein, Bill Blauvelt, Denton Cairnes, Ruth A. Rouff, and Tanya Savory for the help they provided along the way. We owe special thanks to two Townsend Press editors without whose efforts this book, quite literally, would not exist. We are grateful to Barbara Solot, who has once again created a layout and full-color text design that are as clear as they are inviting. The result of her artistry and painstaking efforts is a strikingly attractive book that both students and teachers will enjoy using. And finally, we thank Beth Johnson, whose diligent work, as both co-author and editor, on the first edition of *Voices and Values* laid the foundation for this Second Edition.

Janet M. Goldstein   *John Langan*

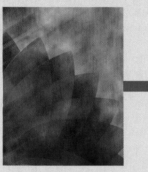

Introduction

1 Becoming a Better Reader

Voices and Values consists of this introductory chapter, a brief chapter on writing, and forty high-interest essays, followed by a unit on the research paper. This introduction will describe the format of the forty essays. It will then explain how understanding the concept of *point and support* can make you a better reader and writer. Finally, it will offer specific strategies for effective reading of the essays. The chapter that follows. "Becoming a Better Writer," will then present in a nutshell what you need to know to write effectively.

Format of the Forty Reading Selections

Each of the forty essays in *Voices and Values* contains the following:

- A *Preview* that presents helpful background information and arouses your interest in the selection.

- A *Words to Watch* section that gives the definitions of some of the words in the selection.

- An activity called *First Impressions* that asks you to write for ten minutes about the selection you have just finished reading.

- A *Vocabulary Check* that helps you learn words in a research-proven way: by seeing how they are actually used in the selection.

- A *Reading Check* that helps you practice and develop important reading skills: recognizing main ideas and the central point, identifying key supporting details, making inferences, and being aware of the writer's craft.

- *Discussion Questions* to help you deepen your understanding of the reading.

- *Two Paragraph Assignments* and *two Essay Assignments*—giving you a choice of topics for writing practice. As a general rule, you will be given both a paragraph and an essay assignment that involve a first-person "I" point of view, in which you are asked to provide evidence from your own personal experience. You will also be given a paragraph and an essay assignment that involve an objective point of view, in which you will be asked to provide evidence from research or your own general knowledge.

Point and Support

The most important principle in this book is that effective writing has two basic parts: (1) a **point** and (2) **support** for that point. The point states what the author thinks, and the support helps you, the reader, understand why the author holds this opinion. By keeping this principle in mind, you can become a better reader *and* writer. When you read, remember that an author's purpose is to make a point and support it with reasons, examples, and other details. When you write, remember that to communicate effectively, you should follow the same basic plan: make a point and support it.

Suppose you are reading a magazine article about flexible working hours. As you read, ask yourself the questions, "What is the author's point?" and "What is the support for the point?" Doing so, you may quickly see that the author's point is that flexible working hours are a good idea. You may then note that the article gives three supporting reasons. Flexible working hours would lead to fewer traffic jams, better use of building space, and more opportunities for parents to work. By asking and answering these two questions, you have found the central meaning of the article. *This strategy can be applied to almost anything you read.*

You should follow the same principle when you write. Let's say you're writing a paper about watching a sports event on television as opposed to going to the game itself. Ask yourself, "What point do I want to make about this topic?" Suppose you decide to argue that watching on TV is better than going to the game. You would then need to think of convincing reasons to support your point. You might explain that the game is cheaper if watched at home; that it's more comfortable to watch it at home without traffic, a noisy crowd, or hard seats; and that it's a more informative experience at home with the advantage of good camera coverage and helpful commentators. By consciously focusing on the point you want to make and on the support you need to give, you can help yourself write a solid, well-reasoned paper.

Reading Strategies

All too often, students have trouble understanding what they read. A familiar complaint is, "I read it, but I didn't understand it." This section explains five strategies that can make you a better reader. You will have many opportunities to apply them in this book. In fact, you will find it helpful to use them for *all* your reading.

Strategy 1: Learn to Read Actively.

One key to improved reading is getting actively involved in each stage of the reading process. Here are some ways to do so.

1 **Preview the selection.** In other words, look over what you will read—quickly but alertly—before you start to read it. Follow these steps:

   a **Make the title into a question.** For example, before reading a short selection titled "TV Commercials and Children," you might ask the question "How do TV commercials affect children?" or "Why are TV commercials directed at children?" Searching for the answer to your question will give you a reason for reading.

   On the lines below, try out this tip by writing two questions based on "He Was First," the title of one of the selections in this book.

   Answers will vary.

   _____

   _____

   Are the questions you wrote on the lines above something like "Who was first?" or "What did he do to be first?" or "How difficult was it to be first?" If so, you've got the idea. Asking basic questions can make you a more active reader.

   b **Read through the first several paragraphs and the last several paragraphs.** They may give you a quick sense of the main idea of the selection.

   c **Look at the first sentence in some of the paragraphs.** You won't get a complete picture of the selection by reading only these sentences, but you will get some idea of the selection's overall organization.

2 **Read the selection straight through for pleasure.** Don't get bogged down; instead, try to understand as much as you can this first time through.

3 **Use any special features the book provides.** In this book, a *Preview* introduces you to each essay. Also, *Words to Watch* defines the difficult words in the selection in the order in which they appear. All these words are then marked in the selection with a small circle (°). Finally, the three *First Impressions* questions after each selection prompt you to jot down some quick reactions

to the selection and its relationship to your own life. Knowing that you'll be writing down your first impressions each time should help you focus your attention when you read the selections in this book. And once you get in the habit of writing about your first impressions, you'll be surprised by how many ideas you have.

4 **Reread the selection, marking key information with a pen or pencil.** Marking material will keep your mind alert and show you what to come back to later. Here are some suggestions on how and what to mark:

a Underline the ideas that seem important.

b Write *Ex* in the margin to set off important examples.

c Put question marks beside any material you don't understand.

d Number any major series of ideas.

Following each selection in this book is a set of questions that help you practice important reading skills. As you strengthen these skills enough to make them habits, your reading ability is sure to improve. Here are the skills:

- Understanding vocabulary in context
- Recognizing the central point and main ideas
- Identifying key supporting details
- Making inferences
- Being aware of the writer's craft

Each skill is itself a "strategy" that can make you a better reader. These skills are explained on the pages that follow.

Strategy 2: Understand Vocabulary in Context.

Building a good vocabulary is essential to becoming a better reader and writer. In fact, people who build strong vocabularies are more likely to be successful in school and in their careers. Yet few of us have the time or desire to open the dictionary every time we meet an unfamiliar word. Luckily, there is another way to learn new words: we can guess their meanings with the help of surrounding words (called **context**).

- Sometimes, the context will contain a **synonym**—a word that means **the same as** the unfamiliar word:

    Nick … felt betrayed and abandoned by friends, and he *declined* into self-pity. Nick might have sunk all the way to rock bottom if it had not been for Kristen.

  The synonym *sunk* suggests that *declined* means "fell."

- Sometimes, the context will contain an **antonym**—a word that means **the opposite of** the unfamiliar word:

    > While there are *myriad* regulations to protect people who work in noisy environments, there are relatively few governing repeated exposure to noise outside the workplace . . .

    The antonym *few* indicates that *myriad* means "many."

- Or the context might include one or more **examples** of the unfamiliar word:

    > Two of Nick's favorite *pastimes* had been cycling and playing basketball . . .

    The examples—*cycling* and *playing basketball*—suggest that *pastimes* means "enjoyable activities."

- But most of the time, you'll need to look at the entire sentence. For example, see if you can figure out the meaning of the word *fluctuate* from its context in this sentence:

    > Desert temperatures can *fluctuate* by as much as fifty degrees between daytime and nighttime.

    With the help of the entire sentence, you can guess that *fluctuate* means "vary."

To help you practice this strategy, following each selection in this book are several vocabulary items. These items will help you learn words by looking at their contexts.

Strategy 3: Look for Point and Support in What You Read.

As you learned from the section titled "Point and Support," a well-written selection has two basic parts: (1) a point and (2) support for that point. The essays in this book are always accompanied by point and support questions:

1 **Recognizing the Central Point and Main Ideas.** The *central point* refers to the point of an entire essay; *main ideas* refer to the points of individual paragraphs. If a central point is not expressed directly in a selection, you can often figure it out by considering the supporting details.

2 **Identifying Key Supporting Details.** The support for central points and main ideas may be in the form of reasons, examples, details, facts, quotations, or personal experiences. Noting these details will help you determine the point an author is making in an essay.

Look, for example, at the following paragraph:

TV Commercials and Children

Television commercials aimed at young children—the kind shown during Saturday morning cartoon shows, for example—should be banned. For one thing, such commercials often promote junk food. They encourage little children to crave sugary snacks and breakfast cereals made of tiny chocolate doughnuts or cookie nuggets. In addition, these commercials urge children to be greedy. At the same time parents are teaching their children to share what they have with others, TV commercials make them want more expensive toys and other products for themselves. The worst thing about these ads, however, is that they take advantage of children who have not yet learned what advertising is or how it works. If a beloved cartoon character tells a child that a cereal or a toy is great, the child believes it. Children can't see how advertisers trick them into wanting a product or how ads make toys or games look better than they really are. Aiming ads at little children is unfair.

Can you find the main idea and the three key supporting details in this paragraph? Answer the questions below, and then read the explanations that follow them.

__B__ 1. Which sentence best expresses the main idea of "TV Commercials and Children"?
   A. All television commercials should be banned.
   B. TV commercials aimed at young children should be banned.
   C. Commercials make young children want to eat junk food.
   D. Advertisers do not care what children eat.

In this paragraph, the main idea is *B,* "TV commercials aimed at young children should be banned." Answer *A* is *too broad*—it refers to all television commercials, not just those aimed at youngsters. Answer *C* is *too narrow*—it is actually one of the supporting details for the main idea. Answer *D* may or may not be true, but it is not what the whole paragraph is about. Only answer *B* states the main idea of the paragraph.

2. On the lines below, write the three key supporting details for the main idea. (Ask yourself, "What specific reasons does the author give for why TV ads are harmful to children?")
   A. They promote junk food.
   B. They encourage greed.
   C. They take advantage of children.

If you wrote answers similar to "They promote junk food," "They encourage greed," and "They take advantage of children," you are correct.

Strategy 4: Make Inferences.

Inferences are the reasonable guesses we make based on the facts presented. For example, if a crowd of people is smiling and talking after leaving a movie, we would probably assume that the movie is an enjoyable one. And if rolled-up newspapers accumulate on a neighbor's porch over a holiday weekend, we could conclude that the family is away on a brief vacation. Or if trucks that usually race along the highway are suddenly observing the speed limit, we could infer that a police radar trap is nearby. We make the same kinds of judgments when we draw conclusions about what we read. In this book, you'll be answering several inference questions each time you read a selection.

Look again at the paragraph on "TV Commercials and Children" (page 8) and answer the following question. Then read the explanation that follows it.

____T____ TRUE OR FALSE? We can infer from the paragraph that young children think that ads tell the truth.

You can find the answer to this question near the end of the paragraph, when the writer explains that young children haven't learned what advertising is. The paragraph goes on to state that if a cartoon character praises a cereal or toy, the child believes that character. Therefore, the author is suggesting that young children believe everything they see on TV—including ads. The inference is true.

Strategy 5: Be Aware of the Writer's Craft.

"Writer's craft" refers to techniques an author uses to communicate ideas. Being aware of these strategies will increase your understanding of what you read as well as improve your own writing. In this book, questions on the writer's craft cover the following:

1 **Introductions and Conclusions.** What does an author do to interest you in reading what he or she has written? Four common kinds of introductions include (1) an entertaining story (sometimes called an *anecdote*), (2) one or more questions, (3) an idea that is the opposite of what will be written about, or (4) a broad statement that narrows down to the central point. Examples of all four introductions are on pages 16–18. Conclusions may include a summary and perhaps a final thought or two.

2 **Type of Support.** How has the author supported his or her central point? As already mentioned, common methods of support include reasons, examples, details, facts, quotations, and personal experiences.

3 **Patterns of Organization.** How have the supporting details been arranged? Authors often use a **time order**—telling the parts of a story in the order that they happened. Common word signals (also called **transitions**) that mark time order are *first, then, before, as, after, next,* and *last.*

An equally popular pattern of organization is a **listing order**—providing a series of reasons, examples, or details. Common word signals or transitions that mark listing order are *first of all, another, in addition, also,* and *finally.*

Another pattern of organization is **comparison-contrast**—showing how two things are alike or (more often) different. Typical transitions for this pattern are *like, just as, similarly, but, however, in contrast,* and *on the other hand.*

A final pattern worth noting is **cause-effect**—explaining the reasons why something happened or the results of something. Typical transitions for this pattern are *because, therefore, effect, consequently,* and *as a result.*

4 **Tone.** Just as a speaker's tone of voice reveals how he or she feels, a writer's tone also communicates feelings. You should be able to tell how an author feels about his or her subject by looking at the wording of the selection. It will often indicate whether a selection's tone is humorous or serious, angry or friendly, formal or informal, self-pitying or sarcastic, encouraging or discouraging, or simply objective (factual).

5 **Purpose.** Decide what type of writing you are reading. Is it intended to **inform** (give people information), to **entertain** (give people pleasure), or to **persuade** (change people's minds about an issue)? Or does it have a combination of these purposes?

6 **Audience.** Decide for what kind of reader the selection was probably written. Was it meant for the general reader (anyone)? Or was the author writing for a smaller audience, such as major-league baseball players, a group of fellow researchers, or parents of high-school students?

7 **Titles.** Most authors choose their titles very carefully. Many times, a title clearly describes the topic of the essay, and sometimes it is the shortest possible summary of the central point of an essay. Look closely at titles for excellent clues about authors' ideas and their attitudes toward their topics.

Final Thoughts about Reading the Essays

Read each selection first to enjoy whatever it may have to say about human nature and life today. Then reread the selection and work on the activities with the intention of learning as much as you can.

To help you learn, answers to the questions on the first selection, "The Blind Vet," appear at the bottom of the last page of questions. Read these answers *after* you have worked through the activities. Be sure you understand why each answer is correct. This information will help prepare you to do well on the remaining selections, for which answers are not given.

Finally, remember that learning is, in the end, up to you. If you have the intention of gaining as much as you can from this book, then *Voices and Values* will offer you a great deal. As you learn to consistently apply the questions "What is the point?" and "What is the support for that point?" you will acquire a powerful learning and reasoning tool—a tool that can make you a skilled and independent learner for the rest of your life. Just as important, you will find that reading the essays will not only improve your mind but also touch your heart. The essays will help you connect with others and realize that all people have the same shared humanity. Someone once wrote, "We read in order to know that we are not alone." We become less isolated as we share the common experiences, emotions, and thoughts that make us human.

2 Becoming a Better Writer

What, in a nutshell, do you need to become a better writer? You need to know the basic goals in writing and to understand the writing process—as explained on the pages that follow.

Two Basic Goals in Writing

When you write a paper, your two basic goals should be (1) to **make a point** and (2) to **support that point**. Look for a moment at the following cartoon:

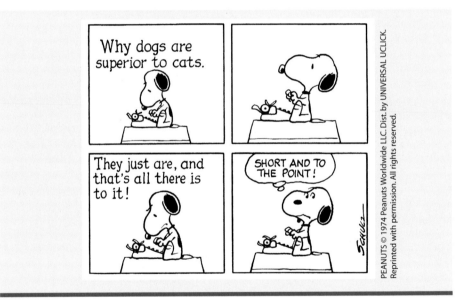

See if you can answer the following questions:

- What is Snoopy's point in his paper?

  Your answer: His point is that ___dogs are superior to cats.___

- What is his support for his point?

  Your answer: ____No support is given.____

Explanation

Snoopy's point, of course, is that dogs are superior to cats. But he offers no support whatsoever to back up his point! There are two jokes here. First, he is a dog and so is naturally going to believe that dogs are superior. The other joke is that his evidence ("They just are, and that's all there is to it!") is a lot of empty words. His somewhat guilty look in the last panel suggests that he knows he has not proved his point. To write effectively, you must provide *real* support for your points and opinions.

Writing Paragraphs

A **paragraph** is a series of sentences about one main idea, or **point**. A paragraph typically starts with a point (also called the **topic sentence**), and the rest of the paragraph provides specific details to support and develop that point.

Look at the following paragraph, written by a student named Carla.

Three Kinds of Bullies

There are three kinds of bullies in schools. First of all, there are the physical bullies. They are the bigger or meaner kids who try to hurt kids who are smaller or unsure of themselves. They'll push other kids off swings, trip them in the halls, or knock books out of their hands. They'll also wait for kids after school and slap them or yank their hair or pull out their shirts or throw them to the ground. They do their best to frighten kids and make them cry. Another kind of bully is the verbal bully. This kind tries to hurt with words rather than fists. Nursery-school kids may call each other "dummy" or "weirdo" or "fatty," and as kids get older, their words carry even more sting. "You are **such a loser**," those bullies will tell their victim, making sure there is a crowd nearby to hear. "Where did you get that sweater—a trash bin?" The worst kind of bully is the social bully. Social bullies realize that they can make themselves feel powerful by making others feel unwanted. Bullies choose their victims and then do all they can to isolate them. They roll their eyes and turn away in disgust if those people try to talk to them. They move away if a victim sits near them at lunch. They make sure the unwanted ones know about the games and parties they aren't invited to. Physical, verbal, and social bullies all have the same ugly goal: to hurt and humiliate others.

● What is the point of the paragraph on the previous page?

There are three kinds of bullies in schools.

● What are the three specific details that Carla has provided to back up her point?   *Wording of answers may vary.*

1. *Physical—try to hurt or frighten kids physically*

2. *Verbal—try to hurt with words*

3. *Social—try to make victims feel unwanted*

The above paragraph, like many effective paragraphs, starts by stating a main idea, or point. In this case, the clear point is that there are three kinds of bullies in schools. An effective paragraph must not only make a point but also support it with specific evidence—reasons, examples, and other details. Such specifics help prove to readers that the point is a reasonable one. Even if readers do not agree with the writer, at least they have the writer's evidence in front of them. Readers are like juries: they want to see the evidence for themselves so that they can make their own judgments.

As you have seen, the author of the paragraph provides plenty of examples to support the idea that there are physical, verbal, and social bullies. To write an effective paragraph, always aim to do what the author has done: begin by making a point, and then go on to back up that point with strong specific evidence.

Writing Essays

Like a paragraph, an essay starts with a point and then goes on to provide specific details to support and develop that point. However, a **paragraph** is a series of sentences about one main idea or point, while an **essay** is a series of paragraphs about one main idea or point—called the **central point** or **thesis**. Since an essay is much longer than one paragraph, it allows a writer to develop a topic in more detail.

Look at the following paragraph, written by Carla after she was asked to more fully develop her paragraph on bullies.

Introductory Paragraph

A Hateful Activity: Bullying

Eric, a new boy at school, was shy and physically small. He quickly became a victim of bullies. Kids would wait after school, pull out his shirt, and punch and shove him around. He was called such names as "Mouse Boy" and "Jerk Boy." When he sat down during lunch hour, others would leave his table. In gym games he was never thrown the ball, as if he didn't exist. Then one day he came to school with a gun. When the police were called, he told them he just couldn't take it anymore. Bullying had hurt him badly, just as it hurts so many other students. Every member of a school community should be aware of bullying and the three hateful forms that it takes: physical, verbal, and social.

First Supporting Paragraph

First of all, there is physical bullying. Bigger or meaner kids try to hurt kids who are smaller or unsure of themselves. They'll push kids into their lockers, knock books out of their hands, or shoulder them out of the cafeteria line. In gym class, a popular bully move is to kick someone's legs out from under him while he is running. In the classroom, bullies might kick the back of the chair or step on the foot of the kids they want to intimidate. Another classic bully move is to corner a kid in a bathroom. There the victim will be slapped around, will have his or her clothes half pulled off, and might even be shoved into a trash can. Bullies will also wait for kids after school and bump or wrestle them around, often while others are looking on. The goal is to frighten kids as much as possible and try to make them cry. Physical bullying is more common among males, but it is not unknown for girls to be physical bullies as well. The victims are left bruised and hurting, but often in even more pain emotionally than bodily.

Second Supporting Paragraph

Perhaps even worse than physical attack is verbal bullying, which uses words, rather than hands or fists, as weapons. We may be told that "sticks and stones may break my bones, but names can never harm me," but few of us are immune to the pain of a verbal attack. Like physical bullies, verbal bullies tend to single out certain targets. From that moment on, the victim is subjected to a hail of insults and put-downs. These are usually delivered in public, so the victim's humiliation will be greatest: "Oh, no; here comes the nerd!" "Why don't you lose some weight, blubber boy?" "You smell as bad as you look!" "Weirdo." "Fairy." "Creep." "Dork." "Slut." "Loser." Verbal bullying is an equal-opportunity event, with girls as likely to be verbal bullies as boys. Meanwhile, the victim retreats further and further into his or her shell, hoping to escape further notice.

Third Supporting Paragraph

As bad as verbal bullying is, many would agree that the most painful type of bullying is social bullying. Many students have a strong need for the comfort of being part of a group. For social bullies, the pleasure of belonging to a group is increased by the sight of someone who is refused entry into that group. So, like wolves targeting the weakest sheep in a herd, the bullies lead the pack in isolating people who they decide are different. They roll their eyes and turn away in disgust if those people try to talk to them. They move away if a victim sits near them at lunch or stands near them in a school hallway or at a bus stop. No one volunteers to work with these victims on class activities, and they are the ones that no one wants as part of gym teams. The bullies make sure the unwanted ones know about the games and parties they aren't invited to. As the victims sink further into isolation and depression, the social bullies—who seem to be female more often than male—feel all the more puffed up by their own popularity.

Concluding Paragraph

Whether bullying is physical, verbal, or social, it can leave deep and lasting scars. If parents, teachers, and other adults were more aware of the types of bullying, they might help by stepping in before the situation becomes too extreme. If students were more aware of the terrible pain that bullying causes, they might think twice about being bullies themselves.

- Which sentence in the introductory paragraph expresses the central point of the essay? _____ The final sentence _____

- How many supporting paragraphs are provided to back up the central point? _3_

The Parts of an Essay

Each of the parts of an essay is explained below.

Introductory Paragraph

A well-written introductory paragraph will normally do the following:

- Gain the reader's interest by using one of several common methods of introduction.

- Present the thesis statement. The **thesis statement** expresses the central point of an essay, just as a topic sentence states the main idea of a paragraph. The central idea in Carla's essay is expressed in the last sentence of the introductory paragraph.

Four Common Methods of Introduction

Four common methods of introduction are (1) telling a brief story, (2) asking one or more questions, (3) shifting to the opposite, or (4) going from the broad to the narrow. Following are examples of all four.

1   **Telling a brief story.** An interesting anecdote is hard for a reader to resist. In an introduction, a story should be no more than a few sentences, and it should relate meaningfully to the central idea. The story can be an experience of your own, of someone you know, or of someone you have read about. Carla uses this method of introduction for her essay on bullying:

> Eric, a new boy at school, was shy and physically small. He quickly became a victim of bullies. Kids would wait after school, pull out his shirt, and punch and shove him around. He was called such names as "Mouse Boy" and "Jerk Boy." When he sat down during lunch hour, others would leave his table. In gym games he was never thrown the ball, as if he didn't exist. Then one day he came to school with a gun. When the police were called, he told them he just couldn't take it anymore. Bullying had hurt him badly, just as it hurts so many other students. Every member of a school community should be aware of bullying and the three hateful forms that it takes: physical, verbal, and social.

2 **Asking one or more questions.** These questions may be ones that you intend to answer in your essay, or they may indicate that your topic is relevant to readers—it is something they care about. If Carla had used this approach, here is how her introductory paragraph might look:

> When you were a kid, were you ever pushed around by bigger children? Were you shoved aside in hallways or knocked out of your seat in classrooms? Were you ever called hurtful names like "fatso," "worm," "dogface," or "retard"? Or were you coldly ignored by other students? Did they turn their backs on you, pretending you didn't exist? If the answer to any of these questions is "yes," then you were a victim of one of three forms of bullying: physical, verbal, or social.

3 **Shifting to the opposite.** Another way to gain the reader's interest is to first present an idea that is the opposite of what will be written about. Using this approach, Carla could have begun her essay like this:

> For many children, school is a happy experience. They like their teachers, they see their friends on a daily basis, and they feel comfortable and welcome. But for the victims of bullies, school is a nightmare. Every day they must face someone bigger or meaner than they are and endure humiliation in a variety of forms—physical, verbal, and social.

4 **Going from the broad to the narrow.** Broad, general observations can capture your reader's interest; they can also introduce your general topic and provide helpful background information. If Carla had used this method of introduction, she might have written first about typical problems in growing up and then narrowed her focus down to one problem: bullying.

> Many unpleasant parts of growing up seem unavoidable. Pimples happen, voices crack, and students worry all the time about their looks and their changing bodies. In time, the pimples disappear, the voices deepen, and the worries recede. But one all-too-common aspect of growing up, bullying, can have lasting negative results. Young people should not have to put up with bullying in any of its forms—physical, verbal, or social.

Supporting Paragraphs

The traditional school essay has three supporting paragraphs. But some essays will have two supporting paragraphs, and others will have four or more. Each supporting paragraph should have its own topic sentence stating the point to be developed in that paragraph.

Notice that the essay on bullying has clear topic sentences for each of the three supporting paragraphs.

Transitional Sentences

In a paragraph, transitional words like *First, Another, Also, In addition,* and *Finally* are used to help connect supporting ideas. In an essay, transitional sentences are used to help tie the supporting paragraphs together. Such transitional sentences often occur at the beginning of a supporting paragraph.

- Look at the topic sentences for the second and third supporting paragraphs in the essay on bullying. Explain how those sentences are also transitional sentences.

  The first few words in each sentence refer to the main idea of the

  paragraph immediately before it.

Concluding Paragraph

The concluding paragraph often summarizes the essay by briefly restating the thesis and, at times, the main supporting points. It may also provide a closing thought or two as a way of bringing the paper to a natural and graceful end.

- Look again at the concluding paragraph of the essay on bullies. Which sentence summarizes the essay? _____First_____ Which sentences provide closing thoughts? _____Second and third_____ How many closing thoughts are there? _Two_

A Note on a Third Goal in Writing

A third important goal in writing is to organize the supporting material in a paper. Perhaps the most common way to do so is to use a **listing order**. In other words, provide a list of three or more reasons, examples, or other details. Use signal words such as *First of all, Another, Secondly, Also,* and *Finally* to mark the items in your list. Signal words, better known as **transitions**, let your reader know that you are providing a list of items.

- Turn back to page 13 and look again at the paragraph on bullies. What signal words does Carla use to mark each of the three kinds of bullies?

    _____First of all_____   _____Another_____   _____worst_____

You'll note that she uses *First of all* to introduce the first kind of bully, *Another* to introduce the second kind of bully, and *worst* to introduce the last kind of bully.

Practice 1: Using a Listing Order

Read the paragraph below and answer the questions that follow.

Drunk Drivers

People caught driving while drunk—even first offenders—should be jailed. For one thing, drunk driving is more dangerous than carrying a loaded gun. Drunk drivers are in charge of three-thousand-pound weapons at a time when they have little coordination or judgment. Instead of getting off with a license suspension, the drunk driver should be treated as seriously as someone who walks into a crowded building with a ticking time bomb. In addition, views on drunk driving have changed. We are no longer willing to make jokes about funny drunk drivers, to see drunk driving as a typical adolescent stunt, or to overlook repeat offenders who have been lucky enough not to hurt anybody—so far. Last of all, a jail penalty might encourage solutions to the problem of drinking and driving. People who go out for an evening that includes drinking would be more likely to select a designated driver. That person would stay completely sober. Bars might promote more tasty and trendy nonalcoholic drinks such as fruit daiquiris and "virgin" piña coladas. And perhaps beer and alcohol advertising would be regulated so that young people would not learn to associate alcohol consumption with adulthood. By taking drunk driving seriously enough to require a jail sentence, we would surely save lives.

- What is the writer's point in this paragraph? _____
  People caught driving while drunk should be jailed.

- What transition introduces the first supporting reason for the point?
  For one thing

- What transition introduces the second supporting reason? *In addition*

- What transition introduces the third supporting reason? *Last of all*

The author's list of reasons and use of transitions—*For one thing, In addition,* and *Last of all*—both help the author organize the supporting material and help the reader clearly and easily understand the supporting material.

Another common way to organize supporting details is to use a time order. In **time order**, supporting details are presented in the order in which they occurred. First this happened; next, this; after that, this; then this; and so on. The events that make up a story are almost always organized in time order.

Practice 2: Using a Time Order

Read the paragraph below, which is organized in a time order. In the spaces provided, write appropriate transitions showing time relationships. Use each of the following transitions once: *Before, Then, When, As, After.*

An Upsetting Incident

An incident happened yesterday that made me very angry. I got off the bus and started walking the four blocks to my friend's house. _____*As*_____ I walked along, I noticed a group of boys gathered on the sidewalk about a block ahead of me. _____*When*_____ they saw me, they stopped talking. A bit nervous, I thought about crossing the street to avoid them. But as I came nearer and they began to whistle, a different feeling came over me. Instead of being afraid, I was suddenly angry. Why should I have to worry about being hassled just because I was a woman? I stared straight at the boys and continued walking. _____*Then*_____ one of them said, "Oooh, baby. Looking fine today." _____*Before*_____

I knew what I was doing, I turned on him. "Do you have a mother? Or any sisters?" I demanded. He looked astonished and didn't answer me. I went on. "Is it OK with you if men speak to them like that? Shouldn't they be able to walk down the street without some creeps bothering them?" _____After_____ I spoke, he and the other boys looked guilty and backed away. I held my head up high and walked by them. An hour later, I was still angry.

The writer makes the main point of the paragraph in her first sentence: "An incident happened yesterday that made me very angry." She then supports her point with a specific account of just what happened. Time words that could be used to help connect her details include the following: "As I walked along"; "When they saw me"; "Then one of them said"; "Before I knew"; "After I spoke."

The Writing Process

Even professional writers do not sit down and write a paper in a single draft. Instead, they have to work on it one step at a time. Writing a paper is a process that can be divided into the following five steps:

Step 1: Getting Started through Prewriting
Step 2: Preparing a Scratch Outline
Step 3: Writing the First Draft
Step 4: Revising
Step 5: Editing

Step 1: Getting Started through Prewriting

What you need to learn, first, are methods that you can use to start working on a writing assignment. These techniques will help you think on paper. They'll help you figure out both the point you want to make and the support you need for that point. Here are three helpful prewriting techniques:

- Freewriting
- Questioning
- List making

Freewriting

Freewriting is just sitting down and writing whatever comes into your mind about a topic. Do this for ten minutes or so. Write without stopping and without worrying in the slightest about spelling, grammar, and the like. Simply get down on paper all the information that occurs to you about the topic.

Below is part of the freewriting done by Carla for her paragraph about bullies. Carla had been given the assignment, "Write about the types of bullying that go on in school." She began prewriting as a way to explore her topic and generate details about it.

Example of Freewriting

> Bullying is part of school most of the time teachers dont have a clue. I really never thought about it and was just glad I wasn't part of it. At least for the most part. I'd see some physical stuff but kind of turned my head not wanting to look at it. The worst thing with girls was words, they meant more than physical stuff. I rember once being called a name and it stung me so bad and it botherd me for weeks. . . .

Notice that there are problems with spelling, grammar, and punctuation in Carla's freewriting. Carla is not worried about such matters, nor should she be—at this stage. She is just concentrating on getting ideas and details down on paper. She knows that it is best to focus on one thing at a time. At this point, she just wants to write out thoughts as they come to her, to do some thinking on paper.

You should take the same approach when freewriting: explore your topic without worrying at all about writing "correctly." Figuring out what you want to say should have all your attention in this early stage of the writing process.

Practice 3: Freewriting

On a sheet of paper, freewrite for at least ten minutes on the best or worst job or chore you ever had. Don't worry about grammar, punctuation, or spelling. Try to write—without stopping—about whatever comes into your head concerning your best or worst job or chore.

Questioning

Questioning means that you generate details about your topic by writing down a series of questions and answers about it. Your questions can start with words like *what, when, where, why,* and *how.*

Here are just some of the questions that Carla might have asked while developing her paper:

Example of Questioning

- Who was bullied?
- Who were the bullies?
- When did bullying take place?
- Where did it happen?
- Were there different kinds of bullying?
- Why were some kids teased and bullied?

Practice 4: Questioning

On a sheet of paper, answer the following questions about your best or worst job or chore.

- When did you have the job (or chore)?
- Where did you work?
- What did you do?
- Whom did you work for?
- Why did you like or dislike the job? (Give one reason and some details that support that reason.)
- What is another reason you liked or disliked the job? What are some details that support the second reason?
- Can you think of a third reason you liked or did not like the job? What are some details that support the third reason?

List Making

In **list making** (also known as **brainstorming**), you make a list of ideas and details that could go into your paper. Simply pile these items up, one after another, without worrying about putting them in any special order. Try to accumulate as many details as you can think of.

After Carla did her freewriting about bullies, she made up a list of details, part of which is shown below.

Example of List Making

some bullies were physical
boys would push kids around
kids would be tripped in hallways
some kids would cry
names would be used
"dummy" or "creep" or "fairy"
no one would sit near some kids
some kids never chosen for games . . .

One detail led to another as Carla expanded her list. Slowly but surely, more supporting material emerged that she could use in developing her paper. By the time she had finished her list, she was ready to plan an outline of her paragraph and to write her first draft.

Practice 5: List Making

On separate paper, make a list of details about the job (or chore). Don't worry about putting them in a certain order. Just get down as many details about the job as occur to you. The list can include specific reasons you liked or did not like the job and specific details supporting those reasons.

Step 2: *Preparing a Scratch Outline*

A **scratch outline** is a brief plan for a paragraph. It shows at a glance the point of the paragraph and the support for that point. It is the logical framework on which the paper is built.

This rough outline often follows freewriting, questioning, list making, or all three. Or it may gradually emerge in the midst of these strategies. In fact, trying to outline is a good way to see if you need to do more prewriting. If a solid outline does not emerge, then you know you need to do more prewriting to clarify your main point or its support. And once you have a workable outline, you may realize, for instance, that you want to do more list making to develop one of the supporting details in the outline.

In Carla's case, as she was working on her list of details, she suddenly discovered what the plan of her paragraph could be. She realized she could describe different kinds of bullies.

Example of a Scratch Outline

> There are three kinds of bullies.
>   1. Physical
>   2. Verbal
>   3. Social

After all her preliminary writing, Carla sat back pleased. She knew she had a promising paper—one with a clear point and solid support. Carla was now ready to write the first draft of her paper, using her outline as a guide.

Practice 6: Scratch Outline

Using the list you have prepared, see if you can prepare a scratch outline made up of the three main reasons you liked or did not like the job.

Answers will vary.

_____ was the best (*or* worst) job (*or* chore) I ever had.

Reason 1: _____

Reason 2: _____

Reason 3: _____

Step 3: *Writing the First Draft*

When you do a first draft, be prepared to put in additional thoughts and details that didn't emerge in your prewriting. And don't worry if you hit a snag. Just leave a blank space or add a comment such as "Do later," and press on to finish the paper. Also, don't worry yet about grammar, punctuation, or spelling. You don't want to take time correcting words or sentences that you may decide to remove later. Instead, make it your goal to develop the content of your paper with plenty of specific details.

Here are a few lines of Carla's first draft:

First Draft

There are different kinds of bullies that can be seen in schools. One kind of bullying that goes on is done by physical bullies. You see kids who will get pushed around on the playground. You see kids getting shoved into lockers and that kind of stuff. There was a girl I knew who was a real bully and a bit crazy because of a really bad home life. She would shove gum into another girl's hair and would also pull her hair. Other bullying went on with words and the calling of names. There were awful names that kids would use with each other, words included "creep" and "wierdo" and names that I don't even want to write here. . . .

Practice 7: First Draft

Now write a first draft of your paper. Begin with your topic sentence stating that a certain job (or chore) was the best or worst one you ever had. Then state the first reason why it was the best or the worst, followed by specific details supporting that reason. Use a transition such as *First of all* to introduce the first reason. Next, state the second reason, followed by specific details supporting that reason. Use a transition such as *Secondly* to introduce the second reason. Last, state the third reason, followed with support. Use a transition such as *Finally* to introduce the last reason.

Don't worry about grammar, punctuation, or spelling. Just concentrate on getting down on paper the details about the job.

Step 4: *Revising*

Revising is as much a stage in the writing process as prewriting, outlining, and doing the first draft. **Revising** means that you rewrite a paper, building upon what has been done, to make it stronger and better. One writer has said about revision, "It's like cleaning house—getting rid of all the junk and putting things in the right order." A typical revision means writing at least one or two more drafts, adding and omitting details, organizing more clearly, and beginning to correct spelling and grammar.

Here are a few lines of Carla's second draft.

Second Draft

> There are three kinds of bullies in schools. First of all, there are the physical bullies. They are the bigger kids who try to hurt smaller kids. They'll push kids off of swings in the playground or shove them into lockers. Other examples are knocking books out of the hands of kids or waiting for them after school and slapping them around or yanking their hair. Another kind of bullying is by verbal bullies. The aim here is to hurt with words rather than with fists. A victim will be called a "creep" or "weirdo" or "fatty" or will be told "You are such a loser." . . .

Notice that in redoing the draft, Carla started by more concisely stating the point of her paragraph. Also, she inserted transitions (*First of all* and *Another*) to clearly set off the kinds of bullies. She omitted the detail about the crazy girl she knew because it was not relevant to a paragraph focusing on bullies. She added more details, so that she would have enough supporting examples for the types of bullies.

Carla then went on to revise the second draft. Since she was doing her paper on a computer, she was able to print it out quickly. She double-spaced the lines, allowing room for revisions, which she added in longhand as part of her third draft, and eventually the paragraph on page 13 resulted. (Note that if you are not using a computer, you may want to skip every other line when writing out each draft. Also, write on only one side of a page, so that you can see your entire paper at one time.)

Practice 8: Revising the Draft

Ideally, you will have a chance to put the paper aside for a while before doing later drafts. When you revise, try to do all of the following:

- Omit any details that do not truly support your topic sentence.

- Add more details as needed, making sure you have plenty of specific support for each of your three reasons.

- Be sure to include a final sentence that rounds off the paper, bringing it to a close.

Step 5: Editing

Editing, the final stage in the writing process, means checking a paper carefully for spelling, grammar, punctuation, and other errors. You are ready for this stage when you are satisfied that your point is clear, your supporting details are good, and your paper is well organized.

At this stage, you must **read your paper out loud**. Hearing how your writing sounds is an excellent way to pick up grammar and punctuation problems in your writing. Chances are that you will find sentence mistakes at every spot where your paper does not read smoothly and clearly. This point is so important that it bears repeating: *To find mistakes in your paper, read it out loud!*

At this point in her work, Carla read her latest draft out loud. She looked closely at all the spots where her writing did not read easily. She used a grammar handbook to deal with the problems at those spots in her paper, and she made the corrections needed so that all her sentences read smoothly. She also used her dictionary to check on the spelling of every word she was unsure about. She even took a blank sheet of paper and used it to uncover her paper one line at a time, looking for any other mistakes that might be there.

Practice 9: Editing

When you have your almost-final draft of the paper, edit it in the following ways:

- Read the paper aloud, listening for awkward wordings and places where the meaning is unclear. Make the changes needed for the paper to read smoothly and clearly. In addition, see if you can get another person to read the draft aloud to you. The spots that this person has trouble reading are spots where you may have to do some revision and correct your grammar or punctuation mistakes.

- Using your dictionary (or a spell-check program if you have a computer), check any words that you think might be misspelled.

- Finally, take a sheet of paper and cover your paper, so that you can expose and carefully proofread one line at a time. Use your handbook to check any other spots where you think there might be grammar or punctuation mistakes in your writing.

Final Thoughts

You have a paper to write. Here in a nutshell is what to do:

1   Write about what you know. If you don't know much about your topic, go onto the Internet by using the helpful search engine Google. You can access it by typing

www.google.com

A screen will then appear with a box in which you can type one or more keywords. For example, if you were thinking about doing a paper on a topic involving bullying in schools, you could type in the keywords *bullying in schools*. Within a second or so you will get a list of over 83 million articles on the Web about bullying in schools!

You would then need to narrow your topic by adding other keywords. For instance, if you typed *solutions to bullying in schools,* you would get a list of more than 3 million items. If you narrowed your potential topic further by typing *solutions to cyberbullying in schools,* you would get a list of 358,000 items. You could then click on the items that sound most promising to you.

Using Google will help you get more information quickly about a given topic; it will also suggest ways you can narrow down your potential topic. For example, you might decide, after looking through a number of articles about cyberbullying, that you will write an essay on the steps that schools should take to prevent cyberbullying.

Keep in mind two notes of caution about use of the Internet:

- Never for a moment believe that "If it's on the Internet, it must be true." Technology today allows anyone to publish anything at any time. For a given article, an author or information provider should be clearly identified. That author or information provider should be a knowledgeable, qualified, impartial, and reliable authority on the data presented.

- Do not use someone else's words in writing your paper. That would be *plagiarizing*—in a word, stealing. Use other people's ideas only as a springboard for developing your own thoughts about a given topic.

2   Use prewriting strategies to begin to write about your topic. Look for a point you can make, and make sure you have details to support it.

3   Write several drafts, aiming all the while for three goals in your writing: a **clear point**, **strong support** for that point, and **well-organized support**. Use transitions to help organize your support.

4   Then read your paper out loud. It should read smoothly and clearly. Look closely for grammar and punctuation problems at any rough spots. Check a grammar handbook or a dictionary as needed.

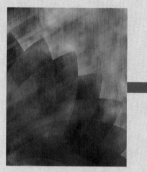

Unit One

Overcoming Obstacles

1 The Blind Vet

Gail Hoffman

Preview

When Nick returned home from the war in Afghanistan blinded by a bomb, he knew his life would never be the same. In so many ways, Nick would have to start all over again, and he wasn't certain he could do it. When Nick's friends slowly stopped coming by to see him, Nick fell into a sadness that threatened to destroy all his hopes. He wanted to give up. But one very special person refused to give up on Nick.

Words to Watch

rivulet (4): small stream
IED (6): improvised explosive device, a homemade roadside bomb that caused significant casualties in Iraq and Afghanistan
apprehension (8): fear
sufficiently (23): enough

1   When Nick boarded the bus, everyone looked at him. A few people shook their heads in pity. It didn't seem right that such a young man should have so much trouble climbing the three short steps up to the bus aisle.

2   "Why does that man have that white stick?" a small girl asked her mother loudly.

3   "Shh!" the mother said quickly. "It's not polite to talk about him, honey. He's blind."

4   But Nick had heard the little girl. In fact, he could feel everyone's eyes on him even though he couldn't see them. Using his cane, Nick carefully measured the height of each step. Gripping the handrail with white knuckles, he slowly made his way to the aisle. Then he used his hands to feel his way. Gratefully, Nick eased into the first set of seats reserved for the disabled. A thin rivulet° of sweat trickled down Nick's forehead, and his hands shook.

5   *Okay. Relax.* Nick tried to calm himself down. *You'll be all right. You'll make it.*

6   Nick, barely 22, had been blind for just over a year. During a tour of duty in Afghanistan, the vehicle Nick had been riding in had run over an IED°. Nick remembered a bright flash, a

terrible explosion, and the screams of his comrades. Then, the bright color of his own blood in his eyes was the last thing Nick ever saw. Fragments of metal and glass had scarred his face and destroyed his eyes.

7   When he came home from the war, Nick was frightened. What would his friends think of him? Two of Nick's favorite pastimes had been cycling and playing basketball, and that's how he had met a lot of his friends. Now he wouldn't be able to do either. Would his friends even want to be around him anymore?

8   But Nick's biggest apprehension° was that his girlfriend, Kristen, would leave him. The two of them had been together since high school, and Nick had secretly planned on proposing to Kristen when he returned from Afghanistan. But he never dreamed that he'd be returning like this. Now Kristen would have to take care of him—if she even wanted to stay with him. *And why would she want to stay with him*, Nick wondered. Kristen was funny and smart. Plus, she was beautiful with long red hair and bright green eyes. *She won't want to waste her time with some blind guy who can't even see her*, Nick thought bitterly. *She'll never marry me now.*

9   At first, Nick's friends came around a lot. They sat and talked with him, trying to get him to laugh at old jokes. They brought him foods he liked and often hung around for hours listening to music or reading the newspaper to Nick. They rarely mentioned basketball or the upcoming cycling races they were

training for—they thought this would make Nick sad. In fact, they rarely even mentioned Nick's blindness because it made them uncomfortable. And, in time, most of Nick's friends' discomfort with his blindness outweighed their concern for him. They ran out of things to talk about. One by one, most of Nick's friends faded away.

10   Now Nick became angry and depressed. He felt betrayed and abandoned by friends, and he declined into self-pity. Nick might have sunk all the way to rock bottom if it had not been for Kristen. During that very difficult first year, Kristen never wavered in her devotion to Nick. She helped him in any way she could, even when Nick's frustration made it hard for her to help him.

11   "I'm blind!" he'd sometimes shout angrily. "Why are you ruining your life by staying with me? I'm no good anymore. Why don't you go find someone who

can *see* you—someone who doesn't have to be treated like a baby?"

12   More than anything, Nick hated his loss of independence. He'd always prided himself on the fact that he was never afraid to try new things and go to new places. Sometimes on long weekend bike rides, Nick would make himself get lost intentionally just to see what kind of adventure it might turn into. Now he couldn't even walk to the corner store without Kristen's help.

13   Kristen knew that Nick needed to feel some sense of independence, or he would only become angrier and sadder. As it was, he often spent entire days doing little more than listening to the radio, sleeping, and drinking beer—something he'd rarely done before. So when Kristen came across an article about a local center for disabled veterans, she mentioned it to Nick.

14   "It's a way for you to meet other men and women like yourself," Kristen explained. "And there's all kinds of help there to get you trained and prepared for a new career."

15   "Career?" Nick asked doubtfully. "What could I do without my eyes?"

16   Kristen walked over and took Nick's hands in hers. "A lot, Nick," she said quietly. "Why don't you go and find out?"

17   Nick agreed to give it a try. There was only one catch. The center didn't open until 9:00, and since Kristen had to be at work at 8:30, she would not be able to drive Nick there every day.

18   "Nick, the city bus stops right in front of the center," Kristen said carefully. "Why don't you learn how to take the bus?"

19   "Take the bus?" Nick replied angrily. "How would I even know where I was going? What if I get lost? I feel like you're abandoning me—just like all my friends did."

20   Kristen thought Nick might respond like this, so she had already figured out a plan. "Look," she said, "I'll make some arrangements at work. I'll ride the bus with you for a week or so until you get the hang of it. What do you think of that?"

21   It took a little more convincing, but Nick finally decided to try. And, actually, he was excited about the idea of something new—something he could do on his own.

22   And so, for a week and a half, Nick and Kristen took the bus together across town. She helped him use his cane to feel for the curb, the bus steps, and the aisle to his seat. They counted the number of stops it took to get from their apartment to the center, and when they arrived, Kristen helped Nick find the sidewalk that led to the center's front door. If Nick stumbled or became confused, Kristen was there to smooth things over and encourage her boyfriend along.

23   Finally, Nick felt sufficiently° confident to ride the bus alone. He'd been enjoying the time spent at the center, and he was looking forward to being independent again. But now as Nick sat on the bus alone for the first time, he wasn't so sure. He heard the little girl ask her mother again what was wrong with the man with the funny

cane. Nick took a deep breath and tried to concentrate.

24   *Two, three, four . . .* Nick counted the stops. Very carefully, he got off at the seventh stop. Just like every day with Kristen, Nick used his cane to walk over the curb and to the sidewalk to the center. His heart was pounding. What if he was going the wrong way? What if he fell? No one was there to help him.

25   "Hey, Nick! Good to see you." Relief flooded Nick. It was one of the instructors at the center. He'd made it!

26   At the end of his first week of riding alone, Nick was hardly nervous at all. Every day had gone well. Only one time had he tripped on the curb, but almost instantly the hand of a stranger had gripped his shoulder to keep him from falling. Nick had said thank you, but the stranger just patted him on the back.

27   Now as Nick carefully made his way down the steps of the bus, the bus driver said, "You sure are one lucky young man."

28   At first, Nick wasn't sure if the bus driver was talking to him. Why would anyone think he was lucky? "Me?" Nick asked.

29   "Yes, you!" the driver said with a friendly laugh.

30   "Why do you say that?"

31   "Well, to have someone looking out for you like that," the driver explained. "Making sure you're okay."

32   "What are you talking about?" Nick asked.

33   "You know," the driver said, sounding a little puzzled by Nick's question. "That pretty woman with the red hair—the one who has been standing on the corner waiting and watching for you every day this week. The one who caught you when you almost fell."

34   Nick was too stunned to say anything at first. Then tears filled his eyes behind his dark glasses.

35   The driver chuckled again and said, "I wish my wife cared that much about me!"

36   Nick smiled through his tears. "She's not my wife," he said quietly. "But she's going to be."

First Impressions

Freewrite for ten minutes on one of the following.

1. Did you enjoy reading this selection? Why or why not?

2. Why do you think Nick's girlfriend didn't let him know that she was watching for him every day at the center?

3. Have you ever known someone like Nick who was disabled in some way? What was his or her outlook on life?

Vocabulary Check

___D___ 1. In the excerpt below, the word *trickled* means
  A. waited.
  B. held.   Sweat drips off one's forehead
  C. pulled.   when one is nervous.
  D. dripped.

  "Gratefully, Nick eased into the first set of seats reserved for the disabled. A thin rivulet of sweat trickled down Nick's forehead, and his hands shook." (Paragraph 4)

___C___ 2. In the excerpt below, the word *pastimes* means
  A. bad habits.
  B. responsibilities.   For many people, spending time
  C. enjoyable activities.   cycling and playing basketball with
  D. promotions.   friends are enjoyable activities.

  "Two of Nick's favorite pastimes had been cycling and playing basketball, and that's how he had met a lot of his friends. Now he wouldn't be able to do either." (Paragraph 7)

___A___ 3. In the excerpt below, the word *declined* means
  A. fell.
  B. climbed.
  C. became angry.   Synonym clue: *sunk.*
  D. refused.

  "Nick . . . felt betrayed and abandoned by friends, and he declined into self-pity. Nick might have sunk all the way to rock bottom if it had not been for Kristen." (Paragraph 10)

___B___ 4. In the excerpt below, the word *wavered* means
- A. gestured.
- B. hesitated.
- C. started.
- D. damp.

The words *helped him in any way she could* suggest that Kristen never hesitated in her devotion.

"During that very difficult first year, Kristen never wavered in her devotion to Nick. She helped him in any way she could . . ." (Paragraph 10)

Reading Check

Central Point and Main Ideas

___B___ 1. Which sentence best expresses the central point of the entire selection?
- A. Nick, a blind vet, returns home from the war to find his world turned upside down.
- B. Kristen's solid devotion to Nick helps Nick through a very difficult time, proving that love can overcome even the greatest obstacles.
- C. Nick ultimately decides to marry Kristen after he realizes what she's done for him and how much she really loves him.
- D. The journey of the disabled veteran is a difficult one, and it is not unusual for friends to disappear just when the vet needs them most.

Answer A covers only paragraphs 1–8. Answer C covers only paragraphs 35–36. Answer D covers only paragraph 9.

___D___ 2. Which sentence best expresses the main idea of paragraph 8?
- A. Nick and Kristen had been very close before he was blinded, but now she was beginning to pull away.
- B. Nick was worried that if he couldn't even see Kristen's beauty, she wouldn't want to be with him.
- C. Nick suddenly realized that Kristen would probably not want to marry him now.
- D. Because he was blind, Nick feared that Kristen would leave him.

Answer A is not supported. Answer B covers only sentences 7–8. Answer C covers only the last sentence.

___D___ 3. Which sentence best expresses the main idea of paragraph 9?
- A. Nick's friends felt reluctant to talk about his blindness, because it made them uncomfortable.
- B. Because Nick could no longer play basketball or cycle, his friends had to think of other things to do with him when they visited.
- C. Nick's friends came around fairly often, but Nick could tell they were going to slowly disappear.
- D. At first, Nick's old friends came to visit him, but because his blindness bothered them, they began to fade away.

Answer A covers only sentences 5–6. Answer B covers only sentences 2–3. Answer C is not supported.

Supporting Details

_C_   4. How long had Nick been blind by the time he was able to ride the bus alone?

     A. Three months

     B. Half a year

     C. A little over a year   See paragraph 6.

     D. Two years

_B_   5. To help walk over curbs and climb the steps on the bus, Nick

     A. asked Kristen to help him.

     B. used his cane to feel for them.

     C. counted his footsteps.   See paragraphs 4, 22, and 24.

     D. asked the bus driver to help him.

Inferences

_C_   6. We can infer that the bus driver

See paragraph 33. If the driver is puzzled by Nick's question, he must have assumed that Nick would know what he was referring to.

     A. had known Nick before he started riding the bus.

     B. was unwilling to help Nick when he boarded the bus.

     C. thought that Nick knew Kristen had been the one who caught him when he fell.

     D. does not get along well with his wife.

_C_   7. The reading suggests that

     A. Nick's friends should not be blamed for feeling uncomfortable and leaving him alone.

See paragraph 10.

     B. the loss of his friends finally sent Nick over the edge.

     C. Nick was more angry than sad about losing his friends.

     D. true friendships with others can survive in spite of hardships.

_D_   8. From this selection, we can conclude that Kristen

     A. had never doubted she would remain Nick's girlfriend.

     B. often grew impatient with Nick's self-pity and anger.

     C. would have broken up with Nick if he had refused to go to the veterans' center.

     D. was worried, at first, about Nick taking the bus to the center alone.

The fact that Kristen secretly watched Nick the first week (paragraphs 26–33) supports this inference.

The Writer's Craft

___B___ 9. What technique does Hoffman use to end "The Blind Vet"?

The reader does not know that Kristen has been watching Nick until the driver tells Nick (paragraph 33).

    A. Mystery: we don't know what will happen to Kristen and Nick

    B. Surprise: we learn that Kristen was waiting on the corner to make sure Nick got to the center

    C. Shock: we find out that Nick isn't really blind after all

    D. Humor: we smile at the bus driver's comment about his wife

___A___ 10. What do you think was the author's purpose in writing "The Blind Vet"?

    A. To entertain readers with an inspirational story about overcoming an obstacle

    B. To inform readers of the particular problems a blind vet faces after returning from combat

    C. To persuade readers that veterans need more support services

    D. All of the above   The author describes how Nick overcame the obstacle of his blindness with the loving help of Kristen.

Discussion Questions

1. Why do children stare at and talk loudly about people who, like the blind vet, are different in some way? Aside from the standard "It's not polite to stare/point/talk," how would you explain to a child why he or she should not stare or point at someone who looks different or behaves differently?

2. How do you think you would feel and react if one of your closest friends suddenly became disabled in some way? Would you find it difficult to be with him or her?

3. Do you think Kristen's behavior toward Nick is how most people would react to a loved one becoming disabled? Or do you think this is an unusual, even unbelievable, story? Explain.

4. Consider this bit of scripture from the Bible: "Three things will last forever—faith, hope, and love—and the greatest of these is love." What do these words mean to you? How might they apply to "The Blind Vet"?

Paragraph Assignments

1. Has someone—for example, a friend, teacher, coach, or parent—ever believed in you and patiently urged you on in spite of your own self-doubt or frustration? Write a paragraph about this experience. Be sure to provide specific details as you answer these questions in your paragraph:

   • Who helped you?

   • Why were you feeling doubtful or frustrated?

   • How did this person help you?

   • What was the outcome?

   • What did you learn from this experience?

2. Most of Nick's friends disappeared one by one, because they felt uncomfortable being around someone who was blind. They weren't sure how to act or what to do. In general, many of us tend to be a little awkward around people with disabilities. However, there are things we can do to put both the disabled person and ourselves at ease—and stop friendships from fading away. Write a paragraph that gives several tips on how to feel at ease with a disabled friend or acquaintance. To get some ideas, try Googling phrases such as "how to interact with disabled people" or "supporting someone with a disability." When giving advice, offer an example to make the advice clear.

Essay Assignments

1. Hoffman writes, "More than anything, Nick hated his loss of independence." Most of us take our ability to do whatever we want for granted. We never question being able to take a trip, drive a car, or even make meals for ourselves, since it's what we're used to. What would you miss most if, due to a disability, you no longer could do whatever you wanted? Write an essay in which you detail three aspects of your life that you would particularly miss if, like Nick, you had to rely on others to take care of you.

   Alternatively, if you personally know someone who has become disabled, write an essay about the changes you have seen in this person. You could write about an elderly person whose loss of vision, hearing, or mobility now keeps him or her from doing some of the things he or she used to love to do—or a younger person who, like Nick, has suffered an injury and can no longer enjoy life in the same way. Choose three different things you know this person can no longer do, and devote a paragraph to describing each one. Include details about what he or she may have said to you about loss of independence and how he or she is coping with these changes.

2. Obviously, returning from war with a serious disability would make life very difficult for a veteran. But many veterans who have suffered no physical injuries at all still find it quite difficult to settle back into civilian life. Their difficulties range from nightmares to depression to problems finding employment to inability to adapt to the sudden freedoms of non-military life.

Write an essay in which you present and describe three different reasons that some veterans struggle with returning to civilian life. If you need to do some research, a Google search of key phrases such as "problems veterans face when returning home" or "difficulties adjusting to civilian life" will provide a great many ideas and articles on this topic.

2 The Scholarship Jacket

Marta Salinas

Preview

All of us have suffered disappointments and moments when we have felt we've been treated unfairly. In "The Scholarship Jacket," originally published in *Growing Up Chicana: An Anthology*, Marta Salinas writes about one such moment in her childhood in southern Texas. By focusing on an award that school authorities decided she should not receive, Salinas shows us the pain of discrimination as well as the need for inner strength.

Words to Watch

scholarship (1): acknowledgment of academic excellence
agile (2): able to move quickly
despaired (3): lost hope
eavesdrop (4): secretly listen
filtered through (7): passed through
muster (12): call forth
mesquite (15): a sweet-smelling thorny tree
clod (15): lump of earth or clay
gaunt (25): thin and bony
vile (29): very unpleasant
adrenaline (31): a hormone that raises the blood pressure and stimulates the heart

1   The small Texas school that I attended carried out a tradition every year during the eighth grade graduation: a beautiful gold and green jacket, the school colors, was awarded to the class valedictorian, the student who had maintained the highest grades for eight years. The scholarship° jacket had a big gold *S* on the left front side, and the winner's name was written in gold letters on the pocket.

My oldest sister, Rosie, had won 2 the jacket a few years back, and I fully expected to win also. I was fourteen and in the eighth grade. I had been a straight-A student since the first grade, and the last year I had looked forward to owning that jacket. My father was a farm laborer who couldn't earn enough money to feed eight children, so when I was six I was given to my grandparents to raise. We couldn't participate in sports at school because there were registration fees, uniform costs, and trips out of town; so even though we were quite agile° and athletic, there would never be a sports school jacket for us. This one, the scholarship jacket, was our only chance.

3   In May, close to graduation, spring fever struck, and no one paid any attention to class; instead we stared out the windows and at each other, wanting to speed up the last few weeks of school. I despaired° every time I looked in the mirror. Pencil thin, not a curve anywhere, I was called "Beanpole" and "String Bean," and I knew that's what I looked like. A flat chest, no hips, and a brain, that's what I had. That really isn't much for a fourteen-year-old to work with, I thought, as I absentmindedly wandered from my history class to the gym. Another hour of sweating during basketball and displaying my toothpick legs was coming up. Then I remembered my P.E. shorts were still in a bag under my desk where I'd forgotten them. I had to walk all the way back and get them. Coach Thompson was a real bear if anyone wasn't dressed for P.E. She had said I was a good forward and once she even tried to talk Grandma into letting me join the team. Grandma, of course, said no.

4   I was almost back at my classroom door when I heard angry voices and arguing. I stopped. I didn't mean to eavesdrop°; I just hesitated, not knowing what to do. I needed those shorts and I was going to be late, but I didn't want to interrupt an argument between my teachers. I recognized the

voices: Mr. Schmidt, my history teacher, and Mr. Boone, my math teacher. They seemed to be arguing about me. I couldn't believe it. I still remember the shock that rooted me flat against the wall as if I were trying to blend in with the graffiti written there.

5   "I refuse to do it! I don't care who her father is, her grades don't even begin to compare to Martha's. I won't lie or falsify records. Martha has a straight-A-plus average and you know it." That was Mr. Schmidt, and he sounded very angry. Mr. Boone's voice sounded calm and quiet.

6   "Look, Joann's father is not only on the Board, he owns the only store in town; we could say it was a close tie and—"

7   The pounding in my ears drowned out the rest of the words, only a word here and there filtered through°. ". . . Martha is Mexican . . . resign . . . won't do it. . . ." Mr. Schmidt came rushing out, and luckily for me went down the opposite way toward the auditorium, so he didn't see me. Shaking, I waited a few

minutes and then went in and grabbed my bag and fled from the room. Mr. Boone looked up when I came in but didn't say anything. To this day I don't remember if I got in trouble in P.E. for being late or how I made it through the rest of the afternoon. I went home very sad and cried into my pillow that night so Grandmother wouldn't hear me. It seemed a cruel coincidence that I had overheard that conversation.

8 The next day when the principal called me into his office, I knew what it would be about. He looked uncomfortable and unhappy. I decided I wasn't going to make it any easier for him, so I looked him straight in the eye. He looked away and fidgeted with the papers on his desk.

9 "Martha," he said, "there's been a change in policy this year regarding the scholarship jacket. As you know, it has always been free." He cleared his throat and continued. "This year the Board decided to charge fifteen dollars— which still won't cover the complete cost of the jacket."

10 I stared at him in shock, and a small sound of dismay escaped my throat. I hadn't expected this. He still avoided looking in my eyes.

11 "So if you are unable to pay the fifteen dollars for the jacket, it will be given to the next one in line."

12 Standing with all the dignity I could muster°, I said, "I'll speak to my grandfather about it, sir, and let you know tomorrow." I cried on the walk home from the bus stop. The dirt road was a quarter of a mile from the highway, so by the time I got home, my eyes were red and puffy.

13 "Where's Grandpa?" I asked Grandma, looking down at the floor so she wouldn't ask me why I'd been crying. She was sewing on a quilt and didn't look up.

14 "I think he's out back working in the bean field."

15 I went outside and looked out at the fields. There he was. I could see him walking between the rows, his body bent over the little plants, hoe in hand. I walked slowly out to him, trying to think how I could best ask him for the money. There was a cool breeze blowing and a sweet smell of mesquite° in the air, but I didn't appreciate it. I kicked at a dirt clod°. I wanted that jacket so much. It was more than just being a valedictorian and giving a little thank-you speech for the jacket on graduation night. It represented eight years of hard work and expectation. I knew I had to be honest with Grandpa; it was my only chance. He saw me and looked up.

16 He waited for me to speak. I cleared my throat nervously and clasped my hands behind my back so he wouldn't see them shaking. "Grandpa, I have a big favor to ask you," I said in Spanish, the only language he knew. He still waited silently. I tried again. "Grandpa, this year the principal said the scholarship jacket is not going to be free. It's going to cost fifteen dollars and I have to take the money in tomorrow, otherwise it'll be given to someone else." The last words came out in an eager rush. Grandpa straightened up tiredly and leaned his chin on the hoe handle. He looked out over the field that was filled with

the tiny green bean plants. I waited, desperately hoping he'd say I could have the money.

17   He turned to me and asked quietly, "What does a scholarship jacket mean?"

18   I answered quickly; maybe there was a chance. "It means you've earned it by having the highest grades for eight years and that's why they're giving it to you." Too late I realized the significance of my words. Grandpa knew that I understood it was not a matter of money. It wasn't that. He went back to hoeing the weeds that sprang up between the delicate little bean plants. It was a time-consuming job; sometimes the small shoots were right next to each other. Finally he spoke again.

19   "Then if you pay for it, Marta, it's not a scholarship jacket, is it? Tell your principal I will not pay the fifteen dollars."

20   I walked back to the house and locked myself in the bathroom for a long time. I was angry with Grandfather even though I knew he was right, and I was angry with the Board, whoever they were. Why did they have to change the rules just when it was my turn to win the jacket?

21   It was a very sad and withdrawn girl who dragged into the principal's office the next day. This time he did look me in the eyes.

22   "What did your grandfather say?"

23   I sat very straight in my chair.

24   "He said to tell you he won't pay the fifteen dollars."

25   The principal muttered something I couldn't understand under his breath, and walked over to the window. He stood looking out at something outside. He looked bigger than usual when he stood up; he was a tall, gaunt° man with gray hair, and I watched the back of his head while I waited for him to speak.

26   "Why?" he finally asked. "Your grandfather has the money. Doesn't he own a small bean farm?"

27   I looked at him, forcing my eyes to stay dry. "He said if I had to pay for it, then it wouldn't be a scholarship jacket," I said and stood up to leave. "I guess you'll just have to give it to Joann." I hadn't meant to say that; it had just slipped out. I was almost to the door when he stopped me.

28   "Martha—wait."

29   I turned and looked at him, waiting. What did he want now? I could feel my heart pounding. Something bitter and vile° tasting was coming up in my mouth; I was afraid I was going to be sick. I didn't need any sympathy speeches. He sighed loudly and went back to his big desk. He looked at me, biting his lip, as if thinking.

30   "Okay, damn it. We'll make an exception in your case. I'll tell the Board, you'll get your jacket."

31   I could hardly believe it. I spoke in a trembling rush. "Oh, thank you, sir!" Suddenly I felt great. I didn't know about adrenaline° in those days, but I knew something was pumping through me, making me feel as tall as the sky. I wanted to yell, jump, run the mile, do something. I ran out so I could cry in the hall where there was no one to see me. At the end of the day, Mr. Schmidt winked at me and said, "I hear you're getting a scholarship jacket this year."

32   His face looked as happy and innocent as a baby's, but I knew better. Without answering I gave him a quick hug and ran to the bus. I cried on the walk home again, but this time because I was so happy. I couldn't wait to tell Grandpa and ran straight to the field. I joined him in the row where he was working and without saying anything I crouched down and started pulling up the weeds with my hands. Grandpa worked alongside me for a few minutes, but he didn't ask what had happened. After I had a little pile of weeds between the rows, I stood up and faced him.

33   "The principal said he's making an exception for me, Grandpa, and I'm getting the jacket after all. That's after I told him what you said."

34   Grandpa didn't say anything; he just gave me a pat on the shoulder and a smile. He pulled out the crumpled red handkerchief that he always carried in his back pocket and wiped the sweat off his forehead.

35   "Better go see if your grandmother needs any help with supper."

36   I gave him a big grin. He didn't fool me. I skipped and ran back to the house whistling some silly tune.

First Impressions

Freewrite for ten minutes on one of the following.

1. Did you enjoy reading this selection? Why or why not?

2. Have you ever felt that you were treated unfairly simply because of your gender, age, ethnicity, or financial situation? Explain.

3. Which person in this story do you admire the most? Why?

Vocabulary Check

_B_ 1. In the excerpt below, the word *falsify* means
   A. write down.
   B. make untrue.
   C. keep track of.
   D. sort alphabetically.

   Synonym clue: *lie.*

   "'I won't lie or falsify records. Martha has a straight-A-plus average and you know it.'" (Paragraph 5)

___B___ 2. In the excerpt below, the words *fidgeted with* mean
- A. folded neatly.
- B. fussed nervously with.   *Synonym-like clues for* nervously:
- C. played happily with.   *uncomfortable, unhappy, looked away.*
- D. calmly examined.

"He looked uncomfortable and unhappy. . . . He looked away and fidgeted with the papers on his desk." (Paragraph 8)

___D___ 3. In the excerpt below, the word *dismay* means
- A. joy.
- B. comfort.   If Marta was "shocked" and received
- C. relief.   unexpected information, she would
- D. disappointment.   make a sound of disappointment.

"I stared at him in shock, and a small sound of dismay escaped my throat. I hadn't expected this." (Paragraph 10)

___D___ 4. In the sentence below, the word *withdrawn* means
- A. not healthy.
- B. curious.   People who are sad and have to
- C. amused.   drag themselves to appointments
- D. not responsive.   are often quiet and unresponsive.

"It was a very sad and withdrawn girl who dragged into the principal's office the next day." (Paragraph 21)

Reading Check

Central Point and Main Ideas

___C___ 1. Which sentence best expresses the central point of the entire selection?
- A. It is more important to be smart than good-looking or athletic.
- B. People who are willing to pay for awards deserve them more than

Answers A, B, and D   people who are not.
are not supported.
- C. By refusing to give in to discrimination, the author finally received the award she had earned.
- D. Always do what the adults in your family say, even if you don't agree.

___B___ 2. Which sentence best expresses the main idea of paragraph 2?
- A. Marta wanted to win the scholarship jacket to be like her sister Rosie.
- B. The scholarship jacket was especially important to Marta because she

Answers A, C, and D   was unable to earn a jacket in any other way.
are not supported.
- C. The scholarship jacket was better than a sports school jacket.
- D. Marta resented her parents for sending her to live with her grandparents.

___B___ 3. Which sentence best expresses the main idea of paragraph 7?
- A. Marta didn't want her grandmother to know she was crying.
- B. Marta was shocked and saddened by the conversation she overheard.
- C. Mr. Schmidt didn't see Marta when he rushed out of the room.
- D. Marta didn't hear every word of Mr. Schmidt's and Mr. Boone's conversation.

Expressions like "ears pounded," "shaking," "fled from the room," and "don't remember" show that Marta was shocked and saddened.

Supporting Details

___B___ 4. Marta was raised by her grandparents because
- A. she wanted to learn to speak Spanish.
- B. her father did not earn enough money to feed all of his children.
- C. she wanted to learn about farming.
- D. her parents died when she was six.

See paragraph 2.

___T___ 5. TRUE OR FALSE? Marta was called by a different name at school.

Marta's teachers and the principal called her "Martha." See paragraphs 5, 7, 9, and 28. (What might be a reason for this change?)

Inferences

Item 6: We suspect the principal is going to tell Marta that there is some sort of problem with the scholarship jacket that he knows she deserves, so it is logical to infer that this is why he looks "uncomfortable and unhappy."

___C___ 6. We can infer from paragraph 8 that the principal was "uncomfortable and unhappy" because
- A. the students had not been paying attention in class during the last few weeks before graduation.
- B. his office was very hot.
- C. he was ashamed to tell Marta that she had to pay fifteen dollars for a jacket that she had earned.
- D. Mr. Boone and Mr. Schmidt were fighting in the hallway.

___B___ 7. The author implies that the Board members were not going to give Marta the scholarship jacket because
- A. she was late for P.E. class.
- B. they wanted to award the jacket to the daughter of an important local citizen.
- C. another student had better grades.
- D. they didn't think it was fair to have two members of the same family win the jacket.

See paragraphs 5–6. Answers A and D are unsupported; answer C is contradicted by paragraph 5.

The Writer's Craft

If the
jacket is beautiful,
it is desirable. If
the author "fully
expected to win" it,
we want to find out
if she does.

_D_ 8. The author begins her story with a description of the scholarship jacket in order to
   A. get readers interested in who will win the jacket.
   B. show that the jacket is desirable.
   C. let readers see exactly what the jacket looks like.
   D. do all of the above.

Starting in paragraph
3, the events of the
story are shown in
the order in which
they happened.

_C_ 9. In general, what is Salinas's pattern of organization in her essay?
   A. Comparison-contrast: She contrasts her school life with her home life.
   B. Listing order: She lists a series of reasons why being charged for the scholarship jacket was unfair.
   C. Time order: She relates the events of the story in the order that they happened.
   D. Cause-effect: She explains the results of overhearing the conversation between her two teachers.

_C_ 10. The tone, or emotion, that the author conveys in paragraph 31 is best described as
   A. acceptance and contentment.
   B. anger and resentment.
   C. joy and excitement.
   D. disappointment and distress.

Words like "great," "as tall as the sky," and "I wanted to yell, jump, run the mile" indicate joy and excitement.

Discussion Questions

1. In her first meeting with the principal, Marta could have challenged him by telling what she had overheard the two teachers saying. Why do you think she stayed silent? What do you think the principal would have said or done if she'd told him she knew the real reason she wasn't being given the jacket?

2. Why do you think the principal gave in during his second meeting with Marta? What do you think will happen when he has to face the Board again? If you were the principal, what would you say to the Board?

3. What values did Marta learn from her grandfather? Where in the story do they demonstrate similar values?

4. Salinas implies that she was discriminated against because of her ethnic background (she was Mexican) and her family's economic condition (they were poor). Have you ever experienced discrimination, or do you know of a friend who has experienced it? Explain.

Paragraph Assignments

1. Write a paragraph about a time when you experienced or witnessed an injustice. Describe the circumstances surrounding the incident and why you think the people involved acted as they did. In your paragraph, describe how you felt at the time and any effect the incident has had on you. Your topic sentence could be something like one of the following:

   - I was angry when my supervisor promoted his nephew even though I was more qualified.

   - A friend of mine recently got in trouble with authorities even though he was innocent of any wrongdoing.

2. In her essay, Salinas tells a story about an example of social injustice that she experienced. "Social injustice" is defined as unfairness in the way society treats one or more groups of people, usually involving a lack of basic human rights or equality. In Salinas's case, she was treated unfairly because of her race.

   Write a paragraph about a different group that is often a target of social injustice. In your paragraph, present a few examples of how this group experiences inequality. You can research specific examples of social injustice by first choosing the group you want to present in your paragraph (for example, elderly people, women, gay people, African Americans, poor people, etc.) and then simply Googling "examples of discrimination against the elderly" (or whichever group you choose).

Essay Assignments

1. This story contains several examples of authority figures—specifically, the two teachers, the principal, and Marta's grandfather. Write an essay describing three qualities that you think an authority figure should possess. Such qualities might include honesty, fairness, compassion, and knowledge, among others.

   Devote each of the supporting paragraphs in the body of your essay to one of those qualities. Within each paragraph, give an example or examples of how an authority figure in your life has demonstrated that quality.

   You may write about three different authority figures that have demonstrated those three qualities to you. Alternatively, one authority figure may have demonstrated all three.

   Your thesis statement might be similar to one of these:

- My older brother, my grandmother, and my football coach have been models of admirable behavior for me.
- My older brother's honesty, courage, and kindness to others have set a valuable example for me.

2. In paragraph 3, Marta recalls her self-consciousness about her skinny body, which made the other students call her "Beanpole" and "String Bean." Her reaction reflects the importance placed on physical appearance in our society.

   Think about the messages teenagers receive regarding their appearance. ("Appearance" could include their bodies, dress, and hairstyles, among other things.) These messages can come from any of the following:

   - other students
   - music videos
   - magazine advertisements
   - television commercials
   - talk shows
   - television shows and movies
   - sports figures

   Write an essay about the types of pressure that teenagers face to look or act a certain way. Examine the consequences—for example, low self-esteem, eating disorders, steroid use—when these ideals are not achieved.

   Focus your essay on three different influences—for example, fashion magazines, popular TV shows, and professional sports—and the consequences of each.

3 Life Over Death

Bill Broderick

Preview

A small, furry body lies on the pavement. It's a daily reality for most of us, living as we do in a world where the automobile rules the road. But in this case, something moved the author to stop and investigate. What he found reminded him that the chance to save a life doesn't come along every day.

Words to Watch

grimaced (2): made a twisted face to express pain or disgust
immobile (2): not moving
ligament (5): a band of tissue which connects bones or supports organs
tendon (5): a tissue which connects muscles to bones and other parts of the body
good Samaritan (6): someone who helps others unselfishly
kinked (7): twisted
resignation (9): acceptance without resistance
dejected (11): depressed
pathetic (11): pitiful

1 The reaction was as it always is when I see an animal lying in the roadway. My heart sank. And a lump formed in my throat at the thought of a life unfulfilled. I then resolved to move him off the road, to ensure that one of God's creations did not become a permanent part of the pavement. Some might ask what difference it makes. If it's already dead, why not just leave it there? My answer is that I believe in death with dignity, for people and for animals alike.

2 So I pulled my car over to the side of the road and walked back to where the cat lay motionless. Two cars passed over him, managing to avoid running him over. With no other cars in sight, I made my way to the lifeless form just as a jogger went by. The jogger grimaced° at the sight of the immobile° cat, blood dripping from his mouth. "How'd it happen?" he asked. I replied that I didn't know; he probably got hit by some careless driver. I just wanted to get him off the road. I reached down for the cat and got the surprise of my life. The little creature lifted his head ever so slightly and uttered a pitiful, unforgettable little

"meow." He was still alive.

3   What was I going to do now? I was already late for work. All I had intended to do was move the cat off the road. I didn't need this. But I knew I had no choice. I sighed deeply, then reached down and carefully cradled the cat in my hands. I asked the jogger to open my car trunk and remove the things from a small box. Then I gently placed the cat in the box. He was in shock, so he probably could not feel the pain from his obvious injuries. "Kinda funny lookin', isn't he?" asked the jogger. I was annoyed by his question, but I had to admit that he was right. This cat looked peculiar. Not ugly, mind you. But he seemed to have a comical look on his face, even at such a dreadful time.

4   "What are you gonna do with him?" the jogger asked. I told him I would take the cat to the local vet and let him decide what to do.

5   The vet was only five minutes away. My wife and I had been bringing our animals to him for several years, and I knew I could rely on him to do what was best for the cat. I brought the cat into the reception room and placed it on the counter. As this was an emergency, the vet was summoned right away. He examined the cat thoroughly, listing the injuries for his assistant to write down. "Broken jaw, that'll have to be set. Two teeth broken. A couple more loose. Possible internal injuries, but they don't look too bad. Uh-oh. This doesn't look good. He doesn't appear to have any movement in his right front leg. Possible break, definite ligament° and tendon° damage."

The vet completed his examination, 6 then looked at me and asked what I wanted to do. I knew what he meant. Did I want to have the cat "put to sleep"? I became uneasy. I clumsily explained that I was hoping to get advice from him on what to do. Fair enough. The jaw would have to be wired shut for six weeks, and the cat would have to wear a cast on its leg for three months. There was no way of knowing if the damage to the leg was permanent. He could have the cast removed and still not be able to use the leg. The cost of all the surgery would be high, but I would get a 50 percent "good Samaritan°" discount if I went ahead with it.

Now I was really at a loss. If I went 7 ahead with the surgery, I'd be paying for a cat which wasn't mine, whose owner I'd probably never find, and who might end up with the use of only three legs. And on top of it, this was one of the funniest-looking cats ever born. Black and white, spotted where it shouldn't be, kinked° tail, and a silly half-smile on its face. I chuckled at that and the entire situation.

8   "What do you want to do, Bill?" asked the vet.

9   I shrugged my shoulders in resignation°. "Dan, I'll choose life over death every time. Let's give it our best shot."

10   I called back later in the day and learned that the surgery had been successful. "You can pick up your cat tomorrow morning," I was told. My cat. I started to say that he was not my cat, but I knew otherwise.

11   The next morning, my wife and I drove to the vet and picked up the cat. He looked ghastly. His jaw was now bandaged, and a cast covered one leg entirely and wrapped around his midsection. We were dejected°. But, as we drove him home, we began thinking that perhaps this cat was not as pathetic° as he looked. As frightened as he must have been, as much pain as he must have felt, he sat calmly in my wife's lap. He purred and stared out the window with his curious half-smile.

12   When we got home, we introduced him to our two Siamese cats, who stared in disbelief at this strange creature. They sensed it might be a cat, but they had never seen one like this. It took him very little time to get used to his new surroundings. It took him longer to get used to the cast, which made even walking a chore. Surely he must have been embarrassed. After all, an animal normally able to glide around quietly should not make a resounding thump every time he moves.

13   In due time, the cast came off. To our relief, Pokey, as we now called him, had about 90 percent mobility in the leg. He got around okay, but he limped whenever he tried to move any faster than a slow walk.

14   All this occurred four years ago. Pokey is still with us today. In fact, he has become our most beloved cat. Because of his injury, he is strictly an indoor cat. This does not seem to bother him at all. It is hard to believe that any cat has ever enjoyed himself more. Maybe it's because he had been slowed after being hit by a car, or perhaps he just has a special individuality. He is never bored. At times he will race around the house like he is leading the Indy 500. Or he'll leap into the air at an imaginary foe. Or he'll purr loudly at the foot of our bed, staring into space with that silly grin on his face. And he couldn't care less that he still looks funny.

15   It would have been easy to let Pokey lie in the middle of the road. And it would have been just as simple to have the vet put him to sleep. But when I think of all the pleasure this cat has given us, and of how much fun he has living with us, I know the right decision was made. And I'd do it again in a second. I'll take life over death every time.

First Impressions

Freewrite for ten minutes on one of the following.

1. Did you enjoy reading this selection? Why or why not?

2. Would you ever stop to remove an animal's dead body from the road? Under what circumstances?

3. Do you consider yourself an animal lover? Explain.

Vocabulary Check

___C___ 1. In the sentence below, the word *resolved* means

    A. forgot.

    B. hid.   If the author wanted to prevent the cat from being crushed

    C. decided.   by other cars, he must have decided to move the cat.

    D. drove.

"I then resolved to move him off the road, to ensure that one of God's creations did not become a permanent part of the pavement." (Paragraph 1)

___B___ 2. In the excerpt below, the word *summoned* means

    A. paid.

    B. called for.   In an emergency, one would call for the

    C. telephoned.   vet right away to examine the cat.

    D. ignored.

"As this was an emergency, the vet was summoned right away. He examined the cat thoroughly. . . ." (Paragraph 5)

___C___ 3. In the excerpt below, the word *ghastly* means

    A. threatening.

    B. appealing.   A cat with a bandaged jaw and a

    C. terrible.   body cast would look terrible.

    D. marvelous.

"He looked ghastly. His jaw was now bandaged, and a cast covered one leg entirely and wrapped around his midsection." (Paragraph 11)

Reading Check

Central Point and Main Ideas

__B__ 1. Which sentence best expresses the central point of the entire selection?
  A. Drivers need to be alert to dangers on the road.
  B. Every life is valuable.
  C. Cats make wonderful pets.
  D. Pokey is strictly an indoor cat because of his injury.

Answer A covers only the seventh sentence of the paragraph. Answer B is contradicted by the vet's statement of what the cat needs. Answer D is incorrect because the author does not know what the vet will recommend. That is why he asks the vet's advice.

__C__ 2. Which sentence best expresses the main idea of paragraph 6?
  A. The author wanted to know if the damage to the cat's leg was permanent.
  B. The vet didn't know what to do with the cat.
  C. To help the author decide what to do, the vet explained what could be done for the cat and what it would cost.
  D. The author expected the vet to say that the cat should be "put to sleep."

__A__ 3. Which sentence best expresses the main idea of paragraph 14?
  A. Pokey is beloved and enjoys life a great deal now.
  B. Pokey sometimes leaps into the air at imaginary enemies.
  C. Pokey must spend the rest of his life indoors.
  D. Pokey was injured four years ago. Answers B, C, and D are too narrow. Answer B covers only the ninth sentence; answer C covers only the third sentence; answer D covers only the first sentence.

Supporting Details

See paragraphs 2 and 3. The author says he "got the surprise of [his] life" when the cat moved and meowed. Answer A is contradicted by sentence 5 in paragraph 2. Answer C is wrong because there is no indication the author is surprised by the jogger. Answer D is wrong because the author says the cat was "not ugly," but peculiar and comical.

__B__ 4. The author
  A. saw a car hit the cat.
  B. was very surprised that the cat was still alive.
  C. was surprised that the jogger came by.
  D. thought that the cat was ugly.

__C__ 5. For Pokey's surgery, the vet charged the author
  A. nothing.
  B. extra, because of the emergency circumstances.
  C. half the usual cost.
  D. the usual cost.

See the last sentence of paragraph 6.

Item 1:
Sentence A is not supported because the selection says nothing about the need for drivers to be alert to dangers. Sentence B is supported by the title of the selection, the author's statements in paragraphs 9 and 15, and the author's actions in saving the cat's life. Sentences C and D cover only paragraph 14.

Inferences

___B___ 6. It is reasonable to conclude that

A. Pokey would have lived if the author had not picked him up.

Paragraph 1 suggests this conclusion. Answers A, C, and D are not supported.

B. this was not the first time the author had moved the body of an animal off the road.

C. the author was angry that the vet charged him for Pokey's surgery.

D. the author's wife does not like cats as much as he does.

___C___ 7. We can conclude from paragraph 3 that the author

A. would have left the cat there if the jogger hadn't been watching.

B. was frequently late to work.

C. knew the cat would not recover without medical attention.

D. knew that the cat's injuries were not very severe.

The facts that the cat is in shock and has obvious injuries suggest answer C and contradict answer D. Answers A and B are not supported.

The Writer's Craft

Answer A: The events are described in a manner that engages and entertains the reader. Answer B: The events show that an animal can be helped to recover. Answer C: See paragraph 15.

___D___ 8. The author's purpose in writing "Life Over Death" was to

A. entertain readers with a charming story about adopting a cat.

B. teach readers that animals can be helped to recover from serious injuries.

C. persuade readers that doing the right thing has its own rewards.

D. do all of the above.

___D___ 9. How does the author support his main point in this selection?

The entire selection describes the author's experience in saving Pokey. Answers A, B, and C are not supported.

A. By giving facts about injured animals

B. By presenting examples of the ways animals can change a person's life

C. By citing results of studies showing how animals benefit people

D. By relating his personal experience with saving an injured cat

___A___ 10. What does Broderick's concluding paragraph do?

A. It offers a final thought.

B. It gives a recommendation to readers.

C. It presents surprising new information.

D. It summarizes the events that took place in the selection.

The concluding paragraph adds a final thought about the value and rewards of doing the right thing and making humane choices.

Discussion Questions

1. In the first paragraph, the author uses the expression "death with dignity." What do you think he means by that expression?

2. When the vet told Broderick that he could pick up his cat at the vet's office, the author began to protest but then stopped. Why do you think Broderick decided the cat was really his?

3. Why do you think that Pokey has become, in Broderick's words, "our most beloved cat"? Do you think Pokey's injuries had an effect on how the author ended up feeling about him? Why or why not?

4. Can—and should—something be done to make the world a better place for hurt and homeless animals like Pokey? Or should our priorities lie elsewhere? Explain your answer.

Paragraph Assignments

1. The author of "Life Over Death" felt he "had no choice"—that he *had* to help the injured cat. For this assignment, write a one-paragraph letter to the author telling him about a time you also did something because you thought it was the only right thing to do. A topic sentence for this letter could be worded something like this: "When I realized my brother was shoplifting, I felt I had no choice but to tell our parents."

    After your topic sentence, describe the situation that faced you, and then explain the decision you made. Conclude by telling what finally happened.

2. Bill Broderick acted as a "good Samaritan" when he saved Pokey—in other words, he unselfishly helped another creature without expecting any reward. Write an essay about one or more good Samaritans you have known and what they have done to help others. In your essay, be sure to answer the following questions:

    - Who was the good Samaritan?
    - Who was the person (or animal) in need?
    - Exactly what did the person do to help?
    - What might have happened if the Samaritan had *not* provided help?

Essay Assignments

1. When the author stopped his car to move a dead cat out of the middle of the road, he would never have guessed that, first, the cat was still alive and, second, the cat would one day be the most beloved cat in his own household! The fact that Broderick just happened to pass by at that exact time and make the unusual decision to stop can be thought of as "a twist of fate." Twists of fate are defined as random occurrences that have far-reaching consequences—like stopping to move a "dead" animal and ending up keeping that animal for the rest of its life. We all experience various twists of fate throughout our lives, events that may entirely change something around us—or about us.

   Write an essay about a twist of fate in your life. Think about how some random action (like turning a corner, driving home a different way, going to an event you didn't really want to attend, taking a class you thought you'd hate, etc.) led to something that profoundly affected your life. In your essay, tell the story of what happened. Organize your essay as Broderick does: First, describe what you were doing and how it led you to the person/thing/animal that would change your life. Next, describe what happened at that moment, how you felt, and what you were thinking. Finally, explain what ultimately resulted from this "twist of fate" and how it has affected your life.

2. Why do people own pets? What do pets contribute to people's lives? Write an essay about some of the reasons people choose to keep pets. For each reason, provide specific details or examples that help illustrate that reason. You might find it helpful to Google a phrase such as "benefits of pets."

   An effective thesis statement for this essay might be one of the following:

   - Pets are important to people for several reasons.
   - Owning a pet guarantees a steady supply of amusing anecdotes, satisfying responsibilities, and—best of all—unconditional love.

4 A Small Victory

Steve Lopez

Preview

There are a million small miseries in a big city, and most of them go unnoticed and unrepaired. But when *Philadelphia Inquirer* columnist Steve Lopez wrote about Ruby Knight, a gracious woman caught in a nightmarish tangle of medical red tape, he touched a nerve in his readers. You may or may not be surprised to learn of the outpouring of response to Lopez's column.

Words to Watch

dog days (1): the hot, humid summer days between early July and early September
metropolis (2): big city
glances (2): flashes
shimmer (2): shine
bureaucracy (6): a system in which complex rules interfere with effective action
inventory (15): the amount of goods on hand
exclusively (40): entirely
sprawling (44): spread out (and therefore hard to deal with)
cynical (53): distrustful of people's motives

First column, written on July 22:

1 On the dog days° of summer, ten floors above Camden [New Jersey], Ruby Knight sets the fan at the foot of her bed and aims it at Philadelphia. Then she sits in the window, breeze at her back, and lets her thoughts carry her across the river to the city where she grew up.

2 She is 71 and has lived—since her husband passed on—in a high-rise near the Ben Franklin Bridge toll plaza. The neighborhood isn't the greatest, but from the tenth floor, Philadelphia is a gleaming metropolis°. The city sprouts above the river, and the sun glances° off skyscrapers that shimmer° in the July heat.

3 Mrs. Knight watches the boats and ships on the river, the cars on the bridge. She looks to North Philly and thinks back on her eighteen proud years as a crossing guard at 17th and Ridge. And she worries about tomorrow.

4   Mrs. Knight, in the quiet of her home, is slowly starving.

5   She beat cancer: Her doctor calls it a near miracle. But now she's wrestling a worse kind of beast.

6   Bureaucracy°.

7   Joseph Spiegel, a Philadelphia surgeon, tells the story:

8   In 1986, a tumor filled Mrs. Knight's throat. Spiegel removed her voice box and swallowing mechanism. Mrs. Knight was fed through a tube to her stomach. It was uncomfortable and painful, but she was happy to be alive.

9   Although she couldn't speak, she learned to write real fast and took to carrying a note pad around. She gets help from an older sister, Elizabeth Woods, who herself beat a form of lung cancer that's often a quick killer.

10   The doctor was impressed by Mrs. Knight's fight. "She said she was placing her faith in my hands and the Lord's," he says.

11   Mrs. Knight had several more operations. But over the years, no sign of cancer. And five months ago—she smiles at the memory—Spiegel removed the tube. She was able to swallow again. After four years.

12   Little did she know the end of one problem was the start of another.

13   Instead of pouring her liquid nutrition down the tube, Mrs. Knight now drank it. The same exact liquid.

14   But Medicare, which paid when it went down the tube, refused to pay when it went down her throat.

15   Mrs. Knight, who lives on a fixed and meager income, kept the liquid cans in the corner of her living room, an open inventory°. She would look at those cans as if they represented the days left in her life. And she began rationing.

16   Mrs. Knight says her fighting weight is close to 100. When it dropped noticeably, she went to the doctor, but had trouble making her point.

17   "I think she was a little embarrassed that she couldn't afford to buy the stuff," Spiegel says.

18   She had lost about ten pounds since her last visit, down to the high eighties. She was on her way, Spiegel says, to starving herself to death.

19   Spiegel got an emergency supply of the liquid—she goes through about six cans a day at one dollar a can—and began calling Medicare. If she ends up in the hospital, Spiegel argued, it'll cost Medicare a lot more than six dollars a day.

20   But Medicare, with built-in safeguards against intentional or accidental use of common sense, wouldn't budge.

21   "This is a federally funded program, and we have specific guidelines for what

we can pay for and can't pay for," Jan Shumate said in an interview. She's director of "Medicare Part B Services" in the Columbia, South Carolina claims office.

22   But it's the same liquid.

23   "Yes, I understand that."

24   It costs less than hospitalization.

25   "Yes, I understand that, but we're mandated to go by the rules."

26   Even if it costs more money?

27   "My only solution I can suggest is if she files again and it gets denied, she can request an informal review."

28   The reasoning is Medicare can't pay for every substance somebody claims to need for survival.

29   Spiegel says Mrs. Knight needs this drink. She can't eat or drink much of anything else. He has told her he may have to put the tube back in her stomach, so Medicare will pay again.

30   At the mere suggestion, Mrs. Knight loses it. No way. Her sister is with her, the two of them confused by it all. They've beaten cancer, cheated the days, and now this.

31   Mrs. Knight hustles to the bathroom and returns with the scale. She puts it by her bed, gets on. The needle hits 83. She stands at the window, frail against the Philadelphia skyline, grace and dignity showing through her despair.

32   The two sisters look at the cans in the corner. There's enough for one month, but Mrs. Knight will try to stretch it. On her pad, she writes:

33   "My trial. God's got to do something."

34   (Dr. Spiegel is at 215-545-3322.)

Follow-up column, written on July 29:

It's the kind of thing I don't get   35
around to often enough. But today, I think some thanks are in order.

The problem is, I won't be able   36
to get to everyone. I don't even know where to begin.

Maybe with last week's column.   37

Those who looked in this corner   38
last Sunday saw a story about Ruby Knight, a retired crossing guard in North Philadelphia. She had throat cancer real bad at one time, but Dr. Joseph Spiegel removed a tumor, and Mrs. Knight has gone nearly five years without a recurrence.

It took four years for Mrs. Knight,   39
now 71, to learn how to swallow again. And it was a big day for her about six months ago when Spiegel removed the feeding tube from her stomach. Finally, she could swallow.

Problem was, she couldn't eat or   40
drink regular food because of discomfort. Her diet was still, exclusively°, a nutritional supplement called Ensure Plus.

Now here's the deal.   41

When Mrs. Knight poured it down   42
the tube, it was covered by Medicare. When she drank the same stuff, Medicare refused to cover it.

Medicare reasons that if you don't   43
need a tube, you don't need a special diet. The rule exists to avoid abuse.

The idea is a good one," Spiegel   44
says. "But Medicare is the biggest, most sprawling° bureaucracy of all." He says its inability to make reasonable exceptions often hurts the elderly poor.

45 Spiegel tried to get Medicare to change its mind, arguing that it would cost the government a lot more if he had to surgically implant the tube back in Mrs. Knight's stomach. But he got nowhere.

46 "We're mandated to go by the rules," a Medicare spokeswoman told me when I asked for an explanation.

47 Meanwhile, Mrs. Knight, without anyone's knowledge, was working on her own solution. She had begun rationing her Ensure Plus.

48 She kept a careful count of the cans, figuring she needed at least four a day to survive. Mrs. Knight stacked the fifty-one cans in her Camden living room, measuring the supply each day against her fixed income.

49 As Spiegel put it, "she was slowly starving herself." She went from nearly one hundred pounds to eighty-three.

50 When I went to visit, I found one of the sweetest, most unassuming people I have met. Mrs. Knight's sister, Elizabeth Woods, is the same way. She's 76 and also beat cancer. They live in the same high-rise apartment house with a fabulous view of Philadelphia, and they help each other through the days.

51 Mrs. Knight can't speak, but she gets her points across just fine. She writes almost as fast as you can talk and she has a world-class hug.

52 The day after the column, Spiegel and his staff got to their Pine Street office at 8 a.m. There were seventy-four messages on the machine. By noon, there were 150. By closing time Monday, more than four hundred people had called.

53 "You can get cynical° about things," Spiegel says, "but then there's this outpouring of help from people. It's just astounding."

54 People called for two reasons. Compassion and anger. Everyone knows somebody who's been seriously ill. Everyone has had trouble with bureaucracy.

55 Ruby Knight hit the daily double.

56 And I would like to begin now with the thank-yous. First to Dr. Spiegel for his sense of compassion and outrage. To his staff—Lori, Gina, Maria, Sally, Laura, Monica and Mike—for patiently handling calls, letters and donations. "It was kind of fun," Maria says.

57 And thanks to readers whose names fill thirteen typed pages compiled by Spiegel's staff. One person gave a year's supply of Ensure Plus. One donated twenty cases. Some sent prayers, holy cards, religious medals.

58 Some thanked Mrs. Knight for her years as a crossing guard at 17th and Ridge. Some people sent as much as four hundred dollars. One sent three one-dollar bills and a note: "I wish I could send more."

59 One sent ten dollars and this note: "May God bless you. I lost my dear husband to leukemia two and a half years ago."

60 Some called Medicare to complain. Some called Ensure Plus, where spokeswoman Sharon Veach said she thought the company could arrange to provide a lifetime supply, if needed.

61 Friday at noon, Spiegel, Maria and Mike drove to Camden and dropped in on Mrs. Knight with thirty cases of

Ensure Plus and a list of donors.

62   Mrs. Knight was beside herself, humble, gracious, overwhelmed. She and her sister kept looking at each other, shaking their heads.

63   "I'm speechless," Mrs. Knight wrote on her pad, and then laughed.

64   She said she would pray for everyone. She kept scribbling that she wishes there were some way she could express thanks and love for the kindness of strangers.

65   And I told her that she had.

First Impressions

Freewrite for ten minutes on one of the following.

1. Did you enjoy reading this selection? Why or why not?

2. Think of someone you know who has gotten involved in a frustrating struggle with a bureaucracy. What happened to this person?

3. Why do you think people responded so strongly to Mrs. Knight's story?

Vocabulary Check

_C_ 1. In the excerpt below, the word *meager* means
   A. stolen.
   B. avoidable.
   C. very small.
   D. enormous.

   If Mrs. Knight couldn't afford the stuff, she must have lived on a very small income.

   "Mrs. Knight . . . lives on a fixed and meager income . . . 'I think she was a little embarrassed that she couldn't afford to buy the stuff,' Spiegel says." (Paragraphs 15 and 17)

_D_ 2. In the excerpt below, the word *mandated* means
   A. not allowed.
   B. scared.
   C. mistaken.
   D. required.

   The words *specific guidelines for what we can . . . and can't pay for* suggest that *mandated* means "required."

   "'This is a federally funded program, and we have specific guidelines for what we can pay for and can't pay for. . . . [W]e're mandated to go by the rules.'" (Paragraphs 21 and 25)

<u>C</u> 3. In the sentence below, the word *recurrence* means
   A. regret.
   B. reduction.
   C. reappearance.   The words *at one time* suggest that she has had no
   D. review.   reappearance of cancer in almost five years.

   "She had throat cancer real bad at one time, but Dr. Joseph Spiegel removed a tumor, and Mrs. Knight has gone nearly five years without a recurrence." (Paragraph 38)

Reading Check

Central Point and Main Ideas

<u>B</u> 1. Which sentence best expresses the central point of the entire selection?
   A. The elderly poor usually suffer unnecessarily.

Answer A is not supported. Answers C and D each cover only one specific detail of the selection.

   B. Individuals were able to solve a problem that bureaucracy failed to handle.
   C. Mrs. Knight's diet is made up almost completely of a liquid supplement.
   D. Ruby Knight lost her voice box to throat cancer.

<u>D</u> 2. Which sentence best expresses the main idea of paragraph 15?
   A. Mrs. Knight lives on a fixed income.

Answers A, B, and C each present only one specific detail of the paragraph, not the main idea.

   B. Mrs. Knight kept her supply of Ensure Plus in her living room.
   C. Mrs. Knight looked every day at the cans of Ensure Plus in her living room.
   D. Since Mrs. Knight could not afford more Ensure Plus, she began rationing the cans she had.

<u>D</u> 3. Which sentence best expresses the main idea of paragraph 52?
   A. Only four hundred people read the author's column.
   B. Dr. Spiegel and his staff begin their work day at 8 a.m.
   C. Dr. Spiegel's office is a busy one.
   D. Many people called Dr. Spiegel in response to the author's column.

Answers A and C are not supported. Answer B covers only one specific detail of the paragraph.

Supporting Details

<u>A</u> 4. Even though she could now swallow, Mrs. Knight
   A. could comfortably take only Ensure Plus.
   B. had lost her taste for regular food.
   C. preferred to feed herself through a tube.   See paragraph 40.
   D. wanted to go to the hospital.

___C___ 5. Dr. Spiegel's argument to Medicare was that
A. government should pay for whatever a person needs to survive.
B. Mrs. Knight had suffered greatly because of her cancer.
C. it would cost the government more if he had to re-insert the tube in Mrs. Knight's stomach.
D. keeping Mrs. Knight out of the hospital would be helpful because the hospitals were already too full.

See paragraphs 19, 24, and 26.

Inferences

___D___ 6. We can assume that Lopez included Dr. Spiegel's phone number

Answers A, B, and C are all logical reasons for Lopez to include the phone number.

A. with Dr. Spiegel's permission.
B. to encourage people to help Mrs. Knight.
C. because he believed people would want to help Mrs. Knight.
D. for all of the above reasons.

___D___ 7. Which of the following statements would the author of this selection be most likely to agree with?
A. All Medicare rules should be eliminated.
B. People helped Mrs. Knight because they knew they would be praised in the newspaper.
C. Ensure Plus is too expensive.
D. The Medicare system should find a way to make reasonable exceptions to its rules.

See paragraph 20.

___B___ 8. What main pattern of organization does Lopez use in this selection?
A. Listing order: Lopez first lists the problems Mrs. Knight had with Medicare, and then he lists the ways people helped her.
B. Time order: Lopez tells the events of Mrs. Knight's story mostly in the order in which they happened.
C. Comparison-contrast: He contrasts the life Mrs. Knight used to have with the life she has now.
D. Cause-effect: He explains why bureaucracy deprived Mrs. Knight of the supplement she needed.

After introducing Mrs. Knight in paragraphs 1–4, Lopez presents the events in time order.

The Writer's Craft

___C___ 9. When the author refers to Mrs. Knight, his tone is
A. humorous and amused.
B. totally objective.
C. admiring and affectionate.
D. critical and disbelieving.

Words and phrases such as *sweetest, unassuming, has a world-class hug, humble,* and *gracious* demonstrate this tone. See paragraphs 50, 51, and 62–65.

_C_ 10. Lopez titles this selection "A Small Victory." Which of the following *best* explains his choice of a title?
  A. Medicare won a small victory over Mrs. Knight.
  B. Mrs. Knight and her sister, Mrs. Woods, each won a small victory over cancer.
  C. By helping Mrs. Knight, people joined together to win a small victory over bureacracy.
  D. Steve Lopez won a small victory by writing such a popular story.

Answer C states the point of the entire selection.

Discussion Questions

1. If Steve Lopez hadn't written about Mrs. Knight, what do you think might have happened to her? Do you think anyone else in the story would have continued to try to help her?

2. What do you think Lopez means when he says in paragraph 20 that Medicare has "built-in safeguards against intentional or accidental use of common sense"? What is Lopez implying by his choice of words?

3. Lopez writes, "Medicare reasons that if you don't need a tube, you don't need a special diet. The rule exists to avoid abuse." What kind of abuse do you think Medicare might be trying to avoid by having such a rule? How might Medicare be taken advantage of by people who wanted to do so?

4. Lopez writes, "People called for two reasons. Compassion and anger" (paragraph 54). Why do you think so many people reacted with such depth of feeling? What events have you read or heard about recently that provoked a similar response in you?

Paragraph Assignments

1. Steve Lopez makes the humorous claim that Medicare has "safeguards against intentional or accidental use of common sense." Think about what "common sense" means to you; then write a paragraph about a time someone you know displayed a lack of common sense. In your paragraph, describe the situation, indicate what a sensible response to the situation would have been, and tell what the person did instead. Your paragraph may be serious or humorous. A topic sentence for this paragraph might be something like this:

- When my little sister's kitten got stuck in a tree, my sister's attempt to rescue it showed a real lack of common sense.
- The first time my brother did his own laundry, his lack of common sense created some colorful problems.

2. Lopez points out, "Everyone has had trouble with bureaucracy." His story about Ruby Knight might seem like an extreme example, but with a little online research, you should be able to uncover other astounding cases of bureaucratic ignorance. Some of what you find might really surprise you. Write a paragraph about one of the cases of bureaucratic error that you find. You can dig up stories by searching for "bureaucratic mistakes" or "how bureaucracy hurts people." If you want to find out about bureaucratic nightmares in specific areas (like welfare, education, health care, and so on), simply add that word to your search.

   When writing your paragraph about the bureaucratic error, make the sequence of events clear by using time transition words such as *first, next, after,* and *finally.* You might want to end your paragraph by offering ideas for how to avoid or change the particular bureaucratic mess that you are writing about.

Essay Assignments

1. In his first column, Steve Lopez wrote about a problem he hoped his readers would help solve. Write an essay for your school newspaper discussing a problem at your school and offering solutions.

   Your thesis statement might be something like any of these:

   - Students, teachers, and administrators could all work together to make our campus a more pleasant place.
   - Our campus could be made safer if a few simple steps were taken.
   - Steps should be taken to help students at our school have a better educational experience.

   Your essay will be richer and more interesting if you provide examples to emphasize your point. For instance, if you are writing about making the campus more attractive, you could provide specific examples of places that are currently unattractive.

2. Lopez emphasizes in his columns that Mrs. Knight is a proud, independent woman who wants to live her life with dignity. But it is also clear that Mrs. Knight's age, income, and physical condition all make it difficult for her to maintain that dignity.

   Write an essay about the challenges that face people who are growing old in America today: physical, mental, social, financial, or other kinds of challenges. Choose any three challenges and provide specific examples of each type. If you need ideas, an online search for "challenges of aging" should yield all the information you will need.

5 Joe Davis: A Cool Man

Beth Johnson

Preview

Drugs and guns, crime and drugs, drugs and lies, liquor and drugs. If there was one constant in Joe Davis's life, it was drugs, the substance that ruled his existence. Personal tragedy was not enough to turn him off the path leading to the brink of self-destruction. Finally Joe was faced with a moment of decision. The choice he made has opened doors into a world that the old Joe barely knew existed.

Words to Watch

option (6): choice
rehabilitated (10): brought back to a good and healthy life
encountered (20): met
unruly (26): disorderly
hushed (27): quiet

1   Joe Davis was the coolest fourteen-year-old he'd ever seen.

2   He went to school when he felt like it. He hung out with a wild crowd. He started drinking some wine, smoking some marijuana. "Nobody could tell me anything," he says today. "I thought the sun rose and set on me." There were rules at home, and Joe didn't do rules. So he moved in with his grandmother.

3   Joe Davis was the coolest sixteen-year-old he'd ever seen.

4   Joe's parents gave up on his schooling and signed him out of the tenth grade. Joe went to work in his dad's body shop, but that didn't last long. There were rules there, too, and Joe didn't do rules. By the time he was in his mid-teens, Joe was taking pills that got him high and even using cocaine. He was also smoking marijuana all the time and drinking booze all the time.

5   Joe Davis was the coolest twenty-five-year-old he'd ever seen.

6   He was living with a woman almost twice his age. The situation wasn't great, but she paid the bills, and certainly Joe couldn't. He had his habit to support, which by now had grown to include heroin. Sometimes he'd work at a low-level job, if someone else found it for him. He might work long enough to

get a paycheck and then spend it all at once. Other times he'd be caught stealing and get fired first. A more challenging job was not an option°, even if he had bothered to look for one. He couldn't put words together to form a sentence, unless the sentence was about drugs. Filling out an application was difficult. He wasn't a strong reader. He couldn't do much with numbers. Since his drug habit had to be paid for, he started to steal. First he stole from his parents, then from his sister. Then he stole from the families of people he knew. But eventually the people he knew wouldn't let him in their houses, since they knew he'd steal from them. So he got a gun and began holding people up. He chose elderly people and others who weren't likely to fight back. The holdups kept him in drug money, but things at home were getting worse. His woman's teenage daughter was getting out of line. Joe decided it was up to him to discipline her. The girl didn't like it. She told her boyfriend. One day, the boyfriend called Joe out of the house.

7   BANG.

8   Joe Davis was in the street, his nose in the dirt. His mind was still cloudy from his most recent high, but he knew something was terribly wrong with his legs. He couldn't move them; he couldn't even feel them. His mother came out of her nearby house and ran to him. As he heard her screams, he imagined what she was seeing. Her oldest child, her first baby, her bright boy who could have been and done anything, was lying in the gutter, a junkie with a .22 caliber bullet lodged in his spine.

The next time Joe's head cleared, he   9
was in a hospital bed, blinking up at his parents as they stared helplessly at him. The doctors had done all they could; Joe would live, to everyone's surprise. But he was a paraplegic—paralyzed from his chest down. It was done. It was over. It was written in stone. He would not walk again. He would not be able to control his bladder or bowels. He would not be able to make love as he had before. He would not be able to hold people up, then hurry away.

Joe spent the next eight months   10
being moved between several Philadelphia hospitals, where he was shown the ropes of life as a paraplegic. Officially he was being "rehabilitated°"—restored to a productive life. There was just one problem: Joe. "To be *re*habilitated, you must have been *habilitated* first," he says today. "That wasn't me." During his stay in the hospitals, he found ways to get high every day.

Finally Joe was released from the   11
hospital. He returned in his wheelchair to the house he'd been living in when

he was shot. He needed someone to take care of him, and his woman friend was still willing. His drug habit was as strong as ever, but his days as a stickup man were over. So he started selling drugs. Business was good. The money came in fast, and his own drug use accelerated even faster.

12   A wheelchair-bound junkie doesn't pay much attention to his health and cleanliness. Eventually Joe developed his first bedsore: a deep, rotting wound that ate into his flesh, overwhelming him with its foul odor. He was admitted to Magee Rehabilitation Hospital, where he spent six months on his stomach while the ghastly wound slowly healed. Again, he spent his time in the hospital using drugs. This time his drug use did not go unnoticed. Soon before he was scheduled to be discharged, hospital officials kicked him out. He returned to his friend's house and his business. But then police raided the house. They took the drugs, they took the money, they took the guns.

13   "I really went downhill then," says Joe. With no drugs and no money to get drugs, life held little meaning. He began fighting with the woman he was living with. "When you're in the state I was in, you don't know how to be nice to anybody," he says. Finally she kicked him out of the house. When his parents took him in, Joe did a little selling from their house, trying to keep it low-key, out of sight, so they wouldn't notice. He laughs at the notion today. "I thought I could control junkies and tell them 'Business only during certain hours.'" Joe got high when his monthly Social Security check came, high when

he'd make a purchase for someone else and get a little something for himself, high when a visitor would share drugs with him. It wasn't much of a life. "There I was," he says, "a junkie with no education, no job, no friends, no means of supporting myself. And now I had a spinal cord injury."

Then came October 25, 1988. Joe   14
had just filled a prescription for pills to control his muscle spasms. Three hundred of the powerful muscle relaxants were there for the taking. He swallowed them all.

"It wasn't the spinal cord injury that   15
did it," he says. "It was the addiction."

Joe tried hard to die, but it didn't   16
work. A sister heard him choking and called for help. He was rushed to the hospital, where he lay in a coma for four days.

Joe has trouble finding the words   17
to describe what happened next.

"I had . . . a spiritual awakening, for   18
lack of any better term," he says. "My soul had been cleansed. I knew my life could be better. And from that day to this, I have chosen not to get high."

Drugs, he says, "are not even a   19
temptation. That life is a thing that happened to someone else."

Joe knew he wanted to turn himself   20
around, but he needed help in knowing where to start. He enrolled in Magee Hospital's vocational rehabilitation program. For six weeks, he immersed himself in discussions, tests, and exercises to help him determine the kind of work he might be suited for. The day he finished the rehab program, a nurse at Magee told him about a

receptionist's job in the spinal cord injury unit at Thomas Jefferson Hospital. He went straight to the hospital and met Lorraine Buchanan, coordinator of the unit. "I told her where I was and where I wanted to go," Joe says. "I told her, 'If you give me a job, I will never disappoint you. I'll quit first if I see I can't live up to it.'" She gave him the job. The wheelchair-bound junkie, the man who'd never been able to hold a job, the drug-dependent stickup man who "couldn't put two words together to make a sentence" was now the first face, the first voice that patients encountered° when they entered the spinal cord unit. "I'd never talked to people like that," says Joe, shaking his head. "I had absolutely no background. But Lorraine and the others, they taught me to speak. Taught me to greet people. Taught me to handle the phone." How did he do in his role as a receptionist? A huge smile breaks across Joe's face as he answers, "I did excellent."

21   Soon, his personal life also took a very positive turn. A month after Joe started his job, he was riding a city bus to work. A woman recovering from knee surgery was in another seat. The two smiled, but didn't speak.

22   A week later, Joe spotted the woman again. The bus driver sensed something was going on and encouraged Joe to approach her. Her name was Terri. She was a receptionist in a law office. On their first date, Joe laid his cards on the table. He told her his story. He also told her he was looking to get married. "That about scared her away," Joe recalls. "She said she wasn't interested in marriage. I asked, 'Well, suppose you did meet someone you cared about, who cared about you, and treated you well. Would you still be opposed to the idea of marriage?' She said no, she would consider it then. I said, 'Well, that's all I ask.'"

23   Four months later, as the two sat over dinner in a restaurant, Joe handed Terri a box tied with a ribbon. Inside was a smaller box. Then a smaller box, and a smaller one still. Ten boxes in all. Inside the smallest was an engagement ring. After another six months, the two were married in the law office where Terri works. Since then, she has been Joe's constant source of support, encouragement, and love.

24   After Joe had started work at Jefferson Hospital, he talked with his supervisor, Lorraine, about his dreams of moving on to something bigger, more challenging. She encouraged him to try college. He had taken and passed the high-school general equivalency diploma (GED) exam years before, almost as a joke, when he was recovering from his bedsores at Magee. Now he enrolled in a university mathematics course. He didn't do well. "I wasn't ready," Joe says. "I'd been out of school seventeen years. I dropped out." Before he could let discouragement overwhelm him, he enrolled at Community College of Philadelphia (CCP), where he signed up for basic math and English courses. He worked hard, sharpening study skills he had never developed in his earlier school days. Next he took courses toward an associate's degree in mental health and social services, along with a certificate

in addiction studies. Five years later, he graduated from CCP, the first member of his family ever to earn a college degree. He then went on to receive a B.A. in mental health from Hahnemann University in Philadelphia and an M.A. in social work from the University of Pennsylvania.

25   Today, Joe is employed as a psychotherapist at John F. Kennedy Mental Health Center in Philadelphia. He does his best to get into the "real world," the world of young men and women immersed in drugs, violence, and crime. Whenever he can, he speaks at local schools through a program called Think First. He tells young people about his drug use, his shooting, and his experience with paralysis.

26   At a presentation at a disciplinary school outside of Philadelphia, Joe gazes with quiet authority at the unruly° crowd of teenagers. He begins to speak, telling them about speedballs and guns, fast money and bedsores, even about the leg bag that collects his urine. At first, the kids snort with laughter at his honesty. When they laugh, he waits patiently, then goes on. Gradually the room grows quieter as Joe tells them of his life and then asks them about theirs. "What's important to you? What are your goals?" he says. "I was still in school at age 40 because when I was young, I chose the dead-end route many of you are on. But now I'm doing what I have to do to get where I want to go. What are *you* doing?"

27   He tells them more, about broken dreams, about his parents' grief, about the former friends who turned away from him when he was no longer a source of drugs. He tells them of the continuing struggle to regain the trust of people he once abused. He tells them about the desire that consumes him now, the desire to make his community a better place to live. His wish is that no young man or woman should have to walk the path he's walked in order to value the precious gift of life. The teenagers are now silent. They look at this broad-shouldered black man in his wheelchair, his head and beard close-shaven, a gold ring in his ear. His hushed° words settle among them like gentle drops of cleansing rain. "What are *you* doing? Where are *you* going?" he asks them. "Think about it. Think about me."

28   Joe Davis is the coolest fifty-one-year-old you've ever seen.

First Impressions

Freewrite for ten minutes on one of the following.

1. Did you enjoy reading this selection? Why or why not?

2. Why do you think Joe tried to kill himself?

3. Have you ever known someone who has turned his or her life around, as Joe has? What were the circumstances?

Vocabulary Check

___C___   1. In the sentence below, the word *restored* means
        A. held back.
        B. punished.   The hospital staff would want to bring
        C. returned.   someone back to a productive life.
        D. paid.

        "Officially he was being 'rehabilitated'—restored to a productive life."
        (Paragraph 10)

___A___   2. In the sentence below, the word *accelerated* means
        A. increased.
        B. grown less serious.   Synonym-like clue: "The money came in
        C. disappeared.   [that is, increased] fast . . ."
        D. helped.

        "The money came in fast, and his own drug use accelerated even faster."
        (Paragraph 11)

___B___   3. In the sentence below, the word *ghastly* means
        A. quite small.
        B. very unpleasant.   A "deep, rotting wound" that eats
        C. caused by a gun.   into the flesh and smells terrible
        D. illegal.   would be very unpleasant.

        "He was admitted to Magee Rehabilitation Hospital, where he spent
        six months on his stomach while the ghastly wound slowly healed."
        (Paragraph 12)

___C___   4. In the sentence below, the word *immersed* means
        A. totally ignored.
        B. greatly angered.   Doing something for six weeks that
        C. deeply involved.   includes discussions, tests, and exercises
        D. often harmed.   would keep a person deeply involved.

        "For six weeks, he immersed himself in discussions, tests, and exercises to
        help him determine the kind of work he might be suited for." (Paragraph
        20)

Reading Check

Central Point and Main Ideas

<u>B</u> 1. Which sentence best expresses the central point of the entire selection?

Answers A and D are not mentioned in the selection. Answer C covers only paragraphs 2–4.

    A. Most people cannot improve their lives once they turn to drugs and crime.

    B. Joe Davis overcame a life of drugs and crime and a disability to lead a rich, meaningful life.

    C. The rules set by Joe Davis's parents caused him to leave home and continue a life of drugs and crime.

    D. Joe Davis's friends turned away from him once they learned he was no longer a source of drugs.

<u>A</u> 2. A main idea may cover more than one paragraph. Which sentence best expresses the main idea of paragraphs 21–23?

    A. The first sentence of paragraph 21

    B. The second sentence of paragraph 21

    C. The first sentence of paragraph 22

    D. The first sentence of paragraph 23

The "positive turn" referred to generally in the first sentence is then described in detail.

<u>C</u> 3. Which sentence best expresses the main idea of paragraph 24?

Answers A and B are too specific. Answer D is too general.

    A. It was difficult for Joe to do college work after being out of school for so many years.

    B. Lorraine Buchanan encouraged Joe to go to college.

    C. Joe overcame a lack of academic preparation and eventually earned two college degrees and a master's degree.

    D. If students stayed in high school and worked hard, they would not have to go to the trouble of getting a high-school GED.

Supporting Details

<u>C</u> 4. Joe Davis quit high school

    A. when he was 14.

    B. when he got a good job at a hospital.

    C. when he was in the tenth grade.

    D. after he was shot.

See the first sentence of paragraph 4.

<u>A</u> 5. Joe tried to kill himself by

    A. swallowing muscle-relaxant pills.

    B. shooting himself.

    C. overdosing on heroin.

    D. not eating or drinking.

See paragraphs 14–16.

___B___ 6. According to the selection, Joe first met his wife
  A. in the hospital, where she was a nurse.
  B. on a city bus, where they were both passengers.
  C. on the job, where she was also a receptionist.   See paragraph 21.
  D. at the Community College of Philadelphia, where she was also a student.

___C___ 7. Joe decided to stop using drugs
  A. when he met his future wife.
  B. right after he was shot.
  C. when he awoke from a suicide attempt.   See paragraph 18.
  D. when he was hired as a receptionist.

Inferences

___A___ 8. We can conclude from paragraph 26 that

The second sentence
lists some of the
personal information
that Joe reveals.

  A. Joe is willing to reveal very personal information about himself in order to reach young people with his story.
  B. Joe was angry at the Philadelphia students who laughed at parts of his story.
  C. Joe is glad he did not go to college directly from high school.
  D. Joe is still trying to figure out what his life goals are.

The Writer's Craft

___D___ 9. When the author writes, "Joe Davis was the coolest fourteen- [or sixteen- or twenty-five-] year-old he'd ever seen," she is actually expressing

Joe's present-day
view of his past life
(see paragraph 26)
supports answer D.

  A. her approval of the way Joe was living then.
  B. her envy of Joe's status in the community.
  C. her mistaken opinion of Joe at these stages in his life.
  D. Joe's mistaken opinion of himself at these stages in his life.

___B___ 10. To conclude her essay, Johnson uses
  A. a series of statistics.
  B. an anecdote followed by a personal comment.
  C. a summary of her main idea.
  D. a prediction of what will happen to Joe in the future.

Paragraphs 26 and 27 are the anecdote. Paragraph 28
is Johnson's personal comment.

Discussion Questions

1. When speaking of his suicide attempt, Joe said, "It wasn't the spinal cord injury that did it. It was the addiction." What do you think Joe meant? Why do you think he blamed his addiction, rather than his disability, for his decision to try to end his life?

2. Why do you think the students Joe spoke to laughed as he shared personal details of his life? Why did they later quiet down? What effect do you think his presentation had on these students?

3. Joe speaks of wanting to "regain the trust of people he once abused." In other words, he hopes they will give him a second chance. Have you ever given a second chance to someone who had abused your trust? Alternatively, have you ever sought a second chance from someone you had wronged? What happened?

4. Joe wants young people to learn the lessons he has learned without having to experience his hardships. What lessons have you learned in your life that you would like to pass on to others?

Paragraph Assignments

1. Like Joe Davis, many of us have learned painful lessons from life. And like him, we wish we could pass those lessons on to young people to save them from making the same mistakes.

   Write a one-paragraph letter to a young person you know. In it, use your experience to pass on a lesson you wish he or she would learn. Begin with a topic sentence in which you state the lesson you'd like to teach, as in these examples:

   - My own humiliating experience taught me that shoplifting is a very bad idea.
   - I learned the hard way that abandoning your friends for the "cool" crowd will backfire on you.
   - The sad experience of a friend has taught me that teenage girls should not give in to their boyfriends' pressure for sex.
   - Dropping out of high school may seem like a great idea, but what happened to my brother should convince you otherwise.

2. Although Joe's parents loved him, they weren't able to stop him from using drugs, skipping school, and doing other self-destructive things. Think of a time that you have seen someone you know (or have read or heard about) doing something destructive to himself or herself. Who else got involved? How did the situation turn out?

Write a paragraph in which you describe the situation and its outcome. In it, make sure you answer the following questions:

- What was the person doing?
- Why were these actions dangerous?
- Who might have helped the person?
- Did anyone take any action?
- How did the situation finally turn out? Was this a good outcome? Why or why not?

Essay Assignments

1. One of Joe's goals was to regain the trust of the friends and family members he abused during his earlier life. Have you ever given a second chance to someone who treated you poorly? Write an essay about what happened. You could begin with a thesis statement something like this: "Although my closest friend betrayed my trust, I decided to give him another chance."

    You could then go on to structure the rest of your essay in this way:

    - In your first supporting paragraph, explain what the person did to lose your trust. Maybe it was an obviously hurtful action, like physically harming you or stealing from you. Or perhaps it was something more subtle, like insulting or embarrassing you.

    - In your second supporting paragraph, explain why you decided to give the person another chance.

    - In your third supporting paragraph, tell what happened as a result of your giving the person a second chance. Did he or she treat you better this time? Or did the bad treatment start over again?

    - In your concluding paragraph, provide some final thoughts about what you learned from the experience.

    Alternatively, write an essay about a time that you were given a second chance by someone whose trust you had abused. Follow the same pattern of development.

2. Obviously, young people often do not learn from the experiences of others. For example, despite all the evidence about how harmful smoking is to health, young people continue to smoke. The same can be said for careless driving, drug and alcohol abuse, and other reckless behaviors.

    Write an essay in which you explore possible reasons why young people often disregard the experience of others and, instead, learn their lessons the hard way.

6 Migrant Child to College Woman

Maria Cardenas

Preview

Maria Cardenas grew up in a family of migrant workers. As the family moved from state to state, following the fruit and vegetable harvest, Maria became used to backbreaking labor, poverty, and violence. The brutality she encountered, as well as her own lack of education, could have snuffed out her hopes for a better life. But, as this selection will show, Maria has found the courage both to dream and to make her dreams become reality.

Words to Watch

abducted (18): taken away by force
taunted (22): cruelly teased
briskly (24): in a lively manner
GED (24): general equivalency diploma (equal to a high-school diploma)

1   As I walk into the classroom, the teacher gazes at me with her piercing green eyes. I feel myself shrinking and burning up with guilt. I go straight to her desk and hand her the excuse slip. Just like all the other times, I say, "I was sick." I hate lying, but I have to. I don't want my parents to get in trouble.

2   I'm not a very good liar. She makes me hold out my hands, inspecting my dirty fingernails and calluses. She knows exactly where I've been the past several days. When you pick tomatoes and don't wear gloves, your hands get rough and stained from the plant oils. Soap doesn't wash that out.

3   In the background, I can hear the students giggling as she asks her usual questions: "What was wrong? Was your brother sick, too? Do you feel better today?" Of course I don't feel better. My whole body aches from those endless hot days spent harvesting crops from dawn to dusk. I was never absent by choice.

4   That year, in that school, I think my name was "Patricia Rodriguez," but I'm not sure. My brother and I used whatever name our mother told us to use each time we went to a new school. We understood that we had to be registered as the children of parents who were in the United States legally, in case Immigration ever checked up.

5   My parents had come to the States in the late '60s to work in the fields and earn money to feed their family. They paid eight hundred dollars to someone who smuggled them across the border, and they left us with our aunt and uncle in Mexico. My five-year-old brother, Joel, was the oldest. I was 4, and then came Teresa, age 3, and baby Bruno. The other kids in the neighborhood teased us, saying, "They won't come back for you." Three years later, our parents sent for us to join them in Texas. My little heart sang as we waved good-bye to those neighbor kids in Rio Verde. My father did love us!

6   My parents worked all the time in the fields. Few other options were open to them because they had little education. At first, our education was important to them. They were too scared to put us in school right away, but when I was 8 they did enroll us. I do remember that my first-grade report card said I was "Antonietta Gonzales." My father made sure we had everything we needed—tablets, crayons, ruler, and the little box to put your stuff in. He bragged to his friends about his children going to school. Now we could talk for our parents. We could translate their words for the grocer, the doctor, and the teachers. If Immigration came by, we could tell them we were citizens, and because we were speaking English, they wouldn't ask any more questions.

7   In the years to come, I often reminded myself that my father had not forgotten us like the fathers of so many kids I knew. It became more important for me to remember that as it became harder to see that he loved us. He had hit my mother once in a while as I was growing up, but when his own mother died in Mexico in 1973, his behavior grew much worse. My uncles told me that my father, the youngest of the family, had often beaten his mother. Maybe it was the guilt he felt when she died, but for whatever reason, he started drinking heavily, abusing my mother emotionally and physically, and terrorizing us kids. The importance of our education faded away, and now my papa thought my brother and I should work more in the fields. We would work all the time—on school vacations, holidays, weekends, and every day after school. When there were lots of tomatoes to pick, I went to school only every other day.

8   If picking was slow, I stayed home after school and cooked for the family. I started as soon as I got home in the afternoon. I used the three large pots my mother owned: one for beans, one

for rice or soup, and one for hot salsa. There were also the usual ten pounds of flour or *maseca*, ground corn meal, for the tortillas. I loved this cooking because I could eat as much as I wanted and see that the little kids got enough before the older family members finished everything. By this time there were three more children in our family, and we often went to bed hungry. (My best subject in school was lunch, and my plate was always clean.)

9   Other than lunchtime, my school life passed in a blur. I remember a little about teachers showing us how to sound words out. I began to stumble through elementary readers. But then we'd move again, or I'd be sent to the fields.

10   Life was never easy in those days. Traveling with the harvest meant living wherever the bosses put us. We might be in little houses with one outdoor toilet for the whole camp. Other times the whole crew, all fifty or one hundred of us, were jammed into one big house. Working in the fields meant blistering sun, aching muscles, sliced fingers, bug bites, and my father yelling when we didn't pick fast enough to suit him.

11   But we were kids, so we found a way to have some fun. My brother and I would make a game of competing with each other and the other adults. I never did manage to pick more than Joel, but I came close. One time I picked 110 baskets of cucumbers to Joel's 115. We made thirty-five cents a basket.

12   Of course, we never saw any of that money. At the end of the week, whatever the whole family had earned was given to my father. Soon he stopped working altogether. He just watched us, chatted with the field bosses, and drank beer. He began to beat all of us kids as well as our mother. We didn't work fast enough for him. He wanted us to make more money. He called us names and threw stones and vegetables at us. The other workers did nothing to make him stop. I was always scared of my father, but I loved him even though he treated us so badly. I told myself that he loved us, but that alcohol ruled his life.

13   I knew what controlled my father's life, but I never thought about being in control of my own. I did as I was told, spoke in a whisper, and tried not to be noticed. Because we traveled with the harvest, my brothers and sisters and I attended three or four different schools in one year. When picking was good, I went to the fields instead of school. When the little kids got sick, I stayed home to watch them. When I did go to school, I didn't understand very much. We spoke only Spanish at home. I don't know how I got through elementary school, much less to high school, because I only knew how to add, subtract, and multiply. And let's just say I got "introduced" to English writing skills and grammar. School was a strange foreign place where I went when I could, sitting like a ghost in a corner alone. I could read enough to help my mother fill out forms in English. But enough to pick up a story and understand it? Never. When a teacher told the class, "Read this book, and write a report," I just didn't do it. I knew she wasn't talking to me.

14   In 1978, my mother ran away after

two weeks of terrible beatings. Joel and I found the dime under the big suitcase, where she had told us it would be. We were supposed to use it to call the police, but we were too scared. We stayed in the upstairs closet with our brothers and sisters. In the morning, I felt guilty and terrified. I didn't know whether our mother was alive or dead. Not knowing what else to do, I got dressed and went to school. I told the counselor what had happened, and she called the police. My father was arrested. He believed the police when they said they were taking him to jail for unpaid traffic tickets. Then the police located my mother and told her it was safe to come out of hiding. My father never lived with us again although he continued to stalk us. He would stand outside the house yelling at my mother, "You're gonna be a prostitute. Those kids are gonna be no-good drug addicts and criminals. They're gonna end up in jail."

15   My father's words enraged me. I had always had a hunger for knowledge, always dreamed of a fancy job where I would go to work wearing nice clothes and carrying a briefcase. How dare he try to kill my dream! True, the idea of that dream ever coming true seemed unlikely. In school, if I asked about material I didn't understand, most of the teachers seemed annoyed. My mother would warn me, "Please, don't ask so many questions."

16   But then, somehow, when I was 14, Mrs. Mercer noticed me. I don't remember how my conversations with this teacher started, but it led to her offering me a job in the Western clothing store she and her husband owned. I helped translate for the Spanish-speaking customers who shopped there. I worked only Saturdays, and I got paid a whole twenty-dollar bill. Proudly, I presented that money to my mother. The thought "I can actually do more than field work" began to make my dreams seem like possibilities. I began to believe I could be something more. The month of my sixteenth birthday, Mrs. Mercer recommended me for a cashier's job in the local supermarket. I worked there for six weeks, and on Friday, January 16, 1981, I was promoted to head cashier. I was on top of the world! I could not believe such good things were happening to me. I had a good job, and I was on my way to becoming my school's first Spanish-speaking graduate. I thought nothing could go wrong, ever again.

17   But that very night, my dreams were shattered again—this time, I thought, permanently. The manager let me off at nine, two hours early. I didn't have a ride because my brother was not picking me up until 11:00 p.m. But I was in luck! I saw a man I knew, a friend of my brother's, someone I had worked with in the fields. He was a trusted family friend, so when he offered me a lift, I said, "Of course." Now I could go home and tell everybody about the promotion.

18   I never made it home or to my big promotion. The car doors were locked; I could not escape. I was abducted° and raped, and I found myself walking down the same abusive road as my mother. My dreams were crushed. I had failed.

In my old-fashioned Mexican world, I was a "married woman," even if I wasn't. To go home again would have been to dishonor my family. When I found I was pregnant, there seemed to be only one path open to me. I married my abductor, dropped out of tenth grade, and moved with him to Oklahoma.

19   "My father was right," I thought. "I am a failure." But dreams die hard. My brother Joel was living in the same Oklahoma town as I was. He would see me around town, my face and body bruised from my husband's beatings. But unlike the workers in the fields who had silently watched our father's abuse, Joel spoke up. "You've got to go," he would urge me. "You don't have to take this. Go on, you can make it."

20   "No!" I would tell him. I was embarrassed to have anyone know what my life had become. I imagined returning to my mother, only to have her reprimand me, saying, "What's the matter with you that you can't even stay married?"

21   But Joel wouldn't give up. Finally he told me, "I don't care what you say. I am going to tell Mother what is going on."

22   And he did. He explained to our mother that I had been forced to go with that man, that I was being abused, and that I was coming home. She accepted what he told her. I took my little girl and the clothes I could carry, threw everything into my car, and left Oklahoma for Florida. My husband taunted° me just as my father had my mother: "You'll be on food stamps! You can't amount to anything on your own!" But I proved him wrong. I worked days in the fields and nights as a cashier, getting off work at midnight and up early the next day to work again. I don't know how I did it, but I kept up the payments on my little car, I didn't go on food stamps, and I was happy.

23   But as Antonietta grew up and started school, I began to think my little triumphs were not enough. I was thrilled to see her learning to read, doing well in school. And when she would bring me her simple little books and trustingly say, "Read with me!" it filled me with joy. But I realized the day would come, and come soon, that I would be unable to read Antonietta's books. What would she think of me when I said, "I can't"? What would I think of myself?

24   Teaching myself to read became the most important goal in my life. I began with Antonietta's kindergarten books. I thought sometimes how people would laugh if they saw me, a grown woman, a mother, struggling through *The Cat in the Hat*. But with no one to watch me, I didn't care. Alone in my house, after my daughter was asleep, I read. I read everything we had in the house—Antonietta's books, cereal boxes, advertisements that came in the mail. I forced myself through them, stumbling again and again over unfamiliar words. Eventually I began to feel ready to try a real story, a grown-up story. But my fears nearly stopped me again. We lived near a library. Antonietta had asked again and again to go there. Finally I said "all right." We walked in, but panic overwhelmed me. All those people, walking around so briskly°, knowing where to find the

books they wanted and how to check them out! What was someone like me doing there? What if someone asked me what I wanted? Too intimidated to even try, I insisted that we leave. I told Antonietta to use the library at her school. I struggled on in private, eventually earning my GED°.

25   The years passed, and I married a wonderful man who loved me and my daughter. He was proud that I had some real education, and he knew that I wanted more. But I couldn't imagine that going on in school was possible.

26   Then, in 1987, I was working for the Redlands Christian Migrant Association. They provided services for migrant children. One day, in the office, I spotted something that made my heart jump. It was a book called *Dark Harvest*. It was filled with stories about migrant workers. Although my reading skills had improved, I had still never read a book. But this one was about people like me. I began reading it, slowly at first, then with more and more interest. Some of the people in it had gone back for a GED, just as I had! Even more—some had gone on to college and earned a degree in education. Now they were teaching. When I read that book, I realized that my dream wasn't crazy.

27   My husband and I took the steps to become legally admitted residents of the United States. Then, my husband found out about a federal program that helps seasonal farm workers go to college. I applied and found I was eligible. When I took my diagnostic tests, my reading, English, and math skills turned out to

be seventh-grade level. Not as bad as I thought! The recruiter asked if I would mind attending Adult Basic Education classes to raise my scores to the twelfth-grade level. Mind? I was thrilled! I loved to study, and in spite of a serious illness that kept me out of classes for weeks, my teacher thought I was ready to try the ABE exams early. Her encouragement gave my confidence a boost, and I found my scores had zoomed up to a 12.9 level.

28   Then, in the fall of 1994, I took the greatest step of my academic life. Proud and excited, I started classes at Edison Community College in Florida. Of course, I was also terrified, trembling inside almost like that scared little girl who used to tiptoe up to the teacher's desk with her phony absence excuses. But I wasn't a scared little kid anymore. My self-confidence was growing, even if it was growing slowly.

29   I laugh when I look back at that day I fled in terror from the library. My family and I might as well live there now. We walk in with me saying, "Now, we have other things to do today. Just half an hour." Three hours later, it's the kids saying to me, "Mom, are you ready yet?" But it's so exciting, knowing that I can learn about anything I want just by picking up a book! I've read dozens of how-to books, many of them about gardening, which has become my passion. I can't put down motivational books, like Ben Carson's *Gifted Hands* and *Think Big*. I love Barbara Kingsolver's novels. One of them, *The Bean Trees*, was about a young woman from a very poor area in

Kentucky whose only goal, at first, was to finish school without having a child. I could understand her. But my favorite author is Maya Angelou. Right now, I'm re-reading her book *I Know Why the Caged Bird Sings*. She writes so honestly about the tragedy and poverty she's lived with. She was raped when she was little, and she had a child when she was very young. And now she's a leader, a wonderful writer and poet. When I see her—she read a poem at President Clinton's inauguration—I am very moved. And I can't talk about my life now without mentioning Kenneth and Mary Jo Walker, the president of Edison Community College and his wife. They offered me a job in their home, but so much more than that: they have become my friends, my guardian angels. I am constantly borrowing books from them, and they give me so much encouragement that I tell them, "You have more faith in me than I do myself."

30   Sometimes I have to pinch myself to believe that my life today is real. I have a hard-working husband and three children, all of whom I love very much. My son Korak is 11. Whatever he studies in school—the Aztecs, the rainforest, Mozart—he wants to find more books in the library about it, to learn more deeply. Jasmine, my little girl, is 7, and is reading through the *Little House on the Prairie* books. Like me, the children have worked in the fields, but there is little resemblance between their lives and mine as a child. They are in one school the whole year long. They work at their own pace, learning the value of work and

of money—and they keep what they earn. Antonietta, who inspired me to begin reading, is 17 now. Although she's only a junior in high school, she's taking college calculus classes and planning to study pre-med in college, even though her teachers have encouraged her to become a journalist because of her skill in writing.

31   And guess what! My teachers compliment my writing too. When I enrolled in my developmental English class at Edison, my teacher, Johanna Seth, asked the class to write a narrative paragraph. A narrative, she explained, tells a story. As I thought about what story I could write, a picture of a scared little girl in a schoolroom popped into my head. I began writing:

32   *As I walk into the classroom, the teacher gazes at me with her piercing green eyes. I feel myself shrinking and burning up with guilt. I go straight to her desk and hand her the excuse slip. Just like all the other times, I say, "I was sick." I hate lying, but I have to. I don't want my parents to get in trouble.*

33   I finish my narrative about giving my phony excuses to my grade-school teachers and hand it in. I watch Mrs. Seth read it and, to my horror, she begins to cry. I know it must be because she is so disappointed, that what I have written is so far from what the assignment was meant to be that she doesn't know where to begin to correct it.

34   "Did you write this?" she asks me. Of course, she knows I wrote it, but she seems disbelieving. "You wrote this?" she asks again. Eventually I realize that

she is not disappointed. Instead, she is telling me something incredible and wonderful. She is saying that my work is good, and that she is very happy with what I've given her. She is telling me that I can succeed here.

An Update

35   And she was right. I graduated from Edison as a member of Phi Theta Kappa, the national academic honors society for junior colleges. I went on to Florida Gulf Coast University, where I earned my bachelor's degree in elementary education. I've had the pleasure of seeing my children make their successful ways in the world: Antonietta is a lawyer, Korak is a college student, and Jasmine is serving in the military. Most wonderfully of all, I am a third-grade teacher. My students are Hispanic, and many of them are the children of migrant workers, like me. But unlike me, they do not sit in the back of the classroom, scared and ignored. Unlike me, they do not hear that they will never do more than travel the country picking crops. They are growing up knowing that, like their teacher, they can achieve much in life. It is my great joy that I can help teach them that.

Maria Cardenas with her third-grade students

First Impressions

Freewrite for ten minutes on one of the following.

1. Did you enjoy reading this selection? Why or why not?

2. Have you ever known anyone who frequently moved from one town (or school) to another? What effects did all that moving have on the person?

3. Why do you think Maria didn't immediately leave her first husband when he began to beat her? If you were in Maria's situation, what would you have done?

Vocabulary Check

_D_ 1. In the excerpt below, the word *options* means
   A. opinions.
   B. pleasures.
   C. gifts.
   D. choices.

   If Maria's parents had little education, they would have few choices other than working in the fields.

   "My parents worked all the time in the fields. Few other options were open to them because they had little education." (Paragraph 6)

_A_ 2. In the sentence below, the word *reprimand* means
   A. scold.
   B. ignore.
   C. compliment.
   D. support.

   The mother is scolding her daughter when she says, "What's the matter with you that you can't even . . ."

   "I imagined returning to my mother, only to have her reprimand me, saying, 'What's the matter with you that you can't even stay married?'" (Paragraph 20)

_C_ 3. In the excerpt below, the word *intimidated* means
   A. thoughtful.
   B. bored.
   C. fearful.
   D. critical.

   If she is overcome by panic, she must be fearful.

   "We walked in, but panic overwhelmed me. . . . What was someone like me doing there? What if someone asked me what I wanted? Too intimidated to even try, I insisted that we leave." (Paragraph 24)

Reading Check

Central Point and Main Ideas

The other choices are all too narrow. Sentence A does not include her difficulties and how she overcame them. Sentences C and D cover only paragraphs 26 and 27, respectively.

_B_ 1. Which sentence best expresses the central point of the entire selection?
   A. Maria Cardenas's goal was to graduate from college and teach migrant children to achieve their dreams.
   B. With hard work and courage, Maria Cardenas was able to overcome great difficulties and achieve her dream of a better life.
   C. Some books are filled with inspirational stories that can help us all.
   D. Maria Cardenas's story proves that certain skills, including writing and mathematical abilities, are necessary if we want to succeed in college.

_A_ 2. The topic sentence of paragraph 10 is its
A. first sentence.
B. second sentence.   The second, third, and last sentences give details
C. third sentence.   of what was hard about Maria's life in those days.
D. last sentence.

_B_ 3. Which sentence best expresses the main idea of paragraph 26?

Answers A, C, and D   A. In 1987, Maria worked for the Redlands Christian Migrant
are too narrow.   Association.
Answer A covers only
sentence 1.   B. The book *Dark Harvest* convinced Maria that her dream for a better
Answer C covers only   education wasn't crazy.
the minor detail in
sentence 2.   C. The Redlands Christian Migrant Association provided services for
Answer D ignores the   migrant children.
last sentence of the
paragraph, which   D. The book *Dark Harvest* contained stories about migrant workers,
describes how the book   including some who had gone on to college and became teachers.
affected her.

Supporting Details

_D_ 4. To see if Maria had been working in the fields, her teacher inspected her
A. clothing.
B. homework.   See paragraph 2. Maria's "dirty fingernails and
C. shoes.   calluses" prove she's been working in the fields.
D. hands.

_C_ 5. Maria was encouraged to leave her abusive husband by her
A. mother.
B. daughter.
C. brother.   See paragraph 19.
D. employer.

Inferences

_C_ 6. We can infer from paragraph 14 that

The father's   A. Maria's father should have been given another chance to live with his
stalking and yelling   wife and children.
at Maria's mother
is evidence for   B. Maria's mother didn't care about her children.
answer C. Answers
A, B, and D are   C. Maria's father was angry that he no longer had control over his wife
unsupported.   and children.

D. Maria's father spent several years in jail.

We can assume that by sharing her story, Maria wants to give other people in similar situations the courage to take control of their lives. Answer A is unsupported. Answer C is contradicted by paragraph 24. Answer D is contradicted by paragraph 34.

__B__ 7. We can conclude from the selection that

   A. most migrant workers prefer working in the fields to other types of employment.

   B. Maria hopes that her story will inspire others, just as the book *Dark Harvest* inspired her.

   C. it was easy for Maria to teach herself to read.

   D. Maria's teacher, Mrs. Seth, suspected that Maria had paid someone to write her narrative for her.

The Writer's Craft

__B__ 8. Cardenas introduces her essay by

See paragraphs 1–3. Maria tells a story about one of the times she returned after an absence.

   A. making general statements about the life of a migrant worker.

   B. telling a story about her experience in school.

   C. asking questions about creating better schools for migrant children.

   D. presenting an opposite idea: imagining herself as a teacher.

__D__ 9. In paragraph 29, the author's tone is mainly

   A. humorous and playful.

   B. warm and nostalgic.

   C. detached and instructive.

   D. enthusiastic and appreciative.

Maria shows enthusiasm and appreciation for reading and for the Walkers, who gave her a job and befriended her as well.

__B__ 10. What do you think was Cardenas's purpose in writing this selection?

   A. She hoped to inform readers of the benefits of attending community college.

   B. She wanted to both entertain readers with an inspiring story and persuade them to never give up on dreams.

   C. She wanted to inform readers about the many obstacles faced by young people who speak English as a second language.

   D. She hoped to both persuade readers to help migrant children and to inform readers of ways to do so.

For "inspiring story," see, in particular, paragraphs 26–35. For "never give up on dreams," see paragraphs 15–16, 19–22, 24, 26–29, and 34–35. Answers A and C are too narrow; answer D is not covered in the selection.

Discussion Questions

1. Maria's children worked in the fields, as their mother did when she was younger. In what ways were those children's lives different from Maria's life when she was a child working in the fields?

2. Why might it have been so important to Maria to learn to read after her daughter began school? What do you think she imagined might happen if she did *not* learn to read?

3. Why do you think Mrs. Seth cried upon reading Maria's narrative about giving phony excuses to her grade-school teacher? Why might Maria have thought that Mrs. Seth was disappointed with what she had written?

4. What do you think Maria means when she says she encourages migrant children to "stand on their own two feet"? What do you think *all* children must learn in order to "stand on their own two feet"?

Paragraph Assignments

1. All through her adult life, Maria Cardenas made herself do things that were very scary or difficult for her. For example, she left an abusive husband, despite not knowing how she would cope on her own. She made herself learn to read. She forced herself to begin college. She did all these things because she believed the long-term benefits would outweigh the short-term difficulties.

   When have you made yourself do something difficult, even though it would have been easier not to? Maybe it was one of these:

   - Apologizing for something you did wrong
   - Starting a new class or job
   - Moving to a new town
   - Speaking up for yourself to someone who was treating you badly

   Write a paragraph about what you did and why. In it, answer these questions:

   - What did I do that was difficult?
   - Why did I find doing it so hard or frightening?
   - Why did I think doing it would be worthwhile?
   - How did I feel about myself after I'd done it?

You might begin with a topic sentence similar to one of the following:

- One of the hardest things I've ever had to do was to transfer to a new school halfway through my freshman year.

- Apologizing to my sister for playing a cruel trick on her was a difficult moment for me.

2. Cardenas writes that she found herself "walking down the same abusive road as my mother." As much as she had hated seeing her father abuse her mother, she found herself married to the same kind of man. Although it doesn't seem to make any sense that a child of an abusive father would stay with a man who beats her, it happens all the time.

   Write a paragraph explaining why you believe this unfortunate situation continues to happen. If you need help with ideas, searching "why women stay in abusive relationships" will give you a great deal of information. Choose the reasons that make the most sense to you, and include these in your paragraph. Be sure to support each reason with one or more vivid examples.

Essay Assignments

1. Maria Cardenas feels a strong drive to help migrant children learn to speak English and to "stand on their own two feet." If you were offered the chance to help three different groups of people, who would those groups be? (You might choose, for example, to help politicians, world leaders, salespeople, teachers, students, waiters or waitresses, bosses, gamblers, smokers, drinkers, professional athletes, slow or fast drivers, motorcycle riders, TV or Internet addicts, gang members, teenage girls or boys, senior citizens, city dwellers, suburbanites . . .) Write an essay in which you explain which groups you would help and why, and describe what you would do in each case to help those involved. Your essay can be either humorous or serious.

2. Like Maria, many people reach adulthood without having learned to read well. Unlike Maria, many of those people live the rest of their lives as non-readers. Learning to read as an adult is challenging for a number of reasons. Some of those reasons are as follows:

   - Easy-to-read material is often written for small children, and such material may seem boring or insulting to adults.

   - Adults are often ashamed of being poor readers, and they may fear they will be further humiliated if they seek help.

   - Adults often have work and family commitments that make attending classes difficult.

Keeping those challenges in mind, write an essay in which you describe a plan for teaching adults in your community to read. You could begin with a thesis statement something like this: "For an adult-literacy program to succeed, it will have to deal with several challenges." Then go on to organize your essay by addressing a specific challenge in each paragraph and explaining how to overcome it.

7 He Was First

John Kellmayer

Preview

Jackie Robinson is widely known as the superb athlete who broke major-league baseball's "color line" in 1947. But as this selection indicates, it is worth remembering just what Robinson went through to achieve that breakthrough. The Robinson story also shows how professional baseball's white establishment, spurred both by self-interest and a growing distaste for racism, pinned its hopes on Robinson, his skills, and—most of all—his character.

Words to Watch

rampant (6): widespread
staunch (7): strong
conclave (14): meeting
cantankerous (21): ill-tempered
prestigious (29): highly respected
tumultuous (31): noisy
adulation (31): great admiration

1   Today few people under 70 can remember what it was like *not* to see blacks in professional baseball.

2   But until April 15, 1947, when Jackie Robinson played his first game with the Brooklyn Dodgers, the world of major-league baseball was a whites-only world.

3   The transition was not an easy one. It took place largely because Branch Rickey, owner of the Dodgers, held onto a dream of integrating baseball and because Jackie Robinson had the character, talent, and support to carry him through an ugly obstacle course of racism.

4   Even before he arrived in professional baseball, Robinson had to combat discrimination. Robinson entered the army with a national college reputation as an outstanding athlete. Still, he was denied permission to play on the football and baseball teams at Fort Riley, Kansas, where he was stationed. He had been allowed to practice with the football team, but when the first game against an opposing team came up,

Robinson was sent home on a pass. His exclusion from the baseball team there was more direct. A member of that team recalls what happened: "One day we were out at the field practicing when a Negro lieutenant tried out for the team. An officer told him, 'You have to play with the colored team.' That was a joke. There was no colored team." Robinson walked silently off the field.

5   Eventually, Robinson was granted an honorable discharge, and soon after, he signed a contract to play baseball in the Negro American League.

6   At this time Branch Rickey was waiting for his opportunity to sign a black ballplayer and to integrate major-league baseball. He understood not only that the black ballplayer could be good box office but also that bigotry had to be fought. While involved with his college baseball team, he had been deeply moved by a nasty scene in which his star catcher, an outstanding young black man, was prohibited from registering at a hotel with the rest of the team. Rickey then became determined to do something about the rampant° racism in baseball.

7   By 1944, the social climate had become more accepting of integration, in large part because of the contribution of black soldiers in World War II. Also, when the commissioner of baseball, a staunch° opponent of integration, died in 1944, he was replaced by a man named Happy Chandler. Chandler was on record as supporting integration of the game: "If a black man can make it at Okinawa and go to Guadalcanal, he can make it in baseball."

Rickey knew the time had come. He 8 began searching for the special black ballplayer with the mix of talent and character necessary to withstand the struggles to follow. When he learned about a star player in the Negro American League named Jackie Robinson, he arranged to meet with him.

At their meeting, Rickey said, "Jack, 9 I've been looking for a great colored ballplayer, but I need more than a great player. I need a man who will accept insults, take abuse, in a word, carry the flag for his race. I want a man who has the courage not to fight, not to fight back. If a guy slides into you at second base and calls you a black son of a bitch, I wouldn't blame you if you came up swinging. You'd be right. You'd be justified. But you'd set the cause back twenty years. I want a man with courage enough not to fight back. Can you do that?"

10   Robinson thought for a few minutes before answering, "If you want to take this gamble, I promise you there'll be no incidents." The promise was not easily made. Robinson had encountered plenty of racism in his life, and he was accustomed to fighting for black rights. He was known by his teammates in the Negro American League to have a quick temper. Consequently, keeping his promise to Rickey was going to require great personal will.

11   After signing with the Dodgers in October 1945, Robinson did not have to wait long to put his patience to the test. Even before he began to play in the Dodger organization, he and his wife, Rachel, encountered the humiliation of Southern racism.

12   It began when the Robinsons flew from Los Angeles to spring training in Florida, two weeks after they got married. On a stop in New Orleans, they were paged and asked to get off the plane. They later learned that in the South, whites who wanted seats on a flight took preference over blacks already seated. Their places had been given to a white couple. They had to wait a day to get another flight and then were told to get off for yet another white couple at a stop in Pensacola, Florida. The Robinsons then had to take a segregated bus the rest of the way to Jacksonville, where Branch Rickey had a car waiting for them. Of that trip, Rachel Robinson later said, "It sharpened for us

the drama of what we were about to go into. We got a lot tougher thereafter."

13   Soon after, during an exhibition game in Florida, Jackie suffered another humiliation, the first of many more to come on the diamond. During the first inning of that game, a police officer came onto the field and told Jackie, "Your people don't play with no white boys. Get off the field right now, or you're going to jail." Jackie had no choice but to walk quietly off the field. Not one of his teammates spoke up for him then.

14   Robinson's assignment to the Dodger minor-league team in Montreal was evidence of Rickey's careful planning for the breaking of the color barrier, as there was little racism in the Canadian city. That fact became important in supporting the spirits of Jackie and Rachel against the horrible outpouring of hate that greeted him at each stop on the road. Baseball historian Robert Smith wrote that when Robinson first appeared in Syracuse, "the fans reacted in a manner so raucous, obscene, and disgusting that it might have shamed a conclave° of the Ku Klux Klan." It was during this game that a Syracuse player threw a black cat at Jackie and yelled, "Hey, Jackie, there's your cousin." In Baltimore, the players shouted racist insults, threw balls at his head, and tried to spike him. In addition, as would be the case at many stops through the years, Jackie wasn't allowed to stay at the same hotel as the rest of the team.

15   Robinson's manager at Montreal was Clay Hopper, a Mississippi native adamantly opposed at first to the

presence of Robinson on his ball club. Rickey once stood near Hopper during a game when Robinson made a superb dive to make an out, and Rickey commented that Robinson seemed "superhuman." Hopper's reply was, "Do you really think he's a human being?"

16   No civil rights legislation could have turned Clay Hopper around the way Jackie Robinson did. By the end of a season in which Robinson led his team to the minor-league World Series, Hopper told Robinson, "You're a great ballplayer and a fine gentleman. It's been wonderful having you on the team." Hopper would later remark to Rickey, "You don't have to worry none about that boy. He's the greatest competitor I ever saw, and what's more, he's a gentleman."

17   It was clear that Jackie Robinson's next stop was the big leagues, the Brooklyn Dodgers. Not surprisingly, though, the prospect of a black major-league player was not met by all with open arms. Just how much resistance there was, however, could be seen in the meeting of the baseball club owners in January of 1947 in which every owner but Rickey voted against allowing Jackie to play.

18   Fortunately, commissioner Happy Chandler had another point of view. He later told Rickey, "Mr. Rickey, I'm going to have to meet my Maker some day. If He asked me why I didn't let this man play, and I answered, 'Because he's a Negro,' that might not be a sufficient answer. I will approve of the transfer of Robinson's contract from Montreal to Brooklyn." So the color barrier was broken, and Robinson became a member of the Brooklyn Dodgers.

19   Robinson's talent meant less to some of the Brooklyn players than race. The prospect of a black teammate prompted a Dodger outfielder, a Southerner by the name of Dixie Walker, to pass among the other Southern players a petition urging Rickey to ban Robinson from their team. Walker gathered signatures and his petition gained momentum until he approached shortstop Pee Wee Reese, a Kentucky native. Robinson had originally been signed on as a shortstop and could have posed a real threat to Reese's job. Nonetheless, Reese refused to sign the petition. Reese was one of the leaders of the Brooklyn "Bums," so his acceptance of Robinson was of great importance in determining how the rest of the Dodgers would react.

20   As expected, Robinson's presence triggered an ugly racial response. It began with hate mail and death threats against him and his wife and baby boy. In addition, some of his teammates continued to oppose him. Some even refused to sit near him.

21   The opposing teams, however, were much worse, and the hatred was so intense that some of the Dodger players began to stand up for Jackie. In Philadelphia, players cried out such insults as "They're waiting for you in the jungles, black boy," and "Hey, snowflake, which one of you white boys' wives are you dating tonight?" The first Dodger to stand up for Robinson on the field was a Southerner, the cantankerous° Eddie "The Brat" Stanky. When the Phillies pointed their bats at Robinson

and made machine-gun-like noises in a cruel reference to the threats on his and his family's lives, Stanky shouted, "Why don't you yell at someone who can answer back?"

22   Other opposing teams were no better. In an early-season game in Cincinnati, for instance, players yelled racial epithets at Jackie. Rex Barney, who was a Dodger pitcher then, described Pee Wee Reese's response: "While Jackie was standing by first base, Pee Wee went over to him and put his arm around him, as if to say, 'This is my man. This is the guy. We're gonna win with him.' Well, it drove the Cincinnati players right through the ceiling, and you could have heard the gasp from the crowd as he did it."

23   In the face of continuing harassment, Jackie Robinson, a hot-tempered young man who had struggled against racism all his life, chose to fight his toughest battle, not with his fists or foul language, but with the courage not to fight back. Instead, he answered his attackers with superior play and electrifying speed.

24   Within the first month of the 1947 season, it became apparent that Robinson could be the deciding factor in the pennant race. His speed on the base paths brought an entirely new dimension to baseball. Robinson used bunts and fake bunts and steals and fake steals to distract opposing pitchers and force basic changes in strategy in the game.

25   Undoubtedly, one reason many Dodger players rallied around Robinson was that they saw him as a critical, perhaps the critical, factor in their pursuit of the pennant. Like Rickey's, their motives reflected a mixture of personal ambition and a genuine concern for doing what was right.

26   And many did do what was right, even off the field. For example, Robinson at first waited until all his teammates had finished their showers before he would take his. One day, outfielder Al Gionfriddo patted Robinson on the butt and told him to get into the showers with everybody else, that he was as much a part of the team as anyone. Robinson smiled and went to the showers with Gionfriddo.

27   The ballplayers' wives also extended the hand of friendship to Robinson and his wife. Pitcher Clyde King related an incident that was typical of the efforts put forth to make the Robinsons feel part of the Dodger family. At Ebbets Field, an iron fence ran from the dugout to the clubhouse, keeping the fans from the players. After the games, the Dodger wives would be allowed inside the fence to wait for their husbands. Rachel Robinson, reluctant to join the other wives, would wait for Jackie outside the fence among the fans. King remembers that his own wife, Norma, a North Carolina girl, made sure that Rachel joined her and the other Dodger wives inside.

28   For Jackie, a series of such small but significant events may have meant the difference between making it and exploding under the enormous pressure that followed him throughout that first baseball season.

29   As the season passed, he gained the support not only of many of his

teammates but of much of the baseball world in general. On September 12, *Sporting News*, the leading publication in baseball, selected Robinson as its Rookie of the Year—the first of many prestigious° awards he would receive during his term with the Dodgers.

30   In the article announcing the award, there was a quote from none other than Dixie Walker, the same Dodger who had started the petition in the spring to ban Robinson from playing for Brooklyn. Walker praised Robinson for his contributions to the club's success, stating that Robinson was all that Branch Rickey had said and more.

31   On September 22, the Dodgers defeated the St. Louis Cardinals to clinch the National League pennant—against a team in whose town Jackie had to stay in a "colored" hotel. Fittingly enough, the following day was proclaimed Jackie Robinson Day at the Dodger ballpark. Robinson was honored with a tumultuous° outpouring of affection from the Brooklyn fans, an unbroken peal of adulation° that shook the very foundations of Ebbets Field.

32   Americans learned something that year about competition and excellence, about character and race. The fire that Jackie Robinson fanned swept across the years to follow, resulting in a permanent change in the makeup of the game. He had demonstrated that not only could blacks play on the same field with white players; they could excel. People brought their families hundreds of miles to see him play. The floodgates opened for the signing of the black ballplayer. The same major-league team owners who had voted against hiring blacks soon followed Rickey's lead. In the next few years came Willie Mays, Ernie Banks, Henry Aaron, and more—an endless list of black stars.

33   For some, Jackie Robinson is simply one of the greatest second basemen of all time. For others, he is much more. He is an individual who stood up and opposed the ugliness of racism with a relentless intensity. He was the first to brave the insults and the ignorance, the first to show that major-league baseball could be raised from the depths of segregation. His victory is a model of what one determined person can accomplish.

First Impressions

Freewrite for ten minutes on one of the following.

1. Did you enjoy reading this selection? Why or why not?

2. Were you already familiar with who Jackie Robinson was and what he had done? Were you surprised by any of the details revealed in this story? Explain.

3. In what ways do you think that attitudes have changed since Jackie Robinson's day? In what ways have they perhaps *not* changed?

Vocabulary Check

__B__ 1. In the sentence below, the word *raucous* means
   A. cold and silent.
   B. loud and disorderly.
   C. warm and welcoming.
   D. shocked and confused.

   > The sentences that follow this one describe people throwing things and shouting insults. This suggests that the reaction was loud and disorderly.

   "Baseball historian Robert Smith wrote that when Robinson first appeared in Syracuse, 'the fans reacted in a manner so raucous, obscene, and disgusting that it might have shamed a conclave of the Ku Klux Klan.'" (Paragraph 14)

__B__ 2. In the sentence below, the word *adamantly* means
   A. weakly.
   B. stubbornly.
   C. secretly.
   D. pleasantly.

   > The third sentence in paragraph 15 tells us that Hopper's opposition was not secret. Hopper's remark was certainly not pleasant or weak. We can conclude, therefore, that his opposition was stubborn because it took a long time for him to change his mind about Robinson.

   "Robinson's manager at Montreal was Clay Hopper, a Mississippi native adamantly opposed at first to the presence of Robinson on his ball club." (Paragraph 15)

__C__ 3. In the sentence below, the word *momentum* means
   A. a deliberate insult.
   B. opposition.
   C. forward movement.
   D. defeat.

   > What would more signatures add to a petition?

   "Walker gathered signatures and his petition gained momentum until he approached shortstop Pee Wee Reese . . ." (Paragraph 19)

_A_ 4. In the excerpt below, the word *epithets* means
A. insults.
B. poetry.
C. encouragements.
D. questions.

The words *ugly racial response* suggest that *epithets* means "insults."

"As expected, Robinson's presence triggered an ugly racial response. . . . In an early-season game in Cincinnati, for instance, players yelled racial epithets at Jackie." (Paragraphs 20 and 22)

Reading Check

Central Point and Main Ideas

_C_ 1. Which sentence best expresses the central point of the entire selection?
A. Until 1947, there were no blacks in professional baseball.
B. Jackie Robinson, a man of principle and courage, became the best second baseman in baseball.
C. Baseball became integrated because of the courage of Branch Rickey and Jackie Robinson, who proved blacks could excel in major-league baseball.
D. The integration of American society was not easily accomplished.

Answers A and B are too narrow; answer D is too broad.

_D_ 2. Which sentence best expresses the main idea of paragraph 7?
A. Happy Chandler became baseball commissioner in 1944.
B. Black soldiers fought for the United States during World War II.
C. A commissioner of baseball who was opposed to integration died in 1944.
D. By 1944, society had become more open to integrating baseball.

Answers A, B, and C are too narrow.

_B_ 3. Which sentence best expresses the main idea of paragraph 12?
A. In the South at that time, blacks who were already seated on an airplane had to give up their seats for whites who wanted them.
B. Although the Robinsons' trip to Florida was marked by irritating incidents of racism, what was to come later was worse.
C. While on their way to Florida, the Robinsons were forced off two planes because white passengers wanted their seats.
D. Branch Rickey was waiting for the Robinsons in Jacksonville, Florida.

The main idea (answer B) is expressed in the last two sentences of the paragraph. Answers A, C, and D are specific details from the paragraph.

Supporting Details

_C_ 4. Branch Rickey had wanted to do something about racism in baseball ever since
    A. he saw Jackie Robinson denied a chance to play sports in the army.
    B. he himself had been a victim of racism.
    C. he saw a member of his college baseball team denied a room in a whites-only hotel.
    D. he saw Pee Wee Reese's acceptance of a black teammate.

See paragraph 6.

_F_ 5. TRUE OR FALSE? During Robinson's first year with the Dodgers, none of his teammates accepted him.   See paragraphs 25–26 and 29.

_A_ 6. Robinson encountered racism
    A. on and off the field in both the North and the South.
    B. only during baseball games.
    C. mainly in Canada.
    D. until he joined the major leagues.

There are many examples throughout. See, for example, paragraphs 12 and 21.

Inferences

_T_ 7. TRUE OR FALSE? The author implies that the Dodgers won the 1947 National League pennant largely because of Jackie Robinson.

See the first sentence of paragraph 25.

_C_ 8. Which of the following inferences is best supported by paragraph 19?
    A. All Southern players were racist.
    B. Pee Wee Reese felt threatened by Jackie Robinson.
    C. Reese put principle ahead of personal concern.
    D. Without Pee Wee Reese, baseball would not have become integrated.

Several examples prove answer A to be inaccurate. Answer B is not mentioned in the story, but the fact that Reese stood up for Robinson suggests otherwise.

The Writer's Craft

Answer C is correct because Reese did what was right, not what was convenient. Answer D is unsupported.

_B_ 9. In which paragraph does the author, through his choice of words, first begin to reveal his attitude towards Jackie Robinson?
    A. Paragraph 1
    B. Paragraph 3
    C. Paragraph 8
    D. Paragraph 9

The statement *Jackie Robinson had the character [and] talent . . . to carry him through an ugly obstacle course of racism* indicates the writer's attitude toward Robinson.

_____A_____ 10. The main purpose of this selection is to

   A. inform readers about how major-league baseball became integrated, thanks in large part to Branch Rickey and Jackie Robinson.

   B. simply entertain readers with an account of Jackie Robinson's first major-league season.

   C. persuade readers that Branch Rickey deserves all the credit for integrating baseball.

   D. persuade readers that Jackie Robinson was the greatest second baseman of all time.   Paragraph 3 states this idea, and the rest of the selection develops the point in a direct and informative manner. Answer B is too narrow. Answer C is contradicted by the details about Robinson and by the title of the selection. Answer D is not supported.

Discussion Questions

1. Kellmayer writes, "By 1944, the social climate had become more accepting of integration, in large part because of the contribution of black soldiers in World War II." Why do you think the contribution of black soldiers in World War II would be such an influence on the progress of integration in the United States?

2. An ongoing question about history is whether individuals cause important changes in society or whether it is circumstances that lead to changes—once the circumstances are right, the right individuals will emerge. In the integration of baseball, how important do you think the times were? How important were the individuals involved?

3. Do you think Branch Rickey was right to make Robinson agree "not to fight back"? Explain your answer.

4. Robinson had to face a great deal of racism. Unfortunately, despite the greater integration of today, racism still exists. Have you experienced any racial insults yourself or seen anyone else treated badly because of the racial or ethnic group he or she belongs to? Tell what happened, and how you or the other person reacted.

Paragraph Assignments

1. Pee Wee Reese used his position as a team leader to stop the anti-Robinson momentum. When have you seen an individual stand up to a group and speak up for another point of view? Write a paragraph that describes what happened. Your topic sentence could be similar to one of the following:

- I'll never forget the day my shy sister finally spoke up for herself.

- When my cousin heard his parents criticizing a family of another race that had moved onto their street, he stood up for the new family.

- By inviting several unpopular kids to his party, my friend Peter showed he wouldn't go along with the crowd and its cruelty.

Be sure to include details such as what the mood of the group was, what actions you or the individual took, and how the group responded.

2. Branch Rickey asked Robinson to accept insults, take abuse, and not fight back when attacked either verbally or physically. He felt that if Robinson responded with anger or violence, it would "set the cause back twenty years." During the Civil Rights Movement, many African Americans were divided on which approach was best in the struggle for fair and equal treatment. Many, like Dr. Martin Luther King, Jr., believed that peaceful protest and refusing to fight back was more effective. Others, like Malcolm X, felt that peaceful protest conveyed only weakness and that black people should express their anger.

   Do you agree that the way to deal with the hatred and violence of others is to remain silent and peaceful and to turn the other cheek? Why or why not? Write a paragraph defending your point of view. Give specific reasons for why you believe that it is either better to fight back or, as Rickey asked Robinson to do, remain silent.

   To get some ideas for this paper, try researching "peaceful protest versus violent protest" or "Is peaceful protest effective?"

Essay Assignments

1. Because of his great skill and his inner strength, Jackie Robinson became a national hero. But every community, school, and even family has its "everyday heroes"—people who have quietly and courageously dealt with obstacles in their lives. Write an essay about someone you know personally whom you consider an everyday hero. Perhaps it is a single mother who has done a great job raising her children. Or maybe it is a young man who has achieved an education, despite receiving little support at home. In your essay, make it clear why you consider this person an everyday hero, what obstacles have stood in his or her way, and what effect you think his or her actions have had on others.

2. Why do some people react with such violent hatred to others whom they perceive as "different"? Write an essay in which you discuss several possible explanations for hate crimes. For more information for this assignment, Google "hate crimes" or "crimes against minorities." A thesis statement for this paper could be something like the following: "I believe that people who commit hate crimes are driven by their upbringing, their fears, and their desire to impress their friends."

8 Into the Light

Tanya Savory

Preview

What would you do if you were convinced that people would reject, even despise you if they knew who you really were? Would you dare to be yourself and risk their condemnation? Or would you do your best to conform to their expectations? In this selection, Tanya Savory tells how she came to terms with her identity as a gay woman.

Words to Watch

commonplace (15): routine
heterosexuality (18): desire for someone of the opposite sex
murky (23): dark and gloomy
boycotted (23): stayed away from
prissy (24): overly prim and proper
orientation (27): direction

1   One night in April when I was barely seven years old, my mother told me to put on my Sunday dress—Dad was taking the family to a church across town. None of this made sense to me. After all, it was a Thursday, it was nearly bedtime, and our church was right next door. Dad was the minister, so all we did was walk across a parking lot to get to church. Why were we going across town?

2   After what seemed like an endless drive, we were winding slowly through a neighborhood I'd never seen before. Suddenly we were in front of a big wooden building with no windows. Streams of people were pouring in, all of them quiet and many of them hugging or holding hands. When our family walked into the church, many people turned to stare at us for a moment—nearly everyone in the church was black, and we were white. But then a friend of my father's, a young black minister, rushed over to greet us and led us to a pew.

3   Throughout that evening, the tall black woman sitting next to me turned to smile at me again and again even though there were tears in her eyes. I was amazed by her hat full of flowers and even some bird feathers, so I smiled back. No one wore hats like that in our church. I gazed at her hat until I became

105

drowsy and drifted in and out of sleep, occasionally waking up to hear voices joined in song. Many songs were sung that night that I knew, but at the end of the service everyone joined hands and sang a slow, moving song that I'd never heard before: *We shall overcome, we shall overcome, we shall overcome some day…* The tall woman next to me put one arm around me and lifted the other into the air, tears streaming down her face.

4   It was April 4th, 1968, and Martin Luther King, Jr., had been shot and killed just five hours earlier.

5   When I was a senior in high school, I sat on the front porch with my dad one warm South Carolina afternoon and asked him about that night.

6   "Weren't you afraid?" I asked.

7   "Afraid? Of what?" my dad asked, giving me a kind of funny look.

8   "Well, you know," I said awkwardly, "afraid of the kind of white people who hate blacks. What if they had found out that we were at that service that night? Weren't you afraid of what they might think or do?"

9   My dad stared at me for a long moment before he answered. "Your mother and I have never been *afraid* of what bigots think of us. And we certainly weren't going to be bullied into hiding the way we felt just because some racists thought we were wrong."

10   "Yeah, but when everyone found out, you lost a lot of friends. Even Aunt Jo still doesn't speak to you," I pointed out.

11   "Not a lot of friends—a few. But that's a small price to pay to be true to yourself. I'm sorry to lose some friends,

but I'd be sorrier to be living my life according to how other people think I should live it."

12   "Really? I asked. "You really think that?"

13   "Yes. I really *know* that," my dad answered.

14   That night I lay awake for hours thinking about what my dad had said. I knew he was right, but I was 100% afraid to be true to myself. I was in a small town in the South in 1978, and I was afraid, very afraid, that I was someone that even open-minded people would despise. Someone who, if I *were* true to myself, would be laughed at, abandoned by my friends, and worse. Someone whose own mother and father might turn against her. I was afraid I was gay.

15   This was decades before gay characters on TV or in the movies had become commonplace°. The words "gay marriage" would only have been heard in a punch line to a joke, and, in fact, most people still believed that homosexuality was a mental illness or a crime. In the town where I grew up, it was illegal to be gay—police used to stake out a little rundown cinderblock bar on the other side of the tracks where, supposedly, gay men gathered. It was not uncommon for the police to rough up and handcuff men they saw coming out of this bar. Then they were thrown in the jail for the night for little or no real reason. Most of the townspeople thought this was a good idea.

16   Every day in the halls at school, I would wonder and worry if my classmates could tell by looking at me.

I pretty much looked and acted like any other seventeen-year-old girl. I passed notes in geometry, wore too much mascara, and worried about what I would wear to the prom in April. And like most of my friends, I had a boyfriend that I loved. But something had begun to creep into my consciousness about a year earlier—something like the slightest pinprick of light that had grown just a bit brighter every day until I was sure that everyone could see it like a spotlight on me: I didn't love my boyfriend, Mark, the same way I loved my best friend, Karla. I loved her more—I was *in* love with her. Midway through my senior year in high school, I became so afraid and confused about how I felt that I simply made the choice to stop being friends with Karla. The way I saw it, if I turned off the spotlight, no one would be able to see the real me.

17 In the darkness, it was easier to hide. I made new friends that I didn't really care too much about. I lost interest in anything that was special or unique about me, not wanting to draw attention to who I was. I went entirely overboard in my devotion to Mark, even suggesting that we get married as soon as we graduated from high school. College and my future no longer mattered to me. All that mattered was escaping the light, the fear of who I really was. It didn't matter that I was confused and miserable as long as I was hidden.

18 Strange as it may sound today, I was actually relieved when, one Sunday morning, I came across a short and angry article in a Christian magazine that insisted that homosexuality was a sin and that it was a choice. Apparently, all one had to do was change his or her mind about who they loved, *choose* to hate that kind of love, and everything would be okay. Supposedly it was as simple as deciding not to rob a bank or choosing not to eat too much pie. Choose heterosexuality° and you get heaven. Otherwise, you get hell. I had made the right choice! In a burst of satisfaction, I decided to tell my father everything I had been through and how I had made the right decision. After all, he was a minister. Surely he'd be proud of me.

19 Thankfully, he was not.

20 "Is your decision based on who you really are or who you want people to think you are?" was my dad's first question.

21   I was stunned. This was not how I had expected my father to respond at all. No one I knew had ever said anything about it being okay to be gay. In fact, no one ever talked about it at all except to make fun of it. I paused for a long time before answering. Finally, I quietly said, "I'm not sure."

22   I don't remember what else was said, but my father hugged me. And that was a great turning point, a great source of light in my life.

23   Decades later, I look back on that year as a strange, murky° time full of confusion about myself and about the world around me. Luckily, I had parents who, though they worried about how the world around me would treat me, did not try to change me. They never once suggested that there was anything "wrong" with me. But most of the gay people I know who grew up in that same era were not so lucky: One friend tells a story of his 75-year-old grandmother chasing him down the street with a shotgun when she found out he was gay. "She thought I'd be better off dead," he explained. "Luckily, her aim was bad." Another friend describes how her parents changed the locks on the doors, leaving a note that simply read, "Don't come back." Perhaps worst of all was a friend whose own family boycotted° his funeral when he died of AIDS.

24   It's hard to imagine where that kind of hate comes from. What is it about love between two people of the same sex that creates such anger and hostility? Some people, like my friend's 75-year-old grandmother, have an uninformed idea of what gay people are like. They believe all the ridiculous stereotypes that they've read about or seen on TV or in the movies. The stereotypes are frightening to them—and fear is always one step away from hate. To them, gay people are a big group of creepy and weird outcasts full of prissy° men who wear dresses and angry women who look like lumberjacks. In reality, of course, gay people are no different from anyone else. We work in the same jobs, eat the same foods, have the same worries, and experience the same joys and sorrows as any other human beings.

25   Other people, like the parents who locked their daughter out of their house, feel that it is immoral—that it is just plain wrong for two people of the same sex to fall in love. They feel that it is best to just lock it out and hope it goes away. This, in fact, was the same way many people felt about black and white people falling in love years ago. It just seemed wrong, and it made people feel uneasy. They didn't want to have to see it or think about it. So until 1948, it was against the law in the United States for interracial couples to marry. But laws designed to keep people from loving one another, and labeling something "immoral" just because it makes some people uncomfortable, are always bad ideas.

26   Still other people, like the family that refused to attend their own son's funeral, claim that God doesn't approve of homosexuality. Like the author of the article I had read so many years ago, they feel it's a sin. There is rarely any argument one can present that can change the minds of people who point to the Bible as their reason for disliking, even hating,

gay people. But using religion to justify the way we can mistreat other people, however, is nothing new. In the past, the Bible has been used to justify slavery, segregation, and even denying women the right to vote. As the daughter of a minister, all of this seems strange to me. Like my father, I would like to think that religion is better suited to promoting love—not hate.

27   Luckily, attitudes are changing fast. Today, the world is far from the dark and mysterious place for a young gay person that it was when I was seventeen. It is definitely no longer considered funny or socially acceptable to make fun of gay people or tell jokes about them based on their sexual orientation°. In fact, the majority of young people in the United States agree that making fun of gay people isn't cool.

28   And though it was pretty much unthinkable when I was growing up, now more and more states are making it legal for gay couples to marry. In only a handful of decades, gay Americans have gone from being afraid to carefully hold hands in a darkened movie theater to publicly (and legally) celebrating a wedding! That's some incredible progress. By law, marriage can no longer be defined as being only between a man and a woman. Many feel and hope that it will not be long before gay marriage is legal throughout the entire country. After all, gay marriage is already legal in more than a dozen countries, including our next-door-neighbor, Canada.

29   Even so, there is still plenty of progress to be made. In nineteen states, it is still perfectly legal to discriminate against a person for being gay. This means that, by law, you can fire someone, refuse to hire someone, and even deny housing to someone just because you don't approve of whom they love. These are the same states that will certainly fight against legalizing gay marriage with everything they've got. And beyond all the legalities, there are still many Americans who dislike, even hate, gay people. As was proven with the Civil Rights Movement, changing laws is easier than changing the hearts and minds of people who hate others for who they are.

30   Not long ago, I read a story that made me very angry. In a small town in the Midwest, an elderly woman named Sarah had just lost her partner of forty-two years, Laura, to leukemia. As Laura lay dying in the hospital, Sarah pleaded with the hospital staff to allow her to see Laura, but the staff refused. Sarah and Laura lived in one of those states where gay people can still be denied rights. Only family was allowed in the rooms of critical patients. That was the law. Laura died alone, and Sarah never got to tell her goodbye.

31   Within a couple days of Laura's death, Laura's only surviving relative, a nephew who hadn't seen his great-aunt in twenty years, came to claim possession of the home Sarah and Laura had shared for decades. The home was in Laura's name, so now the law said it belonged to the nephew. Additionally, the nephew was happy to be legally entitled to all of the home's possessions and all of the money in his aunt's savings. Sarah was left with nothing—

no laws protected her because no laws recognized her relationship with Laura. Legally, Sarah and Laura were no more than strangers to one another. Sarah would spend her remaining years in a rundown facility for penniless elderly people.

32   And, legally, Sarah could even have been denied the right to attend her partner's funeral if the nephew hadn't wanted her there. However, the nephew had no interest in attending the service once he secured the deed to Laura's house.

33   On a cold April morning, Sarah and a handful of friends gathered at Laura's gravesite. But just as the service began, shouts were heard. Ten members of an anti-gay hate group had gathered across the road from the rural cemetery. Somehow, they had gotten wind of the fact that a gay person was about to be buried. Standing in a line and holding signs with slogans such as "Fags Burn in Hell" and "God Hates Homos," the group shouted cruel and angry comments throughout the funeral service. *Legally*, they had the right to do this.

34   As I read this story and looked at the pictures of the faces of those holding the signs and yelling, I felt hate. I felt like jumping in my car and driving nonstop to that little town and giving them a dose of their own darkness.

35   But then, near the end of the story, a comment by the elderly woman, Sarah, stopped me in my tracks. Reporters, who had crassly rushed to the scene, asked Sarah how she felt about the group picketing across the street. "Well," she had said, "I'm sorry they feel that way. But it won't do no good to hate them back."

36   And suddenly, Sarah's words were like a light—a light that seemed to shine all the way back to nearly forty years ago. It shone on a night in April amidst a group of mourners who chose to sing and hold hands in response to hate and violence—a group that was certainly angry and weary of being treated unfairly. And surely, somewhere during that evening, the young black minister who had led us to a seat must have reminded the congregation of Dr. King's own words: "Darkness can not drive out darkness; only light can do that. Hate can not drive out hate; only love can do that."

First Impressions

Freewrite for ten minutes on one of the following.

1. Did you enjoy reading this selection? Why or why not?

2. What part of this essay surprised you the most? Why do you think it surprised you?

3. Has reading this essay changed, in any way, your feelings about gay rights? Explain.

Vocabulary Check

___D___ 1. In the excerpt below, the word *hostility* means
   A. envy.
   B. discomfort.   When people hate something,
   C. sadness.   they show strong opposition to it.
   D. strong opposition.

   "It's hard to imagine where that kind of hate comes from. What is it about love between two people of the same sex that creates such anger and hostility?" (Paragraph 24)

___A___ 2. In the excerpt below, the word *crassly* means
   A. rudely.
   B. sensitively.   It is rude to rush to the scene of a burial service
   C. violently.   and interview the mourners.
   D. cleverly.

   "Reporters, who had crassly rushed to the scene, asked Sarah how she felt about the group picketing across the street. 'Well,' she had said, 'I'm sorry they feel that way. But it won't do no good to hate them back.'" (Paragraph 35)

Reading Check

Central Point and Main Ideas

Answer A covers only paragraphs 14–18. Answer B covers only paragraphs 15 and 27–28. Answer D is mentioned several times but ignores the issues of being true to oneself and of using love to drive out hate.

___C___ 1. Which sentence best expresses the central point of the entire selection?
   A. The author had a difficult time growing up in a small town in the South.
   B. Attitudes toward homosexuality have changed over the past few decades.
   C. Over time, the author learned to accept her gayness and love her enemies.
   D. Gays have often been the target of cruel and unfair treatment.

Answer A covers only sentences 2–4. Answer B covers only the middle of the paragraph. Answer C covers only the next-to-last sentence.

___D___ 2. Which sentence best expresses the main idea of paragraph 16?
   A. During high school, Savory looked and acted like any other seventeen-year-old girl.
   B. During high school, Savory had a boyfriend, but realized she was in love with her best friend, Karla.
   C. Midway though her senior year, Savory decided to stop being friends with Karla.
   D. During high school, Savory was afraid and confused that she might be gay.

___A___ 3. Which sentence best expresses the main idea of paragraph 31?

    A. Despite their long-term relationship, Sarah was left with nothing after Laura died.

    B. Laura's nephew, not Sarah, inherited her house and money.

    C. Laura's only surviving relative was a nephew who hadn't seen his great-aunt in twenty years.

    D. Sarah spent her remaining years in a rundown facility for penniless elderly people.

Answer B covers only sentences 2–3. Answer C covers only sentence 1. Answer D covers only the last sentence.

Supporting Details

___B___ 4. Savory first became aware that she might be gay

    A. when she was seven years old.

    B. when she was seventeen.

    C. as a college student.

    D. in her early thirties.

See paragraphs 14 and 16.

___B___ 5. The hospital staff told Sarah she could not see her partner Laura because

    A. Laura had a highly contagious disease.

    B. Sarah was not a family member.

    C. Sarah was gay.

    D. Laura didn't want any visitors.

See paragraph 30, the fifth sentence.

___D___ 6. According to this selection, the majority of Americans

    A. still despise homosexuals.

    B. think that gays will always be outcasts.

    C. believe in gay marriage.

    D. think gays should be treated the same as anyone else.

See the last two sentences of paragraph 27.

Inferences

___D___ 7. We can infer that Savory's father took his family to the black church the night of Martin Luther King's assassination

    A. to prove to bigots that he wasn't afraid of them.

    B. because he was in the habit of visiting different churches.

    C. to learn more about black church services.

    D. to show their support for the black community.

See paragraph 9 and paragraph 36, sentence 2.

___D___ 8. In telling the story of Sarah and Laura, the author implies that

    A. Sarah should have inherited Laura's home, possessions, and money.

    B. Laura's nephew didn't care about Laura; all he cared about was her money.

    C. Sarah is a forgiving person.

    D. all of the above.

For answer A, see paragraph 31. For answer B, see the second sentence of paragraph 32. For answer C, see the last sentence of paragraph 35.

The Writer's Craft

___C___ 9. In paragraph 28, the author mainly

Phrases such as *have gone from* and *no longer* signal a contrast of the perceptions from the past with the perceptions today.

A. compares American and Canadian attitudes toward gay marriage.

B. provides reasons that American attitudes toward gay marriage have changed.

C. contrasts how gay marriage would have been perceived when she was growing up with how it is perceived now.

D. lists examples of how attitudes toward gay marriage have changed.

___D___ 10. The word that best describes the tone of the last paragraph of the selection is

A. light-hearted.

B. ironic.

C. apologetic.

D. forgiving.

Anyone who responds to unfairness and hatred with love must be forgiving. The details of the paragraph— "words . . . like a light," "chose to sing and hold hands in response to hate and violence," and Dr. King's words—indicate the tone.

Discussion Questions

1. How does Savory's attitude toward homosexuality change in the course of the selection? What incident marks the turning point in her attitude toward her own sexuality?

2. What comparison does Savory draw between the treatment of blacks and the treatment of gays? In your view, is this comparison convincing? Explain.

3. What did Savory feel was so unjust about the story of Sarah and Laura? If you agree with her attitude toward the couple, what steps could be taken to make sure that unfortunate situations like these no longer occur?

4. In paragraph 28, Savory states, "Many feel and hope that it will not be long before gay marriage is legal throughout the entire country." Do you agree? What are your feelings about gay marriage?

Paragraph Assignments

1. Savory was outraged by the picketers who appeared at Laura's funeral. Although most of us have probably not experienced this level of hatred, we've all seen or heard about situations which have awakened our sense of injustice. Write a paragraph about a situation you've experienced or learned about whose injustice outraged you. Describe in detail what happened, your reaction, and why you reacted as you did.

2. Although, as Savory points out, gay people are now more accepted by society than they once were, gay marriage is still a controversial topic. Write a paragraph either in support of or in opposition to the idea of gay marriage. Explain the reasons you have for your position.

Essay Assignments

1. Clearly, Savory's minister father was an important figure in her life. Not only did he show her that it was important to stand up for her beliefs and to treat others with respect, but he also made it easier for her to accept her own sexual orientation. Write an essay about a person in your life who has had a positive influence on you. Provide whatever background information is necessary for the reader to understand your relationship with this person. Your thesis will be a general statement that summarizes the person's impact on your life, such as this one: "_____ helped me in several ways that greatly affected my life." Then continue your introduction by listing three specific ways that person influenced you, and write about each way in a separate paragraph. An example of such a plan-of-development sentence might be: "He helped me to believe in myself, showed me that it was important to listen to others, and taught me the value of hard work."

2. In the final paragraph of her essay, Savory quotes Dr. Martin Luther King, Jr.: "Darkness can not drive out darkness; only light can do that. Hate can not drive out hate; only love can do that." Dr. King's words are a fervent plea for love and understanding—as Savory witnessed in the black church, forty years earlier—as a response to hatred and violence.

   What other situations can you think of in which a nonviolent response would be far preferable to a violent one? Brainstorm a list of two or three tense situations from current events, recent history, or your own community in which a peaceful approach was successful in defusing a potentially violent situation. Then write an essay about one of these events. What caused the conflict? Who chose to address it with tact, diplomacy, or even love? What was the outcome? In your conclusion, suggest that Dr. King's words are still relevant today . . . and why.

   Alternatively, you could write about three such events, devoting a separate paragraph to each.

   For ideas for your essay, you might try Googling "peaceful protest" or "nonviolent response."

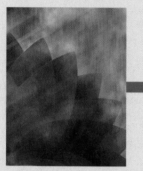

Unit Two

Understanding Ourselves

9 Night Watch

Roy Popkin

Preview

How often have you seen the advice, "Practice random acts of kindness"? The following selection belongs in this category. It proves, in the words of its author, that "there are people who care what happens to their fellow human beings."

Words to Watch

smudged (2): dirty with streaks or stains
relayed (3): passed along
boondocks (3): a rural region
maneuvers (3): military exercises
sedated (5): drugged with a pain reliever
oblivious (7): unaware
condolence (9): sympathy

1 The story began on a downtown Brooklyn street corner. An elderly man had collapsed while crossing the street, and an ambulance rushed him to Kings County Hospital. There, during his few returns to consciousness, the man repeatedly called for his son.

2 From a smudged°, oft-read letter, an emergency-room nurse learned that the son was a Marine stationed in North Carolina. Apparently, there were no other relatives.

3 Someone at the hospital called the Red Cross office in Brooklyn, and a request for the boy to rush to Brooklyn was relayed° to the Red Cross director of the North Carolina Marine Corps camp. Because time was short—the patient was dying—the Red Cross man and an officer set out in a jeep. They located the sought-after young man wading through marshy boondocks° on maneuvers°. He was rushed to the airport in time to catch the one plane that might enable him to reach his dying father.

4 It was mid-evening when the young Marine walked into the entrance lobby of Kings County Hospital. A nurse took the tired, anxious serviceman to the bedside.

5 "Your son is here," she said to the old man. She had to repeat the words several times before the patient's eyes

117

opened. Heavily sedated° because of the pain of his heart attack, he dimly saw the young man in the Marine Corps uniform standing outside the oxygen tent. He reached out his hand. The Marine wrapped his toughened fingers around the old man's limp ones, squeezing a message of love and encouragement. The nurse brought a chair, so the Marine could sit alongside the bed.

6   Nights are long in hospitals, but all through the night the young Marine sat there in the poorly lighted ward, holding the old man's hand and offering words of hope and strength. Occasionally, the nurse suggested that the Marine move away and rest a while. He refused.

7   Whenever the nurse came into the ward, the Marine was there. His full attention was on the dying man, and he was oblivious° of her and of the night noises of the hospital—the clanking of an oxygen tank, the laughter of night-staff members exchanging greetings, the cries and moans and snores of other patients. Now and then she heard him say a few gentle words. The dying man said nothing, only held tightly to his son through most of the night.

8   Along toward dawn, the patient died. The Marine placed on the bed the lifeless hand he had been holding, and went to tell the nurse. While she did what she had to do, he relaxed—for the first time since he got to the hospital.

9   Finally, she returned to the nurse's station, where he was waiting. She started to offer words of condolence° for his loss, but the Marine interrupted her. "Who was that man?" he asked.

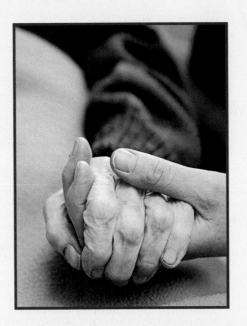

"He was your father," she answered, startled.   10

"No, he wasn't," the Marine replied. "I never saw him before in my life."   11

"Why didn't you say something when I took you to him?" the nurse asked.   12

"I knew right off there'd been a mistake, but I also knew he needed his son, and his son just wasn't here. When I realized he was too sick to tell whether or not I was his son, I figured he really needed me. So I stayed."   13

With that, the Marine turned and left the hospital. Two days later a routine message came in from the North Carolina Marine Corps base informing the Brooklyn Red Cross that the real son was on his way to Brooklyn for his father's funeral. It turned out there had been two Marines with the same name and similar serial numbers in the camp. Someone in the personnel office had pulled out the wrong record.   14

15   But the wrong Marine had become the right son at the right time. And he proved, in a uniquely human way, that there are people who care what happens to their fellow human beings.

First Impressions

Freewrite for ten minutes on one of the following.

1. Did you enjoy reading this selection? Why or why not?

2. Should the young Marine have immediately told the people at the hospital that the old man wasn't his father? Why or why not?

3. Have you ever spent time with an ill or injured person in the hospital? What do you remember most about the experience? How did it affect you?

Vocabulary Check

_D_ 1. In the sentence below, the words *enable him* mean

By catching the plane, he might be able to reach his dying father.

    A. stop him.
    B. encourage him.
    C. delay him.
    D. make it possible for him.

> "He was rushed to the airport in time to catch the one plane that might enable him to reach his dying father." (Paragraph 3)

_B_ 2. In the excerpt below, the word *dimly* means

    A. clearly.
    B. unclearly.
    C. rarely.
    D. often.

If he is drugged and difficult to awaken, he would see the man unclearly.

> "She had to repeat the words several times before the patient's eyes opened. Heavily sedated because of the pain of his heart attack, he dimly saw the young man. . . ." (Paragraph 5)

___D___ 3. In the sentence below, the word *condolence* means
  A. excuse.
  B. bitterness.
  C. surprise.
  D. sympathy.

If she thinks he just lost his father, what kind of words would she offer?

"She started to offer words of condolence for his loss, but the Marine interrupted her." (Paragraph 9)

___C___ 4. In the sentence below, the words *uniquely human* mean
  A. impossible for humans.
  B. scary to humans.
  C. done only by humans.
  D. not human.

What animals besides human beings would do what the Marine did?

"And he proved, in a uniquely human way, that there are people who care what happens to their fellow human beings." (Paragraph 15)

Reading Check

Central Point and Main Ideas

___B___ 1. Which sentence best expresses the central point of the entire selection?
  A. A mistake led to the wrong Marine being sent to the bedside of a dying man.
  B. In order to comfort a dying man, a young Marine pretended to be the old man's son.
  C. Because the dying man was heavily sedated, he did not realize that the young man at his bedside was not his son.
  D. A young Marine sat all night at the bedside of a dying old man.

Answer A covers only paragraph 14. Answer C covers only paragraph 5. Answer D covers only paragraphs 6 and 7.

___D___ 2. Which sentence best expresses the main idea of paragraph 6?
  A. The Marine refused the nurse's suggestion to rest.
  B. Nights are long in a hospital.
  C. The hospital ward where the dying man lay was poorly lighted.
  D. The Marine spent the whole night keeping the old man company.

Answer A covers only sentence 2. Answers B and C each cover only part of sentence 1.

___A___ 3. Which sentence best expresses the main idea of paragraph 14?
  A. Two days after the man died, the mixup was explained.
  B. The real son and the Marine shared the same name.
  C. Someone in the Marine personnel office had pulled the wrong Marine's record.
  D. The real son was on his way to his father's funeral.

Answer B covers only sentence 3. Answer C covers only sentence 4. Answer D covers only part of sentence 2.

Supporting Details

___D___ 4. People at the hospital learned the son's name
  A. when the son called the hospital, looking for his father.
  B. from the elderly man, who told them his son's name and that he was in the Marines.
  C. from a Marine Corps officer. *See the first sentence of paragraph 2.*
  D. from a letter the old man had with him.

___C___ 5. The Marine realized the old man was not his father
  A. after the man had died.
  B. midway through the night. *See the first sentence of paragraph 13.*
  C. as soon as he saw him.
  D. when he was on maneuvers.

Inferences

Item 6: ___A___ 6. We can assume that
The Marine must have had an elderly father; otherwise, he would not have gone to Brooklyn to see the man he thought was his dying father. Also, he was anxious (paragraph 4), presumably because he was expecting to see his dying father.

  A. the Marine also had an elderly father.
  B. the Marine was glad to be relieved of his military duties for a while.
  C. the Marine did not get along well with his own father.
  D. the Marine's father was dead.

  ___A___ 7. In paragraph 5, the author implies that
  A. the old man's poor vision led him to believe the Marine was his son.
  B. the old man did not want to embarrass the Marine by saying he wasn't his son.
  C. the old man was growing stronger.
  D. the nurse realized that the Marine was not the old man's son.

We are told that the old man was "heavily sedated" and that he only "dimly saw" the man in a Marine uniform.

The Writer's Craft

___B___ 8. Why do you think Popkin titled his essay "Night Watch"?
  A. The Marine didn't arrive at the hospital until late at night.
  B. Soldiers are often assigned "night watch" (night patrol) in the military, so the phrase has a double meaning in this essay.
  C. Even though the soldier wasn't the old man's son, he watched him for a very long time that night.
  D. Popkin wants to suggest that the nurse and old man were "in the dark" about who the soldier really was.

The double meaning of the title also suggests that the Marine was "doing his duty" as a human being to support another human being who was in great need.

_C_ 9. Which of the following best describes the author's purpose in writing this essay?

There is nothing in the essay that informs or persuades. The selection is intended to engage the reader in this story of human compassion.

A. To inform readers of the type of people who join the Marines
B. To inform readers that careless mistakes are made in hospital and Marine offices
C. To entertain readers with an inspirational story of a young man's compassion for a dying man
D. To persuade readers to provide clear instructions about how to contact relatives in case of emergency

_B_ 10. In the final paragraph of the essay, the author
A. quotes the nurse.
B. gives his own thoughts about the Marine's actions.
C. suggests that Americans should be proud of the Marines.
D. predicts what will happen to the Marine.

In the final paragraph, the author steps outside the story of the Marine and suggests the meaning of that story.

Discussion Questions

1. Were you surprised by the way this selection ended? How did the ending affect you? Explain.

2. Why didn't the Marine immediately reveal that a mistake had been made? Do you think his decision was the right one? Why or why not?

3. If you had been the man's son, how might you have felt when you learned what had happened?

4. The author refers to the "uniquely human way" in which the Marine showed "that there are people who care what happens to their fellow human beings." Have you seen other examples of people going out of their way to help strangers? What do you think motivates people to help people they don't know?

Paragraph Assignments

1. The Marine said he stayed with the old man because "I figured he really needed me." Write a paragraph about a time that you felt needed. Explain who needed you and in what way, how you responded to the person's need, and the positive or negative feelings you had about being needed. Here's a sample topic sentence for such a paragraph: "When my mom took a full-time job, she really needed me to help out more at home."

2. If you had an elderly parent (or grandparent) who lived alone, what things might you want him or her to do to be safe? Write a paragraph that details a few ideas. Consider dangers that might present themselves around the house, in the car, or out in public. What, for example, might the elderly man in this story have done to ensure that in the event of an accident, his son could be properly contacted?

Essay Assignments

1. When people are facing death, they often realize what is most important to them in life. In the case of the old man in this story, for example, he wanted more than anything else to see his son.

   If you knew that your life would end soon, what are some things that you would want to accomplish while you still had time? Maybe there are adventures or experiences that you would make a priority. For example, you may have always wanted to learn to snowboard, but have never gotten around to it. Or maybe there is unfinished business between you and a loved one that you would want to resolve. You might, for instance, want to patch up an argument with an old friend, or see a relative that you've lost touch with. Write an essay about several things that you would want to do before you died. Explain not only what those actions are, but why they are so important to you. Possible thesis statements for such an essay might be like these:

   - If I knew that I had only a short time left on earth, I would want to see the Pacific Ocean and go deep-sea fishing there with my brother.

   - Three things that I would want to accomplish before my life ended would be to visit the Grand Canyon, to read a great book such as Charlotte Bronte's *Jane Eyre*, and to spend more time with my grandparents.

2. It's not uncommon to see people reach out to help their loved ones. But the final paragraph of "Night Watch" states that "in a uniquely human way . . . there are people who care what happens to their fellow human beings"—in other words, they care about people to whom they have no particular obligation. Think of experiences you have had, or heard about, in which people went out of their way to assist someone they did not know well, if at all. Write an essay that tells the stories of two or three such incidents. You might conclude your essay by writing about what, if anything, the "givers" in such situations gain by their actions.

   If you need ideas for your paper, the search term "good Samaritan" or "pay it forward" should turn up many examples of people who have shown that they truly care about others.

10 The Most Hateful Words

Amy Tan

Preview

For years, a painful exchange with her mother lay like a heavy stone on Amy Tan's heart. Ongoing arguments and misunderstandings only made the stone grow heavier. In the following essay, Tan tells the story of how that weight was finally lifted.

Words to Watch

tormented (3): hurt or tortured
forbade (3): would not allow
impenetrable (3): impossible to get inside
frantically (9): excitedly, with great worry
bequeathed (15): willed to, left to

1   The most hateful words I have ever said to another human being were to my mother. I was sixteen at the time. They rose from the storm in my chest, and I let them fall in a fury of hailstones: "I hate you. I wish I were dead. . . ."

2   I waited for her to collapse, stricken by what I had just said. She was still standing upright, her chin tilted, her lips stretched in a crazy smile. "Okay, maybe I die too," she said between huffs. "Then I no longer be your mother!" We had many similar exchanges. Sometimes she actually tried to kill herself by running into the street, holding a knife to her throat. She too had storms in her chest. And what she aimed at me was as fast and deadly as a lightning bolt.

3   For days after our arguments, she would not speak to me. She tormented° me, acted as if she had no feelings for me whatsoever. I was lost to her. And because of that, I lost, battle after battle, all of them: the times she criticized me, humiliated me in front of others, forbade° me to do this or that without even listening to one good reason why it should be the other way. I swore to myself I would never forget these injustices. I would store them, harden my heart, make myself as impenetrable° as she was.

4   I remember this now, because I am also remembering another time, just a few years ago. I was forty-seven, had become a different person by then, had become a fiction writer, someone who uses memory and imagination. In fact, I was writing a story about a girl and her mother, when the phone rang.

5   It was my mother, and this surprised me. Had someone helped her make the call? For a few years now, she had been losing her mind through Alzheimer's disease. Early on, she forgot to lock her door. Then she forgot where she lived. She forgot who many people were and what they had meant to her. Lately, she could no longer remember many of her worries and sorrows.

6   "Amy-ah," she said, and she began to speak quickly in Chinese. "Something is wrong with my mind. I think I'm going crazy."

7   I caught my breath. Usually she could barely speak more than two words at a time. "Don't worry," I started to say.

8   "It's true," she went on. "I feel like I can't remember many things. I can't remember what I did yesterday. I can't remember what happened a long time ago, what I did to you. . . ." She spoke as a drowning person might if she had bobbed to the surface with the force of will to live, only to see how far she had already drifted, how impossibly far she was from the shore.

9   She spoke frantically°: "I know I did something to hurt you."

10   "You didn't," I said. "Don't worry."

11   "I did terrible things. But now I can't

Amy Tan today

remember what. . . . And I just want to tell you . . . I hope you can forget, just as I've forgotten."

12   I tried to laugh so she would not notice the cracks in my voice. "Really, don't worry."

13   "Okay, I just wanted you to know."

14   After we hung up, I cried, both happy and sad. I was again that sixteen-year-old, but the storm in my chest was gone.

15   My mother died six months later. By then she had bequeathed° to me her most healing words, as open and eternal as a clear blue sky. Together we knew in our hearts what we should remember, what we can forget.

First Impressions

Freewrite for ten minutes on one of the following.

1. Did you enjoy reading this selection? Why or why not?

2. Do you ever have moments when you feel you hate someone—or moments when you wish you were dead? Explain.

3. What do you think are common reasons why children fight with their parents? Why are these fights often so painful?

Vocabulary Check

____A____ 1. In the excerpt below, the word *stricken* means
   A. wounded.
   B. amused.
   C. annoyed.
   D. bored.

   What might cause Amy Tan's mother to collapse?

   "The most hateful words I have ever said to another human being were to my mother. . . : 'I hate you. I wish I were dead. . . .'

   "I waited for her to collapse, stricken by what I had just said." (Paragraphs 1–2)

____C____ 2. In the excerpt below, the word *humiliated* means
   A. complimented.
   B. spoke to.
   C. embarrassed.
   D. forgot.

   How is someone who is criticized in front of others likely to feel?

   ". . . the times she criticized me, humiliated me in front of others, forbade me to do this or that without even listening to one good reason why it should be the other way." (Paragraph 3)

____A____ 3. In the excerpt below, the word *injustices* means
   A. wrongs.
   B. compliments.
   C. limits.
   D. messages.

   The first two sentences (as well as the rest of the paragraph) describe some of the wrongs that Tan feels were done to her by her mother.

   "For days after our arguments, she would not speak to me. She tormented me, acted as if she had no feelings for me whatsoever. . . . I swore to myself I would never forget these injustices. I would store them, harden my heart, make myself as impenetrable as she was." (Paragraph 3)

Reading Check

Central Point and Main Ideas

__C__ 1. Which sentence best expresses the central idea of the entire selection?
   A. Alzheimer's disease made the author's mother forget the angry words the two of them had said to one another.

Answers A and D are too narrow. Answer B is too broad.

   B. Amy Tan had a difficult relationship with her mother.
   C. A painful relationship between Amy Tan and her mother was healed when her mother expressed regret shortly before her death.
   D. Amy Tan's mother suddenly became aware that something was wrong with her mind and that she had somehow hurt her daughter.

__A__ 2. Which sentence best expresses the main idea of paragraph 3?
   A. Because Tan's mother hurt her so much, Tan was determined to never forgive or forget the injustices.

See the last two sentences of paragraph 3. Answers B, C, and D are specific details from the paragraph.

   B. Tan's mother constantly humiliated and criticized the author in front of other people.
   C. Tan's mother won all of their fights, which only upset the author more.
   D. Tan's mother refused to listen to the author's side of any argument the two of them had.

__A__ 3. Which sentence best expresses the main idea of paragraph 8?
   A. Tan's mother had a disturbing moment of insight into her illness.
   B. Alzheimer's disease causes people to become confused and unable to remember things clearly.
   C. Tan's mother could not remember what she had done the day before.
   D. Tan's mother suddenly thought she was drowning.

Answers B and D are not stated. Answer C is too narrow.

Supporting Details

__A__ 4. When she was a young girl, the author swore that she would
   A. never forget her mother's cruelty.
   B. never be like her mother.
   C. publicly embarrass her mother by writing about her.
   D. never have children.   See the last two sentences of paragraph 3.

__C__ 5. When Tan's mother called her and spoke to her, Tan was immediately shocked because
   A. she and her mother hadn't spoken in years.

See paragraph 7.

   B. she couldn't understand what her mother was saying.
   C. her mother had not been able to say more than two words at a time for quite a while.
   D. her mother could not seem to remember why she had even called her.

Inferences

See paragraph 15. Answers A, C, and D are not supported.

___B___ 6. We can infer that the author of this selection
   A. does not have children of her own.
   B. loved her mother deeply in spite of their fights.
   C. got along with her father much better than her mother.
   D. wishes she had had the conversation with her mother in person instead of over the phone.

Item 7: The final sentence suggests Tan and her mother will remember the love they shared and forget the pain. Answers B, C, and D are not supported.

___A___ 7. The final line of this selection suggests that
   A. the author and her mother forgave each other for pain in the past.
   B. the author would always remember their most painful fights.
   C. the author's mother died before forgiving her daughter.
   D. the author had few good memories of her mother.

___D___ 8. By the end of the selection, the overall emotion that Tan seems to be expressing is
   A. anger.
   B. regret.
   C. confusion.
   D. sympathy.

Tan's responses to her mother (paragraphs 10 and 12) and her reaction to the phone call (paragraphs 14 and 15) support answer D.

The Writer's Craft

Item 9:
Tan links the beginning and the end of her essay by using the words *the storm in my chest* in paragraph 1 and paragraph 14. She emphasizes the contrast by changing the "hateful words" that "fall in a fury of hailstones" (paragraph 1) to "most healing words, as open and eternal as a clear blue sky" (paragraph 15).

___B___ 9. Tan begins her essay by remembering one of the worst fights she had with her mother because
   A. she needs to vent the anger she still feels toward her mother.
   B. it provides a touching and striking contrast with one of her final conversations with her mother.
   C. it explains why Tan decided to become a writer.
   D. argument was the most memorable kind of interaction Tan ever had with her mother.

___D___ 10. Tan probably wrote this selection to
   A. persuade readers not to hold grudges against their parents.
   B. inform readers of the difficulties of dealing with Alzheimer's patients.
   C. inform readers of the steps one can take to change a relationship with a parent.
   D. entertain readers with an honest and heartfelt episode from her life.

There is nothing that informs or persuades us in the selection. Tan merely presents this touching episode from her life in an engaging and human manner.

Discussion Questions

1. How do you think you would react to a parent who, like Tan's mother, tormented you and acted as though she had no feelings at all for you? Are you surprised that Tan even remained in contact with her mother? Why or why not?

2. Did you have a difficult relationship with one or both of your parents? Were the problems more the result of your behavior (possibly as a teenager), or of their behavior? Looking back, what do you think one or both of you could have done to make the relationship better?

3. Tan finally has a sense of peace regarding her and her mother's relationship shortly before her mother dies. Have you (or has someone you know) ever reached reconciliation with someone just in time? If so, how? Or, on the other hand, have you (or has a person you know) lost someone with whom reconciliation was, sadly, not possible? Explain.

4. Tan ends her piece by saying that she knew in her heart what she should remember and what she could forget. What is it that Tan will remember? What will she forget? Is it ever possible to forget things that, at one time in our lives, were very important or painful to us? If so, what are the advantages and disadvantages?

Amy Tan and her mother

Paragraph Assignments

1. At some point, we all have a fight or strong disagreement with a parent. Write a paragraph that describes the fight and how you eventually resolved things (if you did). What happened? How did you feel afterward? Did you, like Amy Tan, say things you regretted? Use dialogue to bring the argument to life for the reader. Conclude your paragraph with a statement about what you may have learned from this experience.

2. This essay makes the reader think of the phrase "forgive and forget." But is this advice always fair—or even realistic? Are there times when it is better to hold someone responsible for his or her actions than to forgive and forget? Is it sometimes impossible to forgive? Explain your response in a paragraph, supporting your point with specific examples.

Essay Assignments

1. Tan begins her essay by remembering a particularly horrible fight with her mother when Tan was 16. She then moves on to recall the years of fighting with her mother and the ways they responded to each other. Finally, she describes a recent phone call and the sense of peace that followed.

   Using, as Tan says, "memory and imagination," write an essay about how a relationship with someone you love has changed over time. Construct your essay, as Tan has done, using time order to tell your story. The relationship you follow and describe over time can be with a parent, sibling, friend, spouse/partner, or even a boss or coworker. Be sure to include specific details about how you felt and what was said.

   Of course, the relationship you write about does not necessarily have to be one that was/is difficult. Describing how a relationship has continued to improve can make a wonderful essay, too.

   Like Tan, you may want to consider using your concluding paragraph to make a point about what this evolving relationship has taught you.

2. Although Tan regretted the "most hateful words" she used as a teenager, one doesn't get the sense that she regrets the often-fiery relationship she had with her mother. That was how she and her mother interacted, and though it assuredly was not always pleasant, it was real and memorable. Some people are reluctant to fight with those they love, thinking that it means they have a bad relationship. However, arguing and airing out issues is actually recommended for maintaining a healthy relationship.

Imagine that you are a relationship counselor. Write an essay that persuades your readers that conflict between two people who love each other is actually healthy and productive. Come up with your own arguments to support your thesis, and research the topic by typing into Google or another search engine such phrases as "why conflict in relationships is healthy" or "fighting helps relationships" or "how to argue with others."

11 A Door Swings Open

Roxanne Black

Preview

No one can stay a child forever. For some, the events that mark childhood's end are barely remembered. For others, a sudden, unforgettable occurrence forever marks the boundary between childish innocence and adult understanding. In "A Door Swings Open," author Roxanne Black describes such a moment.

Words to Watch

foreboding (15): a feeling that something bad is going to happen
chronic (18): lasting for a long time; continuing to occur
remission (21): lessening of the symptoms of a disease
terse (30): brief and to the point
intoned (37): said something in a slow and serious way
muster (39): gather

1 I sat at my bedroom window in my wheelchair, watching my high-school rowing team pull away from the shore, eight friends smiling and waving as they moved into the choppy water. Not long ago, I'd been one of them.

2 I loved everything about rowing: the feeling of freedom, the teamwork, the sense of strength and accomplishment. When I rowed, I was at peace and forgot about my problems. Not that I'd had many then. In most ways, I was a typical New Jersey teenager, a shy high-school freshman who lived with her mother in a small row house that overlooked Lake's Bay. My mother and I didn't have two dimes to rub together, but with that view from our windows, we considered ourselves rich.

3 It was after rowing one afternoon that I had the first warning that something might be wrong with me—a sharp stab of back pain that took my breath away.

4 "What's the matter?" my mother asked when she saw me wincing.

5 "I don't know," I said, stretching. "I guess I strained a muscle."

6 By evening, the pain was almost too painful to bear. My mother filled

a hot bath with Epsom salts, and later gave me a heating pad. I took a couple of Tylenol and decided I'd stay away from crew practice for a few days. In my young life, this had been the antidote for any ailment. Eventually everything passed, given time and a little rest.

7   But not this time. Instead of decreasing, the pain grew so intense that I could barely sit up in bed the next morning.

8   My mother took one look at me and said, "I'm taking you to the doctor."

9   But by the time we arrived at the office, the pain had subsided; and the doctor advised that we simply continue with the heating pad and baths.

10   Two days later, I developed chest pains that by evening were so acute I could barely breathe. Now I was beginning to worry.

11   This time the doctor prescribed antibiotics, thinking I might have an infection. The pains intensified over the next few days; then they too vanished.

12   This pattern of new symptoms that appeared, intensified, then vanished continued with an itchy red rash, which covered my body. After it mysteriously disappeared, my ankles swelled so severely that I was unable to fit into any of my shoes.

13   Although the doctor tracked my reports, took bloodwork, and examined me closely, he couldn't figure out what was wrong. My symptoms were elusive; it was hard to pin them down.

14   Finally he referred me to a specialist. By the day of my appointment, all my symptoms had subsided except for my

swollen ankles. My mother and I arrived at his office, expecting this new doctor would prescribe another medication for what was probably an allergic reaction.

15   Although I'd never seen this doctor's face before, his cool, sober expression as we walked in gave me a sense of foreboding°.

16   After a routine examination, he studied my bloodwork, then touched my ankles, which were so full of fluid they could be molded like lumps of clay.

17   Then he looked up and a strange word floated from his mouth. Lupus. I saw it, like in a cartoon caption, odd and ominous, hanging in the air.

18   The word meant nothing to me, but my mother's reaction did; she covered her face with her hands. In her work as a nurse, she'd spent years caring for patients with chronic° illness. As I watched her sniff and take out a Kleenex, it hit me that this must be serious, something that Tylenol and bed rest weren't going to solve.

19   My health had always been part of my identity, something I was as certain of as my strong legs and pumping heart. Now I was being told baffling facts about kidney function, inflammation, and antibodies.

20   But when the doctor said I was to be admitted to a children's hospital in Philadelphia the following day for testing, I realized a chapter of my life was suddenly ending and a new one was about to start.

21   When I returned home, I looked up lupus in our medical dictionary: a chronic autoimmune disease, potentially weakening and sometimes fatal, that was first discovered in the Middle Ages. The illness follows an unpredictable course, with episodes of activity, called flares, alternating with periods of remission°. During a flare, the immune system attacks the body's cells and tissue, resulting in inflammation and tissue damage.

22   The words "sometimes fatal" stood out to me, as if they were written in blood. Just as alarming were the lists of possible signs: dermatological, musculoskeletal, hematological, renal, hepatic, pulmonary. What else was there?

23   How had this ancient disease—that only affected one in many hundreds in the United States—ended up in Atlantic City, residing in a teenager like me?

24   For that, there was no answer.

25   "There's always one moment in childhood when the door opens and lets the future in," Graham Greene wrote. I don't know if most people remember that moment, but I do.

26   At the children's hospital, I shared a room with a three-year-old girl with a charming face and shiny black hair cut in a bob. She was so energetic and lively, I assumed she was someone's daughter or sister, until I glimpsed a tiny hospital ID bracelet on her wrist.

27   Her name was Michelle, and we bonded from the moment we met. She brought a herd of plastic ponies to my bedside, and we brushed their manes and made up stories.

28   "Why's she here?" I asked when her parents arrived, looking drawn and worried.

29   "She has a hole in her heart," her mother told me. "She's having open-heart surgery tomorrow."

30   A steady stream of doctors arrived to talk to Michelle's parents. I heard the terse° murmur of their voices behind the curtain that separated our room. Through it all, Michelle dashed between the beds, oblivious to the drama around her. She was so vital and energetic, it was hard to believe that anything serious was wrong with her.

31   I'd never known a sick child before, and now I was in a hospital full of them. It seemed unnatural seeing toddlers on IV's, babies on ventilators, adolescents with leg braces, struggling to walk. A parade of pediatric malfunction passed my door, children smashed in motor accidents, suffering from muscular dystrophy and leukemia. This alternate world had existed all along, behind my formerly sunny, innocent life.

32   The next day I was to find out the results of my kidney biopsy, and Michelle was headed to surgery. Before

she left, she walked over and hugged me so tightly that I could smell the baby shampoo in her hair. Then she solemnly handed me a drawing she'd made of a house, a girl, and a tree.

33 "This is you, isn't it?"

34 She nodded.

35 "Well it's beautiful, thanks. I'll see you later."

36 I waited all day for them to bring Michelle back, trying to distract myself by reading and crocheting, but it was no use. Breakfast came and went, then lunch, and still there was no sign of her.

37 Early in the evening, I was talking on the pay phone in the hallway when an alarm sounded, and doctors began running down the hall from all directions. A woman's voice intoned° a code over the loudspeakers, a foreign babble.

38 As I hung up, I saw two new figures running down the hallway. Their features grew terribly familiar as they approached. It was Michelle's parents, their faces smeared with tears, heading in the same direction as the doctors.

39 My mother came out and hurried me back into the room. When she shut the door, I stood there, looking at Michelle's bed, at the picture on the table she had drawn for me. I took out a little prayer book I'd brought along and began a prayer, filling it with all the love and intention I could muster°. A long, terrible female scream pierced the silence.

40 A young floor nurse walked in a short while later. Her sad face was statement enough, but then she told us. Michelle hadn't made it. She'd suffered a heart attack and died.

41 So there it was, and I had to face it: Life wasn't fair. Prayers weren't always answered. The young and innocent could be lost. The door had swung open, and I had been pushed through to the other side.

First Impressions

Freewrite for ten minutes on one of the following.

1. Did you enjoy reading this selection? Why or why not?

2. Had you heard of lupus before reading this piece? Are you familiar with it, or with any similar disease?

3. Do you know anyone who, like Roxanne Black, has a chronic illness? What are some ways it affects that person's life?

Vocabulary Check

___A___ 1. In the excerpt below, the word *subsided* means
    A. became less.
    B. gotten worse.
    C. returned.
    D. stayed the same.

> If the doctor suggests continuing the same treatment, it must have had the desired result—the pain became less.

"My mother took one look at me and said, 'I'm taking you to the doctor.'
"But by the time we arrived at the office, the pain had subsided; and the doctor advised that we simply continue with the heating pad and baths." (Paragraphs 8–9)

___D___ 2. In the excerpt below, the word *elusive* means
    A. difficult to treat.
    B. difficult to see.
    C. difficult to forget.
    D. difficult to define.

> The synonym-like clue *hard to pin . . . down* suggests that *elusive* means "difficult to define."

"Although the doctor tracked my reports, took bloodwork, and examined me closely, he couldn't figure out what was wrong. My symptoms were elusive; it was hard to pin them down." (Paragraph 13)

___A___ 3. In the excerpt below, the words *oblivious to* mean
    A. unaware of.
    B. saddened by.
    C. confused by.
    D. conscious of.

> If Michelle is dashing back and forth in the room, she is unaware of the drama around her.

"A steady stream of doctors arrived to talk to Michelle's parents. I heard the terse murmur of their voices behind the curtain that separated our room. Through it all, Michelle dashed between the beds, oblivious to the drama around her." (Paragraph 30)

Reading Check

Central Point and Main Ideas

Answer A covers only paragraphs 19–24. Answer B is suggested by paragraphs 39–40. Answer C covers part of paragraph 19.

___D___ 1. Which sentence best expresses the central point of the entire selection?
    A. Black was shocked to learn that she had a chronic disease.
    B. Black was saddened when a little girl she met in the hospital died.
    C. Before becoming ill with lupus, Black had been in excellent health.
    D. As the result of her own chronic illness and the death of a child, Black realized that life isn't fair.

Answer D, the central point, is suggested in the concluding paragraph.

_C_ 2. Which sentence best expresses the main idea of paragraph 2?
A. When Black rowed, she forgot about her problems.
B. Black lived with her mother in a small row house overlooking Lake's Bay.
C. In most ways, Black, who loved rowing, was a typical teenager.
D. Although Black and her mother didn't have much money, they considered themselves rich. Answers A, B, and D each cover only one sentence of the paragraph.

Supporting Details

_D_ 3. Black first thought the intense pain she was experiencing was
A. an insect bite.
B. an allergic reaction. See paragraph 5.
C. an infection.
D. a muscle strain.

_C_ 4. When the doctor told Black she had lupus, her mother
A. told the doctor he was wrong.
B. screamed and then broke out into loud sobs.
C. covered her face with her hands and took out a Kleenex.
D. said she knew it all along. See paragraph 18.

_B_ 5. Michelle was in the hospital because she had
A. leukemia.
B. a hole in her heart. See paragraph 29.
C. a brain tumor.
D. been injured in an auto accident.

Inferences

_A_ 6. It is reasonable to conclude that
A. in most respects, Michelle was a typical little girl.
B. Graham Greene had also known a child who died young.
C. Black blames the doctors for not saving Michelle's life.
D. all of the above. Michelle is "energetic and lively," likes toy animals, is friendly, and draws pictures—just like most little girls.

_C_ 7. The author implies that
A. Michelle was terrified of having open-heart surgery.
B. Michelle appeared sickly to most people.
C. Black realized that Michelle had died even before hearing the news from the nurse.
D. Black will never pray for anyone again. See paragraphs 37–40.
The alarm, the behavior of Michelle's parents, and the nurse's sad face all reflect the terrible fact that Michelle didn't make it through surgery.

The Writer's Craft

_B_ 8. Black begins her story with the image of herself watching the rowers because
   A. the rowers remind her of Michelle, her hospital roommate.
   B. she wants to contrast her life before lupus with her life now.
   C. rowing is what caused her to develop lupus.
   D. she had always wanted to learn to row, but was never able to.
   Black was a normal teenager until she contracted lupus. Answers A and C are unsupported. Answer D is contradicted by paragraphs 1–2.

Black's "elusive" symptoms could also have been due to a muscle strain, an infection, or an allergic reaction.

_A_ 9. In paragraphs 6–13, the details that Black provides
   A. demonstrate why her illness was difficult to diagnose.
   B. show that her doctor didn't really care about her condition.
   C. make it clear she was unconcerned about her condition.
   D. demonstrate that she complained a lot about her problems.

_D_ 10. Black uses Michelle's death as a symbol of her realization that
   A. she, too, would die.
   B. she had no hope of ever being cured.
   C. she needed religious faith.
   D. life is not fair.   See paragraph 41. The "door" that has "swung open" for Black refers to the realization that in the real world, prayers are not always answered, and innocent people die.

Discussion Questions

1. When Black enters the hospital, she becomes aware of an "alternate world" that "had existed all along, behind my formerly sunny, innocent life." What is this "alternate world"? What, in particular, does she find surprising about it?

2. Black quotes Graham Greene, who wrote, "There's always one moment in childhood when the door opens and lets the future in." What might this statement mean? According to Black's story, when did this experience happen to her? Why do you think she was so upset afterward?

3. Have you ever known anyone who, like Black, suffers from chronic illness? If so, how does it affect his or her life? What adjustments has the person made in order to live with this condition?

4. Do you remember a moment in _your_ life when "the door opened and let the future in"? Describe the event, and explain what it made you realize.

Paragraph Assignments

1. When Black was diagnosed with lupus, she writes, "I realized a chapter of my life was suddenly ending and a new one was about to start." In your own life, when has there been a change that felt like a chapter ending and a new one starting? Write a paragraph about that change in your life.

2. Even in the face of tragic events, such as the death of Michelle, some people will say, "Everything happens for a reason." Do you believe that "everything happens for a reason"? Write a paragraph in which you explain your answer.

Essay Assignments

1. After developing lupus, Black looked back with new appreciation at the healthy body she had once taken for granted. What are some qualities of your own self that you appreciate? You might think of physical or mental abilities, or aspects of your personality. Write an essay about three things that you like about yourself. Provide details about how those abilities or qualities enhance your life.

2. In the course of "A Door Swings Open," Roxanne Black is faced not only with the onset of her own serious illness, but also with the tragic death of a little girl she had only recently befriended. Such unforeseen circumstances raise the question of how much responsibility we as a society have toward those whom life has treated unfairly. In your opinion, should government play a role in helping individuals overcome crisis situations, or should responsibility rest with the individual? Write an essay supporting your position. Your thesis might look like one of these:

   - Government should play a leading role when life treats people unfairly.
   - Whatever life brings, it is up to the individual to look after him- or herself.

   To support your thesis statement, describe three specific situations in which people face serious challenges. These challenges may involve health care, natural disasters, education, housing, jobs, childcare, providing for the elderly, and so on. Explain in each case what role you envision the individual playing and what role (if any) you envision the government playing. You may discuss situations that have actually occurred or ones that might occur.

12 Responsibility

M. Scott Peck

Preview

The Road Less Traveled, a well-known book by psychiatrist and author M. Scott Peck, begins with this famous line: "Life is difficult." Unlike most "self-help" authors, Dr. Peck does not suggest that once his readers do A and B, they will permanently lose weight, find the perfect mate, never again feel depressed, or suddenly become rich. Instead, Peck encourages people to embrace the messy difficulties that make up life, stressing that growth and development are achieved only through hard work. The following excerpt from *The Road Less Traveled* emphasizes one of Peck's favorite themes: personal responsibility.

Words to Watch

self-evident (1): not requiring any explanation
ludicrous (2): laughable because of being obviously ridiculous
clarified (19): made clear
amenable (23): agreeable
glared (37): stared angrily

1   We cannot solve life's problems except by solving them. This statement may seem idiotically self-evident°, yet it is seemingly beyond the comprehension of much of the human race. This is because we must accept responsibility for a problem before we can solve it. We cannot solve a problem by saying, "It's not my problem." We cannot solve a problem by hoping that someone else will solve it for us. I can solve a problem only when I say, "This is my problem, and it's up to me to solve it." But many, so many, seek to avoid the pain of their problems by saying to themselves: "This problem was caused by other people, or by social circumstances beyond my control, and therefore it is up to other people or society to solve this problem for me. It is not really my personal problem."

2   The extent to which people will go psychologically to avoid assuming responsibility for personal problems,

while always sad, is sometimes almost ludicrous°. A career sergeant in the army, stationed in Okinawa and in serious trouble because of his excessive drinking, was referred for psychiatric evaluation and, if possible, assistance. He denied that he was an alcoholic, or even that his use of alcohol was a personal problem, saying, "There's nothing else to do in the evenings in Okinawa except drink."

3   "Do you like to read?" I asked.

4   "Oh yes, I like to read, sure."

5   "Then why don't you read in the evening instead of drinking?"

6   "It's too noisy to read in the barracks."

7   "Well, then, why don't you go to the library?"

8   "The library is too far away."

9   "Is the library farther away than the bar you go to?"

10   "Well, I'm not much of a reader. That's not where my interests lie."

11   "Do you like to fish?" I then inquired.

12   "Sure, I love to fish."

13   "Why not go fishing instead of drinking?"

14   "Because I have to work all day long."

15   "Can't you go fishing at night?"

16   "No, there isn't any night fishing in Okinawa."

17   "But there is," I said. "I know several organizations that fish at night here. Would you like me to put you in touch with them?"

18   "Well, I really don't like to fish."

19   "What I hear you saying," I clarified°, "is that there are other things to do in Okinawa except drink, but the thing you like to do most in Okinawa is drink."

20   "Yeah, I guess so."

21   "But your drinking is getting you in trouble, so you're faced with a real problem, aren't you?"

22   "This damn island would drive anyone to drink."

23   I kept trying for a while, but the sergeant was not the least bit interested in seeing his drinking as a personal problem which he could solve either with or without help, and I regretfully told his commander that he was not amenable° to assistance. His drinking continued, and he was separated from the service in mid-career.

24   A young wife, also in Okinawa, cut her wrist lightly with a razor blade and was brought to the emergency room, where I saw her. I asked her why she had done this to herself.

25   "To kill myself, of course."

26   "Why do you want to kill yourself?"

27   "Because I can't stand it on this dumb island. You have to send me back to the States. I'm going to kill myself if I have to stay here any longer."

28   "What is it about living on Okinawa that's so painful for you?" I asked.

29   She began to cry in a whining° sort of way. "I don't have any friends here, and I'm alone all the time."

30 "That's too bad. How come you haven't been able to make any friends?"

31 "Because I have to live in a stupid Okinawan housing area, and none of my neighbors speak English."

32 "Why don't you drive over to the American housing area or to the wives' club during the day so you can make some friends?"

33 "Because my husband has to drive the car to work."

34 "Can't you drive him to work, since you're alone and bored all day?" I asked.

35 "No. It's a stick-shift car, and I don't know how to drive a stick-shift car, only an automatic."

36 "Why don't you learn how to drive a stick-shift car?"

37 She glared° at me. "On these roads? You must be crazy."

First Impressions

Freewrite for ten minutes on one of the following.

1. Did you enjoy reading this selection? Why or why not?

2. Do you agree with Peck that many people refuse to take responsibility for their own problems? Explain your answer.

3. What do you think of the sergeant and young wife that Peck describes? How do you think either could improve his or her situation?

Vocabulary Check

_B_ 1. In the sentence below, the word *comprehension* means
   A. definition.
   B. understanding.
   C. confusion.
   D. absence.

   A statement like this one is something people would try to understand.

   "We cannot solve life's problems except by solving them. This statement . . . is seemingly beyond the comprehension of much of the human race." (Paragraph 1)

_____A_____ 2. In the sentence below, the word *extent* means

    A. lengths.

    B. fright.

    C. surprise.

    D. humor.

> The rest of the selection gives two specific examples of the lengths to which people will go to avoid assuming responsibility for personal problems.

"The extent to which people will go psychologically to avoid assuming responsibility for personal problems, while always sad, is sometimes almost ludicrous." (Paragraph 2)

_____D_____ 3. In the sentence below, the word *excessive* means

    A. good-natured.

    B. unwilling.

    C. moderate.

    D. beyond what is normal.

> Drinking beyond normal amounts can cause a person serious trouble.

"A career sergeant ... in serious trouble because of his excessive drinking, was referred for psychiatric evaluation and, if possible, assistance." (Paragraph 2)

Reading Check

Central Point and Main Ideas

_____C_____ 1. Which sentence best expresses the central point of the entire selection?

See the title of the selection and the first paragraph. Answers A, B, and D are too narrow. Each covers only the two examples Peck gives and ignores the idea presented in the title and the first paragraph.

    A. In Okinawa, Peck met two people who refused to take responsibility for their own problems.

    B. People demonstrate healthy creativity in the excuses they make for their irresponsibility.

    C. Many people, like the sergeant and the young wife, won't solve their problems because they refuse to take responsibility for them.

    D. The sergeant and the young wife would rather see their careers and lives ruined than take responsibility for their problems.

_____D_____ 2. Which sentence best expresses the main idea of paragraphs 2–22?

    A. A career sergeant was in trouble because of his drinking.

    B. The sergeant denied that he had a problem with alcohol.

    C. Peck was expected to evaluate the sergeant and, if possible, help him.

    D. People will go to ridiculous lengths to avoid responsibility for their problems.

> Answers A, B, and C are facts presented in paragraphs 2–22. Answer D states the main idea illustrated by these paragraphs.

___D___ 3. Which sentence expresses the main idea of paragraph 23?
  A. Peck tried for some time to help the sergeant.
  B. Drinking has destroyed the lives of many people.
  C. Peck told the commander that he could not help the sergeant.
  D. The sergeant, whom Peck was unable to help, had to leave the service.
  <small>Answers A and C cover only part of the first sentence of the paragraph.
  Answer B is not mentioned. Answer D summarizes the whole paragraph.</small>

Supporting Details

___C___ 4. The author claimed that the sergeant "was not amenable to assistance."
  What evidence did he have for that statement?
  A. The sergeant did not like to fish.   See paragraphs 5–22.
  B. The sergeant did not like to read.
  C. The sergeant refused every one of Peck's suggestions.
  D. All of the above

___B___ 5. The young wife first saw Peck because she
  A. was drinking too much.
  B. had cut her wrist.
  C. had tried to return to the United States.   See paragraph 24.
  D. wanted to learn to drive.

___A___ 6. The young wife said she could not drive to the wives' club because
  A. she could not drive a stick-shift car.
  B. she had to be away at work all day.
  C. none of the other wives spoke English.   See paragraph 35.
  D. she and her husband did not own a car.

Inferences

___A___ 7. Which statement would Peck be most likely to make to the young wife?

Answers B, C, and D are incorrect because they would help the wife avoid taking responsibility for her own problems, and Peck's point is that people need to take responsibility.

  A. "Your unwillingness to learn to drive a stick-shift car indicates that you don't really want to help yourself."
  B. "Your neighbors really should learn English so that they can communicate with you."
  C. "No one could be expected to be happy living in your circumstances."
  D. "The military should make better arrangements for spouses who are living far away from home."

Answers B, C, and D are not supported. Answer A states the point Peck is making by choosing these two people as examples.

  ___A___ 8. We can infer that the sergeant and the young wife
  A. wanted someone else to take responsibility for their problems.
  B. knew each other.
  C. were good at taking responsibility for themselves back in the States.
  D. became happier and better adjusted after their meetings with Peck.

The Writer's Craft

    _B_ 9. The author states, "The extent to which people will go psychologically to avoid assuming responsibility for personal problems . . . is sometimes almost ludicrous." He supports this statement with

Peck gives two examples from his practice—the sergeant who drinks excessively (paragraphs 2–23) and the wife who wants to leave the island (paragraphs 24–37).

A. evidence from psychological textbooks.

B. examples from his own practice.

C. statistics and other figures from sociological studies.

D. examples from news stories.

    _B_ 10. What audience did Peck seem to have in mind when he wrote this selection?

Although Peck's examples are from the military, the problem they illustrate—the failure to accept responsibility for a problem—can be found in all walks of life. In addition, the level of the language is geared to a general audience.

A. Psychiatrists and other doctors who deal with patients like the two examples presented here

B. People who tend to make excuses for their behavior

C. His past patients who refused to see their problems as their own responsibility

D. People in the military based overseas who are facing problems

Discussion Questions

1. Peck refers to the "ludicrous"—that is, ridiculous—lengths people will go to to avoid taking responsibility for their problems. What do you think he finds ludicrous about the sergeant's behavior? The young wife's? Do you find their behavior ridiculous? Why or why not?

2. What problems—big or small—do you observe around you that result from people refusing to take responsibility for their own behavior?

3. What do you think Peck means when he says that "we must accept responsibility for a problem before we can solve it"? Can you give an example from your (or someone else's) experience to illustrate the meaning of his statement?

4. Why do you think so many people find it difficult to take responsibility for their own problems? How might they be helped to do so?

Paragraph Assignments

1. Write a paragraph about a time you have seen someone avoiding responsibility for his or her own problem. Begin with this topic sentence: "Just like M. Scott Peck, I have seen someone refuse to take responsibility for his (*or* her) own problem." Then go on to develop your paper by explaining who the person is, what the person's problem was, how he or she helped to create it, and how he or she blamed others or circumstances rather than accept responsibility.

2. Peck is drawing examples of irresponsible behavior from his practice as a military psychiatrist. But you can find examples of people dodging responsibility everywhere. What kinds of responsibility do students often avoid? Write a paragraph giving details about two or three ways students try to escape their responsibilities. Explain what kind of excuses they frequently make for their behavior. Your paragraph may be either serious or humorous.

Essay Assignments

1. Peck explains that the only way to solve a problem is to solve it—in other words, to take responsibility for the problem and find a solution. Write an essay about a time in your own life when you had to accept responsibility for a problem and figure out a solution for it. As you decide on a topic, you might list areas in which you have experienced problems. Here is one imaginary student's list:

   - Getting along with parents
   - Breaking off with friends who were a bad influence
   - Managing money
   - Holding a job
   - Keeping up with schoolwork

   Once you have decided on a topic to write about, you might begin with a statement like this: "After blaming my teachers for my problems in school, I finally accepted responsibility for my own poor grades."

   Alternatively, write about two or three problems you've had to face and solve.

2. How could this country be improved through people accepting more responsibility for themselves? Write an essay in which you show how several of this country's big problems are related to a lack of personal responsibility. Indicate how those problems would be lessened or eliminated if people were more willing to act responsibly. You may find it helpful to Google a phrase such as "responsibilities of citizens and government." If you prefer, instead of focusing on the whole country, you can write about problems in your state, city, neighborhood, or school.

13 Thank You

Alex Haley

Preview

For most of us, Thanksgiving has become a day marked by overeating, football, and sleepy conversation with similarly overstuffed relatives. Rarely do people observe the day by acting out its meaning. For Alex Haley, the celebrated author of *Roots*, the inspiration to do just that came on an unusual Thanksgiving spent far from home. This story of how Haley practiced true thanksgiving was first published in *Parade* magazine.

Words to Watch

destination (1): the place toward which something or someone is going
fo'c'sle (3): short for *forecastle*, the front part of a ship where the crew's quarters are located
afterdeck (4): the part of a ship's deck located toward the rear of the ship
draughts (4): inhalations
reflex (5): automatic reaction
waning (6): coming to an end
nostalgia (16): a longing for something or someone in the past
jostling (19): pushing and shoving
nigh (25): nearly
yearning (25): desiring
buoyant (27): light-hearted

1   It was 1943, during World War II, and I was a young U.S. coastguardsman, serial number 212-548, a number we never seem to forget. My ship, the USS *Murzim*, had been under way for several days. Most of her holds contained thousands of cartons of canned or dried foods. The other holds were loaded with five-hundred-pound bombs packed delicately in padded racks. Our destination° was a big base on the island of Tulagi in the South Pacific.

2   I was one of the *Murzim*'s several cooks and, quite the same as for folk ashore, this Thanksgiving morning had seen us busily preparing a traditional dinner featuring roast turkey.

3   Well, as any cook knows, it's a lot of hard work to cook and serve a big meal, and clean up and put everything

149

away. But finally, around sundown, with our whole galley crew just bushed, we finished at last and were free to go flop into our bunks in the fo'c'sle°.

4   But I decided first to go out on the *Murzim*'s afterdeck° for a breath of open air. I made my way out there, breathing in great, deep draughts° while walking slowly about, still wearing my white cook's hat and the long apron, my feet sensing the big ship's vibrations from the deep-set, turbine diesels and my ears hearing that slightly hissing sound the sea makes in resisting the skin of a ship.

5   I got to thinking about Thanksgiving. In reflex°, my thoughts registered the historic imagery of the Pilgrims, Indians, wild turkeys, pumpkins, corn on the cob and the rest.

6   Yet my mind seemed to be questing for something else—some way that I could personally apply to the waning° Thanksgiving. It must have taken me a half hour to sense that maybe some key to an answer could result from reversing the word "Thanksgiving"—at least that suggested a verbal direction, "Giving thanks."

7   Giving thanks—as in praying, thanking God, I thought. Yes, of course. Certainly.

8   Yet my mind continued nagging me. Fine. But something else.

9   After awhile, like a dawn's brightening, a further answer did come— that there were people to thank, people who had done so much for me that I could never possibly repay them. The embarrassing truth was I'd always just accepted what they'd done, taken all of

Alex Haley in his Coast Guard uniform

it for granted. Not one time had I ever bothered to express to any of them so much as a simple, sincere "Thank you."

10   At least seven people had been particularly and indelibly helpful to me. I realized, with a gulp, that about half of them had since died—so they were forever beyond any possible expression of gratitude from me. The more I thought about it, the more ashamed I became. Then I pictured the three who were still alive and, within minutes, I was down in the fo'c'sle.

11   Sitting at a mess table with writing paper and memories of things each had done, I tried composing genuine statements of heartfelt appreciation and gratitude to my dad, Simon A. Haley, a professor at the old AMNC (Agricultural Mechanical Normal College) in Pine Bluff, Arkansas, now a branch of the University of Arkansas; to my grandma, Cynthia Palmer, back in our little

hometown of Henning, Tennessee; and to the Rev. Lonual Nelson, my grammar school principal, retired and living in Ripley, six miles north of Henning.

12   I couldn't even be certain if they would recall some of their acts of years past, acts that I vividly remembered and saw now as having given me vital training, or inspiration, or directions, if not all of these desirables rolled into one.

13   The texts of my letters began something like, "Here, this Thanksgiving at sea, I find my thoughts upon how much you have done for me, but I have never stopped and said to you how much I feel the need to thank you—" And briefly I recalled for each of them specific acts performed in my behalf.

14   For instance, something uppermost about my father was how he had impressed upon me from boyhood to love books and reading. In fact, this graduated into a family habit of after-dinner quizzes at the table about books read most recently and new words learned. My love of books never diminished and later led me toward writing books myself. So many times I have felt a sadness when exposed to modern children so immersed in the electronic media that they have little to no awareness of the wondrous world to be discovered in books.

15   I reminded the Reverend Nelson how each morning he would open our little country town's grammar school with a prayer over his assembled students. I told him that whatever positive things I had done since had been influenced at least in part by his morning school prayers.

16   In the letter to my grandmother, I reminded her of a dozen ways she used to teach me how to tell the truth, to be thrifty, to share, and to be forgiving and considerate of others. (My reminders included how she'd make me pull switches from a peach tree for my needed lesson.) I thanked her for the years of eating her good cooking, the equal of which I had not found since. (By now, though, I've reflected that those peerless dishes are most gloriously flavored with a pinch of nostalgia°.) Finally, I thanked her simply for having sprinkled my life with stardust.

17   Before I slept, my three letters went into our ship's office mail sack. They got mailed when we reached Tulagi Island.

18   We unloaded cargo, reloaded with something else, then again we put to sea in the routine familiar to us, and as the days became weeks, my little personal experience receded. Sometimes, when we were at sea, a mail ship would rendezvous and bring us mail from home, which, of course, we accorded topmost priority.

19   Every time the ship's loudspeaker rasped, "Attention! Mail call!" two-hundred-odd shipmates came pounding up on deck and clustered about the raised hatch atop which two yeomen, standing by those precious bulging gray sacks, were alternately pulling out fistfuls of letters and barking successive names of sailors who were, in turn, hollering "Here! Here!" amid the jostling°.

20   One "mail call" brought me responses from Grandma, Dad and the Reverend Nelson—and my reading of

their letters left me not only astounded, but more humbled than before.

21   Rather than saying they would forgive that I hadn't previously thanked them, instead, for Pete's sake, they were thanking me—for having remembered, for having considered they had done anything so exceptional.

22   Always the college professor, my dad had carefully avoided anything he considered too sentimental, so I knew how moved he was to write me that, after having helped educate many young people, he now felt that his best results included his own son.

23   The Reverend Nelson wrote that his decades as a "simple, old-fashioned principal" had ended with grammar schools undergoing such swift changes that he had retired in self-doubt. "I heard more of what I had done wrong than what I did right," he said, adding that my letter had brought him welcome reassurance that his career had been appreciated.

24   A glance at Grandma's familiar handwriting brought back in a flash memories of standing alongside her white wicker rocking chair, watching her "settin' down" some letter to relatives. Frequently touching her pencil's tip to pursed lips, character by character, each between a short, soft grunt, Grandma would slowly accomplish one word, then the next, so that a finished page would consume hours. I wept over the page representing my Grandma's recent hours invested in expressing her loving gratefulness to me—whom she used to diaper!

25   Much later, retired from the Coast Guard and trying to make a living as a writer, I never forgot how those three "thank you" letters gave me an insight into something nigh° mystical in human beings, most of whom go about yearning° in secret for more of their fellows to express appreciation for their efforts.

26   I discovered in time that, even in the business world, probably no two words are more valued than "thank you," especially among people at stores, airlines, utilities and others that directly serve the public.

27   Late one night, I was one of a half-dozen passengers who straggled weary and grumbling off a plane that had been forced to land at the huge Dallas/Fort Worth Airport. Suddenly, a buoyant°, cheerful, red-jacketed airline man waved us away from the regular waiting room seats, saying, "You sure look bushed. I know a big empty office where you can stretch out while you wait." And we surely did. When the weather improved enough for us to leave, "Gene Erickson" was in my notebook; and, back home, I wrote the president of that airline describing his sensitivity and his courtesy. And I received a thank you!

28   I travel a good deal on lecture tours, and I urge students especially to tell their parents, grandparents, and other living elders simply "thank you" for all they have done to make possible the lives they now enjoy. Many students have told me they found themselves moved by the response. It is not really surprising, if one only reflects how it must feel to be thanked after you have given for years.

29   Now, approaching Thanksgiving of 1982, I have asked myself what will I wish for all who are reading this, for our nation, indeed for our whole world—since, quoting a good and wise friend of mine, "In the end we are mightily and merely people, each with similar needs." First, I wish for us, of course, the simple common sense to achieve world peace, that being paramount for the very survival of our kind.

30   And there is something else I wish—so strongly that I have had this line printed across the bottom of all my stationery: "Find the good—and praise it."

First Impressions

Freewrite for ten minutes on one of the following.

1. Did you enjoy reading this selection? Why or why not?

2. If you've traveled, did being far from home affect your feelings about the people and things in your life? In what ways?

3. Who are some people whom you would like to thank for making a special contribution to your life? What did each of these people do for you?

Vocabulary Check

___B___ 1. In the sentence below, the word *indelibly* means
   A. unwillingly.
   B. permanently.
   C. foolishly.
   D. cruelly.

   "At least seven people had been particularly and indelibly helpful to me." (Paragraph 10)

   These people had influenced Haley in his youth. The fact that he continued to remember them as a young man (in 1943) and even as an older man almost forty years later (1982) suggests that *indelibly* means "permanently."

_____D_____ 2. In the sentence below, the word *immersed* means
- A. disgusted with.
- B. improved by.
- C. uninterested in.
- D. deeply involved in.

> If the children have no awareness of the "wondrous world" of books, they must be deeply involved in electronic media.

"So many times I have felt a sadness when exposed to modern children so immersed in the electronic media that they have little to no awareness of the wondrous world to be discovered in books." (Paragraph 14)

_____B_____ 3. In the excerpt below, the word *rendezvous* means
- A. sink.
- B. meet at a prearranged time and place.
- C. pass without stopping.
- D. speed up.

> To deliver mail to a transport ship at sea, the mail ship would have to meet it at a prearranged time and place.

"Sometimes, when we were at sea, a mail ship would rendezvous and bring us mail from home . . ." (Paragraph 18)

_____D_____ 4. In the sentence below, the word *paramount* means
- A. unneeded luxury.
- B. similar.
- C. not possible.
- D. of greatest importance.

> How significant is world peace to the survival of human beings?

"First, I wish for us, of course, the simple common sense to achieve world peace, that being paramount for the very survival of our kind." (Paragraph 29)

Reading Check

Central Point and Main Ideas

_____B_____ 1. Which sentence best expresses the central point of the entire selection?
- A. Haley was ashamed to realize that he had never gotten around to thanking several important people in his life who were now dead.
- B. By writing letters of thanks to three important people in his life, Haley demonstrated his belief that we should be more appreciative of one another.
- C. When Haley's father, grammar school principal, and grandmother received their letters, they in turn thanked Haley for writing them.
- D. Haley believes he owes much of his success to his father, his grammar school principal, and his grandmother.

> Answer A covers only paragraph 10, sentence 3. Answer C covers only paragraph 21. Answer D covers only paragraphs 11 and 12.

___B___ 2. Which sentence best expresses the main idea of paragraph 23?

This main idea is
stated in the final
sentence. Answer A
covers only part
of sentence 1.
Answers C and D
each cover only part
of sentence 2.

    A. Reverend Nelson was an old-fashioned man.

    B. Haley's letter reassured Reverend Nelson that he had been a good principal.

    C. Reverend Nelson had retired filled with self-doubts.

    D. People had complained about the things Reverend Nelson had done wrong.

___D___ 3. Which sentence best expresses the main idea of paragraph 27?

See sentences 5–6.
Answer A covers
only sentence 1.
Answer B covers
only sentences 2–3.
Answer C is too
broad.

    A. Haley's plane was forced to land at the Dallas/Fort Worth airport.

    B. An airline representative, Gene Erickson, was kind to Haley and his fellow passengers.

    C. Airline representatives can be helpful in an emergency.

    D. Haley's letter to the airline president describing Gene Erickson's kindness to him and his fellow passengers was appreciated.

Supporting Details

___C___ 4. As Haley thought about Thanksgiving, his very first thoughts were of

    A. his need to thank God.

    B. the need to thank people who had helped him.

    C. Pilgrims, Indians, turkey, and pumpkins.   See paragraph 5.

    D. his grandmother.

___A___ 5. Haley writes that the people who appreciate words of thanks most are

    A. people who directly serve the public.

    B. college students.

    C. people serving in the military.   See paragraph 26.

    D. retired teachers.

Inferences

Item 6: ___D___ 6. In paragraph 16, the author implies that

That she was loving
is shown in sentence
1. That she was
strict is shown in
sentence 2. Answer
A is contradicted by
sentence 3.
Answers B
and C are not
supported.

    A. he disliked his grandmother's cooking.

    B. he feels his grandmother was abusive to him.

    C. his grandmother spent little time with him as a child.

    D. his grandmother was both loving and strict.

___D___ 7. From reading paragraph 19, we can conclude that

    A. few sailors on the *Murzim* received letters from home.

    B. mail calls happened every day on the *Murzim*.

    C. Haley got more mail from home than anyone else on board ship.

    D. getting mail from home was of great importance to the sailors.

Answers A, B, and C are not supported.

The Writer's Craft

_____ D _____ 8. In paragraphs 14–16, Haley
   A. describes the personalities of his father, principal, and grandmother.
   B. explains how his father, principal, and grandmother each taught him about gratitude.

Each paragraph gives a specific example of how one of these people helped him.

   C. contrasts the positive and negative characteristics of each of the people he wrote to.
   D. lists the specific reasons he was thanking his father, principal, and grandmother.

_____ B _____ 9. In paragraph 24, we get a vivid image of the author's grandmother through Haley's sharing with us
   A. the reasons that he loved his grandmother.

Haley describes in detail how hard she worked on the letter she wrote him.

   B. a meaningful personal experience he had with her.
   C. facts about his grandmother's life.
   D. endearing quotations from his grandmother.

_____ B _____ 10. In the final paragraph of his essay, Haley
   A. quotes his grandmother's favorite saying.
   B. restates his central point.
   C. predicts what will happen if readers follow his advice.
   D. asks a question.

   "Find the good—and praise it" sums up the point of Haley's stories about his Thanksgiving letters and his airplane experience.

Discussion Questions

1. What did the three replies that Haley received have in common? Why do you think Haley was surprised by what they said? What did these replies teach him about human nature?

2. Do you ever write personal letters or e-mail? To whom? And do you, like Haley and his shipmates, enjoy receiving mail? Is receiving a letter or e-mail better than receiving a telephone call? Why or why not?

3. Haley believes we need to say "thank you" more often. But most of us say and hear "thanks" many times a day. What's the difference between everyday "thank you's" and the kind of thanks that Haley is talking about? Give an example of each.

4. Haley urges readers, "Find the good—and praise it." Some people can do this easily; others cannot. Have you ever experienced this difficulty? Explain. Why do you think people might have difficulty expressing gratitude or praise?

Paragraph Assignments

1. Alex Haley didn't have to write those thank-you letters. He decided to write them simply because he felt it was the right and kind thing to do. Write a paragraph about a time you did something kind, not because anyone told you to do it, but just because you wanted to. Maybe you stopped in to visit a friend you knew was feeling depressed, or surprised someone with a gift, or did some chores around the house without being asked. In your paragraph, explain what you did, how you felt about it, and any response you received. You might want to start the paragraph with a sentence like "I felt real satisfaction the day I decided to _____."

2. Haley writes, "So many times I have felt a sadness when exposed to modern children so immersed in the electronic media that they have little to no awareness of the wondrous world to be discovered in books." Since Haley wrote his essay, more than thirty years ago, electronic media have become much more prevalent, and young people are even more "immersed" in them. Other than the amazing worlds that books open up to young people, what else are young people (and adults!) missing out on today due to their obsession with electronic devices? Write a paragraph describing one or more activities that seem to have lost the popularity contest with computers, televisions, and smartphones. To research this topic, consider asking older people what they did for fun and relaxation before computers existed. Googling "What did people do before computers?" will also bring up some interesting and entertaining ideas.

Essay Assignments

1. As you look back on your life, to which three persons are you especially grateful? Write an essay showing exactly how these persons have made a difference in your life. Devote each supporting paragraph to one of these persons, including one especially dramatic example or several smaller examples of what that person has done. In either case, provide plenty of details to illustrate each person's influence on you. Alternatively, you may write your entire essay about one person, devoting each supporting paragraph to an aspect of that person's important role in your life.

   An effective thesis statement for this essay might be one of the following:

   - I will never forget my best friend in first grade, my sixth-grade English teacher, and my wonderful grandmother.

   - My grandmother's constant physical presence and her financial and emotional support have made a real difference in my life.

2. Most people, Haley writes, "go about yearning in secret for more of their fellows to express appreciation for their efforts." Select three categories of people who you think deserve more appreciation than they generally receive. Write an essay in which you explain, for each category, why these people deserve thanks and how the people whose lives they affect could show appreciation. Here are some categories of people you might write about:

- Parents
- Teachers
- Waiters and waitresses
- Store clerks
- Police officers
- Cleaning people
- Church volunteers
- School volunteers

To gather information for your essay, try searching "gratitude toward _____," filling in each category of people you plan to write about.

14 The Ugly Truth about Beauty

Dave Barry

Preview

Why are women so very critical of the way they look? And why are men so very . . . not? Humorist Dave Barry explores this difference between the sexes in a way that ties together supermodels, lawn care, and a well-known plastic doll.

Words to Watch

regimen (5): process
mutation (8): an organism resulting from a DNA change
bolster (9): make stronger

1   If you're a man, at some point a woman will ask how she looks.

2   "How do I look?" she'll ask.

3   You must be careful how you answer this question. The best technique is to form an honest yet sensitive opinion, then collapse on the floor with some kind of fatal seizure. Trust me, this is the easiest way out. Because you will never come up with the right answer.

4   The problem is that women generally do not think of their looks in the same way that men do. Most men form an opinion of how they look in the seventh grade, and they stick to it for the rest of their lives. Some men form the opinion that they are irresistible stud muffins, and they do not change this opinion even when their faces sag and their noses bloat to the size of eggplants and their eyebrows grow together to form what appears to be a giant forehead-dwelling tropical caterpillar.

5   Most men, I believe, think of themselves as average-looking. Men will think this even if their faces cause heart failure in cattle at a range of 300 yards. Being average does not bother them; average is fine, for men. This is why men never ask anybody how they look. Their primary form of beauty care is to shave themselves, which is essentially the same form of beauty care that they give to their lawns. If, at the end of his four-minute daily beauty regimen°, a man has managed to wipe most of the shaving cream out of his hair and is not

bleeding too badly, he feels that he has done all he can, so he stops thinking about his appearance and devotes his mind to more critical issues, such as the Super Bowl.

6   Women do not look at themselves in this way. If I had to express, in three words, what I believe most women think about their appearance, those words would be: "not good enough." No matter how attractive a woman may appear to be to others, when she looks at herself in the mirror, she thinks: woof. She thinks that at any moment a municipal animal-control officer is going to throw a net over her and haul her off to the shelter.

7   Why do women have such low self-esteem? There are many complex psychological and societal reasons, by which I mean Barbie. Girls grow up play-ing with a doll proportioned such that, if it were human, it would be seven feet tall and weigh 81 pounds, of which 53 pounds would be bosoms. This is a difficult appearance standard to live up to, especially when you contrast it with the standard set for little boys by their dolls . . . excuse me, by their action figures. Most of the action figures that my son played with when he was little were hideous-looking. For example, he was very fond of an action figure (part of the He-Man series) called "Buzz-Off," who was part human, part flying insect. Buzz-Off was not a looker. But he was extremely self-confident. You could not imagine Buzz-Off saying to the other action figures: "Do you think these wings make my hips look big?"

8   But women grow up thinking they need to look like Barbie, which for most

women is impossible, although there is a multibillion-dollar beauty industry devoted to convincing women that they must try. I once saw an Oprah show wherein supermodel Cindy Crawford dispensed makeup tips to the studio audience. Cindy had all these middle-aged women applying beauty products to their faces; she stressed how important it was to apply them in a certain way, using the tips of their fingers. All the women dutifully did this, even though it was obvious to any sane observer that, no matter how carefully they applied these products, they would never look remotely like Cindy Crawford, who is some kind of genetic mutation°.

9   I'm not saying that men are superior. I'm just saying that you're not going to get a group of middle-aged men to sit

in a room and apply cosmetics to themselves under the instruction of Brad Pitt, in hopes of looking more like him. Men would realize that this task was pointless and demeaning. They would find some way to bolster° their self-esteem that did not require looking like Brad Pitt. They would say to Brad: "Oh *yeah*? Well, what do you know about *lawn care,* pretty boy?"

10   Of course many women will argue that the reason they become obsessed with trying to look like Cindy Crawford is that men, being as shallow as a drop of spit, *want* women to look that way. To which I have two responses:

11   1. Hey, just because *we're* idiots, that does not mean *you* have to be; and

12   2. Men don't even notice 97 percent of the beauty efforts you make anyway. Take fingernails. The average woman spends 5,000 hours per year worrying about her fingernails; I have never once, in more than 40 years of listening to men talk about women, heard a man say, "She has a nice set of fingernails!" Many men would not notice if a woman had upward of four hands.

Anyway, to get back to my original 13 point: If you're a man, and a woman asks you how she looks, you're in big trouble. Obviously, you can't say she looks bad. But you also can't say that she looks great, because she'll think you're lying, because she has spent countless hours, with the help of the multi-billion-dollar beauty industry, obsessing about the differences between herself and Cindy Crawford. Also, she suspects that you're not qualified to judge anybody's appearance. This is because you have shaving cream in your hair.

First Impressions

Freewrite for ten minutes on one of the following.

1. Did you enjoy reading this selection? Why or why not?

2. Barry says that most women think their appearance is "not good enough." Aside from Barbie dolls, what factors might influence women to feel that way?

3. Do you agree that men are less critical of their own appearance than women are of theirs? Why do you think there is less pressure on men to look attractive?

Vocabulary Check

_____D_____ 1. In the sentence below, the word *bloat* means
   A. bleed.
   B. run.
   C. sneeze.
   D. expand.

> For a man's nose to become the size of an eggplant, it would have to expand.

"Some men form the opinion that they are irresistible stud muffins, and they do not change this opinion even when their faces sag and their noses bloat to the size of eggplants and their eyebrows grow together to form what appears to be a giant forehead-dwelling tropical caterpillar." (Paragraph 4)

_____B_____ 2. In the excerpt below, the word *dutifully* means
   A. oddly.
   B. obediently.
   C. quickly.
   D. carelessly.

> If the women were applying products exactly as Cindy told them to, they were being obedient.

"Cindy had all these middle-aged women applying beauty products to their faces; she stressed how important it was to apply them in a certain way, using the tips of their fingers. All the women dutifully did this, even though it was obvious to any sane observer that, no matter how carefully they applied these products, they would never look remotely like Cindy Crawford, who is some kind of genetic mutation." (Paragraph 8)

_____A_____ 3. In the excerpt below, the word *demeaning* means
   A. insulting.
   B. difficult.
   C. strange.
   D. disgusting.

"I'm just saying that you're not going to get a group of middle-aged men to sit in a room and apply cosmetics to themselves under the instruction of Brad Pitt, in hopes of looking more like him. Men would realize that this task was pointless and demeaning." (Paragraph 9)

> The passage suggests that men have enough self-esteem to view efforts to improve their looks as insulting.

Reading Check

Central Point and Main Ideas

<u> C </u> 1. Which sentence best expresses the implied central point of the selection?

Answer A covers only parts of paragraphs 7 and 8. Answer B does not address the contrasting attitudes of men and women toward appearance. Answer D covers only paragraphs 1–3 and 13.

A. Women have been brought up to believe that they should look like real-life Barbie dolls, even though this is impossible.

B. In our society, women tend to have lower self-esteem than men.

C. Because of the way they have been brought up, most women spend far more time worrying about their appearance than men do.

D. It is impossible for men to tell women the truth about how they look because women will not believe them.

<u> D </u> 2. The implied main idea of paragraphs 8 and 9 is that

The two paragraphs contrast what men and women have been led to believe about their looks. Answers A and C cover only paragraph 8. Answer B is not supported.

A. middle-aged women who try to look like Cindy Crawford are foolish.

B. men have more important things to do than to compare themselves to Brad Pitt.

C. the beauty industry convinces many women that they should try to look like Cindy Crawford, an impossible task.

D. in contrast to women, men have not been led to believe that their looks are the most important thing about them.

Supporting Details

<u> B </u> 3. The author's son played with an action figure that was

A. attractive and self-confident.

B. hideous-looking but self-confident.

C. neither attractive nor self-confident.

D. worried about the size of his hips.

See paragraph 7. Buzz-Off is an example of a hideous-looking action figure who is nonetheless self-confident.

<u> D </u> 4. One thing the author has never heard a man say is

A. "I'm shallow as a drop of spit."

B. "Honey, you look bad."

C. "Honey, you look great."

D. "She has a nice set of fingernails!"

See paragraph 12.

Inferences

Answers A and B are unsupported. The humorous tone of the selection indicates that the Super Bowl is not really a critical issue. Therefore answer D is incorrect.

<u> C </u> 5. We can infer from paragraph 5 that the author believes that

A. most men are ugly, not average-looking.

B. most men are afraid to ask people how they really look.

C. most men don't spend much time grooming themselves or thinking about the way they look.

D. the Super Bowl is a critical issue.

_____A_____ 6. On the basis of paragraph 6, we can infer that the author believes that

Barry says that most women think their appearance is "not good enough." Answers B, C, and D are not supported. (D is not supported because the words *impossible* and *ever* make it too absolute.)

    A. most women have an unrealistically negative view of their own appearance.

    B. most women waste time in front of mirrors because they're spoiled and lazy.

    C. many women become uncontrollably angry when they see themselves in a mirror.

    D. it is impossible for a woman to ever be pleased with her appearance.

_____A_____ 7. We can conclude from the last two paragraphs that many women

Barry says that men don't notice 97% of the beauty efforts women make. Answers B, C, and D are not supported because the paragraphs do not discuss these issues.

    A. overestimate the amount of attention men pay to women's appearances.

    B. dislike men because they care so little about their own appearance.

    C. are annoyed that the beauty industry forces them to spend countless hours worrying about their appearance.

    D. believe that men with shaving cream in their hair are big trouble.

The Writer's Craft

_____D_____ 8. Barry probably titled his essay "The Ugly Truth about Beauty"

    A. to attract the reader's attention with the surprising suggestion that there's something ugly about beauty.

    B. to suggest the "ugly truth" that men don't even notice most of the efforts women make to look beautiful.

    C. to make the point that being overly concerned about one's physical appearance is not a good way to live.

    D. for all the above reasons.   Answer A is supported by the seeming contradiction of *beauty* and *ugly truth*. Answer B is supported by paragraph 12. Answer C is supported by Barry's exaggerated descriptions of women's concern for their appearance.

_____B_____ 9. Which pattern of organization does Barry mainly use in "The Ugly Truth about Beauty"?

    A. Time order: Barry provides a history, from ancient times to today, of women's concerns with their appearance.

    B. Contrast: Barry points out the differences between men's and women's opinions of their appearance.

    C. Comparison: Barry shows that men and women are actually similar in their approach to improving their appearance.

    D. Listing order: Barry presents a series of details about women's beauty treatments.

The first sentence of paragraph 4 suggests that the essay will contrast men's and women's opinions of their appearance. For the balance of the selection, Barry contrasts specific standards men and women have for judging how they look.

_C_ 10. What type of conclusion does Barry use in the final paragraph of his essay?
  A. A summary of his thesis
  B. A summary of his thesis and main supporting details
  C. A summary and a closing thought
  D. A summary, a closing thought, and a recommendation for further action

The first three sentences summarize the selection. The final two sentences add a closing thought.

Discussion Questions

1. Although Barry's essay is written for laughs, he obviously has something serious to say about women and men and their feelings about their appearance. In non-humorous language, how would you rephrase his main points?

2. Think about the women you know. How much time would you say that they devote to clothing, hairstyles, and makeup? On the basis of your answer, do you agree with the author's view that women spend far too much time worrying about how they look? Why or why not?

3. Do you agree or disagree with the author's negative view of the role Barbie dolls play in shaping American girls' image of themselves? Once the girls have grown up, to what extent would you say that external forces, such as the media and the fashion industry, influence their feelings about their own appearances? Explain your reasoning.

4. Do you agree with Barry that men are generally satisfied with their own appearance? Why might their standards be so different from those of women?

Paragraph Assignments

1. Do you think Barbie dolls really influence girls—and, later, women—to have unrealistic expectations about their looks? Why or why not? Write a paragraph defending your answer.

2. Most people would agree that there's nothing wrong with wanting to look good. But wanting to look good too often turns into insecurity and unhappiness with one's appearance. Write a paragraph that explains the difference between a healthy and an unhealthy concern for one's looks.

Essay Assignments

1. Whether we like it or not, beauty matters. Research has shown that better-looking people tend to be more popular, earn more money, and even get better seats at restaurants. Think about three people you know (you can include yourself, if you want) who vary in appearance from not all that attractive to pretty darned attractive. How does each person's appearance make a difference in his or her life and interactions with other people? Are there any differences in these people's confidence and self-image? Write an essay that presents each person and describe how each individual's beauty, or lack of it, affects his or her life.

2. This essay focuses on the different emphases that women and men put on their own physical appearance. But there are numerous other ways that men and women tend to think and act differently. Write an essay in which you spell out three ways in which, in your experience, men and women are different in the ways they think, act, and react. Provide examples to support your claims.

15 Dealing with Feelings
Rudolph F. Verderber

Preview

When you are angry, are you inclined to "get it off your chest" or to "bite your tongue"? When you're happy, do you let the world know it, or keep it to yourself? How does the way you express your emotions make you feel about yourself? How does it make the people around you feel? In this excerpt from the college textbook *Communicate!*, Sixth Edition, the author explores three ways of dealing with feelings and the consequences of each.

Words to Watch

self-disclosure (1): revealing oneself
decipher (2): interpret
seethe (2): boil with emotion
perceived (3): seen
undemonstrative (3): tending not to express feelings
inconsequential (4): unimportant
interpersonally (7): involving relations between people
potential (12): possible
net (14): final
triggered (16): set off
elated (17): very happy

1   An extremely important aspect of self-disclosure° is the sharing of feelings. We all experience feelings such as happiness at receiving an unexpected gift, sadness about the breakup of a relationship, or anger when we believe we have been taken advantage of. The question is whether to disclose such feelings, and if so, how. Self-disclosure of feelings usually will be most successful not when feelings are withheld or displayed but when they are described. Let's consider each of these forms of dealing with feelings.

Withholding Feelings

Withholding feelings—that is, keeping 2 them inside and not giving any verbal or nonverbal cues to their existence—

neuroses and psychoses. Moreover, people who withhold feelings are often perceived° as cold, undemonstrative°, and not much fun to be around.

Is withholding ever appropriate? 4 When a situation is inconsequential°, you may well choose to withhold your feelings. For instance, a stranger's inconsiderate behavior at a party may bother you, but because you can move to another part of the room, withholding may not be detrimental. In the example of Doris seething at Candy's behavior, however, withholding could be costly to Doris.

Displaying Feelings

Displaying feelings means expressing 5 those feelings through a facial reaction, body response, and/or spoken reaction. Cheering over a great play at a sporting event, booing the umpire at a perceived bad call, patting a person on the back when the person does something well, or saying, "What are you doing?" in a nasty tone of voice are all displays of feelings.

Displays are especially appropriate 6 when the feelings you are experiencing are positive. For instance, when Gloria does something nice for you, and you experience a feeling of joy, giving her a big hug is appropriate; when Don gives you something you've wanted, and you experience a feeling of appreciation, a big smile or an "Oh, thank you, Don" is appropriate. In fact, many people need to be even more demonstrative of good feelings. You've probably seen the bumper sticker "Have you hugged your

is generally an inappropriate means of dealing with feelings. Withholding feelings is best exemplified by the good poker player who develops a "poker face," a neutral look that is impossible to decipher°. The look is the same whether the player's cards are good or bad. Unfortunately, many people use poker faces in their interpersonal relationships, so that no one knows whether they hurt inside, are extremely excited, and so on. For instance, Doris feels very nervous when Candy stands over her while Doris is working on her report. And when Candy says, "That first paragraph isn't very well written," Doris begins to seethe°, yet she says nothing—she withholds her feelings.

3   Psychologists believe that when people withhold feelings, they can develop physical problems such as ulcers, high blood pressure, and heart disease, as well as psychological problems such as stress-related

kid today?" It reinforces the point that you need to display love and affection constantly to show another person that you really care.

7   Displays become detrimental to communication when the feelings you are experiencing are negative— especially when the display of a negative feeling appears to be an overreaction. For instance, when Candy stands over Doris while she is working on her report and says, "That first paragraph isn't very well written," Doris may well experience resentment. If Doris lashes out at Candy by screaming, "Who the hell asked you for your opinion?" Doris's display no doubt will hurt Candy's feelings and short-circuit their communication. Although displays of negative feelings may be good for you psychologically, they are likely to be bad for you interpersonally°.

Describing Feelings

8   Describing feelings—putting your feelings into words in a calm, nonjudgmental way—tends to be the best method of disclosing feelings. Describing feelings not only increases chances for positive communication and decreases chances for short-circuiting lines of communication; it also teaches people how to treat you. When you describe your feelings, people are made aware of the effect of their behavior. This knowledge gives them the information needed to determine whether they should continue or repeat that behavior. If you tell Paul that you really feel flattered when he visits you,

such a statement should encourage Paul to visit you again; likewise, when you tell Cliff that you feel very angry when he borrows your jacket without asking, he is more likely to ask the next time he borrows a jacket. Describing your feelings allows you to exercise a measure of control over others' behavior toward you.

Describing and displaying feelings   9 are not the same. Many times people think they are describing when in fact they are displaying feelings or evaluating.

If describing feelings is so important   10 to communicating effectively, why don't more people do it regularly? There seem to be at least four reasons why many people don't describe feelings.

1. *Many people have a poor vocabulary*   11 *of words for describing the various feelings they are experiencing.* People can sense that they are angry; however, they may not know whether what they are feeling might best be described as annoyed, betrayed, cheated, crushed, disturbed, furious, outraged, or shocked. Each of these words describes a slightly different aspect of what many people lump together as anger.

2. *Many people believe that describing*   12 *their true feelings reveals too much about themselves.* If you tell people when their behavior hurts you, you risk their using the information against you when they want to hurt you on purpose. Even so, the potential° benefits of describing

your feelings far outweigh the risks. For instance, if Pete has a nickname for you that you don't like, and you tell Pete that calling you by that nickname really makes you nervous and tense, Pete may use the nickname when he wants to hurt you, but he is more likely to stop calling you by that name. If, on the other hand, you don't describe your feelings to Pete, he is probably going to call you by that name all the time because he doesn't know any better. When you say nothing, you reinforce his behavior. The level of risk varies with each situation, but you will more often improve a relationship than be hurt by describing feelings.

13 3. *Many people believe that if they describe feelings, others will make them feel guilty about having such feelings.* At a very tender age, we all learned about "tactful" behavior. Under the premise that "the truth sometimes hurts," we learned to avoid the truth by not saying anything or by telling "little" lies. Perhaps, when you were young, your mother said, "Don't forget to give Grandma a great big kiss." At that time you may have blurted out, "Ugh—it makes me feel yucky to kiss Grandma. She's got a mustache." If your mother responded, "That's terrible—your grandma loves you. Now you give her a kiss, and never let me hear you talk like that again!" then you probably felt guilty for having this "wrong" feeling. But the point is that the thought of kissing your grandma made you feel "yucky" whether it should have or not. In this case, what was at issue was the way you talked about the feelings— not your having the feelings.

4. *Many people believe that describing* 14 *feelings causes harm to others or to a relationship.* If it really bothers Max when his girlfriend, Dora, bites her fingernails, Max may believe that describing his feelings to Dora will hurt her so much that the knowledge will drive a wedge into their relationship. So it's better for Max to say nothing, right? Wrong! If Max says nothing, he's still going to be bothered by Dora's behavior. In fact, as time goes on, Max will probably lash out at Dora for other things because he can't bring himself to talk about the behavior that really bothers him. The net° result is that not only will Dora be hurt by Max's behavior, but she won't understand the true source of his feelings. By not describing his feelings, Max may well drive a wedge into their relationship anyway.

If Max does describe his 15 feelings to Dora, she might quit or at least try to quit biting her nails; they might get into a discussion in which he finds out that she doesn't want to bite them but just can't seem to stop, and he can help her in her efforts to stop; or they might discuss the problem, and Max may see that it is really a small thing and not let it bother him as much. The point is that in describing feelings, the chances of a successful outcome are greater than they are in not describing them.

16   To describe your feelings, first put the emotion you are feeling into words. Be specific. Second, state what triggered° the feeling. Finally, make sure you indicate that the feeling is yours. For example, suppose your roommate borrows your jacket without asking. When he returns, you describe your feelings by saying, "Cliff, I [indication that the feeling is yours] get really angry [the feeling] when you borrow my jacket without asking [trigger]." Or suppose that Carl has just reminded you of the very first time he brought you a rose.

You describe your feelings by saying, "Carl, I [indication that the feeling is yours] get really tickled [the feeling] when you remind me about that first time you brought me a rose [trigger]."

17   You may find it easiest to begin by describing positive feelings: "I really feel elated° knowing that you were the one who nominated me for the position" or "I'm delighted that you offered to help me with the housework." As you gain success with positive descriptions, you can try negative feelings attributable to environmental factors: "It's so cloudy; I feel gloomy" or "When the wind howls through the cracks, I really get jumpy." Finally, you can move to negative descriptions resulting from what people have said or done: "Your stepping in front of me like that really annoys me" or "The tone of your voice confuses me."

First Impressions

Freewrite for ten minutes on one of the following.

1. Did you enjoy reading this selection? Why or why not?

2. What do you normally do when you have strong feelings—withhold them, display them, or describe them? Give an example.

3. When have you been on the receiving end of a negative display of feelings? A positive display? How did you respond to either of them?

Vocabulary Check

___B___ 1. In the excerpt below, the word *exemplified* means
    A. contradicted.
    B. illustrated.   The poker player is an example (illustration)
    C. surprised.   of withholding feelings.
    D. ignored.

    "Withholding feelings is best exemplified by the good poker player who develops a 'poker face,' a neutral look . . ." (Paragraph 2)

___D___ 2. In the sentence below, the word *detrimental* means
    A. useful.
    B. private.
    C. helpless.   In the example given, withholding may not be harmful.
    D. harmful.

    "For instance, a stranger's inconsiderate behavior at a party may bother you, but because you can move to another part of the room, withholding may not be detrimental." (Paragraph 4)

___C___ 3. In the sentence below, the word *premise* means
    A. question.
    B. surprise.   "The truth sometimes hurts" is a belief. It is not
    C. belief.   a question, a choice, or a disagreement.
    D. disagreement.

    "Under the premise that 'the truth sometimes hurts,' we learned to avoid the truth by not saying anything or by telling 'little' lies." (Paragraph 13)

___B___ 4. In the excerpt below, the words *attributable to* mean
    A. that cannot be explained by.
    B. that can be explained by.
    C. unrelated to.
    D. confused by.

    "As you gain success with positive descriptions [of feelings], you can try negative feelings attributable to environmental factors: 'It's so cloudy; I feel gloomy . . .'" (Paragraph 17)

                           The negative feelings are due to and explained by environmental factors.

Reading Check

Central Point and Main Ideas

___B___ 1. Which sentence best expresses the central point of the entire selection?

Answer A is too broad. Answer C covers only paragraph 2. Answer D covers only paragraph 7.

    A. Everyone has feelings.

    B. There are three ways to deal with feelings; describing them is most useful for educating others about how you want to be treated.

    C. Withholding feelings means not giving verbal or nonverbal clues that might reveal those feelings to others.

    D. Expressing feelings often leads to problems with others.

___D___ 2. Which sentence best expresses the main idea of paragraphs 2 and 3?

    A. Withholding negative feelings may lead to physical problems.

    B. Withholding negative feelings may lead to psychological problems.

    C. Withholding positive feelings can make one seem cold.

    D. Withholding feelings has several disadvantages.   Answers A, B, and C are too narrow. Each describes only one disadvantage.

___A___ 3. Which sentence best expresses the main idea of paragraph 6?

Answer B covers only part of sentence 2. Answer C is not supported. Answer D covers only sentence 5.

    A. When people have positive feelings, they should display them.

    B. Giving someone a hug is appropriate when he or she does something nice for you.

    C. Women are usually more demonstrative of positive feelings than men are.

    D. In order to reassure others of your love, you need to constantly demonstrate that love.

Supporting Details

___A___ 4. According to the author, you are more likely to create physical problems for yourself by

    A. withholding your feelings.   See the first sentence in paragraph 3.

    B. displaying your positive feelings.

    C. describing your positive feelings.

    D. describing your negative feelings.

___F___ 5. TRUE OR FALSE? Withholding feelings is never appropriate.

See paragraph 4.

Inferences

_B_   6. From the reading, we can conclude that consistently displaying negative feelings

See paragraph 7. Answers A and D are not supported. Answer C is contradicted by paragraph 7.

    A. is often the best way to solve problems.
    B. will probably alienate those around you.
    C. will make those around you feel better about themselves.
    D. is a good way to deal with superiors.

_B_   7. Which of the following can we conclude is an example of describing a feeling?

Answer A is an example of withholding feelings. Answers C and D are examples of displaying feelings.

    A. Rachel moves to a different table in the library rather than ask nearby students to stop talking.
    B. Mrs. Hawkins tells her husband, "It annoys me when you leave your dirty socks on the floor."
    C. The football fan jumps out of his seat and shouts "YES!" as his team makes a touchdown.
    D. "You dumb jerk!" Hal shrieks at another driver who cuts him off in traffic.

The Writer's Craft

_B_   8. What pattern of organization does the author use in paragraph 3?

Sentence 1 lists physical and psychological problems. Sentence 2 lists problems in how people may view you.

    A. Time order: the author explains what happens over time if one withholds feelings.
    B. Listing order: the author lists problems associated with withholding feelings.
    C. Cause-effect: the author gives reasons that people withhold feelings.
    D. Comparison-contrast: the author compares those who withhold feelings to those who don't.

_C_   9. The author's tone in "Dealing with Feelings" is best described as

    A. critical.
    B. humorous.
    C. matter-of-fact.
    D. sentimental.

The author unemotionally presents descriptions and examples of three forms of self-disclosure.

The author defines and, in a straightforward manner, describes three ways of dealing with feelings. He also provides examples of each way and explains when each is appropriate. Answer A applies only to paragraph 7. Answers C and D are not supported.

_B_   10. The main purpose of this selection is to

    A. inform readers that displaying feelings is often harmful to interpersonal relations.
    B. inform readers of the different ways to deal with feelings and when each way is appropriate.
    C. entertain readers with stories of how people deal with their feelings.
    D. persuade people that they should always describe their feelings.

Discussion Questions

1. What is the difference between describing feelings and displaying them? How might Doris describe her feelings (rather than displaying them) to Candy after Candy says, "That first paragraph isn't very well written" (paragraph 2)?

2. In paragraph 13, Verderber discusses "tactful" behavior, also known as "little lies." Do you think Verderber approves of these "little lies"? Why or why not?

3. Verderber devotes most of his essay to describing feelings. Why do you think he emphasizes describing feelings over the other two methods of dealing with feelings?

4. What are some examples from your own experience of withholding, expressing or displaying, and describing feelings? How useful was each method?

Paragraph Assignments

1. What was the usual way of expressing feelings in your home as you were growing up? Were you encouraged to describe your feelings? Or were your family members more inclined to display or withhold them? Write a paragraph in which you describe the atmosphere regarding feelings in your home. In your topic sentence, state which way (or ways) of expressing feelings were most common in your home. Here are sample topic sentences for this assignment:

   - When it came to expressing feelings, my family definitely fell into the "displaying" category.

   - In my home, my father usually withheld his feelings, while my mother was more able to describe hers.

   Include specific examples of the behavior or behaviors you have chosen to write about.

2. It's often been said that men withhold or hide their feelings more than women do. Do you think this statement is true, or is it just a stereotype? If you think it's true, write a paragraph explaining why men might withhold feelings. If you need help coming up with reasons, typing "why men hide their feelings" into a search engine will bring up a large collection of ideas and opinions.

   On the other hand, if you feel that the statement is a stereotype, write a paragraph defending your belief. How or why might this stereotype have begun? Why is it incorrect? You might consider how men express their feelings differently or, perhaps, how women misinterpret men's silences and the ways they express themselves.

In developing your paragraph, be sure to provide specific and thoughtful details; avoid generalizations or personal comments.

Essay Assignments

1. Write an essay in which you show yourself dealing with one situation three different ways. To begin, invent a situation that you know would stir up negative emotions in you. Examples of such a situation might be these:

   - An encounter with a very critical relative
   - Dealing with a difficult customer at work
   - Sitting near a table full of very noisy people in a restaurant
   - Being called a nickname that you really hate
   - Discussing a bad grade on a test or paper with a teacher

   In your essay, describe the annoying situation in enough detail to show your reader just how it would make you feel. Then write out three scenes in which you deal with the situation in each of the ways explained in this selection—by withholding, displaying, and describing your feelings. End your essay by saying which of the three approaches you think would work best in that situation and why.

2. "Dealing With Feelings" lists and discusses several ways to handle emotions. Write a paper in which you present three ways to do something else. Your tone may be serious or humorous. For example, you might write about three ways to . . .

   - cut expenses.
   - ruin a meal.
   - meet people.
   - embarrass your friends.
   - criticize in a helpful manner.
   - hurt a relationship.

   Here is a possible opening sentence for this assignment: "In order to ruin a meal, you must follow three simple steps."

16 The Bystander Effect
Dorothy Barkin

Preview

Most of us think of ourselves as decent, helpful people. We certainly wouldn't turn our backs on someone in obvious need of help...or would we? Sociologists' experiments confirm what occasional, shocking news stories suggest: Many of us, when faced with a person who seems to be in desperate trouble, do absolutely nothing. In this essay, Dorothy Barkin explores some of the possible explanations for this troubling "bystander effect."

Words to Watch

intervene (2): interfere
phenomena (4): facts
apathy (23): indifference
diffusion (32): spreading thin
paralysis (32): inability to act

1 It is a pleasant fall afternoon. The sun is shining. You are heading toward the parking lot after your last class of the day. All of a sudden, you come across the following situations. What do you think you'd do in each case?

   Situation One: A man in his early twenties dressed in jeans and a T-shirt is using a coat hanger to pry open a door of a late-model Ford sedan. An overcoat and a camera are visible on the back seat of the car. You're the only one who sees this.

   Situation Two: A man and woman are wrestling with each other. The woman is in tears. Attempting to fight the man off, she screams, "Who are you? Get away from me!" You're the only one who witnesses this.

   Situation Three: Imagine the same scenario as in Situation Two except that this time the woman screams, "Get away from me! I don't know why I ever married you!"

Situation Four: Again imagine Situation Three. This time, however, there are a few other people (strangers to you and each other) who also observe the incident.

2 Many people would choose not to get involved in situations like these. Bystanders are often reluctant to intervene° in criminal or medical emergencies for reasons they are well aware of. They fear possible danger to themselves or getting caught up in a situation that could lead to complicated and time-consuming legal proceedings.

3 There are, however, other, less obvious factors which influence the decision to get involved in emergency situations. Complex psychological factors, which many people are unaware of, play an important part in the behavior of bystanders; knowing about these factors can help people to act more responsibly when faced with emergencies.

4 To understand these psychological phenomena°, it is helpful to look at what researchers have learned about behavior in the situations mentioned at the beginning of this essay.

Situation One: Research reveals a remarkably low rate of bystander intervention to protect property. In one study, more than 3,000 people walked past 214 staged car break-ins like the one described in this situation. The vast majority of passers-by completely ignored what appeared to be a crime in progress. Not one of the 3,000 bothered to report the incident to the police.

Situation Two: Another experiment involved staging scenarios like this and the next situation. In Situation Two, bystanders offered some sort of assistance to the young woman 65 percent of the time.

Situation Three: Here the rate of bystander assistance dropped down to 19 percent. This demonstrates that bystanders are more reluctant to help a woman when they believe she's fighting with her husband. Not only do they consider a wife in less need of help; they think interfering with a married couple may be more dangerous. The husband, unlike a stranger, will not flee the situation.

Situation Four: The important idea in this situation is being a member of a group of bystanders. In more than fifty studies involving many different conditions, one outcome has been consistent: bystanders are much less likely to get involved when other witnesses are present than when they are alone.

5 In other words, membership in a group of bystanders lowers the likelihood that each member of the group will become involved. This finding may seem

surprising. You might think there would be safety in numbers and that being a member of a group would increase the likelihood of intervention. How can we explain this aspect of group behavior?

6   A flood of research has tried to answer this and other questions about bystanders in emergencies ever since the infamous case of the murder of Kitty Genovese.

7   In 1964 in the borough of Queens in New York City, Catherine "Kitty" Genovese, twenty-eight, was brutally murdered in a shocking crime that outraged the nation. As reported two weeks later in an account published on the front page of the *New York Times*, this is what happened:

8   The crime began at 3 a.m. Kitty Genovese was coming home from her job as manager of a bar. After parking her car in a parking lot, she began the hundred-foot walk to the entrance of her apartment. But she soon noticed a man in the lot and decided instead to walk toward a police call box. As she walked by a bookstore on her way there, the man grabbed her. She screamed.

9   Lights went on and windows opened in the ten-story apartment building.

10   Next, the attacker stabbed Genovese. She shrieked, "Oh, my God, he stabbed me! Please help me! Please help me!"

11   From an upper window in the apartment house, a man shouted, "Let that girl alone!"

12   The assailant, alarmed by the man's shout, started toward his car, which was parked nearby. However, the lights in

the building soon went out, and the man returned. He found Genovese struggling to reach her apartment—and stabbed her again.

13   She screamed, "I'm dying! I'm dying!"

14   Once more, lights went on and windows opened in the apartment building. The attacker then went to his car and drove off. Struggling, Genovese made her way inside the building.

15   But the assailant returned to attack Genovese yet a third time. He found her slumped on the floor at the foot of the stairs and stabbed her again, this time fatally.

16   The murder took over a half hour, and Kitty Genovese's desperate cries for help were heard—according to the *New York Times* article—by at least thirty-eight people. Not a single one of the thirty-eight who later admitted to having witnessed the murder bothered to pick up the phone during the attack and call the police. One man called after Genovese was dead.

17   Comments made by bystanders after this murder provide important insight into what group members think when they consider intervening in an emergency.

18   These are some of the comments:

19   "I didn't want my husband to get involved."

20   "Frankly, we were afraid."

21   "We thought it was a lovers' quarrel."

22   "I was tired."

23   Although some of the details in the *New York Times* article are now in doubt, including the actual number of

witnesses, the Genovese murder itself profoundly affected the way Americans think about individual responsibility in the face of violence. The crime sparked a national debate on the questions of public apathy° and fear and became the basis for thousands of sermons, editorials, classroom discussions, and even a made-for-television movie. The same question was on everybody's mind—how could thirty-eight people have done so little?

24   Nine years later, another well-publicized incident provided additional information about the psychology of a group witnessing a crime.

25   On a summer afternoon in Trenton, New Jersey, a twenty-year-old woman was brutally raped in a parking lot in full view of twenty-five employees of a nearby roofing company. Though the workers witnessed the entire incident and the woman repeatedly screamed for help, no one came to her assistance.

26   Comments made by witnesses to the rape were remarkably similar to those made by the bystanders to the Genovese murder. For example, one witness said, "We thought, well, it might turn out to be her boyfriend or something like that."

27   It's not surprising to find similar excuses for not helping in cases involving a group of bystanders. The same psychological principles apply to each. Research conducted since the Genovese murder indicates that the failure of bystanders to get involved can't be simply dismissed as a symptom of an uncaring society. Rather, the "bystander effect," as it is called by social scientists, is the product of a complex set of psychological factors.

28   Two factors appear to be most important in understanding the reactions of bystanders to emergencies.

29   First is the level of ambiguity involved in the situation. Bystanders are afraid to endanger themselves or look foolish if they take the wrong action in a situation they're not sure how to interpret. A person lying face down on the floor of a subway train may have just suffered a heart attack and be in need of immediate medical assistance—or he may be a dangerous drunk.

30   Determining what is happening is especially difficult when a man is attacking a woman. Many times lovers do quarrel, sometimes violently. But they may strongly resent an outsider, no matter how well-meaning, intruding into their affairs.

31   When a group of bystanders is around, interpreting an event can be even more difficult than when one is alone. Bystanders look to others for cues as to what is happening. Frequently other witnesses, just as confused, try to look calm. Thus bystanders can mislead each other about the seriousness of an incident.

32   The second factor in determining the reactions of bystanders to emergencies is what psychologists call the principle of moral diffusion°. Moral diffusion is the lessening of a sense of individual responsibility when someone is a member of a group. Responsibility to act diffuses throughout the crowd. When a member of the group is able to escape the collective paralysis° and

take action, others in the group tend to act as well. But the larger the crowd, the greater the diffusion of responsibility, and the less likely someone is to intervene.

33   The more social scientists are able to teach us about how bystanders react to an emergency, the better the chances that we will take appropriate action when faced with one. Knowing about moral diffusion, for example, makes it easier for us to escape it. If you find yourself witnessing an emergency with a group, remember that everybody is waiting for someone else to do something first. If you take action, others may also help.

Also realize that any one of us 34 could at some time be in desperate need of help. Imagine what it feels like to need help and have a crowd watch you suffer—and do nothing. Remember Kitty Genovese.

First Impressions

Freewrite for ten minutes on one of the following.

1. Did you enjoy reading this selection? Why or why not?

2. Have you ever encountered someone who seemed to be in an emergency situation? How did you respond?

3. In your experience, is it true that people take less responsibility when they are in a group than when they are alone? What examples can you think of to support this idea?

Vocabulary Check

___C___ 1. In the sentence below, the word *scenario* means
   A. fight.
   B. relationship.
   C. suggested scene.
   D. quotation.

   Situation Two has described a suggested scene.

   "Imagine the same scenario as in Situation Two except that this time the woman screams, 'Get away from me! I don't know why I ever married you!'" (Paragraph 1)

___D___ 2. In the excerpt below, the word *assailant* means

A. observer.

B. bystander.

C. victim.

D. attacker.

> If someone shouted while the attack was in progress, who would be scared away? The word *attacker* in the first sentence is a synonym clue.

"Next, the attacker stabbed Genovese.... From an upper window in the apartment house, a man shouted, 'Let that girl alone!'

"The assailant, alarmed by the man's shout, started toward his car ...'"
(Paragraphs 10–12)

___B___ 3. In the excerpt below, the word *ambiguity* means

A. argument.

B. uncertainty.

C. lack of interest.

D. crowding.

> If the bystanders are in a situation they are not sure how to interpret, there is a level of uncertainty involved.

"First is the level of ambiguity involved . . . Bystanders are afraid to endanger themselves or look foolish . . . in a situation they're not sure how to interpret." (Paragraph 29)

Reading Check

Central Point and Main Ideas

Answer A ignores the issue of why people don't want to be involved. Answer B covers only paragraphs 7–16. Answer C is contradicted by paragraph 27.

___D___ 1. Which sentence best expresses the central point of the entire selection?

A. People don't want to get involved in emergencies.

B. Kitty Genovese was murdered because no one came to her assistance or called the police.

C. People don't care what happens to others.

D. Understanding why bystanders react as they do in a crisis can help people act more responsibly.

Answer A covers only sentence 1. Answer B covers only sentence 3. Answer C is contradicted by sentence 3.

___D___ 2. Which sentence best expresses the main idea of paragraph 27?

A. Bystanders always have the same excuses for not helping.

B. There has been research on bystanders since the Genovese murder.

C. The "bystander effect" is a symptom of an uncaring society.

D. Research shows that a number of psychological factors, not a simple lack of caring, keeps bystanders from getting involved.

___D___ 3. The sentence that makes up paragraph 28 states the main idea of

A. paragraph 29.

B. paragraphs 29–30.

C. paragraphs 29–31.

D. paragraphs 29–32.

> Paragraph 28 says there are two factors. Paragraphs 29–31 describe the first factor (introduced by the word *First*). Paragraph 32 describes the second factor (introduced by the word *second*).

Supporting Details

___C___ 4. Bystanders are most likely to help
   A. a woman being attacked by her husband.
   B. in any emergency when others are around.
   C. a woman being attacked by a stranger.
   D. when property is being stolen.

   See paragraph 4.

___C___ 5. The author supports her statement that "bystanders are much less likely to get involved when other witnesses are present" with
   A. opinions.
   B. quotations from experts.
   C. research and examples.
   D. no evidence.

   The examples are the Genovese murder and the Trenton rape. The research-based information precedes and follows the examples.

Inferences

___C___ 6. The reading suggests that people tend to believe
   A. theft is justified.
   B. loss of property is worse than bodily harm.
   C. bodily harm is worse than loss of property.
   D. rape is worse than murder.

   See "Situation One" and "Situation Two" in paragraph 4.

___D___ 7. From the essay, we can conclude that Kitty Genovese's killer
   A. knew his victim.
   B. was unaware of the witnesses.
   C. stabbed her too quickly for her to get help.
   D. kept attacking when he realized no one was coming to help her.

   See paragraphs 12–15.

___B___ 8. In which of the following situations can we conclude that a bystander is most likely to get involved?
   A. A man passes a clothing store with a smashed window from which people are carrying away clothes.
   B. A college student sees a man collapsing on a street where no one else is present.
   C. A neighbor sees a father and son fighting in their yard.
   D. A softball team sees the coach angrily yelling at and shoving his wife.

   See paragraphs 4–5. They suggest that bystanders tend not to help in cases of loss of property or family feuds, and when others are around.

The Writer's Craft

___A___ 9. Barkin introduces her essay by

In paragraph 1, sentence 5, Barkin asks, "What do you think you'd do in each case?"

   A. asking one or more questions.
   B. telling an interesting story about an incident that actually happened.
   C. presenting an idea that is the opposite of what she ends up writing about.
   D. making a broad statement and narrowing it down to the central point.

___D___ 10. The main purpose of this essay, as suggested in the closing paragraphs, is to

In particular, see the second sentence in paragraph 3, and also paragraphs 33–34.

   A. inform people of the existence of the phenomenon called "the bystander effect."
   B. inform readers that Kitty Genovese and others like her could have been saved if bystanders had taken action.
   C. entertain readers with vivid stories involving crisis situations.
   D. persuade people to recognize the bystander effect and be on guard against it in their own lives.

Discussion Questions

1. Have you ever been in a situation in which the bystander effect played a part? How did you respond? Would your behavior be any different in light of what you have learned from this essay?

2. The author states in paragraph 31, "Bystanders look to others for cues as to what is happening. Frequently other witnesses, just as confused, try to look calm." Why do you think witnesses might try to look calm during an emergency?

3. One witness to the Trenton rape said, "We thought, well, it might turn out to be her boyfriend or something like that." If the rapist had been her boyfriend—or her husband—should that fact have affected whether witnesses interfered? Why or why not?

4. Judging from your experience, are there ways other than those described in this essay that people act differently in groups than they act when they are alone? What other effects can being in a group have on individuals?

Paragraph Assignments

1. Barkin's essay suggests that people act differently when they're alone and when they're part of a group. Select an individual you know (for example, "My friend Reba") and write a paragraph that contrasts that person's behavior when he or she is alone versus when he or she is in a particular public setting. Examples of public settings might be a party, a basketball game, a dance, a family gathering, or a shopping mall. Your paragraph may be serious or humorous in tone. Provide lively examples to illustrate your points. You could begin with a topic sentence such as the following: "My friend Reba behaves very differently depending on whether she is with others or alone."

   Alternatively, write the paragraph about yourself.

2. Barkin writes about the impact of emergency situations on people's behavior. Selecting a lighter, less serious topic, write a paragraph in which you show the effects of some other factor on the way people act. You might, for example, write about the effects of final exams on college students, the impact of football season on family life, or the influence of the remote control on people's television-viewing habits. Discuss at least two ways in which the factor you have chosen affects behavior, illustrating each with lively examples from your own experiences or those of people you know. Title your paragraph something like "The Football Effect" or "The Remote-Control Effect."

Essay Assignments

1. "The Bystander Effect" is filled with anecdotes of people who stood back when help was needed, preferring to wait for someone else to act. Think of an individual you know of who has acted in the opposite way: someone who perceived a need and offered assistance. Then write an essay showing how this person went out of his or her way to help someone in need. Explain specifically what the problem was (perhaps it was a crime, a car accident, or a health emergency; or perhaps it was a more long-term need such as an illness or financial problem); what the individual did; and how the situation turned out. Include clear, striking details to help your reader picture the sequence of events. In your conclusion, you may wish to explain what might have happened if help had not been given. A possible thesis statement for this essay might be: "When I had to miss several weeks of school recently, my cousin Oscar came to my rescue in more ways than one."

2. Crises such as those described in "The Bystander Effect" are *not* the only events in which people behave inappropriately. Think of another situation in which people sometimes fail to act responsibly. Then write an essay exploring the possible reasons for this failure. You could, for example, write about why some parents avoid disciplining their children, why some college students fail to pay back their academic loans, or why some teachers are careless in grading student work. Come up with several explanations for the behavior, and be sure to provide convincing examples to illustrate your points.

For help with this topic, use the Internet to research any of the following:

- Why people sometimes fail to act in emergency situations
- Why some parents avoid disciplining their children
- Why some students fail to repay their academic loans
- Why some teachers are careless in grading student work

Alternatively, think of another "failure to act responsibly" to research.

17 Soft Addictions

Tim Bashard

Preview

We usually think of addictions as being habits involving harmful substances that can destroy our lives. But what about some of our common day-to-day habits? Can spending too much time on the Internet or drinking too much coffee be considered an addiction? And if so, can these "soft addictions" actually disrupt our lives?

Words to Watch

transfixed (4): fascinated
proliferation (6): a large number or abundance of something
indispensable (10): necessary or very important

1 What images come into your mind when you think of the word *addiction*?

2 Most people would respond to that question with something dramatic: a junkie nodding off in a crack house; tearful confessions at an AA meeting; a celebrity going off to rehab; a smoker lighting one cigarette from the burning butt of another.

3 Those are images of the "hard addictions"—addictions to drugs, alcohol, and nicotine. Those are the addictions that can and do destroy countless lives, families, and careers. They're the images that make the headlines, the TV shows, and the movies.

4 But there are other addictions whose images are less dramatic. Think of a group of teens swigging their bottles of Red Bull, or a home where the television is never turned off, or a person sitting transfixed° for hours in front of a computer screen. Are these people addicted in the same way a person is chemically addicted to heroin, whiskey, or nicotine? Most people would say not. And yet, giving up their use of caffeine, television, or the Internet would cause these people intense anxiety and discomfort. Is this dependence also a form of addiction?

5 According to a growing number of experts, the answer is yes. Behavioral scientists are increasingly interested in the concept of "soft addictions," which are defined as everyday habits that have gotten powerful enough to interfere with normal life. And dependence on

caffeine, television, and the Internet are three of the most common forms of "soft addictions."

6   Having a cup of coffee in the morning has been a part of many adults' daily routine for generations. In our grandparents' day, that cup was most likely made from powdered instant coffee, and it yielded about 60 milligrams of caffeine. Such a modest intake of caffeine would have little addictive effect. But in today's fast-paced world, it's routine to indulge in several caffeinated pick-me-ups during the day. And those aren't your grandfather's cup of Maxwell House. The proliferation° of sleek coffee shops like Starbucks has made "designer coffee" chic. A "tall" (12 ounce) brewed coffee from Starbucks has 260 milligrams of caffeine. A "grande" cup provides 330 milligrams, and a "venti" a whopping 415 milligrams. The caffeine content of drinks such as lattes and cappuccinos depends on whether they contain a single, double, or triple shot of espresso—each shot equals 75 milligrams. And, of course, today's Americans are not getting their caffeine fix from coffee alone. A 12-ounce Diet Coke, for instance, provides about 45 milligrams of caffeine, and a Mountain Dew as much as 55 milligrams. Then there are the so-called "energy drinks," which are basically delivery systems for high doses of sugar and caffeine. Monster, Red Bull, and Rockstar, three of the most popular brands, each provide about 80 milligrams of caffeine per bottle.

7   The bottom line is that a great many people are consuming massive quantities of caffeine on a daily basis, and that their need for caffeine has become a soft addiction. Their choice of coffee or soda or an energy drink has ceased to be merely a pleasant beverage. The caffeine these drinks provide has become a necessity. When caffeine addicts wake up in the morning, the first thing they think of is getting that initial caffeine hit. Until they have had it, they tend to be grouchy, groggy, and unwilling to interact with people. If they are in a situation where their caffeinated beverage of choice isn't available, they become almost frantic. They are nervous and shaky, often have a raging headache, and cannot concentrate on anything until they've found a caffeine source. This cycle often repeats itself in mid-afternoon and early evening, when

the need for more caffeine hits. They have to take breaks, even if it means neglecting their work or interrupting an important conversation, to seek out another caffeine fix. At day's end, their brains are still buzzing with the effects of caffeine, and they sleep poorly. They awaken groggy and ill-tempered, and the cycle begins again.

8   Television viewing is another activity that can slip over the line from a harmless pastime to a soft addiction. Again, in the past, excessive TV watching was less common. There were only a few major networks, so the choices of what to view were limited. Today, by contrast, the choices are almost limitless, including hundreds of cable channels, network shows, and instant-view movies. According to the most recent AC Nielsen study, the average American watches 34 hours of TV a week, plus another three to six hours of taped programs. That adds up to the equivalent of a 40-hour workweek. And of course, that's only the *average* viewer, meaning that half of all viewers watch more—sometimes much, much more. In some cases, it's almost impossible to measure how much television a person actually watches, because the TV is on virtually all the time.

9   But why does excessive TV watching qualify as a "soft addiction," when we would not use that term to describe most other leisure activities, such as gardening or playing tennis? The answer is in the way TV addicts describe their own feelings about their habit. Unlike the way gardeners or tennis players describe their hobbies, TV mega-watchers report that they feel unhappy about the amount they watch, but are powerless to stop it. They say that their excessive TV watching has damaged their social lives—that they see less and less of their friends and even family. They report that after watching a lot of TV, they feel *less* relaxed, less happy, and less able to concentrate than they were before. But because watching TV is their go-to activity when they're feeling depressed, their response to feeling unhappy is to watch more TV.

10   A final soft addiction is one that did not exist a generation ago. In only a few short decades, the Internet has become an indispensable° part of almost everyone's daily life. The advantages have been enormous. Communication has become easier than ever before, and ordinary men and women now have access to a literally limitless world of information.

11   But it is that very quality—the unlimited promise of the Internet— that has made it so addictive. A person can sit down at his laptop—or pick up his smartphone or open his tablet— fully intending to look up one simple fact. But to enter the Internet is to fall down a bottomless rabbit hole of possibilities. There are e-mails to read, instant messages to respond to, Facebook statuses to like or update, and headlines to look over. A friend on the other side of the world may suddenly appear on Skype. There are urgent invitations to join games, to sign petitions, to watch cute kitten videos. The minute that our person intended to spend looking up that one fact can

12   easily turn into hours as he is sucked into the endless tunnel of facts and entertainment.

    For a person who has difficulty setting limits on his Internet usage, time spent online can easily get out of control. Like television watching, an Internet addiction can cut into time spent with real-world friends, healthful physical exercise, and the development of offline social skills. While the promise of the Internet is enormous, it is, at the end of the day, just a glowing screen in a dark room. After hours of interacting with that screen, the Internet addict, like the TV addict, is likely to feel vaguely depressed, with a sense of having accomplished very little.

    While hard addictions to drugs 13 or alcohol are clearly very serious, soft addictions can be far from harmless. Whenever any activity—even drinking coffee, watching TV, or using the Internet—gets out of control, it can upset the balance that people should aim for in everyday life. It's often said that "knowledge is power." We would all benefit from knowing whether any of our everyday habits have become soft addictions.

First Impressions

Freewrite for ten minutes on one of the following.

1. Did you enjoy reading this selection? Why or why not?

2. Do you need caffeine every morning and/or during the day to get going? How do you feel if you don't have any caffeine?

3. Which of the "soft addictions" discussed in the reading is the one that you would have the most trouble giving up? Why is it such an important part of your life?

Vocabulary Check

  _B_ 1. In the excerpt below, the word *modest* means
    A. shy.
    B. small.
    C. measured.
    D. powerful.

If 60 milligrams has little addictive effect, it must be a small amount.

"In our grandparents' day, that cup was most likely made from powdered instant coffee, and it yielded about 60 milligrams of caffeine. Such a modest intake of caffeine would have little addictive effect." (Paragraph 6)

_____A_____ 2. In the sentence below, the word *initial* means
     A. first.
     B. bitter.   *If they have just woken up in the morning, they*
     C. final.   *would be ready for their first caffeine hit of the day.*
     D. secret.

> "When caffeine addicts wake up in the morning, the first thing they think of is getting that initial caffeine hit." (Paragraph 7)

_____D_____ 3. In the excerpt below, the words *the equivalent of* mean
     A. the rest of.
     B. the pleasure of.   *Thirty-four hours plus another 3 to 6*
     C. a substitute for.   *hours is the same as 40 hours.*
     D. the same amount as.

> "According to the most recent AC Nielsen study, the average American watches 34 hours of TV a week, plus another three to six hours of taped programs. That adds up to the equivalent of a 40-hour workweek." (Paragraph 8)

Reading Check

Central Point and Main Ideas

Item 1: _____C_____ 1. Which sentence best expresses the central point of the entire selection?

Answer A is the opposite of the central point; it is contradicted by paragraphs 7, 9, and 12. Answer B is incorrect because the author does not make this sort of judgment about "most people."

     A. Everyday habits that become something we can't live without, like caffeine or television, are harmless and not real addictions.
     B. Most people watch far too much television and waste too much time on the Internet.
     C. Common habits like watching TV or needing caffeine in the morning can become "soft addictions" that may affect our lives in negative ways.
     D. Addictions to drugs, alcohol, and cigarettes are far more dangerous than addictions to everyday habits.

Answer D is suggested in paragraph 13, but it is not the central point of the selection.

_____D_____ 2. Which sentence best expresses the main idea of paragraph 7?
     A. Many people drink far too much caffeine.
     B. Those who are addicted to caffeine continue to get their "fixes" all day long and even into the evening.
     C. People who are dependent on caffeine often suffer from headaches, grogginess, and moodiness.
     D. Although it is considered a "soft addiction," caffeine dependency can create real physical and emotional problems.

Answer A covers only sentence 1. Answer B covers only sentences 8–10. Answer C covers only sentences 5, 7, and 11.

___A___ 3. Which sentence best expresses the main idea of paragraph 11?

Answers B and D each cover only specific details of the paragraph. Answer C is incorrect because the activities listed are not *causes* of the addiction; too much time spent on them is the *result* of being addicted.

A. The Internet is addictive because it offers endless possibilities for information and entertainment.

B. People often go online to look up one small bit of information and then end up spending hours and hours surfing the Internet.

C. Too much time spent online checking Facebook statuses, watching videos of cute kittens, and playing games can lead to Internet addiction.

D. Internet possibilities are endless, ranging from playing games with a friend across town to chatting on Skype with a friend across the continent.

Supporting Details

___D___ 4. Television addicts agree with all of the following **except**

A. they feel less relaxed and happy than before they watch a lot of TV.

B. they now see less of their friends and family.

C. they feel unable to stop watching TV.

D. they fear that excessive TV watching damages their eyesight.

Answers A, B, and C are all stated in paragraph 9.

Inferences

___B___ 5. We can infer that the author puts quotation marks around the words "energy drinks" in paragraph 6 because he believes that

Calling these drinks "delivery systems for high doses of sugar and caffeine" suggests that he does not see them as a healthy way to become energetic.

A. these drinks do not really cause people to become energetic.

B. consuming these drinks is not a healthy way to become energetic.

C. these drinks do not contain as much caffeine as people are led to believe.

D. people who consume these drinks would be better off consuming coffee.

___B___ 6. Paragraphs 6 and 7 suggest that

A. without Starbucks, very few people would be addicted to caffeine.

B. corporations such as Starbucks profit from people's addiction to caffeine.

C. addiction to caffeinated beverages is as harmful as addiction to drugs or alcohol.

D. it is impossible to drink only moderate amounts of coffee.

Answers A, C, and D are not supported.

___C___ 7. The author would probably agree with which of the following statements?

    A. Being addicted to caffeine is just as bad as being addicted to drugs or alcohol.

    B. Young people should be prevented from purchasing energy drinks.

    C. Almost anything done to excess can become a soft addiction.

    D. Being dependent on the Internet is not as bad as being dependent on TV.   See paragraph 5. Answers A, B, and D are not supported.

The Writer's Craft

The paragraph contrasts the amounts of caffeine in our grandparents' coffee with the amount in today's Starbucks coffees. It also contrasts the number of caffeinated drinks our grandparents consumed in a day with the number many people now consume in a day.

___C___ 8. In paragraph 6, Bashard first points out the amount of caffeine that was in our grandparents' cup of coffee and then lists numerous drinks and the amount of caffeine they contain today in order to

    A. support the idea that our grandparents were healthier.

    B. explain the cause of today's caffeine addiction.

    C. contrast the amount of caffeine our grandparents drank with the much larger amount we drink today.

    D. illustrate the numerous choices we have for caffeine consumption.

Bashard gets readers to actively engage in the essay by asking them to think about their own images of addiction.

___A___ 9. Bashard begins his essay with a question in order to

    A. engage his readers and make them curious about his topic.

    B. suggest that addictions are more common than readers think.

    C. entertain his readers and make them laugh.

    D. avoid having to write a full introduction.

___B___ 10. To conclude his essay, Bashard presents

    A. a series of statistics.

    B. a summary of his main idea followed by a recommendation.

    C. a personal story.

    D. new information followed by a warning.

Sentences 1 and 2 contain the summary.
Sentences 3 and 4 provide the recommendation.

Discussion Questions

1. Bashard begins his essay by asking, "What images come into your mind when you think of the word *addiction*?" What images come into *your* mind when you hear that word? And after having read this essay, would you say those images have changed at all?

2. Bashard describes the Internet as an "endless tunnel of facts and entertainment." Have you ever gotten sucked into this tunnel? What draws you into the Internet, and why is it so hard to leave sometimes?

3. It's safe to say that caffeine, television, and the Internet are not the only everyday addictions in our society. Can you think of other soft addictions that many of us indulge in that can affect us negatively?

4. Some people would disagree with the author and say that these pastimes are not really addictions. They would argue that since TV, coffee, and the Internet can't actually destroy one's life (as drugs and alcohol can), they're not worth worrying about seriously. Do you agree? Why or why not?

Paragraph Assignments

1. Bashard ends his essay by pointing out that "knowledge is power" and, therefore, we should all ask ourselves if we might have some kind of soft addiction. In other words, we can all have more power over our own lives if we are honest and acknowledge an everyday habit we have that disrupts our lives. Do you have a soft addiction? Write a paragraph about it. In the paragraph, make sure you answer the following questions:

   - What is the addiction?
   - How much time do you devote to it each day?
   - How does it make you feel?
   - How does this habit disrupt your life?
   - How might you change this addiction?

2. Might any of these soft addictions be mostly harmless? In other words, is the author being overly alarmist about common habits that are not necessarily "addictions"? If so (or just to play devil's advocate), write a paragraph that defends one of these habits. Include specific reasons why the habit is not necessarily bad, how it may even be a positive habit, and why it is not something that should raise concerns among those who enjoy it.

Essay Assignments

1. Whether we are dealing with a soft addiction or a more serious hard addiction, addictions always interfere with our lives. What's more, addiction affects those who care about the addict. Have you ever had a personal relationship (friend, family member, boyfriend or girlfriend) with someone who was addicted to something that was bad for him or her? Write an essay about your experience with this person. You could begin with a thesis statement something like this: "One of my closest friends had an addiction problem that affected both her life and mine."

   You might structure the rest of your essay in this way:

   - In your first supporting paragraph, describe your friend and her addiction. You might explain how the problem got worse over time and how you became aware of it.

   - In your second supporting paragraph, describe how this addiction negatively affected your friend's life. Use specific examples to show how her addiction had a direct impact on her health, social life, and day-to-day activities.

   - In your third supporting paragraph, detail how your friend's problem had an effect on you. Perhaps it made you angry or sad. Perhaps she tried to drag you into her problems. Maybe you tried to help her, and she grew angry or violent with you.

   - In your concluding paragraph, briefly point out what you learned from this experience.

   Alternatively, write an essay about an addiction that *you* struggled with and how your addiction affected both you and a friend or family member.

2. Imagine that you are a counselor writing an article for students on how to break three soft addictions. Choose from the habits described in Bashard's essay or from the following list:

   - shopping
   - eating
   - procrastinating
   - texting
   - talking on the phone
   - dating

   You can also discover other bad habits by Googling "soft addictions" or "harmful bad habits." Then write the article, devoting one paragraph in the body of your essay to each addiction. Briefly describe the addiction, and then give advice on how to control it. In your conclusion, explain to students how much better they will feel about themselves once they've "kicked" these habits.

If you need information about how to work on breaking these soft addictions, a simple search along the lines of "how to stop shopping/ eating/texting so much" should bring up hundreds of ideas.

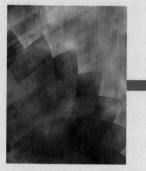

Unit Three

Relating to Others

18 All the Good Things

Sister Helen Mrosla

Preview

Teachers must often wonder if their efforts on behalf of their students are appreciated—or even noticed. In this selection, Sister Helen Mrosla, a Franciscan nun from Little Falls, Minnesota, tells the story of a moment when she learned the answer to that question in a most bittersweet way. Her simple but powerful story has been reprinted many times, as well as widely circulated on the Internet.

Words to Watch

mischievousness (1): minor misbehavior
novice (3): new
deliberately (5): slowly and on purpose
concept (8): idea
taps (16): a bugle call sounded at night and at a military funeral
sheepishly (20): with embarrassment
frazzled (20): worn-out; ragged

1 He was in the first third-grade class I taught at Saint Mary's School in Morris, Minnesota. All thirty-four of my students were dear to me, but Mark Eklund was one in a million. He was very neat in appearance but had that happy-to-be-alive attitude that made even his occasional mischievousness° delightful.

2 Mark talked incessantly. I had to remind him again and again that talking without permission was not acceptable. What impressed me so much, though, was his sincere response every time I had to correct him for misbehaving— "Thank you for correcting me, Sister!" I didn't know what to make of it at first, but before long I became accustomed to hearing it many times a day.

3 One morning my patience was growing thin when Mark talked once too often, and then I made a novice° teacher's mistake. I looked at him and said, "If you say one more word, I am going to tape your mouth shut!"

4 It wasn't ten seconds later when Chuck blurted out, "Mark is talking again." I hadn't asked any of the students to help me watch Mark, but since I had stated the punishment in front of the class, I had to act on it.

5   I remember the scene as if it had occurred this morning. I walked to my desk, very deliberately° opened my drawer, and took out a roll of masking tape. Without saying a word, I proceeded to Mark's desk, tore off two pieces of tape, and made a big X with them over his mouth. I then returned to the front of the room. As I glanced at Mark to see how he was doing, he winked at me.

6   That did it! I started laughing. The class cheered as I walked back to Mark's desk, removed the tape, and shrugged my shoulders. His first words were, "Thank you for correcting me, Sister."

7   At the end of the year I was asked to teach junior-high math. The years flew by, and before I knew it, Mark was in my classroom again. He was more handsome than ever and just as polite. Since he had to listen carefully to my instruction in the "new math," he did not talk as much in ninth grade as he had talked in the third.

8   One Friday, things just didn't feel right. We had worked hard on a new concept° all week, and I sensed that the students were frowning, frustrated with themselves—and edgy with one another. I had to stop this crankiness before it got out of hand. So I asked them to list the names of the other students in the room on two sheets of paper, leaving a space after each name. Then I told them to think of the nicest thing they could say about each of their classmates and write it down.

9   It took the remainder of the class period to finish the assignment, and as the students left the room, each one handed me the papers. Charlie smiled.

Mark said, "Thank you for teaching me, Sister. Have a good weekend."

10   That Saturday, I wrote down the name of each student on a separate sheet of paper, and I listed what everyone else had said about that individual.

11   On Monday I gave each student his or her list. Before long, the entire class was smiling. "Really?" I heard whispered. "I never knew that meant anything to anyone!" "I didn't know others liked me so much!"

12   No one ever mentioned those papers in class again. I never knew if the students discussed them after class or with their parents, but it didn't matter. The exercise had accomplished its purpose. The students were happy with themselves and one another again.

13   That group of students moved on. Several years later, after I returned from a vacation, my parents met me at the airport. As we were driving home, Mother asked me the usual questions about

the trip—the weather, my experiences in general. There was a slight lull in the conversation. Mother gave Dad a sideways glance and simply said, "Dad?" My father cleared his throat as he usually did before something important. "The Eklunds called last night," he began. "Really?" I said. "I haven't heard from them in years. I wonder how Mark is."

14 Dad responded quietly. "Mark was killed in the war," he said. "The funeral is tomorrow, and his parents would like it if you could attend." To this day I can still point to the exact spot on I-494 where Dad told me about Mark.

15 I had never seen a serviceman in a military coffin before. Mark looked so handsome, so mature. All I could think at that moment was, Mark, I would give all the masking tape in the world if only you would talk to me.

16 The church was packed with Mark's friends. Chuck's sister sang "The Battle Hymn of the Republic." Why did it have to rain on the day of the funeral? It was difficult enough at the graveside. The pastor said the usual prayers, and the bugler played taps°. One by one those who loved Mark took a last walk by the coffin and sprinkled it with holy water.

17 I was the last one to bless the coffin. As I stood there, one of the soldiers who had acted as pallbearer came up to me. "Were you Mark's math teacher?" he asked. I nodded as I continued to stare at the coffin. "Mark talked about you a lot," he said.

18 After the funeral, most of Mark's former classmates headed to Chuck's farmhouse for lunch. Mark's mother and father were there, obviously waiting for me. "We want to show you something," his father said, taking a wallet out of his pocket. "They found this on Mark when he was killed. We thought you might recognize it."

19 Opening the billfold, he carefully removed two worn pieces of notebook paper that had obviously been taped, folded and refolded many times. I knew without looking that the papers were the ones on which I had listed all the good things each of Mark's classmates had said about him. "Thank you so much for doing that," Mark's mother said. "As you can see, Mark treasured it."

20 Mark's classmates started to gather around us. Charlie smiled rather sheepishly° and said, "I still have my list. It's in the top drawer of my desk at home." Chuck's wife said, "Chuck asked me to put his list in our wedding album." "I have mine too," Marilyn said. "It's in my diary." Then Vicki, another classmate, reached into her pocketbook, took out her wallet, and showed her worn and frazzled° list to the group. "I carry this with me at all times," Vicki said without batting an eyelash. "I think we all saved our lists."

21 That's when I finally sat down and cried. I cried for Mark and for all his friends who would never see him again.

First Impressions

Freewrite for ten minutes on one of the following.

1. Did you enjoy reading this selection? Why or why not?

2. Do you have any special keepsake or souvenir that you have saved for a long time? What is it? Why is it special to you?

3. Name one teacher you are likely to remember years from now. What is it that you will remember about him or her?

Vocabulary Check

___B___ 1. In the excerpt below, the word *incessantly* means
     A. slowly.
     B. constantly.
     C. quietly.
     D. pleasantly.

> If Mark had to be reminded over and over again to stop talking, how did he talk?

"Mark talked incessantly. I had to remind him again and again that talking without permission was not acceptable." (Paragraph 2)

___A___ 2. In the sentence below, the words *blurted out* mean
     A. said suddenly.
     B. watched for.
     C. ran away.
     D. looked at.

> How did Chuck tell Sister Helen about Mark?

"It wasn't ten seconds later when Chuck blurted out, 'Mark is talking again.'" (Paragraph 4)

___C___ 3. In the sentence below, the word *edgy* means
     A. funny.
     B. calm.
     C. easily annoyed.
     D. happy.

> What describes frustrated and frowning students?

"We had worked hard on a new concept all week, and I sensed that the students were frowning, frustrated with themselves—and edgy with one another." (Paragraph 8)

Reading Check

Central Point and Main Ideas

   B 1. Which sentence best expresses the central point of the entire selection?
   - A. Mark Eklund was a charming, talkative student who appreciated Sister Helen's efforts to teach him.
   - B. Sister Helen found out that an assignment she had given years ago had been very important to a beloved former student and his classmates.
   - C. When Sister Helen was a young teacher, she had some unusual classroom techniques.
   - D. A promising young man, whom Sister Helen had taught and loved, lost his life in the war.   Answers A, C, and D are too narrow.

   C 2. Which sentence best expresses the main idea of paragraphs 1–2?
   - A. Mark Eklund was in the first third-grade class Sister Helen taught at Saint Mary's School.
   - B. Mark Eklund was the most talkative of all Sister Helen's students.
   - C. Although Mark Eklund was talkative and mischievous, he was also very sweet-natured.
   - D. Although Sister Helen kept reminding Mark that talking without permission was not permitted, she was unable to stop him from talking.   Answers A, B, and D are too narrow.

   B 3. Which sentence best expresses the main idea of paragraphs 8–12?
   - A. A difficult math concept had made Sister Helen's students irritable.
   - B. The "good things" assignment made the students feel happy with themselves and others.
   - C. Sister Helen gave up part of her weekend to write out a list of good things about each student.
   - D. At the end of Friday's class, both Charlie and Mark seemed to be in good moods.   Answers A, C, and D are too narrow.

Supporting Details

   B 4. When the students didn't mention the lists after the day they received them, Sister Helen
   - A. assumed that the assignment had been a failure.
   - B. didn't mind, because the assignment had done what she hoped.
   - C. called a few students to ask what they thought of the lists.
   - D. felt angry that the students didn't appreciate what she had done.
          See paragraph 12.

___C___ 5. Sister Helen learned of Mark's death
  A. when her parents called her while she was on vacation.
  B. from Chuck, Mark's old friend.
  C. in the car on the way home from the airport.   See paragraph 14.
  D. from a story in the local newspaper.

___D___ 6. At the funeral, Sister Helen learned that
  A. Mark was the only student who had saved his list.
  B. Vicki and Mark were the only students who had saved their lists.
  C. the lists were more important to the male students than the female students.
  D. all the students in attendance at Mark's funeral had saved their lists.
                                                   See paragraph 20.

Inferences

See paragraphs 18–21. Answer A is contradicted by paragraph 12. Answers B and D are not supported.

___C___ 7. The author implies that
  A. she had known all along how important the lists were to her students.
  B. she did not support the war.
  C. the lists meant more to the students than she had ever realized.
  D. Mark's parents were jealous of her relationship with him.

___A___ 8. It is reasonable to conclude that Mark
  A. cared as much for Sister Helen as she cared for him.
  B. never talked much about his past.
  C. planned to become a math teacher himself.
  D. had not stayed in touch with his classmates.
                                       See paragraphs 2, 6, 9, and 17–20.

The Writer's Craft

___C___ 9. Sister Helen's tone in paragraphs 14–15 is
  A. self-pitying.
  B. matter-of-fact.
  C. sorrowful.
  D. bitter.

Sister Helen remembers exactly where she was when she learned of Mark's death and wishes he could still talk to her—both suggest sadness.

Sister Helen didn't realize, at the time, how much the students' lists would mean to them. She might have wanted readers to think about the powerful effects of kind words. Answers A, C, and D are not supported.

___B___ 10. The author titles this selection "All the Good Things." Which of the following *best* explains her choice of a title?
  A. After years of teaching, Sister Helen chose only to remember good things about her former students.
  B. By asking her students to write good things about each other, Sister Helen had a positive impact on their lives.
  C. At Mark's funeral, Sister Helen learned about all the good things her former students had accomplished in their lives.
  D. Sister Helen believes it was a good thing that she had Mark Eklund as a student.

Discussion Questions

1. In this selection, we read of two classroom incidents involving Sister Helen and her students. In one, she briefly taped a third-grader's mouth closed. In another, she encouraged junior-high students to think of things they liked about one another. In your opinion, what do these two incidents tell about Sister Helen? What kind of teacher was she? What kind of person?

2. Why do you think so many of Sister Helen's students kept their lists for so long? Why were the lists so important to them—even as adults?

3. At the end of her essay, Sister Helen tells us that she "cried for Mark and for all his friends who would never see him again." Do you think she might have been crying for other reasons, too? Explain what they might be.

4. "All the Good Things" has literally traveled around the world. Not only has it been reprinted in numerous publications, but many readers have also sent it out over the Internet for others to read. Why do you think so many people love this story? Why do they want to share it with others?

Paragraph Assignments

1. Although Sister Helen didn't want to do it, she felt she had to tape Mark's mouth shut after announcing that she would do so. When have you done something you didn't really want to do because others expected it? Write a paragraph about that incident. Explain why you didn't want to do it, why you felt pressure to do it, and how you felt about yourself afterward. Here are sample topic sentences for such a paragraph:

   - Even though I knew it was wrong, I told my friend's parents a lie to keep my friend out of trouble.

   - Last year, I pretended I didn't like a guy that I really did like because my friends convinced me he wasn't cool enough.

   - Recently I've gotten into debt because my friends kept encouraging me to just use my credit card.

2. Some people feel that it would be a great gift to be able to see ourselves as others see us. As Sister Helen proved with the students in her math class, what others really think of us could create wonderful memories (or pieces of paper!) that last a lifetime. On the other hand, some

people feel that being able to see ourselves as others see us would be a seriously unpleasant reality check.

What do you think? Write a paragraph explaining why it would be either a blessing or a curse to know what other people really think of us. Present at least three reasons for your opinion. Some questions to consider before you begin to write: Should we care about how other people perceive us? How would knowing what others thought change how we feel about ourselves? How would this knowledge affect our relationships with others? How would it affect how we live our lives?

Essay Assignments

1. If Mark hadn't been killed, Sister Helen might never have found out how much her students appreciated her work with them. Write an essay about someone to whom you are grateful. Begin by explaining who that person is and why you are thankful to him or her. Your thesis statement should be something like any of these:

   - I owe a lot to my Aunt Lydia, who has been like a second mother to me.

   - My best friend, Theresa, has been a constant source of love and support to me.

   - If it wasn't for my seventh-grade science teacher, Mr. Kosinski, I don't think I would be in school today.

   Then tell in detail what that person has done for you and why it has been important in your life.

2. Mark Eklund obviously stood out in Sister Helen's memory. She paints a vivid "word portrait" of Mark as a third-grader. Write an essay about three fellow students who, for positive or negative reasons, you have always remembered. The three may have been your classmates at any point in your life. Your essay should be confined to your memories of those students in the classroom—not on the playground, in the cafeteria, or outside of school. As you describe your memories of those three classmates in that setting, include details that appeal to as many senses as possible—hearing, sight, touch, smell—to make your readers vividly picture those individuals and that time and place in your history.

   Alternatively, you may write an essay about three teachers whom you will always remember.

19 Shame

Dick Gregory

Preview

This excerpt from the autobiography of African American comedian and social activist Dick Gregory describes what it is like to live in poverty. The time was different—Harlem in the 1940s—as were the prices of things, but the human theme of the story resonates in America today. Estimates are that almost 47 million Americans are now living in poverty as our country continues to cope with the longest and deepest recession since the Great Depression of the 1930s.

Words to Watch

nappy (2): kinky, or tightly curled
stoop (2): an outside stairway, porch, or platform at the entrance to a house
mackinaw (28): a short, plaid coat or jacket
googobs (29): Gregory's slang for *gobs*, a large amount

1   I never learned hate at home, or shame. I had to go to school for that. I was about seven years old when I got my first big lesson. I was in love with a little girl named Helene Tucker, a light-complected little girl with pigtails and nice manners. She was always clean, and she was smart in school. I think I went to school then mostly to look at her. I brushed my hair and even got me a little old handkerchief. It was a lady's handkerchief, but I didn't want Helene to see me wipe my nose on my hand. The pipes were frozen again, there was no water in the house, but I washed my socks and shirt every night. I'd get a pot, and go over to Mister Ben's grocery store, and stick my pot down into his soda machine. Scoop out some chopped ice. By evening the ice melted to water for washing. I got sick a lot that winter because the fire would go out at night before the clothes were dry. In the morning I'd put them on, wet or dry, because they were the only clothes I had.

2   Everybody's got a Helene Tucker, a symbol of everything you want. I loved her for her goodness, her cleanness, her popularity. She'd walk down my street, and my brothers and sisters would yell, "Here comes Helene," and I'd rub my tennis sneakers* on the back of my pants and wish my hair wasn't so nappy° and

_____
* All sneakers used to be called "tennis sneakers."

the white folks' shirt fit me better. I'd run out on the street. If I knew my place and didn't come too close, she'd wink at me and say hello. That was a good feeling. Sometimes I'd follow her all the way home, and shovel the snow off her walk and try to make friends with her Momma and her aunts. I'd drop money on her stoop° late at night on my way back from shining shoes in the taverns. And she had a Daddy, and he had a good job. He was a paper hanger.

3   I guess I would have gotten over Helene by summertime, but something happened in that classroom that made her face hang in front of me for the next twenty-two years. When I played the drums in high school, it was for Helene; and when I broke track records in college, it was for Helene; and when I started standing behind microphones and heard applause, I wished Helene could hear it, too. It wasn't until I was twenty-nine years old and married and making money that I finally got her out of my system. Helene was sitting in that classroom when I learned to be ashamed of myself.

4   It was on a Thursday. I was sitting in the back of the room, in a seat with a chalk circle drawn around it. The idiot's seat, the troublemaker's seat.

5   The teacher thought I was stupid. Couldn't spell, couldn't read, couldn't do arithmetic. Just stupid. Teachers were never interested in finding out that you couldn't concentrate because you were so hungry, because you hadn't had any breakfast. All you could think about was noontime, would it ever come? Maybe you could sneak into the cloakroom and

steal a bite of some kid's lunch out of a coat pocket. A bite of something. Paste. You can't really make a meal of paste, or put it on bread for a sandwich, but sometimes I'd scoop a few spoonfuls out of the big paste jar in the back of the room. Pregnant people get strange tastes. I was pregnant with poverty. Pregnant with dirt and pregnant with smells that made people turn away, pregnant with cold and pregnant with shoes that were never bought for me, pregnant with five other people in my bed and no Daddy in the next room, and pregnant with hunger. Paste doesn't taste too bad when you're hungry.

6   The teacher thought I was a troublemaker. All she saw from the front of the room was a little black boy who squirmed in his idiot's seat and made noises and poked the kids around him. I guess she couldn't see a kid who made noises because he wanted someone to know he was there.

7   It was on a Thursday, the day before the Negro payday. The eagle always flew

on Friday.* The teacher was asking each student how much his father would give to the Community Chest**. On Friday night, each kid would get the money from his father, and on Monday he would bring it to the school. I decided I was going to buy a Daddy right then. I had money in my pocket from shining shoes and selling papers, and whatever Helene Tucker pledged for her Daddy, I was going to top it. And I'd hand the money right in. I wasn't going to wait until Monday to buy me a Daddy.

8 I was shaking, scared to death. The teacher opened her book and started calling out names alphabetically.

9 "Helene Tucker?"

10 "My Daddy said he'd give two dollars and fifty cents."

11 "That's very nice, Helene. Very, very nice indeed."

12 That made me feel pretty good. It wouldn't take too much to top that. I had almost three dollars in dimes and quarters in my pocket. I stuck my hand in my pocket and held onto the money, waiting for her to call my name. But the teacher closed her book after she called everybody else in the class.

13 I stood up and raised my hand.

14 "What is it now?"

15 "You forgot me."

16 She turned toward the blackboard. "I don't have time to be playing with you, Richard."

17 "My Daddy said he'd . . ."

18 "Sit down, Richard, you're disturbing the class."

19 "My Daddy said he'd give . . . fifteen dollars."

20 She turned around and looked mad. "We are collecting this money for you and your kind, Richard Gregory. If your Daddy can give fifteen dollars, you have no business being on relief*."

21 "I got it right now, I got it right now, my Daddy gave it to me to turn in today, my Daddy said . . ."

22 "And furthermore," she said, looking right at me, her nostrils getting big and her lips getting thin and her eyes opening wide, "we know you don't have a Daddy."

23 Helene Tucker turned around, her eyes full of tears. She felt sorry for me. Then I couldn't see her too well because I was crying, too.

24 "Sit down, Richard."

25 And I always thought the teacher kind of liked me. She always picked me to wash the blackboard on Friday, after school. That was a big thrill; it made me feel important. If I didn't wash it, come Monday the school might not function right.

26 "Where are you going, Richard!"

27 I walked out of school that day, and for a long time I didn't go back very often. There was shame there.

28 Now there was shame everywhere. It seemed like the whole world had been inside that classroom, everyone had heard what the teacher had said, everyone had turned around and felt

---

* In Gregory's day, ten-dollar bills were known as "eagles." On payday, people would have some ten-dollar bills to spend.

** In Gregory's day, the charitable organization we call the United Way was known as the Community Chest.

---

* welfare

sorry for me. There was shame in going to the Worthy Boys Annual Christmas Dinner for you and your kind, because everybody knew what a worthy boy was. Why couldn't they just call it the Boys Annual Dinner; why'd they have to give it a name? There was shame in wearing the brown and orange and white plaid mackinaw° the welfare gave to three thousand boys. Why'd it have to be the same for everybody so when you walked down the street, the people could see you were on relief? It was a nice warm mackinaw and it had a hood, and my Momma beat me and called me a little rat when she found out I stuffed it in the bottom of a pail full of garbage way over on Cottage Street. There was shame in running over to Mister Ben's at the end of the day and asking for his rotten peaches, there was shame in asking Mrs. Simmons for a spoonful of sugar, there was shame in running out to meet the relief truck. I hated that truck, full of food for you and your kind. I ran into the house and hid when it came. And then I started to sneak through alleys, to take the long way home so the people going into White's Eat Shop wouldn't see me. Yeah, the whole world heard the teacher that day, we all know you don't have a Daddy.

29   It lasted for a while, this kind of numbness. I spent a lot of time feeling sorry for myself. And then one day I met this wino in a restaurant. I'd been out hustling all day, shining shoes, selling newspapers, and I had googobs° of money in my pocket. Bought me a bowl of chili for fifteen cents, and a cheeseburger for fifteen cents, and a Pepsi for five cents, and a piece of chocolate cake for ten cents. That was a good meal. I was eating when this old wino came in. I love winos because they never hurt anyone but themselves.

30   The old wino sat down at the counter and ordered twenty-six cents' worth of food. He ate it like he really enjoyed it. When the owner, Mister Williams, asked him to pay the check, the old wino didn't lie or go through his pocket like he suddenly found a hole.

31   He just said: "Don't have no money."

32   The owner yelled: "Why in hell you come in here and eat my food if you don't have no money? That food cost me money!"

33   Mister Williams jumped over the counter and knocked the wino off his stool and beat him over the head with a pop bottle. Then he stepped back and watched the wino bleed. Then he kicked him. And he kicked him again.

34   I looked at the wino with blood all over his face and I went over. "Leave him alone, Mister Williams. I'll pay the twenty-six cents."

35   The wino got up, slowly, pulling himself up to the stool, then up to the counter, holding on for a minute until his legs stopped shaking so bad. He looked at me with pure hate. "Keep your twenty-six cents. You don't have to pay, not now. I just finished paying for it."

36   He started to walk out, and as he passed me, he reached down and touched my shoulder. "Thanks, sonny, but it's too late now. Why didn't you pay it before?"

37   I was pretty sick about that. I waited too long to help another man.

First Impressions

Freewrite for ten minutes on one of the following.

1. Did you enjoy reading this selection? Why or why not?

2. When you were in elementary school did you, like Gregory, ever have a crush on a classmate? What was it about this person that you liked so much?

3. Were you ever badly embarrassed by a teacher (or did you witness someone else embarrassed by a teacher)? What happened?

Vocabulary Check

___A___ 1. In the excerpt below, the word *pregnant* means

A. full of.
B. empty of.
C. sick of.
D. pleased with.

> Pregnant women's wombs are full of the babies they are carrying, and these women often have strange food cravings. Gregory is full of poverty and hunger, so even paste "doesn't taste too bad. . . ."

"Pregnant people get strange tastes. I was pregnant with poverty . . . and pregnant with hunger. Paste doesn't taste too bad when you're hungry." (Paragraph 5)

___C___ 2. In the excerpt below, the word *pledged* means

A. repeated.
B. studied.
C. promised to give.
D. brought home.

> Each child has been asked how much his or her father would give, so Dick Gregory plans to top whatever amount Helene promises her father will give.

"I had money in my pocket . . . and whatever Helene Tucker pledged for her Daddy, I was going to top it." (Paragraph 7)

___B___ 3. In the excerpt below, the word *function* means

A. enjoy itself.
B. do its job.
C. sound.
D. shut down.

"And I always thought the teacher kind of liked me. She always picked me to wash the blackboard on Friday, after school. That was a big thrill; it made me feel important. If I didn't wash it, come Monday the school might not function right." (Paragraph 25)

> If the blackboard had not been washed Friday afternoon, it would be dirty on Monday; as a result, the school might not be able to do its job right.

_D_   4. In the sentence below, the word *hustling* means

Shining shoes and
selling newspapers all
day are examples of
working energetically.

A. complaining.
B. relaxing.
C. studying hard.
D. working energetically.

"I'd been out hustling all day, shining shoes, selling newspapers, and I had googobs of money in my pocket." (Paragraph 29)

Reading Check

Central Point and Main Ideas

_C_   1. Which sentence best expresses the central point of the entire selection?

Answer A covers
only paragraphs 1–3.
Answer B covers
only paragraph 28.
Answer D covers only
paragraphs 1–2.

A. Dick Gregory had a long-standing crush on a girl named Helene Tucker.
B. The charity Gregory received was given in a way that labeled him as poor, which made him ashamed.
C. As both a receiver and a giver, Gregory learned that giving something the wrong way can cause shame.
D. Gregory grew up in a fatherless, poor family.

_A_   2. Which sentence best expresses the main idea of paragraph 2?

Answer B covers only
the first sentence.
Answer C covers
only sentence 3.
Answer D covers only
the last sentence.

A. The author adored Helene Tucker, a symbol of everything he wanted.
B. Everybody has a symbol of everything he or she wants.
C. Helene Tucker made the author feel ashamed of his looks.
D. Unlike the author, Helene Tucker had a father.

_D_   3. Which sentence best expresses the main idea of paragraph 5?

Answer A is incorrect
because he does not
say he liked to eat it,
only that it doesn't
taste bad if you are
hungry. Answer B covers
only sentences 1–3. Answer C covers only sentence 4.

A. Gregory liked to eat paste.
B. The teacher assumed that Gregory was stupid.
C. The teacher never realized that Gregory was hungry all the time.
D. The teacher assumed that Gregory was stupid and never realized that his poor work was the result of hunger.

Supporting Details

_D_ 4. Gregory could afford to contribute to the Community Chest because he had
   A. worked as a paperhanger.
   See paragraph 7. B. stolen money out of the pockets of coats in the school cloakroom.
   C. earned money by cleaning the blackboard for the teacher.
   D. earned money by shining shoes and selling papers.

_A_ 5. Gregory's mother beat him when he
   A. threw away the jacket that he'd gotten from welfare.
   See paragraph 28. B. dropped his money on Helene's stoop.
   C. didn't stop Mister Williams from beating the wino.
   D. walked out of school.

_B_ 6. After the teacher told the class that Gregory was the type of person the Community Chest helped and that he was fatherless, Gregory
   A. never went back to school.
   B. felt sorry for himself for a while.
   C. stopped working.
   D. felt that Helene Tucker did not feel sorry for him.
   See the first two sentences of paragraph 29.

Inferences

Gregory writes that teachers "were never interested in finding out that you couldn't concentrate because you were so hungry." _C_ 7. In paragraph 5, the author implies that
   A. he is stupid.
   B. teachers understood him well.
   C. it was difficult for him to concentrate in school.
   D. the only way he ever got food was to steal it.

When Mister Williams realizes he isn't going to get money from the wino, he beats him. The beating takes the place of money. _B_ 8. When the wino says, "I just finished paying for [the food]," he is implying that he
   A. had found some money to give Mister Williams.
   B. had paid for it by taking a beating.
   C. had paid for the meal before he ate.
   D. would work for Mister Williams to pay for the meal.

The Writer's Craft

The first ___B___ 9. Gregory organizes his essay by
incident is related in
paragraphs 4–27; the
second, in paragraphs
29–37. Each incident's
details are organized in
the order in which they
happened.

A. listing the types of behavior demonstrated by victims of poverty.

B. relating, in time order, two incidents that taught him the meaning of shame.

C. showing the effects of poverty on a person's educational level.

D. contrasting the ways rich people and poor people relate to others.

___D___ 10. The word that best describes the tone of the last paragraph of the selection is

A. angry.

B. objective.   The words "pretty sick about that" indicate regret.

C. sentimental.

D. regretful.

Discussion Questions

1. Why do you think Gregory included both the classroom story and the restaurant story in his essay? In what ways are the two incidents similar? What is the difference between the shame he felt in the first incident and the shame he felt in the second?

2. The Community Chest incident could have had very different results if Gregory's teacher had handled the situation in another way. What do you think she should have done when Gregory said, "You forgot me"? Or could she have used a different method of collecting money from students? Explain.

3. We say that something is *ironic* when it has an effect that is the opposite of what might be expected. In this reading, Gregory uses irony in several places. In what ways are the following quotations from "Shame" ironic?

   - "I never learned hate at home, or shame. I had to go to school for that."

   - "If I knew my place and didn't come too close, she'd wink at me and say hello. That was a good feeling."

   - "I looked at the wino with blood all over his face and I went over. 'Leave him alone, Mister Williams. I'll pay the twenty-six cents.'
     "The wino got up. . . . He looked at me with pure hate."

4. Has anyone ever tried to help you in a way that embarrassed or hurt you, instead of pleasing you? If so, how did you feel toward that person? Explain. In what ways might activities that are meant to help people also hurt them?

Paragraph Assignments

1. When have you, like Gregory, regretted the way you acted in a particular situation? Perhaps you didn't speak up when someone was being teased, or perhaps you spoke harshly to someone because you were in a bad mood. Write a paragraph that describes the situation and how you acted. You might want to start the paragraph with a sentence like "I still regret the way I acted when _____." Conclude by explaining why you feel you acted wrongly and what you wish you had done instead.

2. Gregory points out that he couldn't concentrate in school because he had often gone without breakfast and was too hungry to think. Although many Americans assume that hunger is not a real problem in a country as wealthy as the United States, the fact is that more than *16 million* children in our country are either underfed or poorly fed. Write a paragraph about the ways hunger harms children. You can research this topic by entering phrases such as "how hunger hurts children" and "effects of malnutrition on children." Conclude your paragraph with either a thoughtful warning or a recommendation for change—or both.

Essay Assignments

1. By embarrassing him in front of the class, Gregory's teacher demonstrated the negative effect that a teacher can have on a student. But teachers also have the potential to be very positive figures in their students' lives. Write an essay about three qualities that you think a good teacher should possess. Some of these qualities might be patience, a sense of humor, insight into students' feelings, and the ability to make a lesson interesting. Illustrate each of those qualities with examples of behavior you have witnessed from real-life teachers. Include your observations on how students benefit when a teacher has the qualities you're writing about.

2. A dictionary defines a word by briefly explaining its meaning. But in an essay, an author can define a term in a different, more personal manner. In this reading, Dick Gregory defines *shame* by describing two incidents in his life in which shame played a central part.

Write an essay in which you define *poverty* by presenting several real-life examples of people in America today coping with poverty. Your central point might be stated something like this: "Many people in America today endure the heartbreak of coping with poverty." Perhaps you can provide an example that comes out of your own life or the life of someone you have heard about or know. Otherwise, or in addition, if you Google "examples of poverty in the U.S.," you will find over 100 million articles on the topic! Look for articles that present vivid specific examples from the real lives of real people dealing with poverty, and use them as the basis for the supporting paragraphs in your essay. In a concluding paragraph, present your thoughts and reactions to what you have learned in researching your paper.

20 Adult Children at Home
Marilyn Mack

Preview

Parents used to expect their children to leave home not long after high school or college. Nowadays, however, children leave home later than ever, and even then they may not be gone for good. Marilyn Mack explains this new pattern and its ups and downs.

Words to Watch

ruefully (2): with regret
phenomenon (10): noteworthy situation or event
cope (12): manage

1   Ruth Patterson remembers the day the last of her children left home. "Dan was 18 and headed off to the state university," said the Pennsylvania housewife. "I cried awhile, and then told myself, 'Cheer up! At last you and Dave have the house to yourselves!'"

2   Six years later, Mrs. Patterson laughs a little ruefully° at that memory. Since her youngest son left for college, three of her four children—one with a three-year-old daughter—have moved back to the family home for at least six months at a time.

3   "The 'empty nest' hasn't been quite as empty as we expected," says Mrs. Patterson.

4   The Pattersons' situation is becoming less unusual all the time. Adult children have been "nesting," or moving back to the family home, in increasing numbers in recent years. In 1970, according to the U.S. Census Bureau, 54 percent of men and 41 percent of women between the ages of 18 and 24 depended on their parents for housing. Lately, those figures have risen much higher. One survey in 2010 found that as many as 85 percent of students graduating from college in the spring planned to move back home.

5   Why are adult children coming home? The case of the Pattersons provides some typical reasons.

6   Their oldest daughter, Suzanne, 35, a bank teller, returned home with her toddler after a painful divorce. Two years later, she is still there, with her mother caring for her little girl. "She needed a place to lick her wounds,"

217

said her mother. "We thought it would be for just a few months, but when we realized what it would cost her to keep Jenny in day care while she worked, it didn't make sense for them to move out again."

7   Five years after high school, their son Peter, now 28, moved back in. The plan was for him to spend a year working on a painting crew while he and his fiancée saved money for the down payment on a house. One year turned into three; long stretches between jobs made it impossible for Peter to make the kind of money he needed. Eventually he and his fiancée married and moved into a tiny apartment. They still hope to buy a house someday, but fear that "someday" may never come.

8   Their daughter Lesley, 30, has moved in and out of the house so many times "we've lost count," says her mother. A legal secretary, Lesley "earns enough to have her own place, if she'd learn to live within her means. But she wants to live like the lawyers she works with." That translates into an expensive car, lots of evenings out, and a wardrobe that bursts the limits of her modest salary.

9   Only the Pattersons' youngest child, Dan, now 24, has followed the route his parents expected. He graduated from college, found a job teaching high-school social studies, and lives on his own in a city apartment.

10   Many factors have contributed to the phenomenon° of nesting. First and foremost is the general slump in the economy. As many commentators have noted, "The rich are getting richer;

the poor are getting poorer; and the middle class is disappearing." Even for college graduates, the prospect of easily finding employment and starting on the path toward home ownership is doubtful. Other contributing factors include the rise in the divorce rate, increased housing costs, college debts, and the trend to delay marriage. Once out on their own, many young people are finding it unexpectedly difficult to maintain the standard of living they hoped for. Apartment rentals, particularly in major cities, can make living alone an impossible option. Even for those fortunate enough to have found steady employment, buying a house can seem unlikely—a first-time home-buyer can expect to pay over 40 percent more today than twenty years ago.

11   Returning home can be a financial lifesaver for struggling young people. Some credit counselors recommend nesting as a solution for people who've gotten in over their heads with credit

cards and rent payments and utility bills. "I was really in a mess financially when I moved back in with Mom and Dad," said Tony Woelk, a 28-year-old Best Buy salesman. "I don't know what I would have done if they hadn't helped me pay off my bills and make a fresh start." Today, after two years of living with his parents, Tony is on his own again and determined to keep his spending under control.

12 Another advantage mentioned by some nesters is the emotional support they were shown by their parents in a time of need. Judy Loewen, 22, moved back in with her family for a month after breaking up with her long-time boyfriend. "I quit my job and left the city where he was," she remembers today. "I really felt that I couldn't cope° unless I got away immediately, and where could I go with no money and no job except to my folks? And bless them, they said, 'Just take it easy here for a while and don't rush into anything.' After a few weeks, I was ready to take a lot more realistic view of the situation and make some good decisions."

13 Parents, too, can find some practical and emotional benefits when their adult children return home. A child's contribution to room and board can help out with household expenses, particularly if the parents are living on a fixed income. In addition, parents may enjoy having a younger person around to help out with household repairs and other chores. "As I get older, taking care of the house and yard has become more of a burden for me," said Bill Robinson, a widower whose 35-year-old son has been sharing the house for the last two years. "Joseph pays some rent, but his real contribution has been to take a lot of those worries off my shoulders."

14 But the nesting phenomenon has its gloomy side as well. Parents and children report the number-one problem as the lack of space and privacy experienced by everyone involved.

15 "Never, never, never again," vowed Vicki Langella, 23, who lived with her parents for six months after losing her job in a township clerk's office. "We get along fine when we visit, but within ten minutes of moving back in, I felt like a twelve-year-old. It was constantly, 'Where are you going? When will you be back? Who are you going to be with?' And I found myself reacting to them as if I really were 12. The worst part of it was knowing that it was my own fault—I'd chosen to move back in with them."

16 "Believe it or not, sixty-year-olds enjoy some privacy too," said Ella Purcell, whose two adult daughters have both returned home for brief periods. "Coming into my own living room to find my daughter and a date smooching on the couch made me feel like an intruder. I finally had to say, 'I love you—but out already!'"

17 Finances can be another difficult area for parents and returned children. Parents often struggle with the decision of whether to ask their children for rent. "When you're letting them stay with you in order to save money, it seems silly to charge rent. But when we saw the way Ed was throwing money around, we began to feel taken advantage of," said the mother of one adult nester.

18   Despite its possible pitfalls, psychologists, family counselors, and others believe that nesting can succeed for many families if some precautions are taken. They offer the following tips on maintaining a happy "nest."

19   ● Regardless of their financial situation, adult children should pay some room and board. Monica O'Kane, the author of *Living with Adult Children,* admits that this can be difficult. "It's hard to squeeze blood from a turnip, especially when it's your own turnip. But paying for room and board helps children grow in financial independence."

20   ● Establish clear expectations about household duties. "I remembered all too well being treated like the family servant when the kids were teenagers," said one experienced mother of a nester. "So when Rob moved back in, I said, 'Fine. Here is your share of the laundry, grocery-shopping, and cleaning duties.' Once it was clear that I was serious, he pitched right in."

● Respect one another. Children   21 should not expect to be treated as guests or to use the parental home as a hotel, coming and going at all hours with no explanations. Parents, on the other hand, should recognize that the nester is no longer a youngster whose activities need constant supervision.

● And, most importantly: Don't let it   22 go on forever. "When a child returns home, everyone should agree on a tentative date for him to move out again," said one family therapist. "If that date is changed later by the mutual consent of everyone concerned, that's OK, but everyone should understand that this isn't a permanent arrangement."

First Impressions

Freewrite for ten minutes on one of the following.

1. Did you enjoy reading this selection? Why or why not?

2. Among your acquaintances, is it common for adult children to move back in with their parents? What are some reasons they give for doing so?

3. If you were a parent, would you want your adult children to move back in with you? Why or why not?

Vocabulary Check

___B___ 1. In the excerpt below, the word *maintain* means
A. avoid.
B. keep up.
C. remember.   What would one want to do to a
D. sum up.   hoped-for standard of living?

"...many young people are finding it unexpectedly difficult to maintain the standard of living they hoped for." (Paragraph 10)

___A___ 2. In the excerpt below, the word *option* means
A. choice.
B. discovery.   High apartment rentals make it
C. failure.   impossible to choose to live alone.
D. limit.

"Apartment rentals . . . can make living alone an impossible option." (Paragraph 10)

___D___ 3. In the excerpt below, the word *tentative* means
A. unchangeable.
B. public.   A date that can be "changed later" is one
C. according to law.   "agreed upon for the time being."
D. agreed upon for the time being.

"'When a child returns home, everyone should agree on a tentative date for him to move out again,' said one family therapist. 'If that date is changed later ... that's OK....'" (Paragraph 22)

Reading Check

Central Point and Main Ideas

___C___ 1. Which sentence best expresses the central point of the entire selection?
A. Parents are not sure if they should ask for rent money from their grown children who live at home.
B. The Pattersons are a good example of nesting.
C. Nesting, which has increased, has advantages and disadvantages, but it can succeed if families take precautions.
D. Between 1970 and 2010, nesting has greatly increased among adult children.   Answers A, B, and D are too narrow.
Each covers only one detail of the selection.

___A___ 2. The main idea of paragraph 10 is expressed in its
   A. first sentence.
   B. second sentence.
   C. third sentence.
   D. last sentence.

The first sentence has a list signal: many factors. The rest of the paragraph lists factors that contribute to nesting.

___A___ 3. The main idea of paragraph 13 is
   A. in the first sentence.
   B. in the second sentence.
   C. in the last sentence.
   D. implied.

The first sentence has a list signal: some practical and emotional benefits. The rest of the paragraph details some of the benefits.

Supporting Details

___D___ 4. Adult children return home
   A. after divorces.
   B. when it's hard to find a job.
   C. so that they can pay their bills.
   D. for all of the above reasons.

See paragraph 10.

___D___ 5. According to the selection, when adult children return home, they
   A. gain privacy.
   B. should be allowed to stay indefinitely.
   C. should be treated like guests.
   D. should help out with finances and household chores.

See paragraphs 19–22.

Inferences

___T___ 6. TRUE OR FALSE? The author implies that money problems are the main reason that adult children return home to live.

See paragraph 10.

Most of the factors contributing to nesting are related to financial problems, suggesting that money is the key reason for the increase in nesting.

___D___ 7. The reading suggests that
   A. only "losers" return home to live with their parents.
   B. going to college is a waste of time and money for many Americans.
   C. most young Americans will never own their own homes.
   D. returning home to live with one's parents is a growing trend.

Answers A, B, and C are not supported.

___C___ 8. We can conclude from the selection that
   A. the negative aspects of returning home to live far outweigh the advantages for both parents and their adult children.
   B. parents should refuse to let their adult children return home to live.
   C. clear communication between parents and their adult children is essential to maintaining a happy "nest."
   D. it is silly for parents to ask their adult children to pay rent.

See paragraphs 18–22, which indicate that with clear expectations, nesting can work for both parents and children.

The Writer's Craft

Ruth's comment, that she and her husband will now have the house to themselves, turns out to be the opposite of what happens.

___B___ 9. Which of the following best describes how the writer introduces this selection?

A. She makes a broad statement that narrows down to a specific point.

B. She introduces an idea that is the opposite of the point of the story.

C. She provides an anecdote that illustrates the point of the story.

D. She asks a challenging question.

___B___ 10. Which of the following statements best describes the writer's purpose?

A. To warn parents against allowing their adult children to return home after moving out

B. To explore reasons adult children are moving home and suggest guidelines for making the arrangement work

C. To criticize parents for being overly demanding of their adult children who need to return home

D. To cite the financial and emotional benefits of having adult children move back home

For reasons, see paragraphs 5–12; for guidelines, see paragraphs 18–22. Answers C and D are too narrow; answer A is unsupported.

Discussion Questions

1. Do you know about any cases of nesting? Why did the children return home? How did it work out?

2. Do you think today's young adults are having a harder time financially than their parents' generation? Or is the "standard of living they hoped for" higher? Or both?

3. Mack mentions the "people who've gotten in over their heads with credit cards and rent payments and utility bills." Why do you think people get into this situation? What advice would you give them?

4. Do you agree that adult children who return home, "regardless of their financial situation," should pay some room and board? If not, what financial situations should excuse adult children from paying room and board?

Paragraph Assignments

1. If you are not living with a parent or parents, would you consider doing so? Under what circumstances? Alternatively, if you had adult children, would you allow them to move back in with you? If so, under what circumstances? Write a paragraph in which you answer one of these questions and explain the reasons for your answer.

2. Think of a family you know in which an adult child has moved back into the parents' home. Does the situation seem to be a positive or a negative one? Write a paragraph in which you describe the situation and tell why it is a good or a bad arrangement.

Essay Assignments

1. Overall, do you think it is a good or a bad thing for adult children to return home? Write an essay in which you develop one of these two thesis statements:

   - There are three reasons I think it is a bad idea for adult children to return to live with their parents.

   or

   - There are three reasons I think it can be a good idea for adult children to return to live with their parents.

   Support your thesis with examples drawn from your own personal experience or the experiences of people you know.

2. The selection ends with a list of suggestions for making the adult-children-at-home living situation go smoothly. Write an essay in which you focus on a different living situation: living with a roommate, living with a spouse or partner, living with teenagers, or living alone. Develop a list of guidelines to make your living situation work well. Devote each of the essay's three main paragraphs to a guideline, giving specific instructions on how that guideline should be put into practice.

21 Abusive Relationships among the Young

Miriam Hill

Preview

It's shocking but true: by the time of high-school graduation, one in three girls will have been involved in an abusive relationship. What begins as a romantic relationship becomes characterized by physical violence, stalking, and emotional abuse. Why are young women so vulnerable to abuse? Why do they stay with and even defend their abusers? What drives young men to hurt and humiliate their girlfriends? And most importantly, how can a girl make the abuse stop? This selection explores a problem that is common but often hidden out of sight, due to the victims' tangled feelings of hurt, guilt, and fear.

Words to Watch

hovering (1): hanging
demographic (4): social group
primarily (6): mainly
intimidate (22): persuade by frightening

1   When Sarah first set eyes on Joe at a back-to-school dance, she thought he was really cute. And when they started dating, he showered her with flowers, compliments, and tickets to the movies. But their relationship quickly went downhill, as Joe began to insult, make demands, and then physically abuse her. The final straw came when Joe kicked her, knocking her into a wall, where she hit her head and lost consciousness. "I woke up and he was hovering° over me," Sarah, now 18, recalls. "I just wanted to get away." Four months after their first date, Sarah stood in line at the family division of the Santa Clara County, California court clerk's office, waiting to pick up a copy of a restraining order.

Kayla Brown's story began much 2 like Sarah's. At first, her high school boyfriend was highly respectful, even calling Kayla's mom to introduce himself. But then he began calling her every hour to see where she was and what she was doing. Finally, he slammed a chair into a table and raised a fist to strike her during an argument in the school cafeteria. Kayla confided in her mother, who had also been involved with an abusive man. When her mother advised her to break off the relationship, Kayla did so. But the process took months. To make sure she was never alone with her ex-boyfriend, she had friends accompany her everywhere, even to the school lavatory.

3   Heather Norris wasn't so lucky. She was 17 when she met her boyfriend, Joshua Bean, and 20 when he stabbed her to death.

4   Why does "love" turn so ugly? What is behind what many are calling an "epidemic" of abusive relationships among the young? The statistics are alarming: one in three girls will have an abusive dating relationship by the time she graduates from high school, and females from the ages of 16 to 24 are the most likely demographic° to experience dating violence. And in today's world, social networking sites and texting are only making it easier for abusers to harass, humiliate, and stalk their victims. It's not only men who abuse women; however, when abuse turns physical, it is the women who wind up in the emergency room.

5   One factor that helps make abusive relationships common is the value our society places on being in a relationship. Whether it's on TV, in movies, in magazines, or on the Internet, the message is that being alone is for losers. Teenage girls, in particular, measure their self-worth by having a boyfriend. Think of it: from an early

age, girls in our culture are taught that being a "princess" is the ideal state of femininity. Is it any wonder they long for a Prince Charming to come and sweep them off their feet?

6   Dr. Jill Murray, an expert in the field of abusive relationships, puts teenage girls' strong need for social acceptance in psychological terms: "Adolescents are primarily° concerned with the way they appear to their peers. That is one reason girls are often desperate for a boyfriend in high school. If their friends are dating, they feel out of place if they are not."

7   Ron Davis agrees. He runs a teen program at a middle school in Walnut Creek, California.

8   "Girls at 16 are looking for love, anybody who's going to show any affection at all," he says. "They fall in love so fast with anybody. That's when they get taken

advantage of." Young people whose parents have neglected them emotionally are even more likely to become involved in abusive relationships.

9   Experts also agree that children who are exposed to violence at home often repeat it in their adult relationships. A girl who sees her father or another male abuse her mother learns to view abuse as a natural part of a relationship. Similarly, when a boy observes his father or another male dominate his mother and sister with emotional and physical abuse, he grows up believing that it is "normal" for him to control a woman by abusing her. Such abuse may include touching his girlfriend inappropriately in public in order to prove to others that she "belongs" to him. It may also include calling her or texting her repeatedly in an attempt to monitor her behavior.

10   In addition, male abusers often hold a stereotyped idea of male and female relationships. In their view, women are inferior to men, so a girlfriend should "know her place." This macho attitude is reinforced by some religious groups, whose teachings emphasize that a man is the natural head of the household and should always be obeyed. Physical or emotional abuse of a female partner is thus viewed as "discipline."

11   Coming from a home where substance abuse takes place is another strong predictor of involvement in an abusive relationship. Abusers generally have a low tolerance for frustration and turn to alcohol or drugs to escape feelings of failure or powerlessness. Alcohol, in turn, lowers inhibitions and increases aggression. Likewise, chronic use of marijuana or crystal meth causes rage and paranoia. In many cases, children of substance abusers adopt their parents' dysfunctional pattern of behavior. Undergoing financial difficulties such as the loss of a job only makes it more likely that people will take out their feelings of frustration on those closest to them.

12   Complicating matters is the fact that young women who have very limited experience in relationships often confuse jealousy and possessiveness with love. At first they are flattered when a boy calls or texts them at all hours. "It shows he loves me," they tell themselves. Shockingly, in one recent study, some teens reported receiving 200 to 300 texts *a day* from boyfriends or girlfriends wanting to know where they were, who they were with, and why. And up to 82 percent of parents had no idea what was happening.

13   "Youths don't recognize that as stalking behavior," says Tatiana Colon, head of the Teen Dating Violence Task Force in Alameda County, California. In other words, it's not about love, it's about control. And control is at the core of abusive behavior.

14   Of course, few girls consciously choose to become involved with an abuser. As in the case of Sarah and Kayla, the relationship usually starts off tenderly. But then a pattern begins to emerge—with abusers emotionally or physically abusive one minute, sweetly apologetic the next.

15   "Honey, I didn't mean it—I'll never do it again," is a common refrain. Furthermore, abusers often have "Dr.

Jekyll" and "Mr. Hyde" personalities. That is, they are careful to present only their good "Dr. Jekyll" side to outsiders. It's not unusual for them to be charming and popular—star athletes and good students. In cases such as these, girls are understandably reluctant to confide that they are being abused for fear of not being believed. When Sarah told school authorities that Joe was abusing her, they ordered him to attend a different school. But other girls told Sarah, "How could you do this to him? He's *so cute*."

16   Another reason girls fail to tell others that they are being abused is that they feel it's their responsibility to fix whatever is wrong in the relationship.

17   "Think of articles in women's magazines," says Dr. Murray. "There is always at least one in which the tone of the article is how to fix your relationship." As Murray points out, there are basically three types of relationship articles: how to catch a man, how to hold onto a man, and how you must fix whatever is wrong in a relationship.

18   Ever notice that men's magazines don't have similar articles?

19   Girls who come from homes where they have been expected to care for a depressed parent are especially likely to fall into this "caretaker" pattern of thinking. Having been trained as children to be "good little helpers," they hold the mistaken belief that they can rescue the abuser. And since few abusers are abusive all the time, they hold out hope that his good side will win out.

20   "He comes from a bad home. I'm all he's got. I can save him," they often think. Although an abuser may express remorse and swear that he will never do it again, experts warn that abuse involves a cycle that feeds itself. It *will not* stop unless drastic action is taken. In fact, 80% of abusers fail to stop their abuse *even with* therapy. According to Murray, an abused woman will typically go back to her abuser seven to nine times before she leaves for good—if she's still alive.

21   Abuse often begins with insults such as "You're fat, you're ugly and stupid. Nobody else would want you." Such hostility is a form of what psychologists term *projection*. In other words, whatever the abuser dislikes about himself, he will "project" onto his partner. By destroying her self-confidence, he feels his power increase. Of course, women can also be guilty of projection. For example, a young woman who cheats on her boyfriend may guiltily accuse him of cheating on her.

22   Emotional abuse generally escalates to physical abuse. At first, an abuser may punch a wall next to his victim or throw something or kick a chair. Such behavior is meant to threaten and intimidate°. An abuser will then graduate to pushing, slapping, pulling hair, kicking, or punching his victim. Sexual abuse is the most serious form of relationship abuse. In fact, date rape accounts for 67% of sexual assaults among teens. Sadly, some young women still believe that it is a male's right to demand sex from his partner whenever he feels like it. Experts disagree. They maintain that if sex is not completely consensual, it is rape.

23   Young women often downplay abuse. "He lost control. It was the alcohol talking, not him," they'll say. Perhaps saddest of all, some young women actually believe their abuser when he insists, "You made me do it."

24   "No one actually loses control," says Scott A. Johnson, author of *When "I Love You" Turns Violent*. "Rather a conscious decision is made . . . to blame the victim." He adds, "If you are being abused, your significant other is telling you loudly and clearly, 'I do not love you!'"

What To Do

25   If you know a young person who is in an abusive relationship, how do you advise him or her to get out? Experts agree that it is best *not* to confront the abuser. Such confrontations can become violent, as the abuser seeks at all costs to reestablish control over his victim. "If I can't have you, no one will," is a classic threat, and one that should be taken at face value.

26   Instead of confronting an abuser, victims should confide in someone trustworthy, such as a teacher, guidance counselor, doctor, friend, or parent. Contact the National Teen Dating Abuse 24/7 Helpline at 1-866-331-9474, **www.loveisrespect.org** or the National Domestic Violence Hotline: 1-800-799-7233. Both organizations help victims of abuse design a personal safety plan to lower the risk of being hurt by an abuser.

27   Remember, there is nothing "loving" about being treated as someone's possession. And no one should have to put up with abusive behavior. So don't be silent if you or someone you know is being abused. You can make it stop, but only if you let others know what's happening.

First Impressions

Freewrite for ten minutes on one of the following.

1. Did you enjoy reading this selection? Why or why not?

2. Do you know anyone who is in an abusive relationship? What has been that person's response to the abuse?

3. Why do you think relationships like Sarah's, Kayla's, and Heather's are becoming more and more common? Or are we just hearing about them more often?

Vocabulary Check

  _A_ 1. In the excerpt below, the word *monitor* means
   A. keep track of.
   B. ignore.
   C. return.
   D. stop.

   What would repeated calling or texting enable a boyfriend to do to his girlfriend's behavior?

   "Such abuse may include touching his girlfriend inappropriately in public in order to prove to others that she 'belongs' to him. It may also include calling her or texting her repeatedly in an attempt to monitor her behavior." (Paragraph 9)

  _B_ 2. In the excerpt below, the word *escalates* means
   A. becomes less frequent.
   B. gets worse.
   C. disappears.
   D. explains.

   Pushing, slapping, pulling hair, kicking, or punching the victim is worse than punching a wall or kicking a chair.

   "Emotional abuse generally escalates to physical abuse. At first, an abuser may punch a wall next to his victim or throw something or kick a chair.... An abuser will then graduate to pushing, slapping, pulling hair, kicking, or punching his victim." (Paragraph 22)

  _B_ 3. In the excerpt below, the word *consensual* means
   A. enjoyable.
   B. agreed to by both parties.
   C. risk-free.
   D. within the bonds of marriage.

   "Sadly, some young women still believe that it is a male's right to demand sex from his partner whenever he feels like it. Experts disagree. They maintain that if sex is not completely consensual, it is rape." (Paragraph 22)

   If sex is demanded by only the male, it is not agreed to by all involved.

Reading Check

Central Point and Main Ideas

_D_ 1. Which sentence best expresses the central point of the entire selection?

Answer A covers only part of paragraph 4 and paragraphs 12–13. Answer B covers only paragraphs 9 and 11. Answer C covers only part of paragraph 20.

    A. Today, modern technology is making it easier for abusers to harass, humiliate, and stalk their victims.

    B. Children who are exposed to violence and substance abuse at home often become involved in abusive relationships.

    C. Abuse involves a cycle that feeds itself and will not stop unless drastic action is taken.

    D. There are a number of factors that cause young people to become involved in abusive relationships.

_C_ 2. The implied main idea of paragraphs 5–8 is that

Paragraph 5 suggests this idea, and paragraphs 6–8 offer support. Answers A and D cover only part of paragraph 5. Answer B covers only paragraph 6.

    A. many girls in our culture long for a Prince Charming to come and sweep them off their feet.

    B. psychologists such as Dr. Jill Murray believe that adolescents are primarily concerned with the way they appear to their peers.

    C. because teenage girls in our culture place such a high value on being in a relationship, they are more likely to become involved in abusive relationships.

    D. TV, the movies, magazines, and the Internet all communicate the message that it's important to be in a relationship.

_A_ 3. The main idea of paragraph 9 is stated in its

    A. first sentence.

    B. second sentence.

    C. third sentence.

    D. fourth sentence.

Answers B and C illustrate the main idea. Answer D describes one kind of abuse that may result.

Supporting Details

_C_ 4. According to the selection, which of the following statements would an abusive male *not* be likely to say?

    A. "She belongs to me."

    B. "Women should know their place."

    C. "It's up to me to fix whatever is wrong in this relationship."

    D. "You made me do it."

Answer C is what an abused female (not an abusive male) might say. For answer A, see paragraph 9. For answer B, see paragraph 10. For answer D, see paragraph 23.

___D___ 5. According to the selection, a girl who sees her father or another male abuse her mother

See paragraph 9, second sentence.

A. is more likely to stay single.
B. is more likely to demand respectful treatment from her partner.
C. is more likely to abuse her male partner.
D. tends to view abuse as natural.

Inferences

The paragraphs point out that basing one's self-worth on having a boyfriend can lead to being taken advantage of. Answers A and B are not supported.

___C___ 6. We can conclude from paragraphs 5–8 that

A. most girls who once pretended to be princesses will become involved in abusive relationships.
B. it is natural for boys to grow up to become "Prince Charming."
C. it's not good for girls to base their self-worth on having a boyfriend.
D. all of the above.

Answer C is supported by the fact that men's magazines do not contain articles about how to fix a relationship (while women's magazines almost always do). Answers A and D are not supported. Answer B is not supported and is also illogical.

___C___ 7. On the basis of paragraphs 16–18, we can conclude that

A. most of the men who read men's magazines aren't interested in women.
B. men's magazines would be more popular if they carried stories about how men should fix romantic relationships.
C. in general, men aren't interested in reading about how to fix romantic relationships.
D. men's magazines deliberately encourage abuse in relationships.

Answer B is supported by paragraphs 9–11, which suggest many teens don't see loving relationships at home. Answers A and D are not supported. Answer C is contradicted by paragraphs 12–13.

___B___ 8. We can infer from the selection that

A. only children who are exposed to violence at home become involved in abusive relationships.
B. many young people today don't know what a loving relationship looks like.
C. loving someone means wanting to know what he or she is doing at all times.
D. young men who are physically unattractive are more likely to become abusive toward women.

The Writer's Craft

___A___ 9. The author begins her essay with

A. a brief story.
B. a series of questions.
C. shifting to the opposite.
D. going from broad to narrow.

Paragraph 1 tells the story of Sarah's abusive boyfriend, Joe, ending with Sarah getting a restraining order.

___D___ 10. To conclude her essay, the author uses
   A. a brief story.
   B. a summary.
   C. a series of questions.
   D. a final thought and recommendation.

   > The author tells readers not to put up with abusive behavior
   > and urges them to let others know if they are being abused.

Discussion Questions

1. Was there anything in this selection that surprised you? If so, what was it, and why did you find it surprising? Was there any information that you disagree with? Explain.

2. Think back to when you were in high school. Was it considered normal to be in a relationship? Were kids who weren't in relationships looked on as "losers"? If so, was dating violence ever discussed? Explain.

3. The selection focuses mainly on males who abuse females. Do you think that women abusing men is also a serious problem? Why or why not?

4. Experts believe that dating violence is on the rise. Whether it is or not, it's clearly a serious problem. In your view, is there anything that can be done to reduce the likelihood that young people will become involved in abusive relationships, either as an abuser or as a victim? If so, what?

Paragraph Assignments

1. As the author explains, it is not wise for a concerned friend to confront an abuser. But if you had a friend in an abusive relationship, what would you *like* to say to the abuser? Write a paragraph that expresses your thoughts.

2. The essay says that many girls' "strong need for social acceptance" is a reason they are likely to end up in abusive relationships. What other evidence is there that teen girls are influenced by the need for social acceptance? Write a paragraph in which you write about some aspect of girls' behavior that seems to be driven by the need to be accepted.

Essay Assignments

1. Abusive relationships are clearly bad relationships. But not all bad relationships are abusive. Write an essay about three relationships you have observed that you think are poor ones, although not necessarily abusive. Perhaps they are bad because the participants have such different personalities, or do not communicate well, or share few common interests.

    Begin with a thesis statement something like this: "Three poor relationships I have observed involve my friend Pam and her boyfriend Rick, my sister and ex-brother-in-law, and my Aunt Frances and Uncle Steve."

    In each case, provide specific details about what (in your view) make the three relationships unsatisfying ones.

2. The essay makes it clear that obsessive attention and being treated as a possession are *not* signs of a healthy love. By contrast, what *are* some signs of a healthy, respectful relationship?

    Pretend you're an advice columnist writing in a magazine for young people. For your next column, you've been asked to write an essay in which you identify three characteristics of a good relationship and give examples of how people in a good relationship demonstrate these characteristics.

    If you need some ideas for this assignment, a search online for "healthy relationships" will bring up an immense supply of information and opinions.

22 Rowing the Bus
Paul Logan

Preview

If you could go back in time and undo one thing you are sorry for, what would it be? Such a long-regretted moment is the focus of Paul Logan's essay. While we can never turn back the clock, this story illustrates how we can do the next best thing: we can turn our regrets into valuable lessons in living.

Words to Watch

musty (3): stale or moldy in odor
brunt (6): greatest part
sinister (7): evil
stoic (13): emotionless
stricken (25): affected by painful emotions

1   When I was in elementary school, some older kids made me row the bus. Rowing meant that on the way to school I had to sit in the dirty bus aisle littered with paper, gum wads, and spitballs. Then I had to simulate the motion of rowing while the kids around me laughed and chanted, "Row, row, row the bus." I was forced to do this by a group of bullies who spent most of their time picking on me.

2   I was the perfect target for them. I was small. I had no father. And my mother, though she worked hard to support me, was unable to afford clothes and sneakers that were "cool." Instead she dressed me in outfits that we got from "the bags"—hand-me-downs given as donations to a local church.

3   Each Wednesday, she'd bring several bags of clothes to the house and pull out musty°, wrinkled shirts and worn bell-bottom pants that other families no longer wanted. I knew that people were kind to give things to us, but I hated wearing clothes that might have been donated by my classmates. Each time I wore something from the bags, I feared that the other kids might recognize something that was once theirs.

4   Besides my outdated clothes, I wore thick glasses, had crossed eyes, and spoke with a persistent lisp. For whatever reason, I had never learned

to say the "s" sound properly, and I pronounced words that began with "th" as if they began with a "d." In addition, because of my severely crossed eyes, I lacked the hand and eye coordination necessary to hit or catch flying objects.

5   As a result, footballs, baseballs, soccer balls and basketballs became my enemies. I knew, before I stepped on the field or court, that I would do something clumsy or foolish and that everyone would laugh at me. I feared humiliation so much that I became skillful at feigning illnesses to get out of gym class. Eventually I learned how to give myself low-grade fevers so the nurse would write me an excuse. It worked for a while, until the gym teachers caught on. When I did have to play, I was always the last one chosen to be on any team. In fact, team captains did everything in their power to make their opponents get stuck with me. When the unlucky team captain was forced to call my name, I would trudge over to the team, knowing that no one there liked or wanted me. For four years, from second through fifth grade, I prayed nightly for God to give me school days in which I would not be insulted, embarrassed, or made to feel ashamed.

6   I thought my prayers were answered when my mother decided to move during the summer before sixth grade. The move meant that I got to start sixth grade in a different school, a place where I had no reputation. Although the older kids laughed and snorted at me as soon as I got on my new bus— they couldn't miss my thick glasses and strange clothes—I soon discovered that there was another kid who received the brunt° of their insults. His name was George, and everyone made fun of him. The kids taunted him because he was skinny, they belittled him because he had acne that pocked and blotched his face, and they teased him because his voice was squeaky. During my first gym class at my new school, I wasn't the last one chosen for kickball; George was.

7   George tried hard to be friends with me, coming up to me in the cafeteria on the first day of school. "Hi. My name's George. Can I sit with you?" he asked with a peculiar squeakiness that made each word high-pitched and raspy. As I nodded for him to sit down, I noticed an uncomfortable silence in the cafeteria as many of the students who had mocked George's clumsy gait during gym class began watching the two of us and whispering among themselves. By letting him sit with me, I had violated an unspoken law of school, a sinister° code of childhood that demands there must always be someone to pick on. I began to realize two things. If I befriended George, I would soon receive the same treatment that I had gotten at my old school. If I stayed away from him, I might

actually have a chance to escape being at the bottom.

8   Within days, the kids started taunting us whenever we were together. "Who's your new little buddy, Georgie?" In the hallways, groups of students began mumbling about me just loud enough for me to hear, "Look, it's George's ugly boyfriend." On the bus rides to and from school, wads of paper and wet chewing gum were tossed at me by the bigger, older kids in the back of the bus.

9   It became clear that my friendship with George was going to cause me several more years of misery at my new school. I decided to stop being friends with George. In class and at lunch, I spent less and less time with him. Sometimes I told him I was too busy to talk; other times I acted distracted and gave one-word responses to whatever he said. Our classmates, sensing that they had created a rift between George and me, intensified their attacks on him. Each day, George grew more desperate as he realized that the one person who could prevent him from being completely isolated was closing him off. I knew that I shouldn't avoid him, that he was feeling the same way I felt for so long, but I was so afraid that my life would become the hell it had been in my old school that I continued to ignore him.

10   Then, at recess one day, the meanest kid in the school, Chris, decided he had had enough of George. He vowed that he was going to beat up George and anyone else who claimed to be his friend. A mob of kids formed and came after me. Chris led the way and cornered me near our school's swing sets. He grabbed me by my shirt and raised his fist over my head. A huge gathering of kids surrounded us, urging him to beat me up, chanting "Go, Chris, go!"

11   "You're Georgie's new little boy-friend, aren't you?" he yelled. The hot blast of his breath carried droplets of his spit into my face. In a complete betrayal of the only kid who was nice to me, I denied George's friendship.

12   "No, I'm not George's friend. I don't like him. He's stupid," I blurted out. Several kids snickered and mumbled under their breath. Chris stared at me for a few seconds and then threw me to the ground.

13   "Wimp. Where's George?" he demanded, standing over me. Someone pointed to George sitting alone on top of the monkey bars about thirty yards from where we were. He was watching me. Chris and his followers sprinted over to George and yanked him off the bars to the ground. Although the mob quickly encircled them, I could still see the two of them at the center of the crowd, looking at each other. George seemed stoic°, staring straight through Chris. I heard the familiar chant of "Go, Chris, go!" and watched as his fists began slamming into George's head and body. His face bloodied and his nose broken, George crumpled to the ground and sobbed without even throwing a punch. The mob cheered with pleasure and darted off into the playground to avoid an approaching teacher.

14   Chris was suspended, and after a few days, George came back to school. I wanted to talk to him, to ask him how he

was, to apologize for leaving him alone and for not trying to stop him from getting hurt. But I couldn't go near him. Filled with shame for denying George and angered by my own cowardice, I never spoke to him again.

15   Several months later, without telling any students, George transferred to another school. Once in a while, in those last weeks before he left, I caught him watching me as I sat with the rest of the kids in the cafeteria. He never yelled at me or expressed anger, disappointment, or even sadness. Instead he just looked at me.

16   In the years that followed, George's silent stare remained with me. It was there in eighth grade when I saw a gang of popular kids beat up a sixth-grader because, they said, he was "ugly and stupid." It was there my first year in high school, when I saw a group of older kids steal another freshman's clothes and throw them into the showers. It was there a year later, when I watched several seniors press a wad of chewing gum into the hair of a new girl on the bus. Each time that I witnessed another awkward, uncomfortable, scared kid being tormented, I thought of George, and gradually his haunting stare began to speak to me. No longer silent, it told me that every child who is picked on and taunted deserves better, that no one—no matter how big, strong, attractive or popular—has the right to abuse another person.

17   Finally, in my junior year, when a loudmouthed, pink-skinned bully named Donald began picking on two freshmen on the bus, I could no longer deny George. Donald was crumpling a large wad of paper and preparing to bounce it off the back of the head of one of the young students when I interrupted him.

18   "Leave them alone, Don," I said. By then I was six inches taller and, after two years of high-school wrestling, thirty pounds heavier than I had been in my freshman year. Though Donald was still two years older than me, he wasn't much bigger. He stopped what he was doing, squinted, and stared at me.

19   "What's your problem, Paul?"

20   I felt the way I had many years earlier on the playground when I watched the mob of kids begin to surround George.

21   "Just leave them alone. They aren't bothering you," I responded quietly.

22   "What's it to you?" he challenged. A glimpse of my own past, of rowing the bus, of being mocked for my clothes, my lisp, my glasses, and my absent father flashed in my mind.

23   "Just don't mess with them. That's all I am saying, Don." My fingertips were tingling. The bus was silent. He got up from his seat and leaned over me, and I rose from my seat to face him. For a minute, both of us just stood there, without a word, staring.

24   "I'm just playing with them, Paul," he said, chuckling. "You don't have to go psycho on me or anything." Then he shook his head, slapped me firmly on the chest with the back of his hand, and sat down. But he never threw that wad of paper. For the rest of the year, whenever I was on the bus, Don and the other troublemakers were noticeably quiet.

25   Although it has been years since my days on the playground and the school bus, George's look still haunts me. Today, I see it on the faces of a few scared kids at my sister's school—she is in fifth grade. Or once in a while I'll catch a glimpse of someone like George on the evening news, in a story about a child who brought a gun to school to stop the kids from picking on him, or in a feature about a teenager who killed herself because everyone teased her. In each school, in almost every classroom, there is a George with a stricken° face, hoping that someone nearby will be strong enough to be kind—despite what the crowd says—and brave enough to stand up against people who attack, tease, or hurt those who are vulnerable.

26   If asked about their behavior, I'm sure the bullies would say, "What's it to you? It's just a joke. It's nothing." But to George and me, and everyone else who has been humiliated or laughed at or spat on, it is everything. No one should have to row the bus.

First Impressions

Freewrite for ten minutes on one of the following.

1. Did you enjoy reading this selection? Why or why not?

2. What do you think would have happened if Paul had stood up for George? Would it have made any difference?

3. Did your elementary or high school have bullies and victims similar to the ones in this selection? How did they behave?

Vocabulary Check

_C_   1. In the sentence below, the word *simulate* means
   A. sing.
   B. ignore.
   C. imitate.
   D. stop.

   "Then I had to simulate the motion of rowing while the kids around me laughed and chanted, 'Row, row, row the bus.'" (Paragraph 1)

   What would the bullies have forced Paul to do while they chanted about rowing the bus?

___B___ 2. In the sentence below, the word *feigning* means
   A. escaping.
   B. faking.
   C. recognizing.
   D. curing.

If he wanted to get out of gym class, he would have faked an illness.

"I feared humiliation so much that I became skillful at feigning illnesses to get out of gym class." (Paragraph 5)

___C___ 3. In the excerpt below, the word *rift* means
   A. friendship.
   B. agreement.
   C. break.
   D. joke.

If he has stopped being friends with George, there would be a break between him and George.

"I decided to stop being friends with George. . . . Our classmates, sensing that they had created a rift between George and me, intensified their attacks on him." (Paragraph 9)

___A___ 4. In the excerpt below, the word *vulnerable* means
   A. easily wounded.
   B. courageous.
   C. cruel.
   D. physically large.

What kind of person would a bully attack, tease, and hurt?

"In each school, in almost every classroom, there is a George . . . hoping that someone nearby will be . . . brave enough to stand up against people who attack, tease, or hurt those who are vulnerable." (Paragraph 25)

Reading Check

Central Point and Main Ideas

Answers A, B, and D are too narrow. Answer A omits all the details about George as well as the story of Paul's eventually standing up to a bully. Answer B covers only paragraphs 6–7. Answer D covers only paragraphs 14–17 and 25–26.

___C___ 1. Which sentence best expresses the central point of the entire selection?
   A. Although Paul Logan was a target of other students' abuse when he was a young boy, their attacks stopped as he grew taller and stronger.
   B. When Logan moved to a different school, he discovered that another student, George, was the target of more bullying than he was.
   C. Logan's experience of being bullied and his shame at how he treated George eventually made him speak up for someone else who was teased.
   D. Logan is ashamed that he did not stand up for George when George was being attacked by a bully on the playground.

___A___ 2. Which sentence best expresses the implied main idea of paragraph 5?

Answers B, C, and D
each cover only one or
two sentences of the
paragraph.

A. Because of Logan's clumsiness, gym was a miserable experience for him in elementary school.
B. Because Logan hated gym so much, he made up excuses to avoid it.
C. The gym teacher caught on to Logan's excuses.
D. Other students did not want Logan to be a member of their team when games were played.

Supporting Details

___D___ 3. When Chris attacked George, George reacted by

See paragraph 13.

A. fighting back hard.
B. shouting for Logan to help him.
C. running away.
D. accepting the beating.

___A___ 4. Logan finally found the courage to stand up for abused students when he saw

See paragraph 17.

A. Donald about to throw paper at a younger student.
B. older kids throwing a freshman's clothes into the shower.
C. seniors putting bubble gum in a new student's hair.
D. a gang beating up a sixth-grader whom they disliked.

Inferences

___C___ 5. We can conclude that when Logan began sixth grade at the new school, he

See paragraphs 5–7.
George is the answer
to Logan's prayers
that he not be the
target of bullying.

A. became quite popular.
B. began to dress more fashionably.
C. was relieved to find someone who was more unpopular than he was.
D. became a bully himself.

___B___ 6. We can infer that by the time Logan was a high-school junior, he

See paragraph 18.
Logan's new height
and weight have given
him the courage to
stand up to a bully.

A. had gained a reputation for being a "psycho."
B. had gained self-confidence as a result of becoming taller and stronger.
C. had done his best to locate George in order to apologize to him.
D. had gotten into several fistfights with bullies.

___B___ 7. The author implies that

 A. the kids who picked on George did not really intend to be cruel.

 B. bullying can lead to terrible tragedies at schools.

 C. his sister is the victim of teasing, much as he was.

 D. George grew up to be a confident, well-adjusted person.

> See paragraph 25. (Sadly, stories about the tragic results of bullying are becoming increasingly common in the news.) Answers A, C, and D are not supported.

The Writer's Craft

___A___ 8. Logan begins his essay with

Logan does not describe the school, ask questions, or mention George in his introduction.

 A. an anecdote that illustrates the humiliation he suffered in elementary school.

 B. a description of his elementary school.

 C. a series of questions about the nature of bullying.

 D. a comparison of his school experience with George's.

___C___ 9. In paragraphs 2–4, the author

Logan mentions his small size, outdated clothing, thick glasses, crossed eyes, lisp, and lack of coordination—all traits that made him a "perfect target" for bullying. Answers A and B are too narrow; answer D is not supported.

 A. describes how his mother did her best to support him.

 B. contrasts his appearance with that of his classmates.

 C. lists specific reasons he was bullied while in elementary school.

 D. explains how he felt about being the target of a group of bullies.

___D___ 10. Logan's tone in paragraph 25 can best be described as

 A. nostalgic.

 B. detached.

 C. depressed.

 D. regretful.

> The phrases "still haunts me" and "a stricken face" indicate that Logan still sympathizes with the targets of bullying and regrets he did not do more to help them.

Discussion Questions

1. Paul Logan titled his essay "Rowing the Bus." Yet very little of the selection actually deals with the incident the title describes—only the first and last paragraphs. Why do you think Logan chose that title?

2. Logan wanted to be kind to George, but he wanted even more to be accepted by the other students. Have you ever found yourself in a similar situation—where you wanted to do the right thing but felt that it had too high a price? Explain what happened.

3. Logan refers to "a sinister code of childhood that demands there must always be someone to pick on." What does the phrase "a sinister code of childhood" mean to you? Why do children need someone to pick on?

4. The novelist Henry James once said, "Three things in human life are important. The first is to be kind. The second is to be kind. And the third is to be kind." Are there things that teachers, school administrators, parents, and other concerned adults can do to encourage young people to treat one another with kindness rather than cruelty?

Paragraph Assignments

1. Logan writes, "In each school, in each classroom, there is a George with a stricken face." Think of a person who filled the role of George in one of your classes. In a paragraph, describe why he or she was the target of bullying and what form that bullying took. Include a description of your own thoughts and actions regarding the student who was bullied. Your topic sentence could be something like the following: "In my eighth-grade class, _____ was a student who was often bullied."

2. Because he was afraid that his life would be made miserable, the author decided to stop being friends with George. How do you feel about that decision? Do you think it was cruel? Understandable? Were there other options Logan might have tried? Write a paragraph in which you evaluate Logan's decision. Suggest at least one other way he could have acted, and describe what the consequences might have been.

Essay Assignments

1. Some students, like the author and George, are singled out as targets for bullying. But other students are singled out for different reasons, positive as well as negative. For instance, besides "The Target," a school might have "The Brain," "The Troublemaker," "The Actor," "The Jock," "The Beauty," "The Clown," and other categories. Write an essay in which you describe two or three of your friends or acquaintances that have been singled out and labeled in this way. In your opinion, what did each of them do to earn this unique status?

2. In his essay, Logan provides vivid descriptions of incidents in which bullies attack other students. Reread those descriptions and consider what they tell you about the nature of bullies and bullying. Then write an essay that supports the following thesis: "Evidence in 'Rowing the Bus' and elsewhere suggests that most bullies share certain characteristics."

From reading this essay, and from your own observations, see if you can pick out several characteristics that many bullies share. You might also research this topic by Googling "characteristics of bullies." In your essay, describe three qualities of bullies. Support your claim with examples from the essay, from stories you have discovered in your research, or from your own experience. Include an introductory paragraph for your essay as well as a final paragraph with concluding thoughts.

23 The Rudeness Epidemic
Gary Wooten

Preview

Does it seem as though more and more people are being rude? If you answered "Yes," you are not alone. But the reason rudeness is spreading in epidemic proportions is more difficult to pin down. Wooten's essay explores what is considered rude, why our society is becoming ruder, and what we can do about it.

Words to Watch

quaint (1): old-fashioned
scenarios (2): situations
appalling (10): terrible
cues (19): signals
collective (24): shared by everyone

1   It is a time-honored practice to look fondly back at the "good old days" and declare that the modern world is going to hell in a handbasket. It is equally common for the younger generation to look back at earlier eras and find them conservative, backwards, and quaint°.

2   One hot-button issue that some-times (but not always) divides people along generational lines is the question of rudeness. Are we, in fact, becoming a ruder society? Or is society just changing, as it always does, to reflect modern ways of acting and thinking? As you consider your answer, read the following four scenarios° and answer the question: Rude or reasonable?

#1. A young woman named Ella is 3 having lunch with a friend at a restaurant. Ella's cell phone rings. She answers it, interrupting her friend's story about her new baby. After listening to the caller for a moment, Ella snaps, "I don't want any of the crap you're selling! Stop calling me, you *!#%!" Noticing her friend's irritated look, Ella shrugs. She defends her behavior because she hates getting sales calls that invade her privacy. She feels that she is the victim of the callers, and as such, she has the right to give them a piece of her mind.

4   **#2.** While driving home from work, in a hurry to pick up his child from school before it gets dark, Kyle sits right on the tail of the car in front of him. The car is in the fast lane but is just barely going the speed limit. Kyle grows increasingly agitated. He begins flashing his headlights at the other driver in an attempt to make him get out of his way. When that doesn't have any effect, Kyle leans on his horn and waves at the other driver to move over. Finally, Kyle angrily passes the car on the right, making a common gesture of rage out the window as he flies by. In Kyle's mind, he is in the right. The other driver deserved it for driving too slowly in the fast lane.

5   **#3.** Two couples are in a casual restaurant with their children, relaxing on a Saturday evening. The children are restless and keep getting out of their chairs. Although the parents tell the children not to wander too far away, they don't really keep a close eye on them. Pretty soon, the kids are running around the restaurant, playing tag, shrieking, and colliding with furniture. Other diners glare at them and their parents. Finally, the owner comes over and quietly asks the parents to restrain the children. One of the fathers gets angry. He points out that this is advertised as a "family restaurant" and that they are paying customers. The children, he says, are just having fun. And

besides, as he reminds the owner, "the customer is always right."

6   **#4.** In the middle of giving a speech to Congress, the president of the United States is interrupted by a member of the House of Representatives, who bellows out, "You lie!" Later, the congressman defends his actions by saying he was angry and upset with the president and wanted his voice to be heard. His supporters agree that he was bravely practicing "freedom of speech."

7   Do any of these scenarios seem shocking, disturbing, the kind of thing that couldn't (or at least shouldn't) really happen? Or do they seem like the kind of thing that you see every day? (Scenarios #1–#3 were invented; #4 actually did happen in 2009.)

8   If you perceive such incidents as both ordinary *and* rude, you're in the majority. According to a recent survey, the average American witnesses *seventeen* acts of what they consider rude behavior every week.

9   While we've all heard older people complain that young people today are not as polite as they were

back when *they* were young, what's happening today is different. Rudeness is not confined to thoughtless or badly-brought-up young people. It's not just the kids; it's *everybody*. Like the flu, rudeness has become contagious. And as a society, we seem to have become more accepting of it, even to the point of defending it.

10   In the world of the workplace, more than half of all workers complain about being unable to focus on their jobs because of inconsiderate coworkers. Loud gum-popping, nail-trimming, nose-blowing, and similar personal hygiene matters occur in shared workspaces. Door slamming and loud private conversations on cell phones (everybody's favorite horrible example) are other leading offenders. In general, there is an appalling° lack of self-awareness, along with an utter disregard for whether one's behavior might be bothering anyone else. As one New York office worker commented, "It's like no one even stops to question whether what they're doing is appropriate anymore."

11   This may sound like whining from stuffy, overly sensitive people. But statistics suggest otherwise. More than 40 percent of employees surveyed admit that they have been so overwhelmed or distracted by rude coworkers that their work suffers. Nearly a quarter of workers say they have actually left a job rather than put up with another worker's rudeness. And the cost of rudeness is not limited to the workplace. It is estimated that "road rage"—certainly an extreme form of rudeness—results in more than

$100 billion a year in accidents! Other incidents of civil misbehavior, from fist fights over parking spaces to shootings over loud music, lead to untold costs associated with medical care, courtroom activity, and the justice system.

12   Beyond the physical damage and expense that rudeness can cause, there is another and less easily measurable cost: the emotional damage that rudeness inflicts on people. Human beings, by nature, are social creatures. We have a deep-seated need for friendship, and we thrive in pleasant, unthreatening environments. When we are frequently bombarded by thoughtless behavior from strangers and friends, we suffer. We become increasingly guarded, unhappy, and depressed.

13   "I know it doesn't seem like a big deal," a woman commented in an interview about rudeness, "but when my best friend and I are together, she always keeps an eye on her phone. In the middle of our conversation, she's updating her status and commenting on other people's pictures. It's constant! It makes me feel like I'm not really there, or that I'm not important to her. It's kind of depressing."

14   Actually, it *is* a big deal. Being treated rudely not only makes people sad; it makes them withdraw and become less sensitive to the needs of others. In other words, it often makes *them* become rude.

15   An experiment in 2009 explored the way rudeness becomes contagious. It was conducted on the first day of classes in the hallways of a college classroom building. An actor, pretending to be a

professor, was placed in a busy hallway. As expected, a number of new students asked the "professor" for directions to a classroom or other typical first-day questions. To half of those students, the professor responded kindly and helpfully. But to the other half, he was extremely rude. "Do I look like a secretary?" was his typical nasty response. "I'm a busy professor. Figure it out for yourself."

16   After every interaction with a student, the fake professor walked away. Now another actor, pretending to be a student, hurried to the same spot and dropped her books all over the floor. The researchers doing the experiment watched to see how the students who had been treated rudely would respond, contrasted with those who had been treated kindly. The results were dramatic. Only 24 percent of the students who had been insulted offered to help the girl. Seventy-five percent of those who had been treated politely hurried to help her pick up her books.

17   The researchers interpreted the results this way: Rudeness actually disrupts our thinking process and makes us less likely to care about others. Furthermore, after repeated exposure to rude or mean behavior, people are far more likely to become rude themselves. And so, rudeness spreads from one person to another, from one group to another, and from coast to coast—the very definition of an epidemic.

18   But how did this epidemic start? The New Yorker quoted earlier said, "It's like no one even stops to question whether what they're doing is appropriate anymore." Why is that? And where did all this rudeness come from?

19   One culprit, in many people's minds, is technology. It isn't as simple as "the Internet is making us mean," but over the last few decades we have plunged abruptly into an online world where real-life etiquette rules don't seem to apply. In face-to-face discussions—the way we've conducted most of our communication for most of human history—we have learned to be sensitive to cues° from the other person. We've listened to tones of voice, watched facial expressions, and noticed body language. When we've seen that the other person was growing uncomfortable, embarrassed, angry, or humiliated, we generally backed off. We didn't want to be rude. Why didn't we? Because it was in our own self-interest to be polite. If we were rude, we estranged members of our own community (or tribe, or clan, or family, or whatever the social unit was), and we needed that community. Because we lived together, worked together, and played together, it made sense to stay on good terms with one another.

20   Not so on the Internet. It's a great deal easier to be unkind when we don't have to look someone in the eye. One-sided "conversations" in which we spout off our opinions and become hostile if anyone disagrees with us are the norm. Internet "trolls," who are aggressively and intentionally mean, get more attention than polite, reasonable people. And if we don't feel like responding to someone's question, invitation, demand, problem, or simple

hello, we don't have to. We can just ignore it.

21 Does all this online rudeness make us equally rude in real life? Many researchers suggest that it does. Over time, electronic socializing can lead to the loss of those real-life social skills. We forget how to make polite conversation or how to listen thoughtfully to someone else's point of view. We're even forgetting how to look someone in the eye. Many people today, instead of looking at their companions, stare constantly at their cell phones.

22 Another possible cause of the rudeness epidemic is a segment of culture that glorifies bullying and humiliation. While there is a great deal of talk about getting rid of bullying in schools, there doesn't seem to be much concern about bullying when it involves adults. Reality TV, in particular, makes stars of adults who are short-tempered, foul-mouthed, and downright rude. Watching strangers humiliate one another on national TV has become popular entertainment. After repeated viewings of this kind of meanness, it's not surprising that more of us have become ill-mannered and disrespectful ourselves. After all, if it's on TV every week, it must be OK . . . right?

23 Still another possible reason for unchecked rudeness is this: everyone is totally stressed out (possibly from dealing with all that rudeness!). Many of us feel we've got too much to do and not enough time to do it. Somehow we think that tailgating, flipping each other off, ignoring real people in favor of our cell phones, and disrespecting authority will not only give us a little more time in our day, but will relieve our stress. And the more acceptable we think these behaviors are, the more widespread and destructive the rudeness epidemic becomes.

24 So what can we do about our collective° rudeness?

25 The good news is that the majority of Americans recognize that we're all being too ill-tempered with one another. Acknowledging that we have a problem is a big step in the right direction. And becoming more polite is not a daunting task. Simply changing a few small behaviors can make a big difference to other people. For example, decide to stay off your phone when you are around friends and family. Smile at strangers. Say hello. Practice saying "please" and "thank you." Perform a random act of kindness every day.

26 And if you're not sure whether your behavior is rude or not, ask yourself: Would you want to be treated the way you're treating those around you?

27 There's a reason that the "Golden Rule" appears in nearly every faith and dates back thousands of years. "Do to others what you want them to do to you" is a simple and worthwhile guideline.

28 Our definitions of rudeness vary. We make excuses for bad manners. We're not even sure just why rudeness is escalating. But the remedy to putting an end to this spreading epidemic is in the hands of each of us. Remember that politeness, just like rudeness, is contagious.

First Impressions

Freewrite for ten minutes on one of the following.

1. Did you enjoy reading this selection? Why or why not?

2. If you had been in the same situation as Ella or Kyle or the children's parents, would you have reacted as they did? Explain.

3. Do you agree that rudeness in our society is epidemic? Why or why not?

Vocabulary Check

_____ B_____ 1. In the excerpt below, the word *restrain* means
   A. leave.
   B. control.
   C. educate.
   D. reward.

> What would a restaurant owner ask the parents to do about children who are running, playing tag, and shrieking?

"Pretty soon, the kids are running around the restaurant, playing tag, shrieking, and colliding with furniture. Other diners glare at them and their parents. Finally, the owner comes over and quietly asks the parents to restrain the children." (Paragraph 5)

_____ C_____ 2. In the sentence below, the word *utter* means
   A. outside.
   B. slight.
   C. complete.
   D. friendly.

> The actions described in the rest of paragraph 10 show a complete disregard for others.

"In general, there is an appalling lack of self-awareness, along with an utter disregard for whether one's behavior might be bothering anyone else." (Paragraph 10)

_____ D_____ 3. In the excerpt below, the word *daunting* means
   A. exciting.
   B. unpopular.
   C. usual.
   D. overwhelming.

> Changing a few small behaviors is not an overwhelming task.

"And becoming more polite is not a daunting task. Simply changing a few small behaviors can make a big difference to other people." (Paragraph 25)

_B_ 4. In the sentence below, the word *escalating* means
      A. dangerous.
      B. increasing rapidly.   The words *spreading epidemic* suggest
      C. historical.   that rudeness is increasing rapidly.
      D. attractive.

      "We're not even sure why rudeness is escalating. But the remedy to putting an end to this spreading epidemic is in the hands of each of us."
      (Paragraph 28)

Reading Check

Central Point and Main Ideas

_C_ 1. Which sentence best expresses the central point of the entire selection?
      A. No one can really understand why our culture is becoming ruder.

See paragraph 28. Answers A and B are not supported. Answer D covers only paragraphs 9–11.

      B. Although most Americans agree that there is a rudeness epidemic, very few people seem willing to help make a change.
      C. Although we are not sure why rude behavior is spreading, we can help end it by being kinder to one another.
      D. Rudeness is not just limited to young people anymore, as is particularly evident in the workplace.

_A_ 2. Which sentence best expresses the main idea of paragraphs 16 and 17?
      A. An experiment revealed that people are inclined to be rude if they are treated rudely.

Answers B, C, and D are not supported.

      B. An experiment revealed that the "rudeness epidemic" is a real problem with no solution.
      C. People behave rudely mainly as a result of an unpleasant experience.
      D. The experiment led researchers to understand why some people are rude, but it didn't help them understand why rudeness is spreading.

_B_ 3. Which sentence best expresses the main idea of paragraph 22?
      A. Although reality TV often involves bullying, it's not really harmful since it's only on television.
      B. Reality TV may encourage rudeness because it glorifies rude behavior.
      C. A great deal of reality TV presents people who are crude, mean, and foul-mouthed.
      D. We would probably be better off avoiding reality TV, since it encourages rude behavior.

      Answer A is not supported. Answer C covers only one detail of the paragraph. Answer D is an inference one might draw, but it is not the main idea of the paragraph.

Supporting Details

_C_ 4. According to the author, rudeness has become
   A. deadly.
   B. a nuisance.
   C. contagious.   See paragraph 9, the next-to-last sentence.
   D. a constant problem in our daily lives.

_D_ 5. When we interact face to face (instead of online), we receive cues from people, such as
   A. tones of voice.
   B. facial expressions.   See paragraph 19, sentence 4.
   C. body language.
   D. all of the above.

Inferences

_C_ 6. We can infer that the author
   A. doesn't own a cell phone.
   B. has been guilty of rude behavior on more than one occasion.
   C. believes that kindness can conquer rudeness.
   D. is bitter about being treated rudely so often.
                                     See paragraphs 25 and 28.

_A_ 7. Paragraphs 19–21 suggest that
   A. we should consider spending more time interacting face to face.
   B. most people who interact primarily on the Internet are usually rude.
   C. technology has damaged our ability to be kind to one another.
   D. we should get rid of our computers and phones.
                   The author indicates that face-to-face interactions make
                   us less rude. Therefore, answer A is a logical inference.

The Writer's Craft

_C_ 8. Wooten wrote this essay in order to
   A. entertain readers with funny and disturbing examples of common rude behavior.
   B. inform readers of the ways people are becoming increasingly rude in our country and how it is hurting us.
   C. persuade readers to consider the rudeness epidemic and act in ways that could help put an end to it.
   D. persuade readers to stop watching reality TV and curb their Internet and phone use.
        The imperatives in paragraph 25 (*decide to, Smile, Say, Practice, Perform*)
     and paragraph 28 (*Remember*) indicate that Wooten wants to persuade people
        to combat the rudeness epidemic. Answer D is not correct because Wooten
        emphasizes things we should *start* doing, not things we should *stop* doing.

_____D_____ 9. At the end of paragraph 22, when Wooten writes, "After all, if it's on TV every week, it must be OK . . . right?" he is
   A. being serious.
   B. expressing anger.
   C. asking the reader's opinion.
   D. being sarcastic.

> The entire selection is about the epidemic of rudeness and how to combat it. Therefore, the author is being sarcastic when he suggests that something that promotes rudeness is OK.

_____D_____ 10. To conclude his essay, the author uses
   A. a brief story.
   B. a series of questions.
   C. a summary.
   D. a final thought and recommendation.

> Recommendation: Being more polite is a way to combat the rudeness epidemic. Final thought: Politeness is contagious.

Discussion Questions

1. Does it surprise you that the majority of Americans think that people are rude and witness an average of seventeen rude acts a week? Why or why not?

2. Consider the examples of rudeness in paragraphs 3, 4, and 5. How would you handle or respond to each situation? Do you think the rude behavior in any of these examples is justified?

3. Do you prefer interacting online or in person? Explain.

4. What reasons—other than the ones presented here—might explain why our culture is growing ruder?

Paragraph Assignments

1. The woman whose friend is constantly looking at her phone when they're together says, "I know it doesn't seem like a big deal," when describing how it makes her feel. However, the author points out that, in fact, feeling ignored by a friend *is* a big deal. More and more, rude behavior seems to get excused and shrugged off, so much so that we may feel reluctant to complain about it or even mention it.

   Can you think of a time when you were treated rudely but, like the young woman in this essay, thought that others might not think it was "a big deal," so you didn't complain? Write a paragraph describing this incident and how it made you feel. Explain why it was clearly "a big deal" to you. How did you end up handling the rudeness?

2. While it may be true that we all witness numerous rude acts every week, we also (hopefully!) witness acts of kindness and thoughtfulness. The less common these random acts of kindness are, the more special

they become. Write a paragraph about several ways people could be kinder in everyday life. In each case, describe how the kind behavior will contrast with the unkind behavior that is all too common today.

Essay Assignments

1. Consider the fact that the majority of Americans think that the majority of Americans are rude. Logically, this would imply that most of us are rude at least some of the time. And some of us are rude a lot of the time.

    Are you ever rude? If you're like most people, you may be reluctant to admit or even acknowledge your not-so-nice behavior (see the four examples at the beginning of this essay). However, if you're also like most people, you're probably willing to make positive changes for the better.

    Write an essay in which you discuss three different times you've been rude or thoughtless. Perhaps these are unusual and isolated cases. Or maybe they're something you do regularly (like tailgating or talking loudly on your phone in public). Either way, describe what you've done or continue to do and why you thought it was justified at the time. Conclude each paragraph by considering how you might have handled things differently and what you might do differently in the future.

    Writing this kind of "confessional" essay may not be easy, but you will definitely learn something about yourself in the process. In addition, with any luck, what you learn may help you be a part of the movement to halt the rudeness epidemic.

2. You have probably heard your parents, grandparents, or other older people say that there was more courtesy back in "their day." It's true that every older generation tends to think the current generation is less polite and more ill-mannered. While this may or may not be the case, what is considered polite definitely changes to some extent from generation to generation.

    Write an essay in which you present three different examples of manners and etiquette that are different today from what they were in the past. You can easily research this topic by typing something like "manners and etiquette 1960s" (or 1950s, 1940s, etc.) into a search engine such as Google.

    In each paragraph, describe one particular example of good manners from an earlier time, and then contrast it with the corresponding behavior today. Be sure to give specific examples and details when describing the modern-day version to show how what is considered acceptable behavior has changed. You might end your essay, as Wooten does, by offering a final thought and recommendation.

24 Unexpected Kindness
Tim Whitaker

Preview

Sometimes the world can feel like a cold and uncaring place. However, as Tim Whitaker's experiences reveal, there are moments when one person's warmth and generosity can change everything.

Words to Watch

heady (10): exciting, stimulating
brusque (14): abrupt, rough
lethal (15): deadly
immaculately (17): flawlessly
robust (17): big and healthy
rhetorical (22): symbolic; a "rhetorical question" is a question that is asked more
    to make a point than to receive an answer
tenacity (39): persistence, drive to succeed
diatribe (63): angry rant
candor (64): honesty
debilitating (82): weakening

1   "Gratitude," the old jazzman Lionel Hampton once said, "is when memory is stored in the heart and not in the mind."

2   My memories of the three men I write about here are stored in my heart.

3   All three popped into my life out of nowhere and did something unexpectedly generous at a moment when I needed a kind turn. Then, nearly as fast as they were there for me, they disappeared. And yet they will always be with me, along with the lesson they taught—to believe in a goodness that lives in all of us.

4   It was *right here!* Where *is* it?

5   Little in life is more soul-crushing than returning to the place where you parked your car and finding it gone.

6   There are only two possibilities.

7   It was either towed or stolen.

8   In my case, the mystery was quickly solved when I looked up and read the

nearby sign: UNAUTHORIZED CARS WILL BE TOWED.

9   At that moment, like so many others back then, I flashed on what my father had been saying to me with a growing impatience for more than a year: Get your head on straight.

10   I was a junior in college at the time and having a pretty tough go of it. My grades were rocky, my mood edgy, and my parents not happy. Too often, instead of going to class, I would hang out with friends and indulge in long and heady° conversations that I somehow thought were critically important at the time. At my best, I would hop a train into the city to help disadvantaged kids with their homework. It sounds commendable, and it would have been, had it not been at the expense of the high-priced education I was receiving courtesy of my parents.

11   I fancied myself as a rebel with a cause or three, but at some level, I knew the truth: I was simply confused. Or, as my parents no doubt would have put it, confused and irresponsible.

12   And now, right on cue, another screwup.

13   I'd been given the family car, despite great reservations, for the weekend while my parents visited friends in Chicago. The weekend was almost over, and my parents would be arriving at the airport in the morning. I was scheduled to pick them up.

14   I called the towing company, and the brusque° voice on the other end told me that if I showed up with sixty bucks—*in cash*—I'd get the car back. No checks, no credit cards. And there was a ten-dollar charge for every extra day the car sat in their fenced-in lot.

15   Sixty dollars was like six times that today—and for a broke college kid, it might as well have been six figures. Nobody I knew had that kind of dough. Calling my parents for help would

unleash a lethal° brew of frustration and renewed gloom about my future. There had to be another way.

16   The situation called for a major sit-down at Campus Hoagies.

17   Every college has a favorite nearby sandwich shop. Ours was Campus Hoagies, owned by George and Marian (we never knew their last name), a kind and middle-aged Greek couple who said little and kept an immaculately° clean shop. Campus Hoagies had everything a college kid needed to escape reality: six stools, four booths, two pinball machines, chips, and robust° sandwiches.

18   It was the default place to go to commiserate over a failing grade or a busted romance. And in my case, a towed family car.

19   "What am I going to do, Hector?"

20   Hector was my college roommate. We had huddled at Campus Hoagies innumerable times in moments of crisis. Our preferred seats were the stools at the front counter where we could watch the sandwiches being made and keep an eye on the front door for cute girls and professors who didn't look kindly on our frequent absences.

21   "Where am I going to get sixty bucks?"

22   The question, considering whom I was talking to, was all but rhetorical°. Hector's family lived in a third-floor walkup in Bedford-Stuyvesant, and Hector himself was surviving on loans and subsidies. Flush for Hector was coming up with enough pocket change to pay for the hoagie in front of him.

23   Most of the time I was sensitive to Hector's fragile economic state. But in this moment only one thing mattered: I needed that car back. I was the one in a jam—not Hector. And why, come to think of it, was I always in jams like this? If I could find a way out of this mess and get that car, I would change for good. There'd be no more trouble.

24   "Where am I going to get sixty bucks?"

25   And then it happened. A miracle. I thought it a miracle then, and I think it a miracle now. Nothing less.

26   In a scene that unfolded in cinematic slow motion, George, the kindly Campus Hoagies proprietor, was stuffing cheese into a long hoagie roll in front of us. He finished, washed his hands, walked over to the cash register, banged it open, and peeled three twenty-dollar bills from the drawer.

27   He handed me the three twenties.

28   "You maybe go get your car back," he said.

29   I don't remember much of what I said. I'm sure I thanked George once, twice, maybe forty times. I'm sure I told him I'd pay him back. I'm sure I thought at that very moment that yes indeed, there certainly is a God and that I would worship him to my dying breath.

30   But, like I said, I don't remember much.

31   In fact, all these decades later, there's only one thing I do recall with certainty: how George made like it was no big deal.

32   *"You maybe go get your car back."*

33   The next morning, I was at the airport to greet my parents right on time. I asked them about their weekend,

told them I had no real news to report, and flipped the keys to my dad.

34   If you're wondering—yes, I did pay George back. It took a full semester and three separate payments, but every cent was paid.

35   Each time I made a payment to George, I would thank him all over again; and each time, he would act like he had forgotten all about it.

36   Today, Campus Hoagies is still in the same spot it was when I was a college student, though it's called the Campus Corner now.

37   George and Marian sold the place decades back, and it's been through several owners since. I drive past it maybe once a year or so, whenever I happen to be in the area. I sometimes think about going in and having a look around, seeing how the place has held up, but I haven't yet and suspect I never will.

38   "What do you know about selling?"

39   I had prepared for the job interview and was ready for the question. Though I had no sales experience, my father had been a successful sales executive, and I remembered the things he used to say about sales, most of which focused on the importance of tenacity°.

40   So I went with tenacity. What I didn't say in the job interview was that I didn't want to be a salesperson at all.

41   I wanted to be a newspaper writer.

42   All my heroes were newspaper writers. Jimmy Breslin and Gay Talese especially, because they were reporters and storytellers. The fact that they got to work in a newsroom, which I considered the coolest workplace in the world,

made the profession seem that much more magical.

43   My problem was I had no experience. I had never written a story for a newspaper. Not even for my high school or college newspaper. I had no clips to show an editor. And with no clips, there was no chance for scoring a job.

44   Which is how I found myself in this interview. If I couldn't *write* for a newspaper, maybe I could sell advertising space for one and work in the same building.

45   "I can do this job, sir. I just need a chance to prove it."

46   And then I talked about the value of tenacity when closing a sale—and it worked.

47   I got the job and was soon assigned a territory.

48   My professional objectives were clear: to hit my sales goals and buddy up to the editors in the building.

49   Being the new guy on the sales team, I was given the new guy sales territory, a part of the city where the businesses were struggling and the business owners were grumpy.

50   Typical exchange on my first few days on the job:

51   Me: "Hi, I'm Tim Whitaker, I'm from the *Globe* newspaper . . ."

52   Business owner: "Not interested, Tim Whitaker from the *Globe* newspaper. If I ever am interested, *I'll* call *you*."

53   Rejection became my constant companion. Still, I kept knocking on doors, selling the benefits of the *Globe* and picking up small sales along the way. Some weeks I'd even make my goal. More weeks, I fell short.

54   "Cold calls are the key to hitting goal," the *Globe*'s ad manager would preach at me when looking at my numbers. "You have to knock on even more doors."

55   "*Hellllllllo*, anyone here? I'm from the *Globe* newspaper."

56   I was standing just inside the doors of Harry's Tiles, a narrow hole-in-the-wall business on a deteriorating business strip. It was my last cold call of the day.

57   "Yeah, so, and I'm supposed to care why?"

58   From behind stacks of tiles and tubes of linoleum in the back of the store, a five-foot-six and slightly hunched-over older man I knew had to be Harry himself emerged and began walking toward me, talking the entire time.

59   "What's a newspaper ad going to do for me? Is it going to bring back the customers that shopped here for thirty years and then ran to the suburbs? Is it going to bring back the customers who used to care about quality and demand customized work? Is it going to stop people from shopping at big franchise stores? How is an ad in your beloved *Globe* going to change all that?"

60   "It's not."

61   That stopped Harry cold.

62   "What? Is that some kind of reverse sales psychology crap?"

63   Harry's diatribe° hit me at the end of an exhausting and futile day on the streets. My sales mojo had run dry. Besides, what Harry said was the truth: no ad in the *Globe* was going to change the course of his business. Time and change had seen to that.

64   Mystified by my candor°, Harry dropped the hard-bitten storekeeper attitude down a notch and asked me what I was hearing from other businesses. He said he had once believed you could make a success of anything with hard work, but was beginning to doubt that truth for the first time in his life.

65   I sat quietly on a stack of tiles and listened.

66   During the following weeks and months, I made Harry's Tiles one of my regular stops. I never tried to sell Harry an ad, and he never fully dropped his gruff persona. Every relationship needs unspoken rules, and those were ours.

67   Over time, I got comfortable enough to tell him I wanted to be a writer. He shook his head and told me about his deceased wife, who did everything right. She wrote him great letters when he was away at war. "She could have taught writing, she was so good," he said, certainty underscoring his words.

68   Thanks to a lot of tenacity, I began to get a few bylines in the newspaper— an occasional movie or book review mostly, the kind of writing I could do on the side nights and weekends. My sales job was another story. I desperately needed to hang onto the job while learning to write, but my sales numbers were flagging and the boss wasn't happy. Things were heading for a nasty showdown if I didn't soon start making goal.

69   The fate of my job came down to this one particular Friday. I had to make my goal. I spent the day knocking on doors and hustling best I could. Nothing.

Before heading back to the office where the week's numbers were being tallied, I stopped by Harry's to tell him I might be moving on. He didn't seem all that interested.

70   At the office, the sales manager greeted me at the door. "You are one lucky bastard," he said.

71   "Really?"

72   "Harry's Tiles just called in and bought four consecutive quarter-page ads. That puts you over goal."

73   The following Monday, when I stopped by to thank Harry, all he said was: "Got to get some beating hearts in this place some damn way."

74   It wasn't too many weeks after that I landed my first writing job at a newspaper. When I told Harry, he said it was about time. I took it as his way of congratulating me.

75   Six months or so after that, I drove back to my old territory to see Harry and found a FOR RENT sign on the door. I peered into the window and saw that the towering stacks of tiles had disappeared and the floor had been swept clean.

76   I didn't have a home address for Harry, and even if I did, I'm not sure he would have wanted me knocking on his door. It didn't seem to comply with our unspoken rules.

77   My car went suddenly dead as I turned the corner where Chestnut meets 20th in the heart of Center City Philadelphia. It was rush hour.

78   I turned the key in the ignition. It wanted to start, sounded like it might, but wouldn't catch. I tried again.

79   Nothing.

80   And again.

81   The cars behind me showed no mercy. First there was one horn. Then there were 117.

82   A debilitating° kind of discomfort seeps in a situation like this.

83   There's no right move. You can't think.

84   I kept turning the key.

85   The car was ten years old. It had been having problems—brakes, electrical, tires.

86   *Why was I always buying tires?*

87   Suddenly, a thump on the trunk. I turned around and saw a wiry guy's face, eyes wide as a big league slugger stepping in against a slow-pitch softball pitcher, flush against my rear window. He had both hands against the rear of my car.

88   "I'm going to push," he shouted. "When I say go, pop the clutch, got it?"

89   He pushed. The car was rolling.

90   "Go!"

91   I popped. Nothing.

92   "Again!"

93   Nothing.

94   He pushed the car to a safe spot along 20th Street and came up to my window.

95   "You're out of gas."

96   "Really?"

97   "All it can be. Battery's not dead. It would have kicked when you popped the clutch. It didn't. No gas."

98   It wasn't impossible. The electrical problems had screwed up the gas gauge. For months I'd been playing a guessing game about how much gas was in the tank. I could have sworn it was at least half full.

99 "I'm going to get gas. You stay here. I live on the street. I need you to watch my rain gear. It's right there."

100 The wiry guy pointed to some stuff against a wall on the sidewalk.

101 I gave him a ten-dollar bill.

102 "All I need is a one."

103 "Please, take the ten."

104 He grabbed it and ran off.

105 I sat in my car, watching his stuff as people walked past on the sidewalk. I started worrying, what if somebody runs off with his rain gear?

106 I had to put his stuff in my car.

107 I jumped out of the car, and when I bent over to get it, I saw it wasn't rain gear at all.

108 It was a rein*deer.*

109 A reindeer vase.

110 I'd clearly misheard the man.

111 The reindeer vase was filled with cards and papers. I'm guessing the cards and papers were of major value to him.

112 *"Where's my reindeer?"*

113 He was back at my car window with a glass Coke bottle in one hand and a Big Gulp cup in the other. He said he had been to the closest gas station, five blocks away.

114 You try to picture the walk back to my car with a Coke bottle and a Big Gulp cup filled with gas. But you just can't, and it may be that you just don't want to.

115 "Reindeer is right here, next to me."

116 "Good, pop the gas cap."

117 A young guy starts crossing the street. He's heading right for the gas tank. He's smoking.

118 "Stop right there."

119 My new friend holds up the cup and the bottle and points to the gas tank.

120 "Right *there.* Unless the day has come to meet your maker, friend."

121 The young guy quickly scurries away.

122 He begins pouring the gas into the tank. It only takes a few minutes, but in those few minutes I learn a few things about my new friend. He's got skills, he tells me. Mechanical skills, handyman skills, you wouldn't believe. But no one seems to care. He has never begged for money and never will.

123 "People work hard for their money, especially these days, and my mother didn't raise me to take advantage."

124 He likes helping people, feeling useful, like he feels right now. He looks for opportunities to be useful. That way maybe he can earn a dollar with his usefulness.

125 "Okay, now get in there and give it a try, should be good for you."

126 He turns the bottle and the cup upside down to get rid of the last drops of gas.

127 I turn the key. The car starts right up.

128 I hand my friend his reindeer and a few bills. He tucks the reindeer under his arm and puts the bills in his pocket without looking.

129 "Happy to help," he says, disappearing into the crowd on the sidewalk.

130 A few minutes later, as I stop at a gas station to fill up, it starts to rain, ever so gently, as it does every spring.

First Impressions

Freewrite for ten minutes on one of the following.

1. Did you enjoy reading this selection? Why or why not?

2. Has a person ever unexpectedly offered you help? Describe the experience.

3. Have you ever offered unasked-for help to a stranger? Why did you do it? How did you feel about yourself afterward?

Vocabulary Check

_D_ 1. In the excerpt below, the word *commendable* means
   A. required.
   B. difficult.
   C. selfish.
   D. admirable.

   > Helping disadvantaged kids is an admirable thing to do.

   "At my best, I would hop a train into the city to help disadvantaged kids with their homework. It sounds commendable, and it would have been, had it not been at the expense of the high-priced education I was receiving courtesy of my parents." (Paragraph 10)

_B_ 2. In the sentence below, the word *unleash* means
   A. tie up.
   B. let loose.
   C. support.
   D. forgive.

   > We have been told that his parents are unhappy with his irresponsibility (paragraphs 9–11). Therefore, it is logical that telling them the car has been towed will let loose a new stream of frustration from them.

   "Calling my parents for help would unleash a lethal brew of frustration and renewed gloom about my future." (Paragraph 15)

_A_ 3. In the excerpt below, the word *commiserate* means
   A. sympathize.
   B. argue.
   C. think.
   D. look.

   > What do friends do when they are upset about something?

   "Every college has a favorite nearby sandwich shop. . . . Campus Hoagies had everything a college kid needed to escape reality: six stools, four booths, two pinball machines, chips, and robust sandwiches.

   "It was the default place to go to commiserate over a failing grade or a busted romance." (Paragraphs 17–18)

_C_   4. In the excerpt below, the word *flagging* means
   A. waving.
   B. growing.   If his boss is getting upset with him, what must
   C. becoming weak.   be happening to his sales numbers?
   D. confusing.

> "My sales job was another story. I desperately needed to hang onto the
> job while learning to write, but my sales numbers were flagging and the
> boss wasn't happy. Things were heading for a nasty showdown if I didn't
> soon start making goal." (Paragraph 68)

Reading Check

Central Point and Main Ideas

_D_   1. Which sentence best expresses the central point of the entire selection?

Answer D is
established in
paragraph 3. Answer
A is not supported.
Answer B is too
general. Answer C
states some details
mentioned in the
selection, but it is not the central point.

   A. It is very rare and unexpected for a stranger to offer help in today's
      society.
   B. Tim Whitaker received unexpected help from various people.
   C. Tim Whitaker was irresponsible as a college student, but hard work
      and determination helped him grow into a successful young man.
   D. Because of the unexpected kindness shown by three people, Whitaker
      came to believe that all people are basically good.

_C_   2. Which sentence best expresses the main idea of paragraph 68?

Answer A is not
supported. Answer
B covers only the
first sentence of the
paragraph. Answer
D covers only the
last two sentences.

   A. Whitaker's boss didn't know that Whitaker was writing articles for
      the paper on the side.
   B. Thanks to his tenacity, Whitaker's dream of becoming a writer was
      slowly coming true.
   C. Whitaker needed to keep his sales job while he learned to write, but
      he wasn't making enough sales.
   D. If Whitaker didn't make his sales goals soon, he and his boss were
      going to have a fight.

Supporting Details

_A_   3. Whitaker's friend, Hector, did not have much
   A. money.
   B. common sense.
   C. luck with girls.   See paragraph 22.
   D. all of the above.

_____C_____ 4. Whitaker needed the car back right away because

A. he had a date that evening.

See paragraphs 2–3.   B. he needed it to get to classes.

C. he had to pick up his parents at the airport in the morning.

D. he needed it to go to an interview at the newspaper.

Inferences

_____D_____ 5. We can infer that Harry finally

A. retired and moved away.

Item 6: The actions   B. sold his tile store to someone else.   Paragraph 75 suggests
of each of the   this inference.
three men   C. regretted buying all those ads.
(paragraphs 31–32,
73, and   _____F_____ 6. TRUE OR FALSE? Whitaker implies that all three men who helped him
128–129)
show this statement   expected something in return, even if they didn't say so.
is false.

_____B_____ 7. We can conclude from this essay that the author

A. did not receive the help he needed on other occasions.

B. was changed in a positive way as a result of the kindness of others.

C. got along better with his parents after he graduated from college.

D. believes that most people would not be as generous as the three men

he describes.   The last sentence of paragraph 3 suggests answer B.

The Writer's Craft

_____B_____ 8. The author begins his essay with Lionel Hampton's definition of

gratitude because

A. gratitude is the opposite of what he is writing about.

B. it expresses how he feels about the three men who helped him.

C. he wants to make sure his readers know what the word *gratitude*

means.

D. he wants to attract his readers' attention by quoting a famous

musician.   See paragraphs 2–3.

_____C_____ 9. The author's main purpose for writing "Unexpected Kindness" was to

A. entertain readers with unusual stories about people from his past.

B. inform readers about how he was able to get out of difficult situations.

C. persuade readers that most people are basically good and kind.

D. persuade readers that tenacity is the key to success.

By telling us about these three men, Whitaker hopes to
persuade us what he believes—that there is "a goodness
that lies in all of us" (paragraph 3).

___D___ 10. The author's tone in this essay is best described as

    A. serious.

    B. sarcastic.

    C. disapproving.

    D. appreciative.

> The appreciative tone is set in paragraphs 2–3 and continues in Whitaker's portrayal of the three men.

Discussion Questions

1. Of the three men who unexpectedly helped Tim Whitaker, whose actions impressed you the most? Why?

2. Harry, the owner of the tile shop, was initially rejecting and even rude to Tim. What do you think changed his attitude? What might Whitaker have learned from this experience? What might *we* learn?

3. Do you think any of the three men who helped Tim Whitaker expected anything in return? Why or why not?

4. In your opinion, would most people respond with kindness to a stranger who needed help? Explain. What might we, as a society, do to encourage even more people to help others?

Paragraph Assignments

1. Write a paragraph *either* about a time you received unexpected help, *or* a time you offered unasked-for help to a stranger. Describe the scene fully, so your reader can picture exactly what happened. Finish your paragraph by telling how you felt afterward. Like Whitaker, did you learn from the experience?

2. It was the Greek philosopher Philo of Alexandria who expressed these words, which have survived through the centuries: "Be kind, for everyone you meet is fighting a hard battle." Write a paragraph in which you explain what you think is meant here. In what ways are many people fighting a hard battle, and why is it important to be kind?

Essay Assignments

1. Whitaker's essay begins with a reference to memories being stored in his heart. Clearly, he will never forget the three men who came to his aid when he needed help the most. Who are three people in your life who have helped you out of troublesome or potentially dangerous situations? Write an essay about these three people and the specific help they gave you at a particular time, devoting a separate paragraph to each person. Your thesis statement could be like one of the following:

   - Like Tim Whitaker, I will never forget three people who were there for me when I most needed them.

   - Three people—_____, _____, and _____—were unexpectedly kind to me when I was in a crisis situation.

   Alternatively, write an essay about three people you remember for negative reasons. As you write, focus on specific incidents that vividly demonstrate the people's bad qualities.

2. Write an essay in which you describe three ways that people could be kinder to each other in everyday life. You may want to research this topic first by Googling "kindness in everyday life." You may also get some ideas for this paper by reading the essay in this book titled "The Rudeness Epidemic."

25 Love
Lisa Scottoline

Preview

Valentine's Day is great—unless you're single. Then it feels like a holiday invented specifically to make you feel like a loser. But according to well-known mystery author and humorist Lisa Scottoline, there's always an opportunity for love on the day of hearts and flowers. It just depends on how you define love.

Words to Watch

Middle Ages (6): a period of time in Europe that lasted from about the 5th to the 15th century
sketchy (9): questionable or unclear
maxim (13): a well-known saying

1　Whenever Valentine's Day comes up, the newspaper, TV, and stores are full of heart-shaped candy boxes, roses, and jewelry for "that special someone." The holiday has become a celebration of romantic love, and that's great if you're in a romance or you're married, which is like having an automatic valentine.

2　But not everyone is so lucky.

3　There are plenty of people who aren't seeing someone right now, which is code for haven't had a date in 55 years. Like me. And that's okay, every day except Valentine's Day.

4　Single people feel like losers on Valentine's Day. They're left out of the hearts and candy. They become wallflowers at the party of life.

5　This is sad, and wrong. I think it's time to revisit the way we think about Valentine's Day. So welcome to another trademark Scottoline time-to-change-things story, wherein my bossy and controlling nature works to my advantage, for once.

6　To begin with, I did some research, and I learned that St. Valentine's Day was intended to celebrate a loving man, a priest so sweet, giving, and devout that he became a saint. Historically, his day had nothing to do with romance. In fact, it wasn't until the Middle Ages°, when Geoffrey Chaucer wrote a poem entitled *The Parliament of Foules*, that St. Valentine's Day became associated with romantic love.

7   Aha! So the link between Valentine's Day and romance is pure fiction. Chaucer made it up, and trust me, he did it to move some poems. Sex sells. Romance novels are bestsellers for a reason, and even my books have sex scenes, which I write from memory.

8   And now I forget.

9   Given that the history of the holiday is so sketchy°, I feel free to write on a clean slate. In other words, I can make it up, too. And if you ask me, Valentine's Day is really about love. Not only romantic love, but also just plain love. And if you're not married or seeing someone, you can still have love in your life.

10   Observe.

11   In my case, I have tons of love in my life. I love my kid, my family, and my friends. I love the people I work with. I love my readers. I love my dogs, cats, and pony. I love spaghetti. I love opera. I love books. I love Brad Pitt in *Legends of the Fall*.

12   In short, I love.

13   If I were going to improve on that maxim° of Descartes, "I think, therefore I am," I'd say, "I love, therefore I am." Or instead of Pope's saying, "To err is human," I'd go with, "To love is human." Plus I agree completely with that great philosopher James Taylor, who tells us to "shower the people you love with love."

14   So I propose that, on Valentine's Day, we celebrate love. Shower the people you love with love. Don't take

each other for granted. Recognize that we grow more valuable to each other as time passes, not less. Raise a glass to someone you love, in celebration of an emotion that powers our best intentions, leads to our greatest happiness, and gives us the stories of the world's greatest operas, movies, and novels.

15   In addition to *Gossip Girl*.

16   Now, there may be some of you reading this who have no one. Maybe you've lost someone, or they're far away, and you're left hiding in your house or apartment, waiting for Valentine's Day to pass.

17   Here's my advice to you:

18   Find the love in your life, because it's all around you. And if you can't find it, make it yourself.

19   Make love.

20   And by that, I don't mean **match. com.**

21   I mean adopt a dog and love it. Buy a pretty collar and walk it around the block. A cat works, too. Cats like pretty collars, even though they're too proud to say so. Or get a fish. There's no shame in love you can buy, even if it has scales. I don't think goldfish get enough credit. Not everybody can look good in orange.

22   Or read a book that everyone says is great. You'll find a story you love, and maybe an author. Or if you don't like to read, go see *Legends of the Fall*. You'll love Brad Pitt, whether you're a man or a woman.

23   And if none of that appeals to you, volunteer at a shelter or a hospital. Cook a meal for the parents at a Ronald McDonald House, like a friend of mine did.

24   Because the thing about love is that we can't control whether we get it, but we can control whether we give it.

25   And each feels as good as the other.

26   Your heart doesn't know whether it's loving a man, a TV show, or a guppy. If your heart were that smart, it would be your brain.

27   All your heart knows is that it's full and happy, and you will feel alive and human.

28   And next time, you will have a wonderful Valentine's Day.

29   And, better yet, a wonderful life.

First Impressions

Freewrite for ten minutes on one of the following.

1. Did you enjoy reading this selection? Why or why not?

2   Do you agree that "single people feel like losers on Valentine's Day"? Why or why not?

3. Some people dislike holidays because they feel as if there is too much pressure to be happy, even if they are not happy. How do you feel about holidays? Are there any holidays you wish *didn't* exist?

Vocabulary Check

___B___ 1. In the excerpt below, the word *wallflowers* means
    A. attractive, likeable people.
    B. shy, unnoticed people.
    C. interruptions.
    D. painful reminders.

> If the single people are left out of the celebration, they will become like shy, unnoticed people at a party.

> "Single people feel like losers on Valentine's Day. They're left out of the hearts and candy. They become wallflowers at the party of life." (Paragraph 4)

___C___ 2. In the excerpt below, the word *propose* means
    A. refuse.
    B. admire.
    C. suggest.
    D. remember.

> The second sentence explains what the author suggests we do to celebrate love.

> "So I propose that, on Valentine's Day, we celebrate love. . . . Raise a glass to someone you love, in celebration of an emotion that powers our best intentions, leads to our greatest happiness, and gives us the stories of the world's greatest operas, movies, and novels." (Paragraph 14)

Reading Check

Central Point and Main Ideas

___D___ 1. Which sentence best expresses the central point of the entire selection?

Scottoline makes this point in the final four paragraphs of the selection. Answer A covers only the detail in paragraph 4, answer B only the detail in paragraph 6, and answer C only the detail in paragraphs 9–12.

    A. Valentine's Day makes many single people feel lonely and unloved.
    B. A holiday that we associate with celebrating romantic love actually had nothing to do with that kind of love originally.
    C. We need to remember that there are many other kinds of love than romantic love.
    D. If you are single, celebrating *any* kind of love on Valentine's Day can make you happier.

___B___ 2. The main idea of paragraphs 6 and 7 is that
    A. we have all been fooled about the history of Valentine's Day.
    B. the connection between Valentine's Day and romance was a fictional idea created by Chaucer.
    C. Chaucer connected Valentine's Day to romantic love in order to sell poems.
    D. the origins of many holidays have nothing to do with how they're observed today.

> Answers A and D are not supported. Answer C covers only one humorous detail in the paragraphs.

___C___ 3. The main idea of paragraphs 18–23 is that
    A. there are various things you can do to take your mind off Valentine's Day.
    B. romantic love is actually not as wonderful as other kinds of love.
    C. love can be experienced and expressed in a number of different ways.
    D. above all, volunteering to help others is the best way to share your love.
           The paragraphs suggest several ways of creating love in your life. Answers A, B, and D are not supported.

Supporting Details

___D___ 4. Saint Valentine was
    A. a poet from the Middle Ages.
    B. a fictional character.
           See the first sentence of paragraph 6.
    C. the creator of Valentine's Day.
    D. a kind and loving priest.

___A___ 5. Scottoline points out that as time passes, we all become more _____ to one another.
    A. valuable
    B. lovable
           See the fourth sentence of paragraph 14.
    C. annoying
    D. distant

Inferences

___C___ 6. We can conclude from this selection that the author
    A. has a lot of single friends.
    B. is often unhappy on Valentine's Day.
           See paragraph 3.
    C. is not married or in a relationship.
    D. is bossy and opinionated.

___B___ 7. We can conclude from this selection that most people
    A. don't particularly like Valentine's Day.
    B. tend to think of Valentine's Day as a day to celebrate only romantic love.
    C. spend Valentine's Day hiding inside their homes and wishing it was over.
    D. find unusual ways to celebrate love on Valentine's Day.
           Paragraph 1 suggests the inference.

The Writer's Craft

8. Which of the following statements best describes the author's purpose in writing this selection?

A. To inform readers about how the holiday of Valentine's Day got started

B. To entertain readers with details about her own private life and the things she loves

C. To entertain readers with amusing sarcasm about what "love" really is

D. To persuade readers to find a way to include love in their lives

9. Overall, what is the author's tone throughout this selection?

A. Humorous but sincere

B. Sincere but sarcastic

C. Thoughtful but irritated

D. Depressed but hopeful

10. What audience did Scottoline seem to have in mind when she wrote this essay?

A. Single older women

B. Young adults who are not in a relationship

C. Recently divorced adults of any age

D. Adults of any age who are single or not in a relationship

Discussion Questions

1. Most people in a relationship feel obligated to get *something* for their loved one on Valentine's Day, even if it's only a card. Retailers, of course, use this holiday to pressure people into buying jewelry, expensive flowers, clothes, and even cars! Do you think Valentine's Day gifts are unnecessary? On the other hand, if you received nothing from the person you love on Valentine's Day, would you feel upset? Explain.

2. Although Valentine's Day places a lot of emphasis on how great it is to be in a romantic relationship, some people actually prefer being single. Why might some people feel this way? Do you think being alone is ever preferable to being half of a couple? Why or why not?

3. Scottoline writes that "the thing about love is that we can't control whether we get it, but we can control whether we give it." What does she mean by this? Do you agree with Scottoline that people can, in fact, control whether or not they give love? Why or why not?

4. Scottoline lists a number of things to love on Valentine's Day other than another person. Can you think of other things that you love and that make your heart "full and happy"? Explain.

Paragraph Assignments

1. What was your very best (or very worst) Valentine's Day? Write a paragraph describing that day and why it was so special or so awful. Be sure to include specific details that make the day real for the reader. What happened? How did you feel? Looking back on that day, did you learn anything from it?

2. We have specific holidays that celebrate love, thankfulness, mothers, fathers, and veterans. Is there a holiday we *should* have that we *don't* have? Can you think of something you think should be celebrated that isn't? Write a paragraph that gives this holiday a name, explains why we should have this new holiday, and describe in detail how the holiday would be celebrated. What new traditions could be started?

Essay Assignments

1. Scottoline, borrowing from the singer James Taylor, suggests that we should "shower the people we love with love." So often, we take the people we love for granted and forget to let them know how we feel. Write an essay about three people you love that you might, occasionally, take for granted. Describe something special that you would do or say to let them know that you love them. What would mean the most to each person? How would you go about providing this special gesture for them, and how do you think they would respond?

2. As Scottoline points out, the origins of Valentine's Day are a little sketchy at best. In fact, there are details about the origins of many holidays that are surprising and unusual. Research the origins of three different holidays, and write an essay that presents unexpected details about the beginnings of each one. You can find helpful information by searching online for "holiday origins," or searching specifically by typing in, for example, "why we celebrate Halloween." You may be surprised by what you find!

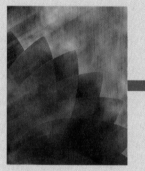

Unit Four

Educating Ourselves

26 The Fist, the Clay, and the Rock
Donald Holland

Preview

Often the best teachers are the ones who challenge us the most. In this selection, the author describes such a teacher. Mr. Gery inspires his students to work hard by using nothing more than his fist, a lump of clay, a rock—and a few well-chosen words. Read how he does it.

Words to Watch

wizard (11): magician
segued (17): moved smoothly onto another subject
vivid (17): strikingly bright; true to life

1 The best teacher I ever had was Mr. Gery, who taught 12th grade English. He started his class with us by placing on the front desk a large mound of clay and, next to it, a rock about the size of a tennis ball. That got our attention quickly, and the class quieted down and waited for him to talk.

2 Mr. Gery looked at us and smiled and said, "If there were a pill I could give you that would help you learn, and help you want to learn, I would pass it out right now. But there is no magic pill. Everything is up to you."

3 Then Mr. Gery held up his fist and kind of shook it at us. Some of us looked at each other. What's going on? we all thought. Mr. Gery continued: "I'd like you to imagine something for me. Imagine that my fist is the real world— not the sheltered world of this school, but the real world. Imagine that my fist is everything that can happen to you out in the real world."

4 Then he reached down and pointed to the ball of clay and also the rock. He said, "Now imagine that you're either this lump of clay or you're the rock. Got that?" He smiled at us, and we waited to see what he was going to do.

5 He went on, "Let's say you're this ball of clay, and you're just sitting around

minding your own business, and then, out of nowhere, here's what happens." He made a fist again, and he smashed his fist into the ball of clay, which quickly turned into a half-flattened lump.

6　　He looked at us, still smiling. "If the real world comes along and takes a swing at you, you're likely to get squashed. And you know what, the real world *will* come along and take a swing at you. You're going to take some heavy hits. Maybe you already have taken some heavy hits. Chances are that there are more down the road. So if you don't want to get squashed, you're better off if you're not a piece of clay.

7　　"Now let's say you're the rock, and the real world comes along and takes a swing at you. What will happen if I smash my fist into this rock?" The answer was obvious. Nothing would happen to the rock. It would take the blow and not be changed.

8　　He continued, "So what would you like to be, people, the clay or the rock? And what's my point? What am I trying to say to you?"

9　　Someone raised a hand and said, "We should all be rocks. It's bad news to be clay." And some of us laughed, though a bit uneasily.

10　　Mr. Gery went on. "OK, you all want to be rocks, don't you? Now my question is, How do you get to be a rock? How do you make yourself strong, like the rock, so that you won't be crushed and demolished even if you take a lot of hits?"

11　　We didn't have an answer right away, and he went on, "You know I can't be a wizard°. I can't pull out a wand and

say, 'Thanks for wanting to be a rock. I hereby wave my wand and make you a rock.' That's not the way life works. The only way to become a rock is to go out and make yourself a rock.

12　　"Imagine you're a fighter getting ready for a match. You go to the gym, and maybe when you start, you're flabby. Your whole body is flab, and it's soft like the clay. To make your body hard like a rock, you're got to train.

13　　"Now if you want to train and become hard like the rock, I can help you. You need to develop skills, and you need to acquire knowledge. Skills will make you strong, and knowledge is power. It's my job to help you with language skills. I'll help you train to become a better reader. I'll help you train to be a better writer. But you know, I'm just a trainer. I can't make you be a fighter.

14　　"All I can do is tell you that you need to make yourself a fighter. You need to become a rock. Because you don't want to be flabby when the real world comes along and takes a crack at you. Don't spend the semester just being Mr. Cool

Man or Ms. Designer Jeans or Mr. or Ms. Sex Symbol of the class. Be someone. *Be someone.*"

15 He then smashed that wad of clay one more time, and the thud of his fist broke the silence and then created more silence. He sure had our total attention.

16 "At the end of the semester, some of you are going to leave here, and you're still going to be clay. You're going to be the kind of person that life can smush around, and that's sad. But some of you, maybe a lot of you, are going to be rocks. I want you to be a rock. Go for it. And when this comes"—and he held up his fist—"you'll be ready."

17 And then Mr. Gery segued° into talking about the course. But his demonstration stayed with most of us. And as the semester unfolded, he would call back his vivid° images. When someone would not hand in a paper and make a lame excuse, he would say, "Whatever you say, Mr. Clay" or "Whatever you say, Ms. Clay." Or if someone would forget a book, or not study for a test, or not do a reading assignment, he would say, "Of course, Mr. Clay." Sometimes we would get into it also and call out, "Hey, Clayman."

18 Mr. Gery worked us very hard, but he was not a tyrant. We all knew he was a kind man who wanted us to become strong. It was obvious he wanted us to do well. By the end of the semester, he had to call very few of us Mr. or Ms. Clay.

First Impressions

Freewrite for ten minutes on one of the following.

1. Did you enjoy reading this selection? Why or why not?

2. What does Mr. Gery mean by "clay"? What is the danger of being clay?

3. What does Mr. Gery mean by "rock"? How does one become a rock?

Vocabulary Check

___B___ 1. In the sentence below, the word *demolished* means
A. delivered.
B. destroyed.
C. easy to see.
D. confused.

> The word *crushed* suggests that *demolished* means "destroyed."

"'How do you make yourself strong, like the rock, so that you won't be crushed and demolished even if you take a lot of hits?'" (Paragraph 10)

_D_   2. In the excerpt below, the word *acquire* means
   A. to ignore.
   B. to be given.
   C. to put away.
   D. to get.

> In addition to helping students develop skills, a teacher can help students get knowledge.

> "'Now if you want to train and become hard like the rock, I can help you. You need to develop skills, and you need to acquire knowledge.'" (Paragraph 13)

_B_   3. In the sentence below, the word *lame* means
   A. reasonable.
   B. weak.
   C. amusing.
   D. crippled.

> The student's excuse must have been weak if it caused Mr. Gery to call the student "Mr. Clay" or "Ms. Clay."

> "When someone would not hand in a paper and make a lame excuse, he would say, 'Whatever you say, Mr. Clay' or 'Whatever you say, Ms. Clay.'" (Paragraph 17)

_A_   4. In the excerpt below, the word *tyrant* means
   A. bully.
   B. leader.
   C. madman.
   D. troublemaker.

> A kind man who wants to help his students is the opposite of a bully.

> "Mr. Gery worked us very hard, but he was not a tyrant. We all knew he was a kind man who wanted us to become strong." (Paragraph 18)

Reading Check

Central Point and Main Ideas

_D_   1. Which sentence best expresses the central point of the entire selection?
   A. Mr. Gery forced his students to become fighters.
   B. Mr. Gery was good at getting his students to pay attention.
   C. Mr. Gery was not a tyrant, but he worked his students hard.
   D. Mr. Gery challenged his students to learn skills that would help them in the real world.

> Answer A is not supported. Answers B and C are too narrow; they do not cover the entire selection.

___B___ 2. Which sentence best expresses the main idea of paragraph 6?

Answer A is not supported. Answer C is too narrow; it covers only a detail in sentence 6. Answer D is contradicted by the last sentence of the paragraph.

    A. Mr. Gery wants his students to know that they're going to take some heavy hits.

    B. Mr. Gery wants his students to prepare themselves to take some heavy hits.

    C. Mr. Gery realizes that some of his students have already taken some heavy hits.

    D. Mr. Gery doesn't want his students to be like rocks.

___C___ 3. Which sentence best expresses the main idea of paragraph 13?

    A. All students need to acquire skills and knowledge in order to be strong.

    B. Mr. Gery's main job is to help students acquire language skills.

    C. Mr. Gery can train his students, but he can't make them "rocks"— they have to do that themselves.

    D. Mr. Gery admits that his training might not be enough to help his students grow stronger. Answers A, B, and D are not supported.

___A___ 4. Which sentence best expresses the main idea of paragraph 17?

    A. When students did not do their work, Mr. Gery often referred to his clay and rock talk by calling the students Mr. or Ms. Clay.

    B. Mr. Gery enjoyed singling out those who were poor students and calling them Mr. and Ms. Clay.

    C. At first, students weren't sure what to make of Mr. Gery calling those who didn't do their work Mr. and Ms. Clay, but in time, even the students joined in.

    D. In spite of Mr. Gery's vivid discussion that first day, some students still made up lame excuses for not turning in work.

Answers B and C are not supported. Answer D covers only sentence 4.

Supporting Details

___D___ 5. Mr. Gery compares his fist to

    A. a rock.

    B. a lump of clay. See paragraph 3.

    C. a magic wand.

    D. everything that can happen out in the real world.

___B___ 6. Mr. Gery's job is to

    A. provide his students with shelter.

    B. help his students with language skills. See paragraph 13.

    C. train his students to become boxers.

    D. teach his students social studies.

Inferences

_____C_____ 7. We can infer that

See the last three
sentences of
paragraph 14.
Answers A, B, and D
are not supported.

    A. Mr. Gery was once a professional boxer.

    B. Mr. Gery had little experience in the real world.

    C. some of the students in Mr. Gery's class weren't used to taking school seriously.

    D. many of Mr. Gery's students failed his course.

_____D_____ 8. We can infer that the author

    A. was one of the students that Mr. Gery called "Mr. Clay" at the end of the semester.

    B. became an English teacher like Mr. Gery.

    C. thought Mr. Gery should have been harder on the class.

    D. learned a great deal from Mr. Gery.

> Answer D is supported by paragraph 1 and by the appreciation the author's words show for Mr. Gery. Answers A, B, and C are not supported.

The Writer's Craft

_____B_____ 9. The main reason Holland wrote "The Fist, the Clay, and the Rock" was to

This reason is
summed up in
paragraph 13.

    A. tell a funny story about one of his favorite teachers from high school.

    B. point out that reading and writing are important skills in the real world.

    C. compare teaching language skills to training a fighter.

    D. describe a teacher's unusual approach.

_____A_____ 10. Holland uses dialogue throughout this selection in order to

    A. make the selection vivid and engaging.

    B. show how funny Mr. Gery was.

    C. make the selection short so that readers won't become bored.

    D. avoid having to write a lot of description.

> By telling most of the story in Mr. Gery's own words, the writer makes us feel as if we are in Mr. Gery's classroom on the first day of school.

Discussion Questions

1. What does Mr. Gery mean by saying that fists will come along in life? Give an example of a time you experienced a fist, or someone you know experienced a fist.

2. If Mr. Gery had been your teacher, what do you think you would have thought of him after that first class? What would you have been thinking during the clay and rock talk?

3. Why is learning to read and write well something that can make you a "rock"?

4. Why does Mr. Gery compare teachers and students to trainers and fighters? Do you think this is a good analogy? Why or why not?

Paragraph Assignments

1. Near the end of his essay, Holland writes, "Mr. Gery worked us very hard, but he was not a tyrant." Have you ever had a teacher (or coach or instructor) who was very strict or demanding, but who turned out to be one of your favorite teachers? Write a paragraph describing this person, how other students might have felt about her or him, and why you liked this particular teacher/coach/instructor so much.

2. Mr. Gery uses the rock, clay, fist demonstration on the first day of class to get his point across in an unusual way. Can you think of an unusual way of getting another important point across? Consider issues like texting and driving, staying in school, underage drinking, bullying, or some other issue that's important to you. Imagine that someone like Mr. Gery is teaching a class and wants to get his or her point across in a way that students will remember. Write a paragraph describing what that person would do and say.

Essay Assignments

1. As Mr. Gery points out, it is each person's individual drive and determination that turns him or her from clay to rock. People can be trained and instructed, but unless they put in the work and focus needed to transform, they will remain soft—like clay. Think about a time in your life when, through hard work and determination, you changed from clay to rock. Perhaps you managed to pass a difficult class. Maybe you struggled with and finally solved a personal problem. Maybe you've transformed yourself physically.

   Write an essay that describes the process you went through to become a rock. In structuring your essay, devote the first supporting paragraph to describing how you felt (frightened, worried, overwhelmed) when you were still clay and were facing the process of becoming rock. Your second paragraph could describe the process you went through. Remember to provide specific details about your experience. Your final supporting paragraph could concern the person you've become and how you've changed.

2. Write an essay about three people who, as Mr. Gery puts it, were "squashed" by the real world. Describe how those people had more than their fair share of "fists" pounding them flat—only to then proceed to overcome the challenges and adversities they faced. Your thesis statement could be something along the lines of, "_____, _____, and _____ are three people who have faced significant obstacles in life, yet had the inner strength and determination needed to rise above them." For each person, provide a supporting paragraph in which you detail how and why that person dealt with a "fist" by being a "rock." You may want to research your topic online by Googling a phrase such as "stories of overcoming adversity."

27 A Change of Attitude
Grant Berry

Preview

No one was more surprised than Grant Berry to find himself in college. His high-school experience did little to prepare him for a life of learning. But somehow, as a father of two with a full-time job, he returned to school to pursue a college degree. Berry's transformation from a reluctant student to a passionate one is the subject of this essay.

Words to Watch

striven (3): tried
suavely (4): in a sophisticated manner
immaculately (4): perfectly clean
tedious (6): boring
trudging (6): moving with great effort
nil (6): zero
smugly (8): in a way that demonstrates self-satisfaction
deprivation (16): state of being without possessions
battering (22): pounding

1 For me to be in college is highly improbable. That I am doing well in school teeters on the illogical. Considering my upbringing, past educational performance, and current responsibilities, one might say, "This guy hasn't got a chance." If I were a racehorse and college was the track, there would be few who would pick me to win, place, or show.

2   When I told my dad that I was going back to school, the only encouragement he offered was this: "Send me anywhere, but don't send me back to school." For my father, school was the worst kind of prison, so I was raised believing that school at its best was a drag. My dad thought that the purpose of graduating from high school was so you never had to go back to school again, and I adopted this working stiff's philosophy.

3   I followed my dad's example like a man who double-crossed the mob follows a cement block to the bottom of the river. My dad has been a union factory worker for more than two

decades, and he has never striven°
to be anything more than average.
Nonetheless, he is a good man; I love
him very much, and I respect him for
being a responsible husband and father.
He seldom, if ever, missed a day of work;
he never left his paycheck at a bar,
and none of our household appliances
were ever carted off by a repo-man. He
took his family to church each week,
didn't light up or lift a glass, and he has
celebrated his silver anniversary with his
first, and only, wife. However, if he ever
had a dream of being more than just a
shop rat, I never knew about it.

4   On the other hand, my dreams
were big, but my thoughts were small. I
was not raised to be a go-getter. I knew
I wanted to go to work each day in a
suit and tie; unfortunately, I could not
define what it was I wanted to do. I told
a few people that I wanted to have a job
where I could dress suavely° and carry a
briefcase, and they laughed in my face.
They said, "You'll never be anything,"
and I believed them. Even now I am
envious of an immaculately° dressed
businessman. It is not the angry type
of jealousy; it is the "wish it were me"
variety.

5   Since I knew I was not going to
further my education, and I didn't know
what I wanted to do except wear a suit,
high school was a disaster. I do not know
how my teachers can respect themselves
after passing me. In every high school
there are cliques and classifications. I
worked just hard enough to stay above
the bottom, but I did not want to work
hard enough to get into the clique with
the honor roll students.

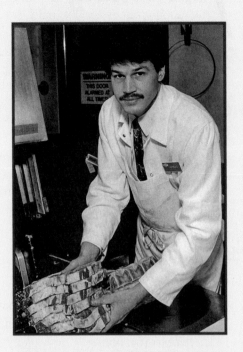

Also, I had always had a problem   6
with reading. When I was a kid, reading
for me was slow and tedious°. My eyes
walked over words like a snail trudging°
through mud. I couldn't focus on what I
was reading, which allowed my young,
active mind to wander far from my
reading material. I would often finish a
page and not remember a single word
I had just read. Not only was reading a
slow process, but my comprehension
was nil°. I wasn't dumb; in fact, I was at
a high English level. However, reading
rated next to scraping dog poop from
the tread of my sneakers. I didn't yet
know that reading could be like playing
the guitar: the more you do it, the
better you get. As far as reading was
concerned, I thought I was stuck in the
same slow waltz forever.

In junior high and high school, I   7
read only when it was absolutely

essential. For example, I had to find out who Spiderman was going to web, or how many children Superman was going to save each month. I also had to find out which girls were popular on the bathroom walls. I'm ashamed to say that my mother even did a book report for me, first reading the book. In high school, when I would choose my own classes, I took art and electronics rather than English.

8   Even though I was raised in a good Christian home, the only things I cared about were partying and girls. I spent all of my minimum-wage paycheck on beer, cigarettes, and young ladies. As a senior, I dated a girl who was twenty. She had no restrictions, and I tried to keep pace with her lifestyle. I would stay out drinking until 3:00 a.m. on school nights. The next morning I would sleep through class or just not show up. It became such a problem that the school sent letters to my parents telling them that I would not be joining my classmates for commencement if I didn't show up for class once in a while. This put the fear of the establishment in me because I knew the importance of graduating from high school. Nonetheless, I never once remember doing homework my senior year. Yet in June, they shook my hand and forked over a diploma as I smugly° marched across the stage in a blue gown and square hat.

9   Since I felt I didn't deserve the piece of paper with the principal's and superintendent's signatures on it, I passed up not only a graduation party, but also a class ring and yearbook. If it were not for my diploma and senior pictures, there would not be enough evidence to convince a jury that I was guilty of attending high school at all. I did, however, celebrate with my friends on graduation night. I got loaded, misjudged a turn, flattened a stop sign, and got my car stuck. When I pushed my car with my girlfriend behind the steering wheel, mud from the spinning tire sprayed all over my nice clothes. It was quite a night, and looking back, it was quite a fitting closure for the end of high school.

10   After graduation I followed my father's example and went to work, plunging into the lukewarm waters of mediocrity. All I was doing on my job bagging groceries was trading dollars for hours. I worked just hard enough to keep from getting fired, and I was paid just enough to keep from quitting.

11   Considering the way my father felt about school, college was a subject that seldom came up at our dinner table. I was not discouraged, nor was I encouraged to go to college; it was my choice. My first attempt at college came when I was nineteen. I had always dreamed of being a disc jockey, so I enrolled in a broadcasting class. However, my experience in college was as forgettable as high school. My habit of not doing homework carried over, and the class was such a yawner that I often forgot to attend. Miraculously, I managed to pull a C, but my dream was weak and quickly died. I did not enroll for the next term. My girlfriend, the one who kept me out late in high school, became pregnant with my child. We were married two days after my final class, which gave

me another excuse not to continue my education.

12   My first job, and every job since, has involved working with my hands and not my head. I enjoyed my work, but after the money ran out, the month would keep going. One evening my wife's cousin called and said he had a way that we could increase our income. I asked, "How soon can you get here?" He walked us through a six-step plan of selling and recruiting, and when he was finished, my wife and I wanted in. Fumbling around inside his large briefcase, he told us we needed the proper attitude first. Emerging with a small stack of books, he said, "Read these!" Then he flipped the books into my lap. I groaned at the thought of reading all those volumes. If this guy wanted me to develop a good attitude, giving me books was having the opposite effect. However, I wanted to make some extra cash, so I assured him I would try.

13   I started reading the books each night. They were self-help, positive-mental-attitude manuals. Reading those books opened up my world; they put me in touch with a me I didn't know existed. The books told me I had potential, possibly even greatness. I took their message in like an old Chevrolet being pumped full of premium no-lead gasoline. It felt so good I started reading more. Not only did I read at night; I read in the morning before I went to work. I read during my breaks and lunch hour, waiting for signal lights to turn green, in between bites of food at supper, and while sitting on the toilet. One of the books I read said that there is no limit to the amount of information our brains will hold, so I began filling mine up.

14   The process of reading was slow at first, just as it had been when I was a kid, but it was just like playing the guitar. If I struck an unclear chord, I would try it again, and if I read something unclear, I would simply read it again. Something happened: the more I read, the better I got at it. It wasn't long before I could focus in and understand without reading things twice. I began feeling good about my reading skills, and because of the types of books I was reading, I started feeling good about myself at the same time.

15   The income from my day job blossomed, while the selling and recruiting business grew demanding, disappointing, and fruitless. We stopped working that soil and our business died, but I was hooked on reading. I now laid aside the self-help books and began reading whatever I wanted. I got my first library card and subscribed to *Sports Illustrated*. I found a book of short stories, and I dove into poetry, as well as countless newspaper articles, cereal boxes and oatmeal packages. Reading, which had been a problem for me, became a pleasure and then a passion.

16   Reading moved me. As I continued to read in a crowded lunch room, sometimes I stumbled across an especially moving short story or magazine article. For example, a young Romanian girl was saved from starvation and deprivation° by an adoptive couple from the U.S. I quickly jerked the reading material to my face to conceal tears

when she entered her new home filled with toys and stuffed animals.

17 Not only did reading tug at my emotions; it inspired me to make a move. All those positive-mental-attitude books kept jabbing me in the ribs, so last fall, at age twenty-seven, I decided to give college another try. Now I am back in school, but it's a different road I travel than when I was a teenager. Mom and Dad paid the amount in the right-hand column of my tuition bill then, but now I am determined to pay for college myself, even though I must miss the sound of the pizza delivery man's tires on my blacktop driveway. I hope to work my way out of my blue collar by paying for school with blue-collar cash.

18 As a meat-cutter, I usually spend between 45 and 50 hours a week with a knife in my hand. Some weeks I have spent 72 hours beneath a butcher's cap. In one two-week period I spent 141 hours with a bloody apron on, but in that time I managed to show up for all of my classes and get all of my homework done (except being short a few bibliography cards for my research paper).

19 Working full time and raising a family leaves me little free time. If I am not in class, I'm studying linking verbs or trying to figure out the difference between compound and complex sentences.

20 There are other obstacles and challenges staring me in the face. The tallest hurdle is a lack of time for meeting all my obligations. For instance, my wife works two nights a week, leaving me to care for my two daughters. A twelve-hour day at work can lead to an evening coma at home, so when Mom's punching little square buttons on a cash register, I hardly have the energy to pour corn flakes for my kids, let alone outline a research paper.

21 Going to college means making choices, some of which bring criticism. My neighbors, for example, hate my sickly, brown lawn sandwiched between their lush, green, spotless plots of earth, which would be the envy of any football field. Just walking to my mailbox can be an awful reminder of how pitiful my lawn looks when I receive an unforgiving scowl from one of the groundskeepers who live on either side of me. It is embarrassing to have such a colorless lawn, but it will have to wait because I want more out of life than a half-acre of green turf. Right now my time and money are tied up in college courses instead of fertilizer and weed killer.

22 But the toughest obstacle is having to take away time from those I love most. I am proud of the relationship I have with my wife and kids, so it tears my guts out when I have to look into my daughter's sad face and explain that I can't go to the Christmas program she's been practicing for weeks because I have a final exam. It's not easy to tell my three-year-old that I can't push her on the swings because I have a cause-and-effect paper to write, or tell my seven-year-old that I can't build a snowman because I have an argument essay to polish. As I tell my family that I can't go sledding with them, my wife lets out a big sigh, and my kids yell, "Pu-leeze, Daddy, can't you come with

us?" At these times I wonder if my dream of a college education can withstand such an emotional battering°, or if it is even worth it. But I keep on keeping on because I must set a good example for the four little eyes that are keeping watch over their daddy's every move. I must succeed and pass on to them the right attitude toward school. This time when I graduate, because of the hurdles I've overcome, there will be a celebration—a proper one.

First Impressions

Freewrite for ten minutes on one of the following.

1. Did you enjoy reading this selection? Why or why not?

2. What is the attitude in your family toward higher education? Is it similar to that of Berry's parents, or is it different? Explain.

3. Do you do any reading for pleasure? If not, what keeps you from enjoying reading?

Vocabulary Check

_C_   1. In the excerpt below, the word *cliques* means
    A. grades.
    B. schools.
    C. groups.
    D. sports.

Synonym clue: *classifications.*

"In every high school there are cliques and classifications. I worked just hard enough to stay above the bottom, but I did not want to work hard enough to get into the clique with the honor roll students." (Paragraph 5)

_D_   2. In the excerpt below, the word *mediocrity* means
    A. luxury.
    B. heavy drinking.
    C. unemployment.
    D. low quality.

Examples of low quality: *worked just hard enough to keep from getting fired; paid just enough to keep from quitting.*

"After graduation I followed my father's example and went to work, plunging into the lukewarm waters of mediocrity. . . . I worked just hard enough to keep from getting fired, and I was paid just enough to keep from quitting." (Paragraph 10)

_C_   3. In the excerpt below, the word *fruitless* means
    A. easy.
    B. illegal.
    C. unsuccessful.   If the business died, it must have been unsuccessful.
    D. enjoyable.

    ". . . the selling and recruiting business grew demanding, disappointing, and fruitless. We stopped working that soil and our business died. . . ." (Paragraph 15)

_C_   4. In the sentence below, the word *scowl* means
    A. sincere smile.
    B. favor.   If Berry's lawn is pitiful, what kind of looks would he
    C. angry look.   get from neighbors whose lawns are green and lush?
    D. surprise.

    "Just walking to my mailbox can be an awful reminder of how pitiful my lawn looks when I receive an unforgiving scowl from one of the groundskeepers who live on either side of me." (Paragraph 21)

Reading Check

Central Point and Main Ideas

_B_   1. Which sentence best expresses the central point of the entire selection?
    A. Berry was never encouraged to attend college or to challenge himself mentally on the job.

Answer A covers only paragraphs 1–2 and 10–12. Answer C covers only paragraph 22. Answer D covers only paragraphs 5–9.

    B. After years of not caring about education, Berry changed his attitude and came to love reading, gain self-esteem, and attend college.
    C. Berry's wife and children often do not understand why he is unable to take part in many family activities.
    D. Berry was given a high-school diploma despite the fact that he did little work and rarely attended class.

_A_   2. Which sentence best expresses the main idea of paragraph 13?
    A. Influenced by self-help books, Berry developed a hunger for reading.
    B. People who really care about improving themselves will find the time to do it and to simplify.
    C. Self-help books send the message that everyone is full of potential and even greatness.
    D. There is no limit to the amount of information the brain can hold.

    Answer B is unsupported; answers C and D are too narrow.

_D_   3. Which sentence best expresses the main idea of paragraph 22?
   A. Berry's decision to attend college is hurting his long-term relationships with his wife and daughters.
   B. Berry has two children, one who is three and another who is seven.
   C. Berry enjoys family activities such as attending his children's plays and building snowmen.
   D. Although he misses spending time with his family, Berry feels that graduating from college will make him a better role model for his children.   *In the first six sentences, Berry describes missing time with his family. The final three sentences show he feels that graduating from college will make him a better role model.*

Supporting Details

_B_   4. The author's reading skills
   A. were strong even when he was a child.
   B. improved as he read more.   *See paragraph 14.*
   C. were strengthened considerably in high school.
   D. were sharpened by jobs he held after high-school graduation.

_D_   5. The first time the author attempted college, he
   A. quit in order to spend more time with his children.
   B. could not read well enough to understand the material.
   C. did so well he immediately signed up for a second course.
   D. often skipped class and rarely did his homework.   *See paragraph 11.*

Inferences

_C_   6. In stating that his graduation night "was quite a fitting closure for the end of high school," Berry implies that
   See paragraph 13. Just as Berry wasted his high school years, he "got wasted" and crashed into a stop sign on graduation night.
   A. he was sorry high school was finally over.
   B. car troubles were a common problem for him in high school.
   C. his behavior had ruined that night just as it had ruined his high-school education.
   D. despite the problems, the evening gave him good memories, just as high school had given him good memories.

_C_   7. We can infer from paragraph 21 that the author
   A. does not tend his lawn because he enjoys annoying his neighbors.
   B. receives a lot of mail.
   C. is willing to make sacrifices for his college education.
   D. has neighbors who care little about the appearance of their property.   *Berry has chosen to spend his time and money on a college education, rather than on lawn care.*

The Writer's Craft

_B_ 8. The first sentence of paragraph 4 indicates which kind of relationship to the material that came before it?

  A. Illustration (the author is giving an example of what he has just explained)

  B. Contrast (the author is showing that what follows is different from what has gone before)

  C. Addition (the author is adding a detail to a list of items)

  D. Time order (the author is telling the next part of the story)

Item 9: See paragraphs 2–3 and 10. Berry calls his father "a good man" whom he loves and respects for being "a responsible husband and father." But he also criticizes his father for prejudicing him against education and for setting an example of "mediocrity."

Contrast transition: On the other hand.

_C_ 9. When Berry refers to his dad, his tone is

  A. sentimental and reverent.

  B. angry and ashamed.

  C. loving and respectful but also critical.

  D. scornful and pessimistic.

_D_ 10. The main purpose of this essay is to

  A. inform readers that it is difficult to attend college while working full time.

  B. persuade readers that they should spend less time with their family and more time reading.

  C. entertain readers with amusing anecdotes about the author's high-school misadventures and busy family life.

  D. inform readers of how Berry's attitude toward education changed after he began reading self-help books.

  Starting in paragraph 13, Berry relates the inspiring story of his turnaround and decision to return to college. Answer A covers only paragraphs 18–22. Answer B is not supported. Answer C covers only paragraphs 8–9 and 19–22.

Discussion Questions

1. As Berry read self-help books, his attitude toward learning improved. In fact, reading those books eventually led him to return to college. Have you ever read a book that influenced the way you thought, acted, or felt about yourself? What was it you read, and how did it affect you?

2. Although Berry's father did not encourage him to go to college, Berry sees many good things about his dad. In what ways was his father a positive role model for him? From Berry's own actions as an adult, what valuable lessons might he have learned from his father's example?

3. Berry discusses some of the difficulties he faces as a result of being in college—struggling to find time to meet his obligations, giving up lawn care, spending less time with his family. If you are in college now, what difficulties do you face as a result of fitting college into your life? If you plan to go to college someday, what do you think will be some of the obstacles you might face?

4. In closing his essay, Berry writes that at his college graduation, "there will be a celebration—a proper one." With what earlier event is he contrasting this graduation? Judging from how Berry describes himself and how he has changed, how do you think the two celebrations will be different?

Paragraph Assignments

1. Children are strongly influenced by their parents and other important adults in their lives. For example, Berry followed his father's example of disliking school and getting a job that did not require him to use his mind.

   Think about your growing-up years and the adults who influenced you, both positively and negatively. Then write a paragraph about one of those persons and his or her influence on you. Provide plenty of specific details to show the reader exactly how the person affected you. Your topic sentence should be something like one of the following:

   - My aunt's example proved to me that I never want to be a teenage mother.
   - From my elementary-school art teacher, I learned that I was a talented and creative person.
   - My father has shown me how to be a loving husband and father.

2. Everyone knows that it's good to have a positive attitude, but *why*, exactly, is it good? How does an optimistic and confident attitude help us in life? Write a paragraph explaining the specific ways that a good mental attitude can propel us in the right direction. When you search "how positive attitude helps us" online, you'll find plenty of ideas and opinions. Think about which responses seem the most important and meaningful to you, and include them in your paragraph. Be sure to provide specific examples and details to support your ideas.

Essay Assignments

1. Berry did not have a realistic idea of what he wanted to do after high school, although he did like to imagine himself in a good-looking suit and carrying a briefcase. What vision do you have of yourself in the future? Write an essay in which you state what you hope to be doing ten years from now. Then describe in your supporting paragraphs three different obstacles or challenges that you will face in pursuing your goal. Explain why those challenges are significant ones for you and just how you plan to overcome them.

2. Berry points out that when he was younger, he wanted to go to college mainly so that he could have a job where he could wear a suit. However, it was not until he was older that Berry slowly came to realize the actual benefits of graduating from college.

   Write an essay in which you present three or more of the benefits of obtaining a college degree. Imagine that your essay is going to be read by high-school students who are unsure of whether or not they should go to college. If you need ideas, simply typing "benefits of a college degree" into a search engine will bring up hundreds of pages. Your thesis statement can be similar to this one: "Obtaining a college degree can benefit you in three important ways."

   For each paragraph that follows, choose a benefit and describe how it can improve students' lives. Including statistics, specific examples, and (brief) actual stories will make your essay stronger. You might conclude your essay by either reviewing the information you've presented, offering a final word of advice or encouragement, or both.

28 Now More Than Ever: Community Colleges

Daniel Wister

Preview

When Miranda left for school at a faraway university, she thought that all her dreams were on their way to coming true. Then, once disappointment set in, friends began suggesting she check out her local community college. Soon, Miranda's life had completely turned around.

Words to Watch

culinary (3): cooking
gourmet (3): fine food
diversity (10): variety
ecstatic (11): thrilled, overjoyed

1   A few years ago, Miranda left home for college at a big four-year university nearly 1500 miles away from the city where she grew up. She had big dreams of being the first person to graduate from college in her family and even bigger dreams of becoming a successful professional some day. At first, Miranda was certain that nothing could get in the way of her dreams coming true. However, Miranda had barely been on campus for more than a few months before she started seeing her high hopes, and her dreams, fade.

2   To begin with, Miranda wasn't particularly comfortable with being so far away from home right after high school. She felt awkward living with a roommate she had never met, and she became increasingly homesick. Making matters worse, Miranda's family didn't have enough money to fly her home more than once during the school year. And that was just the beginning of Miranda's problems. During her second semester, she realized that she really didn't know why she had picked the major she'd picked. She had chosen history because she'd always been kind of interested in the past, but now she wasn't so sure about her decision. However, at a tuition rate of nearly $12,000 a year, Miranda felt pressured to stick with her choice. After all, she had taken out some serious student loans, and she didn't want to waste money by enrolling in a variety of classes in order to make up her mind. Miranda couldn't afford the luxury of taking the time to find out what she really wanted to do with her life.

3   Then Miranda realized that she would need a job in order to help pay for all the added expenses of attending college that her loans didn't cover. Her parents sent some extra money now and then, but it was never nearly enough. Miranda hoped she could work three days a week and take a few of her classes at night or on Saturday. However, Miranda found out that very few night or weekend classes were offered. Compounding her problems, Miranda was beginning to realize that she was not particularly interested in her chosen major, after all. What she had discovered was that she really wanted to major in culinary° arts and become a chef. Gourmet° cooking and creating new recipes had always been a passion of Miranda's. But a culinary arts degree wasn't even offered at her university. Miranda's grades began to drop, and soon she lost interest in college altogether. Finally, at the end of her freshman year, Miranda dropped out. She returned home without a degree but with thousands of dollars to repay for her confusing and upsetting experience at the university. And all her dreams had disappeared.

4   So what's the moral of this story? That it's a bad idea to go to college? Hardly. The moral is more along the lines of "Consider your options before committing to a four-year school." More and more high-school graduates are now turning to community colleges for either their associate degrees or their first two years of college education. Although community college education used to have a reputation for being second best, that is definitely no longer the case. Today, in fact, four out of ten college students who go on to graduate from four-year institutions begin their education in community colleges. With more than 1600 community colleges nationwide and 11 million people enrolled in them, these schools are the fastest growing institutions in higher education. Why are they so popular? Well, consider the rest of Miranda's story.

5   After working full-time at an unfulfilling job for over a year to help pay off her student loans, Miranda was ready to make a change and move on with her life. She was still interested in a culinary arts degree, but this time she didn't want to leave home or spend so much money. She definitely didn't want to take out another loan. Friends had told her about the culinary arts program at the local community college. When Miranda looked into it, she was amazed to see that tuition was only a

little over $1200 a semester! That was about *five times* less expensive than the tuition at the university had been. In fact, community colleges nationwide average only $3000 a year, less than a quarter of what it costs to attend many universities. In addition, now Miranda could live at home, avoiding the huge added expense of living on campus.

6   However, Miranda still wanted to continue working part time in order to pay for school on her own and to eventually save for a car. After her experience at the university, Miranda was afraid that she'd have no choice but to put school off until she had saved all the money she needed. But when she looked at a class schedule, she was relieved to see that nearly all the classes she needed to take were also offered in the evenings. Some were even available on weekends. Because nearly *80 percent* of students who attend community college work either full or part time, most schools arrange classes to fit busy schedules. Miranda realized she could easily fit a part-time working schedule around all her classes.

7   Now, looking at the community college catalog, Miranda wished she had started college there in the first place. She noticed that there were nearly twice as many degrees offered. There was everything from architectural engineering to sign language to web technology. And because classes were so inexpensive, she could have sampled a number of classes before deciding on what exact career she wanted to pursue. The fact is, nearly 70 percent of all college students end up changing majors. Now, if Miranda decided to change her focus from culinary arts, it wouldn't be a big deal—or a big waste of money. And speaking of money, Miranda's college, like most community colleges, was located near the center of the city where she lived. It would be easy and inexpensive to reach by public transportation (unlike a 1500-mile flight!) until she had saved enough for a car. Miranda began to understand why these schools were called "community" colleges.

8   When Miranda began her classes at the college, she worried that her teachers might not be as good as those at a four-year university. What Miranda discovered was a pleasant surprise. These professors weren't better or worse, but they were definitely different. Some of her culinary arts teachers actually worked as chefs in addition to teaching one or two classes a semester. And one of her teachers owned the most popular restaurant in the city! It was a great experience to learn from master chefs who knew exactly what a student needed to know in order to be successful. The years, even decades, of hands-on experience that many of her teachers had was something that Miranda felt was invaluable—and yet the classes were so inexpensive. Also, Miranda found that some of her full-time teachers seemed to have more time for her and her fellow students. In general, this is true at community colleges, because teachers are not required to do research or write papers and books the way they are at four-year universities. All of their time at the community college is devoted solely to teaching.

9   Miranda had also been concerned that she would be older than most of the students in her classes since she had spent several years working and was now in her 20s. At the university, nearly all the students were the same age. Not so at the community college. In many of her classes, students ranged in age from 18 to 65! Miranda became good friends with a 64-year-old woman who said she wanted to open a cupcake bakery when she retired. Miranda also met plenty of people her own age who had not been certain what they wanted to do when they graduated from high school. Some had taken a few years between high school and college to explore and consider their options. Others, like Miranda, had tried four-year schools and realized that direction was not for them.

10   In addition to the broad age range at her college, Miranda was also impressed by the diversity° of the students. Because most community colleges offer courses for developing English-language skills in reading and writing, they attract students for whom English is a second language. These students often need basic courses before progressing on to their career classes. Also, because all community colleges have an open-door policy (meaning no one with a high-school diploma can be turned away, regardless of GPA), Miranda met a number of students who had not done very well in high school, but still wanted a college degree. These students were determined to "re-do" themselves and prove that they could be successful and well educated in spite of their pasts.

11   When Miranda graduated, less than two years after beginning the culinary arts program, the job placement office at the college helped her set up some interviews. Because many of the teachers in the program actually worked at or owned restaurants, they knew where and when jobs were opening. Two of Miranda's chef/teachers let her use them as references. Miranda was ecstatic° when she was offered a job at an upscale French restaurant within three weeks of graduating. Community colleges are often more successful than four-year schools when it comes to placing their graduates in jobs shortly after graduation. This is because many of the degrees offered at two-year schools are in big demand. Popular community college programs such as nursing and computer science have a nearly 100 percent job placement rate.

12   Today, Miranda has worked her way up to sous-chef (one step away from head chef) at the French restaurant. And on weekends she helps out her now-retired classmate in the cupcake bakery. She's not entirely certain that she has any natural talent for decorating cupcakes, but it's a lot of fun and pretty tasty, too. And because Miranda has now finished two years of college, she can transfer to a four-year university as a junior if she decides one day that she'd like to continue her education. Already, Miranda has begun thinking about getting her bachelor's degree in business administration so that she can be better prepared to open her own restaurant some day. So much for faded dreams!

First Impressions

Freewrite for ten minutes on one of the following.

1. Did you enjoy reading this selection? Why or why not?

2. Do you know of anyone who decided that a two-year college would be more financially realistic than a four-year school? Did the decision turn out to be a good one? Why or why not?

3. Miranda got a job shortly after graduating because her culinary arts degree was a marketable one. Think about your major. What are the chances that it will help you get a job in today's world?

Vocabulary Check

_B_ 1. In the sentence below, the word *compounding* means
   A. creating.
   B. increasing.
   C. solving.
   D. without.

   Discovering that one has made a serious and expensive mistake (such as choosing the wrong major) would increase one's problems.

   "Compounding her problems, Miranda was beginning to realize that she was not particularly interested in her chosen major, after all." (Paragraph 3)

_D_ 2. In the excerpt below, the word *moral* means
   A. clearly.
   B. beginning.
   C. funny idea.
   D. lesson.

   The last ten words of the excerpt state the lesson that can be learned from Miranda's story.

   "So what's the moral of this story? That it's a bad idea to go to college? Hardly. The moral is more along the lines of 'Consider your options before committing to a four-year school.'" (Paragraph 4)

_A_ 3. In the excerpt below, the words *devoted . . . to* mean
   A. given to.
   B. attracted to.
   C. saved by.
   D. taken from.

   If teachers have more time, they would be able to give more time to teaching.

   "Also, Miranda found that some of her full-time teachers seemed to have more time for her and her fellow students. . . . All of their time at the community college is devoted solely to teaching." (Paragraph 8)

Reading Check

Central Point and Main Ideas

___B___ 1. Which sentence best expresses the central point of the entire selection?

Answer A is incorrect because the selection describes only Miranda's experience. Answer C covers only paragraphs 6–8. Answer D covers only paragraphs 2–3.

    A. Many students are surprised by how difficult it is to adjust to college.

    B. For a number of reasons, a community college is a better choice for some students than a four-year college.

    C. Community colleges offer more opportunities than four-year colleges, and the teachers have more time to teach.

    D. Four-year schools are often far more expensive and demanding than community colleges.

___C___ 2. The main idea of paragraph 5 is that

Answers A and B each cover only one detail of the paragraph. Answer D is implied in the paragraph, but it is not the main idea.

    A. Miranda had to work at an unfulfilling job to save money.

    B. friends helped Miranda see the advantages of attending community college.

    C. Miranda found out how affordable attending community college could be.

    D. it is not necessary to take out student loans when attending community college.

Supporting Details

___C___ 3. What percentage of community college students work either full- or part-time jobs?

    A. 30 percent

    B. 50 percent

    C. 80 percent   See the next-to-last sentence in paragraph 6.

    D. 100 percent

___D___ 4. According to the author, the reason many professors at community colleges have more time for their students than professors at four-year schools do is that

    A. they teach only part-time.

    B. classes at community colleges tend to be smaller than classes at four-year schools.

    C. they usually live in the community, so they don't have to commute far to work.

    D. they don't have to write papers and books to keep their teaching positions.

See the last two sentences of paragraph 8.

___B___ 5. According to the selection, which community college programs have the highest job placement rate?

A. Culinary arts and law enforcement

B. Computer science and nursing

C. Drafting and interior design

D. Early childhood education and dental assisting

See the last sentence of paragraph 11.

Inferences

___B___ 6. On the basis of the selection, we can reasonably infer that students at community colleges

Paragraph 11 suggests this inference.

A. are usually taught by professors who hold other jobs besides teaching.

B. often major in practical subjects for which there is a strong demand.

C. don't have to do as much school work as students at four-year schools.

D. all of the above.

___A___ 7. The selection suggests that

The last sentence of paragraph 9 suggests this inference.

A. many students automatically enroll in four-year schools without seriously considering community colleges.

B. in the future, most students will attend community college before going on to a four-year school.

C. for most careers, a degree from a four-year college or university is no longer necessary.

D. it is a bad idea to work and attend college at the same time.

The Writer's Craft

___A___ 8. Wister's main purpose in this selection is to

The story of Miranda achieving her dreams is interesting (answer C). However, presenting the benefits of community college (answer A) is Wister's main purpose. This purpose is emphasized by the title of the selection. Answers B and D are not supported.

A. inform readers of the benefits of attending community college.

B. persuade readers to attend community college instead of a four-year college.

C. entertain readers with a true story about how a young woman overcame obstacles to achieve her dreams.

D. persuade readers to take time between high school and college so that they can avoid the mistakes Miranda made.

___C___ 9. Who is Wister's intended audience?

A. General audience of all ages

B. Teachers in higher education

C. Anyone, young or old, who is considering college

D. High-school seniors

The information in the selection would be of particular interest and value to anyone who is considering college.

___D___ 10. In paragraphs 5–9, the author mainly
  A. lists the many kinds of programs available at community colleges.
  B. describes, in time order, the steps in the process of applying to community college.
  C. compares the advantages of community colleges and four-year schools.
  D. contrasts Miranda's concerns about enrolling in community college with the advantages she discovered there.

> Each paragraph describes a concern that Miranda has—cost, timing of classes, quality of teachers, and so forth—and then explains why that concern is not a problem at community college.

Discussion Questions

1. Has reading this selection changed your opinion of community colleges? Explain.

2. As the author points out, community college education has grown rapidly in popularity recently. Why do you think a two-year degree has become more popular?

3. The essay mentions that 70 percent of college students end up changing their majors. What might account for this high percentage? Have you decided what you want to study in college? If so, how did you arrive at this decision?

4. Sometimes people judge community colleges unfairly because of their policy of allowing anyone with a high-school diploma to attend. Do you think that the open-door policy of community colleges makes these colleges better—or worse? Why?

Paragraph Assignments

1. Like Miranda, many of us have big dreams that don't work out exactly as we'd planned. Write a paragraph about a dream you've had that either didn't come true or, as in Miranda's situation, came true in a way different from what you had imagined. In your paragraph, describe your dream, and then describe what actually happened. Conclude your paragraph by pointing out what you learned from the experience.

2. The author points out that the "moral of the story" is definitely *not* that it's a bad idea to go to college. Nonetheless, there are some people who believe that college is a waste of time and money. Have you ever known someone who disapproved of college or thought that it was unnecessary? What was that person like? What was his or her life like? Why, in particular, was this person opposed to college? Write a paragraph that describes this person and his or her point of view.

Essay Assignments

1. Have you ever failed at something, only to discover that the failure actually led to another door opening for you? Think about Miranda's story. She thought she had failed when she had to drop out of college and work at a boring and unfulfilling job. However, coming back home actually led her to the school and career that were right for her.

   Write an essay about how a failure ultimately turned into a success for you. Structure your essay by first discussing your "failure." What happened? Then devote a paragraph to describing how you felt and what you did following this difficult time. Finally, write a paragraph about how this failure eventually resulted in a success. Alternatively, you might write about three separate experiences where disappointment or failure eventually led to better paths and directions.

   You might consider concluding your essay, as Wister does, by looking toward the future and speculating about how your life might become even better.

2. Imagine that you are a high-school counselor. Write an essay for seniors that presents what you believe are the three most important bits of advice to consider before heading to college. Before writing, think about Miranda's experience. She left for a university 1500 miles away without considering that she would not be able to visit home more than once a year, and she became homesick. She didn't enjoy living with someone she had never met. And she clearly had not carefully considered her choice of major or how expensive college life would be. There are, of course, many other unexpected problems that college freshmen might run into. Choose three of these problems, and devote a paragraph to each one. In each paragraph, present the problem, and then suggest ways to be prepared for it or ways to handle the problem when it comes up.

   If you need some help coming up with ideas, search the Internet for phrases such as "common college problems" or "problems faced by college freshmen." As you might imagine, there are plenty of articles about these topics!

29 Reading to Survive
Paul Langan

Preview

In an ideal world, the adults in a child's life are kind and gentle. Surrounded by their love and protection, the child has a safe place to learn and to grow. But what happens when the adults in a child's world are terrifying or, at best, helpless? Growing up in such a world, Ryan Klootwyk learned to create his own safe place—one where books became his protectors, his escape, and, finally, his salvation.

Words to Watch

took its toll (9): demanded a high price
oozing (11): slowly flowing
intimidation (17): fear caused by threats
cycle (19): series of repeated events
drudgery (27): boring, unpleasant work
lingered (30): were slow to disappear
transition (32): change
resentment (39): anger at having been treated unfairly

1 "Drink it. It will make a man out of you."

2 Ryan Klootwyk jerked his head away from the cup of beer that his stepfather Larry was shoving in his face. "But I don't like how it smells," he pleaded. For a moment, Larry just glared drunkenly at the eight-year-old boy, his bloodshot eyes like two cracked windows. Then he raised the cup high in the air and poured the contents on Ryan's head. As Larry stormed out of the room, Ryan sat quietly at the table, drenched in the stinking fluid. He was relieved. Larry could have done much worse; he usually did.

3 Nearly twenty years later, Ryan remembers that moment as if it were yesterday. He tells the story, sitting at another table—his own—with his wife and two young sons. Watching his kids play, Ryan thinks how different their childhood is from his own. "My children will never have to go through what I went through," he says, shaking his head. "Never."

4 Ryan's childhood home was shattered by heroin. Both his parents were addicts. When Ryan was six years old, his father died, an apparent drug-

305

related suicide. Alone and vulnerable, his mother soon brought a new man into their home. This was Larry.

5   When Larry first entered Ryan's life, he seemed friendly. He took Ryan and his brother Frank fishing. He bought new furniture for the house, and Ryan's mother told the kids to call him "Dad." The two lonely young boys started to accept Larry in his new role. But Larry was keeping a secret from the family. Underneath his pleasant exterior, Larry was a monster.

6   Ryan's first glimpse into Larry's true nature occurred a few months after he had moved in with the family. Ryan's dog—one that had belonged to Ryan's father—had an accident on the carpet. High and drunk, Larry announced he was going to kill the dog. Horrified, Frank shouted for him to stop. "That's my dad's dog! That's my dad's dog!" he screamed.

7   Larry ignored Frank's screams, but when their mother heard the commotion and yelled, "Larry, what are you doing?" he snapped. Seven-year-old Ryan watched in helpless horror as Larry beat her, hitting her face with his fists. "My childhood ended that night," Ryan says today. "I hid behind the table and watched him. I had no idea why he acted that way. I only knew I was scared that he would kill one of us." Ryan, Frank and their mother fled into the boys' bedroom. Immediately, Larry cornered them there and issued a stern warning. "Don't you ever, *ever* mention your father to me again," he hissed. Terrified, the little boys could only stare.

8

Ryan Klootwyk today.

As Larry wandered away, Ryan 8 felt emptiness and terror threaten to overwhelm him. There was nowhere to go; there was no one to turn to. But a comforting thought broke through his despair. Reaching under his bed, he pulled out a battered copy of his favorite book, *The Five Chinese Brothers*. Crawling into bed, he quickly lost himself in the familiar pages. Thoughts of Larry's brutality, of fear, of pain, of humiliation faded as he read the story of the brave, clever little brother who saved everyone. Ryan was only seven, but he had already found the lifeline that would keep him afloat through the horrifying years ahead. He had discovered books.

Larry supported himself by robbing 9 nearby households and businesses. With the police constantly trailing him, he had to keep moving. The moves would often occur without notice. "I would come home from school, and we'd be out the door," Ryan remembers. Traveling from motels to shelters, from friends' houses to apartments, Ryan lived in six different states and passed through fifteen separate schools, never staying in one place more than a year and a half. The constant moving took its toll°. "I wanted to be a normal kid," he says, "but transferring from school to school made that impossible. The only people that were constant in my life were my mother and my brother. They were the only ones who knew how bad things were. My biggest fear as a child was that I would lose them, that I would be totally alone."

10   When Ryan was eight years old, that fear almost came true. This time, the family was in Texas. Even drunker and angrier than usual, Larry began kicking and stomping on Ryan's mother. Frank, now nine years old, made a desperate effort to protect her. When he stepped between Larry and his mother, shouting "Don't hit her!" Larry turned on the boy. He kicked him in the face with his heavy black boots. Frank crumpled to the floor.

11   For the rest of that evening, little Ryan watched over his brother and tried to comfort him. "I could see that his eye was swollen shut, and pus and fluid were oozing° out of it," he recalls. "Nothing Larry ever did hurt me inside more than when he hurt my brother like that," says Ryan, his voice wavering. Alone in the darkness with his silent, wounded brother, Ryan quietly sobbed through the night.

The next day Frank was a little 12 better, and his mother took him to the hospital. Ryan went along. Larry instructed the boys to lie about what had happened. "Tell them you were playing baseball and Frank got hit in the head with the bat," Larry said. The boys and their mother obediently lied, but the injury still made people at the hospital suspicious. A police officer questioned the kids, but they stuck to Larry's story.

"I wanted to tell the truth, but we 13 were so afraid of Larry," says Ryan. He still feels the frustration of those days. "We knew what would happen if we told the truth. They would take him away, he would be in jail for a short time, and then he would come out and get us, and he would kill Mom." Without the boys' cooperation, the police could do nothing. And a few weeks later, Larry, aware of the watchful eye of the police, decided to move the family again. In yet another state and another school, the beatings continued.

Amazingly, amidst the constant 14 abuse at home, Ryan did well in school. "School was the one safe place in my life. When I was in school, I was away from Larry. I was free from threats to my family. I could pretend to be a normal kid," recounts Ryan.

As a third-grader, Ryan won a school 15 reading contest. The prize was a copy of *Charlotte's Web*. The book quickly became a new favorite. In it, a little runt pig, Wilbur, has his life saved twice: first by a kind little girl, and then by a clever and loving spider, Charlotte. Charlotte's first word to Wilbur is "Salutations!" Like Wilbur, Ryan had no idea what the word meant. He appreciated Charlotte's explanation to Wilbur: "Salutations are greetings," she said. "When I say 'salutations,' it's just my fancy way of saying hello." Ryan loved Charlotte for her friendship and kindness to lonely little Wilbur.

16   Charlotte and Wilbur joined the five Chinese brothers and Ryan's other favorite characters as pieces in a shield between him and the horrors of his home life. "Reading was a way I could forget about everything," he says. "It was the only thing that was completely in my control. I am not sure if I would have survived without it." He looked for things to read the way a hungry child might look for food that others had overlooked. "Once I even found some old history textbooks in the school trash can. To someone, those old books were trash, but to me they were a treasure. I took them home and read them cover to cover."

17   Ryan's success at school had no effect on his troubled home. Each time he transferred to a new school, he concealed the painful truth of his home, of his mother's addiction, of the constant moves, and of Larry. Ryan's strong grades and good adjustment to school were all his teachers saw. Outwardly he seemed to be doing well. Inwardly, he was begging for help. "Sitting in all those classrooms, I remember thinking, 'Why doesn't anyone do something about what is happening?' I desperately wanted someone to ask about us, to investigate, to care. I was incapable of asking for help. I was ashamed about what was happening to us, ashamed at

what Mom allowed to go on, ashamed that I couldn't do anything about it. And, on top of all that, I was afraid that if someone found out about our family, they might separate my mother and brother and me. I was so scared, I just kept it all inside," he explains. In silence, Ryan endured years of abuse, violence, and intimidation° at the hands of Larry. "I just hoped that we would run away from Larry one day. That is what kept me going."

18   When Ryan was ten years old, his dream almost came true. His mother took the two boys and fled to Michigan, not letting Larry know where they were going. For three months, Ryan was free of the constant threat of violence. But the freedom did not last. Ryan returned from school one day to find Larry sitting on the couch with a smile on his face. "Hi," he said smugly.

19   Ryan could barely speak. "My soul dropped. I just wanted to cry. It was as if something inside me died." Again the cycle° of terror began. This time, Ryan's mother sought legal help. A judge granted her a restraining order that barred Larry from being near her home. Larry's response was to stalk the family. Lying in bed one night soon after the order had been issued, Ryan heard a window break. When he went to investigate, he found Larry punching his mother. She managed to call the police, but Larry ran away before they arrived. For three more years the family ran from Larry, moving from town to town and from school to school.

20   As Ryan grew up, so did his tastes in reading. Instead of make-believe heroes

like Charlotte and the clever Chinese brother, Ryan was drawn to real-life stories of brave men and women. He read biographies of Abraham Lincoln, once a poor boy who would walk miles to borrow a book. He read about Frederick Douglass, a former slave who became a fiery speaker for human rights. Larry's stalking continued until Ryan's mother became involved with a new boyfriend. The two men got into a fight in the street outside Larry's house, and Larry was almost killed. At last, he disappeared from Ryan's life.

21   At the age of 13, Ryan felt that life was starting at last. Ryan's mother overcame her drug addiction and moved into a nicer apartment. For the first time in his life, Ryan was able to attend the same school for more than a year. He began to put down roots, make friends, feel at home. The future looked bright—briefly. Then Ryan's mother announced she could no longer afford the apartment they were living in. They were going to move again.

22   The news that he would have to uproot his life once again shocked Ryan. This time, he rebelled. "I was 13, and I had *had* it," he remembers. "I did not want to move any more. For the first time in my life, I had gotten a chance to have a normal, healthy life, and now someone was going to take it away again." Ryan begged and pleaded for his mother to stay, but she refused. "When we moved, something inside me snapped. It is sad to say, but in ninth grade I just stopped caring. I figured no one ever seemed to care about me, so why should I?"

Ryan's grades reflected his changing   23 attitude. In just months he went from a B+ student to a student who got D's and F's. "I started skipping school, hanging out with the wrong crowd, and then using drugs. I just gave up. All the anger that had built up inside all those years was coming out, and nobody could do anything to stop me." A low point occurred when a cousin called, asking Ryan if he knew someone who would buy stolen jewelry. Ryan arranged the sale. After he and his cousin spent the eighty dollars they'd made on drugs and whiskey, Ryan asked who owned the jewelry. The cousin had stolen it from his own parents, Ryan's aunt and uncle.

Because of Ryan's poor perfor-   24 mance in school, he was sent to a high school for troubled young people. There he was surrounded by students who spent much of their time trying to find a way to smoke marijuana in class. Fights were common. Far more attention was given to discipline than to learning. Once again, overwhelmed by the surrounding violence, Ryan retreated to the one safe place he knew—the world of books.

"I cut school to go to the public   25 library and read," he remembers. "At school, it was clear that the teachers had given up on the students. They were more like babysitters than anything else. But at the library—away from the dangers of school—I could read and learn about anything I wanted." By this time, he was drawn to stories from the pages of military history books. He read about prisoners of war who survived long years of unspeakable torture. One book in particular, *The Forgotten*

Soldier, moved him. It told the story of a man fighting his own personal war against himself as World War II rages around him. The author had been a prisoner. Ryan thought of himself as a kind of prisoner, too. But unlike Ryan, the author had pulled himself out of his prison and into a better life. Ryan was still locked inside his own private jail.

26   Somehow, despite poor grades and a complete lack of direction, Ryan managed to graduate from high school. He went to work as an industrial painter. While working long hours at manual labor, Ryan had time to think about his life since Larry disappeared. "I realized that I had lost control of my life. I asked myself, 'Is this what I want? Is this all there is?'" In order to cope with his own dissatisfaction, Ryan continued reading. "I worked all day and read all night," says Ryan. "I read true stories about people who overcame incredible obstacles, about people who survived wars and concentration camps. I would get depressed because I'd read about people doing amazing things, and I wasn't doing anything except complaining."

27   Ryan's constant reading and the drudgery° of his work forced him to rethink the choices he had made. "I said to myself, 'How did I get here? What am I doing? Where am I taking my life?'" His self-examination was painful. "I became aware of how I had hurt myself, how I had wasted time and made poor choices. But I could not see anything in my future except more of the same. It all seemed like a big nothing. I grew very depressed."

28   Then things got worse. On the job one day, Ryan slipped off a pedestal and shattered his wrist. He couldn't work. His wife was pregnant, and now she had to work more hours to support their household. Feeling scared and sorry for himself, Ryan went to see his brother Frank.

29   "I was looking for sympathy when I went over there," Ryan admits. "I told him I had no income, no food, no money to buy food, no way to support my wife." But Frank didn't want to listen to Ryan's complaints. Instead, Frank gave Ryan the best advice he could think of. With disgust in his voice, Frank said, "Why don't you go back to school and get an education so you can be somebody when you *do* grow up?"

30   "I wanted to punch his lights out," Ryan says. "I had come over to find a friendly, supportive brother, and instead I found someone telling me what to do." Angry and frustrated, Ryan barged out of his brother's home. Yet Frank's words lingered° with him. "The more I thought about it, the more I realized that what Frank said was right. I needed to take charge of my life, and I needed to hear someone say it. Today I thank Frank for telling me the truth."

31   One of the next books to make an impression on Ryan was *Embattled Courage.* In that book, soldiers who fought the long-ago American Civil War spoke of what the war had done to them and their innocent dreams. "Once again, I realized that people who go through hell *can* learn to cope with life."

32   These long-dead soldiers were in Ryan's mind a year later when he

enrolled in Muskegon Community College in Michigan. He was the first one in his family to go to college. The transition° was not easy.

33   "The first day I set foot on campus, I was terrified," he says. "I looked around and saw that I was ten years older than most of my fellow students, and I thought, 'What am I doing here?' I was sure that everyone in the school was looking at me, thinking I was stupid for being so old. Sometimes I still feel that way," he admits.

34   "But worse than anything was my fear of failure. I was afraid that I wasn't prepared for the demands of college, since my high-school years had been such a waste. I thought if I failed, then I would be a complete failure in life, that I wouldn't amount to anything, that everything that happened years earlier would have beaten me."

35   But over the course of his first semester, Ryan's fear faded. His constant reading over so many years had done more than help him to survive: it had helped prepare him for college. Ryan quickly became one of the strongest students in his classes. His love of learning had been buried under the years of abuse and poor choices, but it had not died. "I had given up on school for so long, but when I stepped into college, my mind woke up again," Ryan says. "It was like being reborn." After two years in community college, Ryan was a solid A student.

36   His college work inspired Ryan to decide on a direction for his life. "For years, I survived because I read books about people who kept on fighting, who kept on struggling in the face of horror. At college, I realized that I could teach these same stories to others. It became clear to me that what I wanted to do with my life was to be a history teacher."

Ryan has made his goal a reality. He   37 went on to Grand Valley State University, where he earned a degree in secondary education. He is now teaching history at the same high school where he had once been a student.

"When I read books about extra-   38 ordinary people, when Larry was hurting us or when I was depressed, I would say to myself, 'If they can survive, so can I,'" says Ryan. "Today, there are people everywhere—kids and adults—who are fighting to survive, just as I was. Abuse, drugs, violence—the problems are still out there; they aren't going away. But if just one person can learn to make it, either by my story or the ones I teach, then all that I have been through is worthwhile," he says. "You have to learn from the past to build your future. That is the lesson of history."

"I have another mission too," he   39 says, watching his two sons playing nearby. His older boy, Ryan Richard, is five years old; Reid, his second son, is three. "It is to be something for them that I never had. . . ." He pauses for a moment, picks up Ryan Richard, and gives him a warm hug. "A dad," he says, cradling his son. His eyes are moist when he puts Ryan Richard down. Reid doesn't notice his father coming over to hug him. He is engrossed in his favorite book—*Goodnight Moon*—one which has been read to him so many times that he can recite the words from memory.

Ryan puts his big hand gently on Reid's small shoulder and embraces him. "They are what I live for most," Ryan says, drying his eyes. "When I look in their faces, when I see them looking back at me—safe, secure, and loved—I know why I am here. And despite all my anger and resentment° for so many years, I feel thankful."

40   He sits on the floor with Reid. "Can we read, Daddy?" Reid asks hopefully.

"Yeah, but you have to start," Ryan replies.

41   Reid's childish voice carefully recites the book's first line: *In the great green room there was a telephone and a red balloon . . .*

42   Ryan smiles. He is writing his own kind of book, the book of his life. A painful chapter has ended, and a new one filled with promise and possibilities has begun.

An Update

43   "Reading to Survive" was written in 1997, when Ryan Klootwyk was 31. Before reprinting the story, we checked in with Ryan to ask for an update on his life. This is what we learned:

44   Ryan, who is now 44, spent two and a half years teaching high-school social studies. But as the last-hired "low man on the totem pole," he was laid off when the school reduced its staffing. He was offered another teaching job near Grand Rapids, Michigan, but he and Ronda chose to stay in their hometown. "Ronda loves her job at the hospital, where she maintains surgical supplies," Ryan explained. "And as the boys got older,

we were determined to keep them in one school district, rather than make them go through the sort of uprooting that I experienced so much of." He went to work part-time for an educational publishing company. Contacts he made on that job led him to be hired by a company that provides online programs for long-distance learning. "I'm in sales, which is the last thing I'd ever thought I'd do," Ryan says, "but I love it. It makes all the difference if you're selling a product you truly believe in."

45   In the meantime, Ryan and Ronda's sons have grown up. Ryan Richard has just graduated from high school and will go to the same community college his father attended. Ryan describes his older son as "a great kid; very smart; not *always* as good a student as his dad would like, but with a personality that draws people to him." He is interested in studying journalism, with hopes of becoming a sportscaster. Reid will be starting his junior year in high school. "He's more of the bookworm type," his dad says, adding that Reid pays close attention to his grades, and wants to study to become a pharmacist. Both boys play tennis and the tuba. Ryan takes special pleasure in the fact that both boys have "a great group of friends" who are constantly in and out of the Klootwyk house. "They've got their hideaway in the basement, with a TV and video games, and Ronda cooks for them and generally mothers them all."

46   Ryan's brother Frank still works as a machinist in the area, and the brothers see each other often. Frank's three children are grown and have children of

their own now. Ryan speaks with regret of one much loved nephew who has been in prison since he was 17. The boy had been breaking into houses to steal items. "We love and miss him so much," Ryan says sadly. He adds, "I never think of him without reminding myself, 'That could so easily have been me.'"

47   He gives great credit for his own stable life to Ronda. "We dated for six years and have been married for 21, and through every day of it, she's kept me on the straight and narrow. When I was young and could have so easily gone wrong—more wrong than I did—she was the one who kept me focused on a different kind of life. I love her a lot and owe her everything."

48   Ryan's mom spent some years living in the state of Washington, but has recently returned to live near Ryan and his family. "It's great to have her here and more involved in the boys' lives," he said. "Everyone's happy to be closer together."

49   One thing that has not changed in Ryan's life is his passion for reading. "Oh, that'll never change!" he says with a laugh. "Right now I'm on a self-help book tear. And I read lots of magazines and journals related to my job. But military history will always be my first love. I've got my own little library, and whenever I have time to just read for the fun of it, that's where I go."

Ryan enjoys a late-summer day at home with his wife, Ronda, and their sons, Ryan Richard and Reid.

First Impressions

Freewrite for ten minutes on one of the following.

1. Did you enjoy reading this selection? Why or why not?

2. One of Ryan's favorite first books was *The Five Chinese Brothers*. What was the first book you remember liking? What do you remember about it?

3. When you were a child, what activities did you enjoy most? Why did you like these particular activities?

Vocabulary Check

___A___ 1. In the excerpt below, the word *exterior* means
    A. outward appearance.
    B. threats.
    C. secrets.
    D. genuine kindness.

> The sentences preceding this excerpt describe the pleasant outward appearance that hides what a monster Larry really is.

> "When Larry first entered Ryan's life, he seemed friendly.... But Larry was keeping a secret from the family. Underneath his pleasant exterior, Larry was a monster." (Paragraph 5)

___C___ 2. In the sentence below, the word *commotion* means
    A. radio.
    B. laughter.
    C. noisy confusion.
    D. sudden silence.

> If Frank is screaming at Larry, the mother must have heard noisy confusion.

> "Larry ignored Frank's screams, but when their mother heard the commotion and yelled, 'Larry, what are you doing?' he snapped." (Paragraph 7)

___D___ 3. In the excerpt below, the word *despair* means
    A. confidence.
    B. optimism.
    C. lack of interest.
    D. hopelessness.

> Someone with nowhere to go and no one to turn to is in a state of hopelessness.

> "There was nowhere to go; there was no one to turn to. But a comforting thought broke through his despair." (Paragraph 8)

Reading Check

Central Point and Main Ideas

____D____ 1. Which sentence best expresses the central point of the entire selection?

Answers A and B each cover only parts of paragraphs 1–20. Answer C covers only paragraph 35.

    A. Ryan Klootwyk was abused as a child.

    B. Even though he received no support at home, Ryan Klootwyk developed a love of reading and did very well in elementary school.

    C. Ryan Klootwyk, who loves reading, became a straight-A student in college.

    D. Inspired by books, Ryan Klootwyk overcame child abuse and poor choices and has become a success both as a college graduate and as a parent.

____B____ 2. Which sentence best expresses the main idea of paragraph 17?

Answer A is not supported. Answer C covers only sentence 9. Answer D covers only sentence 12.

    A. Ryan's miserable home life was reflected in his grades at school.

    B. Ryan became used to hiding the truth about his home situation.

    C. Ryan was ashamed that his mother allowed Larry to mistreat them all.

    D. Ryan put up with years of abusive treatment from Larry.

____A____ 3. Which sentence best expresses the main idea of paragraph 26?

See sentences 9–10, in particular. Answer B is not supported. Answer C covers only sentence 1. Answer D covers only sentence 9.

    A. As he read about people he admired and compared himself to them, Ryan became less satisfied with the choices he had made in his own life.

    B. Larry's disappearance brought Ryan contentment with his life.

    C. Although he had made very little effort in high school, Ryan did manage to graduate.

    D. Ryan enjoyed reading about people who had survived difficult situations, including wars and concentration camps.

Supporting Details

____B____ 4. When Ryan was in third grade,

    A. he ran away from home.

    B. he won a copy of *Charlotte's Web*.   See paragraph 15.

    C. he finally told a teacher the truth about Larry.

    D. Larry beat him so badly he had to go the emergency room.

____B____ 5. Ryan rebelled and began doing poorly in school when

    A. Frank moved away from home.

    B. Ryan's mother announced that they were moving again.

    C. Larry and Ryan's mother got married.

    D. Larry killed the dog that had belonged to Ryan's father.

See paragraphs 22–23.

Inferences

See
paragraph 29.
Answers A and B
are not supported.
Answer D is
contradicted in
paragraph 32.

___C___ 6. We can conclude that Ryan's brother Frank
A. lent Ryan money after Ryan hurt his wrist.
B. liked Larry more than Ryan did.
C. wanted Ryan to be more independent and self-reliant.
D. had graduated from college himself.

___D___ 7. From paragraphs 39–42, we can conclude that
A. Ryan Richard has problems with reading.
B. Ryan gets tired of reading *Goodnight Moon* over and over again to Reid.
C. Ryan is unwilling to show much emotion.
D. Ryan has been a much better father to his sons than Larry was to Ryan and his brother.   Answers A and B are not supported. Answer C is contradicted by the passage.

The Writer's Craft

___B___ 8. What technique does Langan use to begin his essay?
A. He presents an unusual idea that is the opposite of the central point of his essay.
B. He tells a story that both grabs the reader's attention and provides important background information.
C. He presents a broad idea and narrows it down to a central point.
D. He tells a story that ultimately presents the thesis statement for the essay.   In paragraphs 1–2, Langan tells the story of one of the specific times Ryan was abused by Larry.

Answer A:
Using Ryan
as an
example, Langan
informs the reader
that reading can be
life-changing.
Answer B: See
paragraphs 8, 16,
and 24. Answer C:
Langan tells Ryan's story in an engaging and interesting manner.

___D___ 9. What do you think was Langan's purpose for writing this essay?
A. He wanted to inform his audience that reading can be life-changing.
B. He wanted to persuade his audience to think of reading as a possible source of comfort and safety.
C. He wanted to entertain readers with a remarkable story of one man's struggle and courage.
D. All of the above.

See paragraphs 8,
16, 24, 26–27, and
38. Answers A,
B, and D are not
supported.

___C___ 10. What is the *best* explanation of the title of this essay, "Reading to Survive"?
A. Ryan's reading gave him an idea of how his family could escape from Larry's abuse.
B. Many of the people Ryan read about used reading as a way to overcome difficult circumstances.
C. Ryan's ability to escape into books helped him survive his life's difficult circumstances.
D. Ryan read a lot because Larry threatened to kill him if he didn't read.

Discussion Questions

1. As a child, Ryan used books as a "lifeline" to escape his troubled home life. When you are troubled or stressed, what do you like to do to make yourself feel better? Does your "lifeline" work as well for you as books worked for Ryan? Explain.

2. Ryan's favorite book was *The Five Chinese Brothers*. Later, he found a new favorite: *Charlotte's Web*. Judging from his story, why do you think these two books appealed so much to Ryan? If you also had a favorite book when you were younger, why did you like it so much? What did it teach you or make you think about?

3. Ryan kept silent about the abuse going on in his home because he was so afraid of Larry. Which people could a child in a similar situation go to for help? How could those people help the child without making the situation worse?

4. "You have to learn from the past to build your future," Ryan says. What lessons has Ryan learned from his past? How, according to the update to Ryan's story, have these lessons helped him build his future? What lessons from *your* past do you think can help you build *your* future?

Paragraph Assignments

1. Ryan was angry when his brother, Frank, gave him stern advice instead of the sympathy Ryan was looking for. Later, though, Ryan realized Frank was right. Have you ever been angry at someone for telling you something you didn't want to hear, only to realize later that he or she was right to say it? Write a paragraph describing what happened. Alternatively, write about a time when you told someone a painful truth that he or she didn't want to hear.

2. Reading books and stories about how people overcame extremely difficult circumstances was a major inspiration to Ryan for working to overcome his own personal battles. As Ryan points out in his story, reading initially saved and ultimately changed his life. Think of a book, short story, song, article, or even a movie that you feel is very inspirational. Why is it inspirational? What might it motivate people to do? What kind of person could it particularly help? Write a paragraph about this inspirational reading/song/film that answers these questions. Start your paragraph with a topic sentence that identifies the item and its special appeal, like either of these:

- The book *I Know Why the Caged Bird Sings* teaches that the human spirit can rise above the most difficult circumstances.

- Anne Frank's *The Diary of a Young Girl* shows that even people with real human failings can have remarkable qualities.

Essay Assignments

1. Ryan could easily write an essay with a thesis like this: "To me, Larry defined the meaning of the word *cruelty*." He would then proceed to describe several different ways that Larry was cruel, or several different incidents that demonstrated Larry's cruelty. Think of a person who defines a certain quality for you. Such a quality might be (among many others) courage, kindness, messiness, selfishness, hospitality, irritability, generosity, carelessness, or cheerfulness. Write an essay in which you make it clear why this person defines that term for you. Use a thesis statement that identifies the person and names the quality, like either of these:

   - After living with my stepfather for five years, I can truly say that for me, he defines the meaning of the word "kindness."

   - When you look up the word "grouchy" in the dictionary, you ought to find a picture of our landlord, Mr. Stevens.

   Include sharp, specific details and illustrations to help your reader clearly see that person.

2. When Ryan first began attending community college, he worried about a number of things. He thought other students would think he was too old and that because he was in college at an older age, he must be stupid. He worried that he would fail again. Finally, he worried that if he did fail at college, he was doomed to fail in life. Ryan's worries are not at all unusual. In fact, fears surrounding starting college are so common that numerous articles and web sites are devoted to discussing, explaining, and calming "college phobia."

   Imagine that you are a college counselor who deals with incoming freshmen. What would you say to help relieve their lingering worries about starting college? Write an essay that addresses some of the most common fears and then offers advice and help. If you need ideas, search key phrases such as "most common college fears," "college freshmen fears," or even "common fears for adults returning to college."

   Your thesis statement might be similar to one of the following:

   - College freshmen may have several fears when starting college, but there are ways to overcome these fears.

   - Starting college can be scary, but for every fear, there is usually a reassuring solution.

30 The Professor Is a Dropout
Beth Johnson

Preview

When Lupe Quintanilla was told "You can't learn," she accepted those humiliating words and left formal education behind her. But when her children were told the same thing, a fire was lit in Lupe's soul. Determined to help her children succeed, Lupe discovered abilities within herself she had never dreamed existed.

Words to Watch

authoritarian (4): expecting obedience without question
fluent (10): able to use language smoothly and easily
radical (16): extreme
plant (29): a person put somewhere to spy
renowned (36): famous
destiny (37): fate; one's path in life

1 Guadalupe Quintanilla is an assistant professor at the University of Houston. She is president of her own communications company. She trains law enforcement officers all over the country. She was nominated to serve as assistant attorney general of the United States. She's been a representative to the United Nations.

2   That's a pretty impressive string of accomplishments. It's all the more impressive when you consider this: "Lupe" Quintanilla is a first-grade dropout. Her school records state that she is retarded, that her IQ is so low she can't learn much of anything.

3   How did Lupe Quintanilla,

"retarded" nonlearner, become Dr. Quintanilla, respected educator? Her remarkable journey began in the town of Nogales, Mexico, just below the Arizona border. That's where Lupe first lived with her grandparents. (Her parents had divorced.) Then an uncle who had just finished medical school made her grandparents a generous offer. If they wanted to live with him, he would support the family as he began his medical practice.

4   Lupe, her grandparents, and her uncle all moved hundreds of miles to a town in southern Mexico that didn't even have paved roads, let alone any schools. There, Lupe grew up helping

her grandfather run his little pharmacy and her grandmother keep house. She remembers the time happily. "My grandparents were wonderful," she said. "Oh, my grandfather was stern, authoritarian°, as Mexican culture demanded, but they were also very kind to me." When the chores were done, her grandfather taught Lupe to read and write Spanish and do basic arithmetic.

5   When Lupe was 12, her grandfather became blind. The family left Mexico and went to Brownsville, Texas, with the hope that doctors there could restore his sight. Once they arrived in Brownsville, Lupe was enrolled in school. Although she understood no English, she was given an IQ test in that language. Not surprisingly, she didn't do very well.

6   Lupe even remembers her score. "I scored a sixty-four, which classified me as seriously retarded, not even teachable," she said. "I was put into first grade with a class of six-year-olds. My duties were to take the little kids to the bathroom and to cut out pictures." The classroom activities were a total mystery to Lupe—they were all conducted in English. And she was humiliated by the other children, who teased her for being "so much older and so much dumber" than they were.

7   After four months in first grade, an incident occurred that Lupe still does not fully understand. As she stood in the doorway of the classroom waiting to escort a little girl to the bathroom, a man approached her. He asked her, in Spanish, how to find the principal's office. Lupe was delighted. "Finally someone in this school had spoken to me with words I

Dr. Quintanilla writes at her desk in her Houston home.

could understand, in the language of my soul, the language of my grandmother," she said. Eagerly, she answered his question in Spanish. Instantly her teacher swooped down on her, grabbing her arm and scolding her. She pulled Lupe along to the principal's office. There, the teacher and the principal both shouted at her, obviously very angry. Lupe was frightened and embarrassed, but also bewildered. She didn't understand a word they were saying.

8   "Why were they so angry? I don't know," said Lupe. "Was it because I spoke Spanish at school? Or that I spoke to the man at all? I really don't know. All I know is how humiliated I was."

9   When she got home that day, she cried miserably, begging her grandfather not to make her return to school. Finally he agreed.

10   From that time on, Lupe stayed at home, serving as her blind grandfather's "eyes." She was a fluent° reader in Spanish, and the older man loved to have her read newspapers, poetry, and novels aloud to him for hours.

11   Lupe's own love of reading flourished during these years. Her vocabulary was enriched and her imagination fired by the novels she read—novels which, she learned later, were classics of Spanish literature. She read *Don Quixote*, the famous story of the noble, impractical knight who fought against windmills. She read thrilling accounts of the Mexican Revolution. She read *La Prensa*, the local Spanish-language paper, and *Selecciones*, the Spanish-language version of *Reader's Digest*.

12   When she was just 16, Lupe married a young Mexican-American dental technician. Within five years, she had given birth to her three children, Victor, Mario, and Martha. Lupe's grandparents lived with the young family. Lupe was quite happy with her life. "I cooked, sewed, cleaned, and cared for everybody," she said. "I listened to my grandmother when she told me what made a good wife. In the morning I would actually put on my husband's shoes and tie the laces—anything to make his life easier. Living with my grandparents for so long, I was one generation behind in my ideas of what a woman could do and be."

13   Lupe's contentment ended when her children started school. When they brought home their report cards, she struggled to understand them. She could read enough English to know that what they said was not good. Her children had been put into a group called "Yellow Birds." It was a group for slow learners.

14   At night in bed, Lupe cried and blamed herself. It was obvious—not only was *she* retarded, but her children had taken after her. Now they, too, would never be able to learn like other children.

15   But in time, a thought began to break through Lupe's despair: Her children didn't seem like slow learners to *her*. At home, they learned everything she taught them, quickly and easily. She read to them constantly, from the books that she herself had loved as a child. *Aesop's Fables* and stories from *1,001 Arabian Nights* were family favorites. The children filled the house with the sounds of the songs, prayers, games, and rhymes they had learned from their parents and grandparents. They were smart children, eager to learn. They learned quickly—in Spanish.

16   A radical° idea began to form in Lupe's mind. Maybe the school was *wrong* about her children. And if the school system could be wrong about her children—maybe it had been wrong about her, too.

17   Lupe visited her children's school, a daring action for her. "Many Hispanic parents would not dream of going to the classroom," she said. "In Hispanic culture, the teacher is regarded as a third parent, as an ultimate authority. To question her would seem most disrespectful, as though you were saying that she didn't know her job." That was one reason Lupe's grandparents had not interfered when Lupe was classified as retarded.

Dr. Quintanilla gets a hug from her daughter, Martha. Martha, an attorney, has served as chief of the Family Violence Division of the Dallas district attorney's office.

"Anglo teachers often misunderstand Hispanic parents, believing that they aren't concerned about their children's education because they don't come visit the schools," Lupe said. "It's not a lack of concern at all. It's a mark of respect for the teacher's authority."

18   At her children's school, Lupe spoke to three different teachers. Two of them told her the same thing: "Your children are just slow. Sorry, but they can't learn." A third offered a glimmer of hope. He said, "They don't know how to function in English. It's possible that if you spoke English at home, they would be able to do better."

19   Lupe pounced on that idea. "Where can I learn English?" she asked. The teacher shrugged. At that time there were no local English-language programs for adults. Finally he suggested that Lupe visit the local high school. Maybe she would be permitted to sit in the back of a classroom and pick up some English that way.

20   Lupe made an appointment with a counselor at the high school. But when the two women met, the counselor shook her head. "Your test scores show that you are retarded," she told Lupe. "You'd just be taking space in the classroom away from someone who could learn."

21   Lupe's next stop was the hospital where she had served for years as a volunteer. Could she sit in on some of the nursing classes held there? No, she was told, not without a diploma. Still undeterred, she went on to Texas Southmost College in Brownsville. Could she sit in on a class? No; no high-school diploma. Finally she went to the telephone company, where she knew operators were being trained. Could she listen in on the classes? No, only high-school graduates were permitted.

22   That day, leaving the telephone company, Lupe felt she had hit bottom. She had been terrified in the first place to try to find an English class. Meeting with rejection after rejection nearly destroyed what little self-confidence she had. She walked home in the rain, crying. "I felt like a big barrier had fallen across my path," she said. "I couldn't go over it; I couldn't go under it; I couldn't go around it."

23   But the next day Lupe woke with fresh determination. "I was motivated by love of my kids," she said. "I was not going to quit." She got up; made breakfast for

her kids, husband, and grandparents; saw her children and husband off for the day; and started out again. "I remember walking to the bus stop, past a dog that always scared me to death, and heading back to the college. The lady I spoke to said, 'I told you, we can't do anything for you without a high-school degree.' But as I left the building, I went up to the first Spanish-speaking student I saw. His name was Gabito. I said, 'Who really makes the decisions around here?' He said, 'The registrar.'" Since she hadn't had any luck in the office building, Lupe decided to take a more direct approach. She asked Gabito to point out the registrar's car in the parking lot. For the next two hours, she waited beside it until its owner showed up.

24   Impressed by Lupe's persistence, the registrar listened to her story. But instead of giving her permission to sit in on a class and learn more English, he insisted that she sign up for a full college load. Before she knew it, she was enrolled in four classes: basic math, basic English, psychology, and typing. The registrar's parting words to her were, "Don't come back if you don't make it through."

25   With that "encouragement," Lupe began a semester that was part nightmare, part dream come true. Every day she got her husband and children off to work and to school, took the bus to campus, came home to make lunch for her husband and grandparents, went back to campus, and was home in time to greet Victor, Mario, and Martha when they got home from school. In the evenings she cooked, cleaned, did

laundry, and got the children to bed. Then she would study, often until three in the morning.

26   "Sometimes in class I would feel sick with the stress of it," she said. "I'd go to the bathroom and talk to myself in the mirror. Sometimes I'd say, 'What are you doing here? Why don't you go home and watch *I Love Lucy*?'"

27   But she didn't go home. Instead, she studied furiously, using her Spanish-English dictionary, constantly making lists of new words she wanted to understand. "I still do that today," she said. "When I come across a word I don't know, I write it down, look it up, and write sentences using it until I *own* that word."

28   Although so much of the language and subject matter was new to Lupe, one part of the college experience was not. That was the key skill of reading, a skill Lupe possessed. As she struggled with English, she found the reading speed, comprehension, and vocabulary that she had developed in Spanish carrying over into her new language. "Reading," she said, "reading was the vehicle. Although I didn't know it at the time, when I was a girl learning to love to read, I was laying the foundation for academic success."

29   She gives credit, too, to her Hispanic fellow students. "At first, they didn't know what to make of me. They were eighteen years old, and at that time it was very unfashionable for an older person to be in college. But once they decided I wasn't a 'plant'° from the administration, they were my greatest help." The younger students

spent hours helping Lupe, explaining unfamiliar words and terms, coaching her, and answering her questions.

30   That first semester passed in a fog of exhaustion. Many mornings, Lupe doubted she could get out of bed, much less care for her family and tackle her classes. But when she thought of her children and what was at stake for them, she forced herself on. She remembers well what those days were like. "Just a day at a time.That was all I could think about. I could make myself get up one more day, study one more day, cook and clean one more day. And those days eventually turned into a semester."

31   To her own amazement perhaps as much as anyone's, Lupe discovered that she was far from retarded. Although she sweated blood over many assignments, she completed them. She turned them in on time. And, remarkably, she made the dean's list her very first semester.

32   After that, there was no stopping Lupe Quintanilla. She soon realized that the associate's degree offered by Texas Southmost College would not satisfy her. Continuing her Monday, Wednesday, and Friday schedule at Southmost, she enrolled for Tuesday and Thursday courses at Pan American University, a school 140 miles from Brownsville. Within three years, she had earned both her junior-college degree and a bachelor's degree in biology. She then won a fellowship that took her to graduate school at the University of Houston, where she earned a master's degree in Spanish literature. When she graduated, the university offered her a job as director of the Mexican-American studies program. While in that position, she earned a doctoral degree in education.

33   How did she do it all? Lupe herself isn't sure. "I hardly know. When I think back to those years, it seems like a life that someone else lived." It was a rich and exciting but also very challenging period for Lupe and her family. On the one hand, Lupe was motivated by the desire to set an example for her children, to prove to them that they could succeed in the English-speaking academic world. On the other hand, she worried about neglecting her family. She tried hard to attend important activities, such as parents' meetings at school and her children's sporting events. But things didn't always work out. Lupe still remembers attending a baseball game that her older son, Victor, was playing in. When Victor came to bat, he hit a home run. But as the crowd cheered and Victor glanced proudly over at his mother in the stands, he saw she was studying a textbook. "I hadn't seen the home run," Lupe admitted. "That sort of thing was hard for everyone to take."

34   Although Lupe worried that her children would resent her busy schedule, she also saw her success reflected in them as they blossomed in school. She forced herself to speak English at home, and their language skills improved quickly. She read to them in English instead of Spanish— gulping down her pride as their pronunciation became better than hers and they began correcting her. (Once the children were in high school and fluent in English, Lupe switched back to

Martha and Mario share a laugh with their mother. Martha is an attorney, and Mario is an emergency room physician.

Spanish at home, so that the children would be fully comfortable in both languages.) "I saw the change in them almost immediately," she said. "After I helped them with their homework, they would see me pulling out my own books and going to work. In the morning, I would show them the papers I had written. As I gained confidence, so did they." By the next year, the children had been promoted out of the Yellow Birds.

35 Even though Victor, Mario, and Martha all did well academically, Lupe realized she could not assume that they would face no more obstacles in school. When Mario was in high school, for instance, he wanted to sign up for a debate class. Instead, he was assigned

to woodworking. She visited the school to ask why. Mario's teacher told her, "He's good with his hands. He'll be a great carpenter, and that's a good thing for a Mexican to be." Controlling her temper, Lupe responded, "I'm glad you think he's good with his hands. He'll be a great physician someday, and he *is* going to be in the debate class."

Today, Lupe Quintanilla teaches at 36 the University of Houston, as she has for more than thirty years. "I keep saying I'm going to retire," she says, "but I would miss my students too much!" At the university, she has developed several dozen courses concerning Hispanic literature and culture. Her cross-cultural training for law enforcement officers, which helps bring police and firefighters and local Hispanic communities closer together, is renowned° throughout the United States. She has served on a national board to keep the White House informed of new programs in law enforcement, been named one of Texas's "100 Most Influential Women of the Past Century," represented the U.S. at the United Nations Institute of Justice, been an ambassador to the World Conference on International Issues and Women's Affairs in Austria, and been the author and subject of several books. She has received numerous awards for teaching excellence, and there is even a scholarship named in her honor. Her name appears in the Hispanic Hall of Fame, and she has been co-chair of the White House Commission on Hispanic Education.

37   The love of reading that her grandfather instilled in Lupe is still alive. She thinks of him every year when she introduces to her students one of his favorite poets, Amado Nervo. Lupe insists that every student in every class she teaches—whether it's Hispanic Women in Literature, Public Speaking in Spanish, or Latin Folklore of the Southwest—memorize a quotation from one of Nervo's poems:

> Porque veo al final de mirudo camino que yo fui el arquitecto de mi propio destino.

> (When I got to the end of my long journey in life, I realized that I was the architect of my own destiny°.)

She explains, "These lines contain, in my opinion, the most important lesson a person can learn: that your future lies in your own hands. You—and only you—are the architect of your own destiny."

38   Lupe is passionate about why it is so important for all her students to realize that they can take control of their lives. "A fascinating study was done here in Houston about why many Latino children, in general, do not do as well in school as Anglo children. One thing that the study found is that most Latino children are less likely to ask questions. When they need help, they don't say so. I see that even at the university level. And I think part of the reason is that, in general, Latino children are accustomed to living in a supportive, protective family environment where they don't *have* to ask for much. Someone is always saying, 'Do you need this? Would you like that? Can I help you?' As a result, these children, according to research, don't learn to speak up and ask for themselves. It's interesting, isn't it, that there is no word for *assertive* in Spanish? The closest is *agresivo*, and the meaning of that is quite different. To be assertive means to be clear about what you want. It means going after what you want. It does not mean being aggressive, or angry, or rude, or somehow unwomanly.

39   "But assertiveness is not a value that our culture promotes. And that is our loss, because if you develop the ability to be assertive, there's no telling what you might accomplish. Let me tell you a story that illustrates what I mean. Some years back I was driving through a pretty neighborhood here in Houston. I thought, 'When I retire, I'd

Mario and his family live near Dr. Quintanilla in Houston. Here, Mario's daughter and son enjoy a moment with their grandmother.

like to live here.' Later I saw a house in that neighborhood come up for sale and called the real estate agent to ask about it. But he told me no, the house was not actually for sale. I said, 'But there's a sign in the yard.' He insisted no, there'd been some mistake, and it wasn't for sale.

40 "Well, I thought about that for a while. I knew the house was for sale; why would the agent tell me it wasn't? Hmm—could it be my Spanish accent? So I had Mario call. He has a Spanish name, of course, but he doesn't have an accent. And he was *Dr.* Quintanilla, the emergency room physician. Well, he got a different answer. The agent told Mario the house *was* for sale, but for a very high price. Then we had a friend of Mario's call. He is an Anglo, a police officer named Robert Jones. The agent told Robert Jones the house was for sale—and for *one-third the price* he had told Mario.

41 "When Robert told me that, I told him to buy the house, but have the contract made out to Robert Jones or his assignees—meaning that Robert could turn the house over to whomever he wanted. Of course, I was actually the buyer. When Mario and I went with Robert to the closing and the real estate agent realized who had really bought the house, he was so furious he would not even speak to us.

42 "And you know what? Since that time, we have bought six more houses in that neighborhood. When we own them all, we'll rename the street 'Quintanilla Drive.'

43 "That's what being assertive can do for you. I say, 'Don't get mad. Get ahead.'"

44   Lupe Quintanilla has certainly lived up to the words of Nervo's poem. Her determination and her passion for reading and learning have helped Lupe create a distinguished destiny. But none of the honors she has received means more to her than the success of her own children, the reason she made that frightening journey to seek classes in English so many years ago. Today Mario *is* a physician. Victor and Martha are lawyers, both having earned doctor of law degrees. Together with their mother, with her Ed..D., they are four "Dr. Quintanillas"—as she laughingly says, "one retarded, and three slow learners."

First Impressions

Freewrite for ten minutes on one of the following.

1. Did you enjoy reading this selection? Why or why not?

2. Have you ever come across students for whom English is a second language? Or is English a second language for you? What problems do these students (or you) face? What are they (or you) doing to cope?

3. When you were younger, did your parents ever talk to your teachers about how you were doing in school? What attitude did they have toward your teachers or your school?

Vocabulary Check

___A___ 1. In the excerpt below, the word *flourished* means
   A. grew.
   B. stood still.
   C. was lost.
   D. was delayed.

   > If Lupe's vocabulary was enriched and her imagination fired, her love of reading must have grown.

   "Lupe's own love of reading flourished during these years. Her vocabulary was enriched and her imagination fired by the novels she read . . . " (Paragraph 11)

___C___ 2. In the excerpt below, the word *undeterred* means
  A. hopeless.
  B. highly educated.
  C. not discouraged.
  D. delighted.

  If Lupe went to the college to ask the same question, she must not have been discouraged by the hospital's rejection of her request.

  "Could she sit in on some of the nursing classes held there? No, she was told, not without a diploma. Still undeterred, she went on to Texas Southmost College in Brownsville." (Paragraph 21)

___C___ 3. In the excerpt below, the word *vehicle* means
  A. obstacle.
  B. loss.
  C. method.
  D. difficulty.

  What was reading in relation to academic success?

  "'Reading,' she said, 'reading was the vehicle. Although I didn't know it at the time, when I was a girl learning to love to read, I was laying the foundation for academic success.'" (Paragraph 28)

___B___ 4. In the sentence below, the word *instilled* means
  A. frightened.
  B. established.
  C. forced.
  D. forgot.

  What did her grandfather do to Lupe's love of reading?

  "The love of reading that her grandfather instilled in Lupe is still alive." (Paragraph 37)

Reading Check

Central Point and Main Ideas

___C___ 1. Which sentence best expresses the central point of the entire selection?

Answers A, B, and D are too narrow. The points made in answers B and D have support in the reading, but neither is the main point of the reading.

  A. Lupe Quintanilla, a first-grade dropout, eventually earned a doctoral degree and created a professional career.
  B. Lupe Quintanilla's experience proves that the educational system must be set up to accommodate children who speak languages other than English.
  C. Through hard work and persistence combined with a love of reading and learning, Quintanilla has created a distinguished career and helped her children become professionals.
  D. In school, Spanish-speaking students may experience obstacles to aiming for a professional career.

_B_   2. Which of the following sentences expresses the main idea of paragraphs 19–24?

A. People at school, a hospital, and a telephone company rejected Quintanilla's requests for an education.

B. Overcoming rejections and disappointment, Quintanilla finally found someone who gave her a chance to learn English by enrolling at a college.

C. Quintanilla discovered that the person who made decisions about who could go to college and who could not was the registrar of the college.

D. The tests Quintanilla took in first grade indicating that she was retarded were a barrier to her desire to learn English.   Answers A, C, and D are too narrow.

_A_   3. Which of the following sentences expresses the main idea of paragraph 34?

A. Quintanilla's children blossomed in school as she continued to speak English to them and was a role model for them.

B. Quintanilla was afraid that her children would resent the busy schedule that kept her from spending as much time with them as she would have liked.

C. Wanting her children to know both English and Spanish, Quintanilla spoke Spanish at home once her children knew English.

D. After helping her children with their homework, Quintanilla would do her own homework.   Answers B, C, and D are too narrow.

Supporting Details

_B_   4. Quintanilla dropped out of school because

A. she had to care for her grandfather, who was going blind.

B. she had been humiliated for speaking to a man in Spanish.

C. her grandfather didn't want her to get an education.

D. she wanted to get married and have children.   See paragraphs 7–9.

_C_   5. Quintanilla realized that her children were *not* slow learners when

A. they got good grades at school.

B. they were put in the group called "Yellow Birds."

C. she saw how quickly they learned at home.   See paragraph 15.

D. they read newspapers, poetry, and novels to her.

_B_ 6. Quintanilla's training for law enforcement officers
- A. teaches them to speak Spanish.
- B. brings police, firefighters, and local Hispanic communities together.
- C. offers a scholarship named in her honor.
- D. teaches Hispanic literature and culture.   See paragraph 36.

Inferences

_D_ 7. From the sentences below, we might conclude that

Quintanilla could not possibly have indicated her intelligence on a test in a language she did not know.

- A. although Quintanilla was not very intelligent at first, she became more intelligent once she learned English.
- B. Quintanilla really did know English.
- C. there are no IQ tests in Spanish.
- D. for school IQ tests to be accurate, they must be given in a language the student understands.

"Once they arrived in Brownsville, Lupe was enrolled in school. Although she understood no English, she was given an IQ test in that language. Not surprisingly, she didn't do very well." (Paragraph 5)

_B_ 8. The last line of the reading suggests that
- A. retarded people can become successful professionals.
- B. people should not blindly accept other people's opinion of them.
- C. Quintanilla's children are smarter than she is.
- D. all of the above.   By using the terms "retarded" and "slow learners," Quintanilla contrasts other people's judgment with her family's actual achievements.

The Writer's Craft

_A_ 9. Johnson begins her essay by describing Quintanilla as a thirteen-year-old first-grade dropout because

The contrast between her situation today and her situation as a thirteen-year-old first-grade dropout makes clear how far she has come.

- A. doing so helps her to illustrate how far Quintanilla has come in life and that others can do the same.
- B. she wants to prove that anyone can go from being a dropout to a university professor.
- C. she wants to make the point that schools in the U.S. don't help the children of immigrants.
- D. she wants to point out that American schools have changed greatly since Quintanilla was a girl.

_C_ 10. In paragraphs 39–42, the story Quintanilla relates illustrates her point that

    A. most Anglos are racists.

    B. there is no word for *assertive* in Spanish.

    C. it's important to be assertive.

    D. it's important to be aggressive.

See the second and third sentences of paragraph 39.

Discussion Questions

1. Quintanilla credits her fellow Hispanic students with being a great help to her in college. Is there anyone in your life—a teacher, family member, or friend—who has helped you through challenging times during your education? Explain what your obstacle was and how this person helped you to overcome it.

2. Quintanilla found that her school responsibilities conflicted with her duties as wife and mother. What kinds of personal responsibilities have you had to juggle as a student? These may include parenthood, a job, a difficult home situation, extracurricular school activities, or anything else that poses a challenge to your academics. How have you balanced these obligations with your role as student?

3. By the end of Quintanilla's story, we see the serious mistakes made by those who called her "retarded" and her children "slow learners." Was there ever a time when you felt people misjudged you? What did they say about you that was wrong, and how did it make you feel? Explain how you reacted to their judgments—did you accept their remarks, or did you fight to disprove them?

4. Quintanilla is an outstanding example of a person who took charge of her life. Would you say that you have taken charge of your life? Describe how you have done so, or describe what you think you must still do to truly be the "architect of your own destiny."

Paragraph Assignments

1. Quintanilla remembers very clearly the bewilderment and humiliation she felt when her first-grade teacher scolded her. What is an embarrassing memory you have from your early school years? Write a paragraph telling what happened, beginning with this topic sentence: "Although it happened years ago, I'll never forget the day when _____." In your paragraph, make clear just who was involved, what the circumstances were, and exactly why you felt embarrassed. Conclude your paragraph by telling how, if at all, your view of the event has changed now that you are older.

2. For many years, Quintanilla truly believed she was stupid and "not even teachable" because of the results of one test given when she was twelve years old in a language that she didn't understand. In reality, it didn't test her intelligence at all.

   All too often, as in Quintanilla's case, IQ test results are used to determine a child's placement in school, evaluate his or her abilities, and predict the child's future. However, even when IQ tests are fairly administered, some people argue that the results should not be seen as a measurement of a child's intelligence and ability.

   Do you think children should be given IQ tests? Write a paragraph arguing against or defending the use of intelligence-measuring tests. Googling phrases such as "pros and cons of IQ testing" and either "why IQ tests are flawed" or "why IQ testing is important" will help you with your argument.

Essay Assignments

1. When Quintanilla ran into obstacle after obstacle in her search to learn English, she nearly gave up. Write an essay that begins with a time you felt extremely discouraged. In your essay, explain what brought you to that point. Then describe what happened next. What options did you consider? How did you proceed? Were you able to improve the situation, or did it remain discouraging? Conclude by explaining how the situation was finally resolved. Your thesis statement might be similar to one of the following:

   - When my first boyfriend (*or* girlfriend) broke up with me, I felt as if my life was over.

   - Failing to make the basketball team was extremely discouraging, but I finally got over it.

2. In order to serve the needs of the largest possible group of people, most schools are designed for students who fall into what might be called the "middle of the road" category—average students without special educational needs. As the story of Quintanilla and her children illustrates, people who fall outside that "middle" category can find school challenging. In your opinion, which types of students are not well served by the average school? You might think of students who are not fluent in English, who have learning differences, who are unusually gifted in some way, who have problems fitting in socially, and so on. In your essay, describe two or three such categories of students. Provide specific examples of people who fall into the categories and of the problems they face in school. As you discuss each category, offer a suggestion or two as to how schools could better serve the needs of those students.

31 The Medium Is the Medium
David Brooks

Preview

When we sit down to surf the Internet, we may watch videos, play games, or listen to music, but mostly, we're reading. Clearly, when we sit down with a book, we're also reading. But are the two activities really the same, or are they vastly different? Furthermore, how does "reading the Internet" affect us compared with reading a book? The answers may surprise you.

Words to Watch

mavens (4): those who are enthusiastic about something

hyperlink (6): a clickable location in an electronic document that leads to another location

contemplation (6): concentration

supposition (9): belief

medium (9): method of communication

deference (11): submission to the judgment of others

contemporary (11): present-day

egalitarian (11): characterized by a belief in equality

savvier (11): more knowledgeable

disputation (11): argument

counterculture (16): a culture whose values differ from those of the larger society it is part of

1 Recently, book publishers got some good news. Researchers gave 852 disadvantaged students 12 books (of their own choosing) to take home at the end of the school year. They did this for three successive years.

2 Then the researchers, led by Richard Allington of the University of Tennessee, looked at those students' test scores. They found that the students who brought the books home had significantly higher reading scores than other students. These students were less affected by the "summer slide"—the decline that especially afflicts lower-income students during

the vacation months. In fact, just having those 12 books seemed to have as much positive effect as attending summer school.

3   This study, along with many others, illustrates the tremendous power of books. We already knew, from research in 27 countries, that kids who grow up in a home with 500 books stay in school longer and do better. This new study suggests that introducing books into homes that may not have them also produces significant educational gains.

4   Recently, Internet mavens° got some bad news. Jacob Vigdor and Helen Ladd of Duke's Sanford School of Public Policy examined computer use among a half-million 5th through 8th graders in North Carolina. They found that the spread of home computers and high-speed Internet access was associated with significant declines in math and reading scores.

5   This study, following up on others, finds that broadband access is not necessarily good for kids and may be harmful to their academic performance. And this study used data from 2000 to 2005, before Twitter and Facebook took off.

6   These two studies feed into the debate that is now surrounding Nicholas Carr's book, *The Shallows*. Carr argues that the Internet is leading to a short-attention-span culture. He cites a pile of research showing that the multidistraction, hyperlink° world degrades people's abilities to engage in deep thought or serious contemplation°.

7   Carr's argument has been challenged. His critics point to evidence

that suggests that playing computer games and performing Internet searches actually improve a person's ability to process information and focus attention. The Internet, they say, is a boon to schooling, not a threat.

But there was one interesting 8 observation made by a philanthropist who gives books to disadvantaged kids. It's not the physical presence of the books that produces the biggest impact, she suggested. It's the change in the way the students see themselves as they build a home library. They see themselves as readers, as members of a different group.

The Internet-versus-books debate is 9 conducted on the supposition° that the medium° is the message. But sometimes the medium is just the medium. What matters is the way people think about themselves while engaged in the two activities. A person who becomes a citizen of the literary world enters a hierarchical universe. There are classic works of literature at the top and beach reading at the bottom.

10   A person enters this world as a novice, and slowly studies the works of great writers and scholars. Readers immerse themselves in deep, alternative worlds and hope to gain some lasting wisdom. Respect is paid to the writers who transmit that wisdom.

11   A citizen of the Internet has a very different experience. The Internet smashes hierarchy and is not marked by deference°. Maybe it would be different if it had been invented in Victorian England, but Internet culture is set in contemporary° America. Internet culture is egalitarian°. The young are more accomplished than the old. The new media is supposedly savvier° than the old media. The dominant activity is free-wheeling, disrespectful, antiauthority disputation°.

12   These different cultures foster different types of learning. The great essayist Joseph Epstein once distinguished between being well informed, being hip and being cultivated. The Internet helps you become well informed—knowledgeable about current events, the latest controversies and important trends. The Internet also helps you become hip—to learn about what's going on, as Epstein writes, "in those lively waters outside the boring mainstream."

13   But the literary world is still better at helping you become cultivated, mastering significant things of lasting import. To learn these sorts of things, you have to defer to greater minds than your own. You have to take the time to immerse yourself in a great writer's world. You have to respect the authority of the teacher.

14   Right now, the literary world is better at encouraging this kind of identity. The Internet culture may produce better conversationalists, but the literary culture still produces better students.

15   It's better at distinguishing the important from the unimportant, and making the important more prestigious.

16   Perhaps that will change. Already, more "old-fashioned" outposts are opening up across the Web. It could be that the real debate will not be books versus the Internet but how to build an Internet counterculture° that will better attract people to serious learning.

First Impressions

Freewrite for ten minutes on one of the following.

1. Did you enjoy reading this selection? Why or why not?

2. Has reading this selection changed your attitude toward the relative merits of the Internet and books? If so, in what ways?

3. Brooks suggests that high-speed Internet access may be harming rather than improving student performance. Do you agree or disagree? Explain.

Vocabulary Check

_A_ 1. In the excerpt below, the word *degrades* means
   A. reduces.
   B. measures.
   C. improves.
   D. fails.

What would the growth of a short-attention-span culture do to people's ability to engage in deep thought or serious contemplation?

"Carr argues that the Internet is leading to a short-attention-span culture. He cites a pile of research showing that the multidistraction, hyperlink world degrades people's abilities to engage in deep thought or serious contemplation." (Paragraph 6)

_C_ 2. In the excerpt below, the word *boon* means
   A. challenge.
   B. distraction.
   C. benefit.
   D. problem.

If something improves a person's ability to process information, it would be a benefit to schooling.

"His critics point to evidence that suggests that playing computer games and performing Internet searches actually improves a person's ability to process information and focus attention. The Internet, they say, is a boon to schooling, not a threat." (Paragraph 7)

_D_ 3. In the excerpt below, the word *hierarchical* means
   A. continually expanding.
   B. free and democratic.
   C. flat and disorganized.
   D. organized according to level of importance.

The words classic works of literature *at the top and beach reading at the bottom suggest that* hierarchical *means "organized according to level of importance."*

"A person who becomes a citizen of the literary world enters a hierarchical universe. There are classic works of literature at the top and beach reading at the bottom." (Paragraph 9)

_C_ 4. In the excerpt below, the word *prestigious* means
   A. confusing.
   B. frequent.
   C. impressive.
   D. stressful.

> Distinguishing the important from the unimportant makes the important more impressive by contrast.

> "The Internet culture may produce better conversationalists, but the literary culture still produces better students.
>   "It's better at distinguishing the important from the unimportant, and making the important more prestigious." (Paragraphs 14–15)

Reading Check

Central Point and Main Ideas

_D_ 1. Which sentence best expresses the central point of the entire selection?

The central point is summarized in paragraphs 14–15. Answer A covers only paragraph 6. Answer B covers only paragraphs 6–7. Answer C covers only paragraphs 1–2.

   A. Studies have shown that the Internet is reducing the ability of people to think deeply about important subjects.
   B. Some people believe that the Internet harms student performance, while others believe that it helps students to focus on specific tasks.
   C. Students who were given books to read during the summer did better than students who weren't.
   D. Although the Internet helps people stay informed, literary culture produces better students and should therefore be encouraged.

_A_ 2. The main idea of paragraphs 1–3 is that

Answer B covers only sentence 3 in paragraph 2. Answer C is not supported. Answer D covers only sentence 2 in paragraph 3.

   A. a number of studies show that having books in the home helps students do better in school.
   B. giving students books to take home during the summer reduced the "summer slide."
   C. book publishers will be pleased with the results of a study conducted by the University of Tennessee.
   D. researchers throughout the world have studied how owning books affects student performance.

_B_ 3. The main idea of paragraphs 12–13 is that

Answer A is an inference one might draw, but it is not the main idea of the paragraphs. Answer C covers only paragraph 12. Answer D is not supported.

   A. there is a big difference between being hip and being cultivated.
   B. Internet culture helps you to know what's going on in the world, while literary culture helps you master great ideas.
   C. being cultivated means being willing to respect the authority of great minds.
   D. today there are two types of learning in the world.

Supporting Details

Item 4:
Answer C
is contradicted
by sentence 2 in
paragraph 11.
Answer A is
supported by
paragraph 12.
Answer B is
supported
by paragraph 4.
Answer D is
supported by
paragraph 11.

___C___ 4. According to the selection, Internet culture has been linked to all of the following **except**
  A. a greater knowledge of current events.
  B. lower math and reading scores.
  C. a respectful attitude toward great writers.
  D. a lack of respect for authority.

___B___ 5. The "summer slide" is
  A. the tendency of students to read easy books rather than difficult books during summer vacation.
  B. the decline in academic performance caused by months off from school during the summer.
  C. the tendency of students to spend more time outdoors instead of on the Internet in the summer.
  D. the unwillingness of many students to do any reading at all during the summer.   See paragraph 2, sentence 3.

___C___ 6. According to author Nicholas Carr, the Internet
  A. leads people to give up reading books.
  B. improves people's conversational skills.
  C. harms people's ability to think deeply about important subjects.
  D. all of the above.   See the last sentence of paragraph 6.

Inferences

___A___ 7. The author suggests that people who immerse themselves in literary culture
  A. are highly respectful of great thinkers.
  B. are often boring.
  C. are often good conversationalists.
  D. don't respect people who get most of their information from the Internet.   See paragraph 13, sentences 2–4.

___B___ 8. We can logically conclude from the selection that
  A. every classroom in America should have high-speed Internet access.
  B. every school-age child should have a home library.
  C. schools should discourage Internet use in the classroom.
  D. if a child dislikes reading books, there's not much anyone can do about it.   See paragraphs 1–3.

The Writer's Craft

_B_ 9. The author begins his essay by
  A. telling an amusing anecdote.
  B. presenting the results of a study.
  C. asking a question.
  D. going from broad to narrow.

> Paragraphs 1 and 2 describe
> a research study done by the
> University of Tennessee.

_D_ 10. Brooks supports his central point by
  A. listing the results of studies measuring the effects of Internet use on student achievement.
  B. providing statistics proving that literary culture is superior to Internet culture.
  C. providing reasons why so many people prefer Internet culture to literary culture.
  D. contrasting the advantages of literary culture with those of Internet culture.

> Paragraphs 11–15 contrast the two cultures. This contrast is
> signaled by the frequent use of the words _different_ and _but_.

Discussion Questions

1. Brooks presents studies that suggest that Internet use may be harmful to academic performance. How has the Internet affected your education? Overall, would you say that its effect has been mostly positive or mostly negative? Explain.

2. If you were (or are) a parent, would you limit the amount of time your child spends on the Internet? Why or why not?

3. Brooks clearly believes that it's important to study the works of great writers and scholars. Yet some would disagree, saying that such study is unnecessary in a rapidly changing world. With whom do you agree? Why?

4. Given that improved test scores are connected with reading books and that most students want to be successful, why, in your opinion, don't more students read books?

Paragraph Assignments

1. Brooks draws a distinction between Internet culture and literary culture. To which culture do you primarily belong? Write a paragraph that explains where you feel most at home—with books and other reading matter, or on the Internet—and why. Given the opportunity, would you like to feel more at home in the "other" culture, or are you comfortable with where you are now?

2. According to the selection, one recent study has connected Internet use among 5th through 8th grade students with declines in reading and math scores. Other studies also suggest that Internet use may harm academic performance. Given this evidence, write a paragraph in which you support the following point:

   > Parents should (*or* should not) limit the amount of time their children spend on the Internet.

Essay Assignments

1. How do you use the Internet? Write an essay in which you break down your Internet activity into three categories. Such categories could include visiting social media sites, playing video games, obtaining news and information, listening to music, watching videos, and the like. In each paragraph, describe which sites you tend to visit most, and why. What conclusions can you draw based on this "inventory" of your Internet use?

2. Brooks describes Internet culture as a society in which "the young are more accomplished than the old" and "the dominant activity is free-wheeling, disrespectful, antiauthority disputation." Think about the positive and negative aspects of such a culture. Then write an essay in which you support one of the following thesis statements:

   - Overall, Internet culture is a good thing for American society.
   - There are definite negative consequences to our society's love affair with the Internet.

   If you need some ideas for your essay, try searching online using phrases such as "advantages of Internet" or "drawbacks of using the Internet."

32 Learning Survival Skills

Jean Coleman

Preview

Sometimes the best teacher is a student. That is certainly the case with Jean Coleman, whose experience as a community-college student has given her a wealth of experience to share with others. You won't find the kind of insight Coleman has in any college catalog. She has gained it the hard way—through experience—and offers it as a gift to you.

Words to Watch

vocational (5): work-related
paralegal assistant (7): a person trained to assist a lawyer
hostile (14): unfriendly
projected (25): gave the impression of
destinies (31): fates

1   For four years I was a student at a community college. I went to night school as a part-time student for three years, and I was able to be a full-time student for one year. My first course was a basic writing course because I needed a review of grammar and the basics of writing. I did well in that course, and that set the tone for everything that followed.

2   It is now eleven years since I started college, and I have a good job with a Philadelphia accounting firm. When I was invited to write this article, the questions put to me were, "What would you want to say to students who are just starting out in college? What advice would you give? What experiences would it help to share?" I thought a lot about what it took for me to be a successful student. Here, then, are my secrets for survival in college and, really, for survival in life as well.

"Be Realistic."

3   The first advice that I'd give to beginning students is: "Be realistic about how college will help you get a job." Some students believe that once they have college degrees, the world will be waiting on their doorsteps, ready to give them wonderful jobs. But the chances

are that unless they've planned, there will be *nobody* on their doorsteps.

4   I remember the way my teacher in a study-skills course dramatized this point in class. He pretended to be a student who had just been handed a college degree. He opened up an imaginary door, stepped through, and peered around in both directions outside. There was nobody to be seen. I understood the point he was making immediately. A college degree in itself isn't enough. We've got to prepare while we're in college to make sure our degree is a marketable one.

5   At that time I began to think seriously about (1) what I wanted to do in life and (2) whether there were jobs out there for what I wanted to do. I went to the counseling center and said, "I want to learn where the best job opportunities will be in the next ten years." The counselor referred me to a copy of the *Occupational Outlook Handbook* published by the United States government. The *Handbook* has good information on what kinds of jobs are available now and which career fields will need workers in the future. In the front of the book is a helpful section on job hunting. The counselor also gave me a vocational° interest test to see where my skills and interests lay.

6   The result of my personal career planning was that I eventually graduated from community college with a degree in accounting. I then got a job almost immediately, for I had chosen an excellent employment area. The firm that I work for paid my tuition as I went on to get my bachelor's degree. It is now

paying for my work toward certification as a certified public accountant, and my salary increases regularly.

7   By way of contrast, I know a woman named Sheila who earned a bachelor's degree with honors in French. After graduation, she spent several unsuccessful months trying to find a job using her French degree. Sheila eventually wound up going to a specialized school where she trained for six months as a paralegal assistant°. She then got a job on the strength of that training—but her years of studying French were of no practical value in her career at all.

8   I'm not saying that college should serve only as a training ground for a job. People should take some courses just for the sake of learning and for expanding their minds in different directions. At the same time, unless they have an unlimited amount of money (and few of us are so lucky), they must be ready

at some point to take career-oriented courses so that they can survive in the harsh world outside.

9 In my own case, I started college at the age of twenty-seven. I was divorced, had a six-year-old son to care for, and was working full time as a hotel night clerk. If I had had my preference, I would have taken a straight liberal arts curriculum. As it was, I did take some general-interest courses—in art, for example. But mainly I was getting ready for the solid job I desperately needed. I am saying, then, that students must be realistic. If they will need a job soon after graduation, they should be sure to study in an area where jobs are available.

"Persist."

10 The older I get, the more I see that life lays on us some hard experiences. There are times for each of us when simple survival becomes a deadly serious matter. We must then learn to persist—to struggle through each day and wait for better times to come—as they always do.

11 I think of one of my closest friends, Neil. After graduating from high school with me, Neil spent two years working as a stock boy at a local department store in order to save money for college tuition. He then went to the guidance office at the small college in our town. Incredibly, the counselor there told him, "Your IQ is not high enough to do college work." Thankfully, Neil decided to go anyway and earned his degree in five years—with a year out to care for his father, who had had a stroke one day at work.

12 Neil then got a job as a manager of a regional beauty-supply firm. He met a woman who owned a salon, got married, and soon had two children. Three years later he found out that his wife was having an affair. I'll never forget the day Neil came over and sat at my kitchen table and told me what he had learned. He always seemed so much in control, but that morning he lowered his head into his hands and cried. "What's the point?" he kept saying in a low voice over and over to himself.

13 But Neil has endured. He divorced his wife, won custody of his children, and learned how to be a single parent. Recently, Neil and I got letters informing us of the twentieth reunion of our high-school graduating class. Included was a short questionnaire for us to fill out that ended with this item: "What has been your outstanding accomplishment since graduation?" Neil wrote, "My outstanding accomplishment is that I have survived." I have a feeling that many of our high-school classmates, twenty years out in the world, would have no trouble understanding the truth of his statement.

14 I can think of people who started college with me who had not yet learned, like Neil, the basic skill of endurance. Life hit some of them with unexpected low punches and knocked them to the floor. Stunned and dismayed, they didn't fight back and eventually dropped out of school. I remember Yvonne, still a teenager, whose parents involved her in their ugly divorce battle. Yvonne started missing classes and gave up at midsemester. There was Alan, whose

girlfriend broke off their relationship. Alan stopped coming to class, and by the end of the semester he was failing most of his courses. I also recall Nelson, whose old car kept breaking down. After Nelson put his last two hundred dollars into it, the brakes failed and needed to be replaced. Overwhelmed by his continuing car troubles, Nelson dropped out of school. And there was Rita, discouraged by her luck of the draw with teachers and courses. In sociology, she had a teacher who wasn't able to express ideas clearly. She also had a mathematics teacher who talked too fast and seemed not to care at all about whether his students learned. To top it off, Rita's adviser had enrolled her in an economics course that put her to sleep. Rita told me she had expected college to be an exciting place, but instead she was getting busywork assignments and trying to cope with hostile° or boring teachers. Rita decided to drop her mathematics course, and that must have set something in motion in her head, for she soon dropped her other courses as well.

15   In my experience, younger students seem more likely to drop out than do older students. I think some younger students are still in the process of learning that life slams people around without warning. I'm sure they feel that being knocked about is especially unfair because the work of college is hard enough without having to cope with other hardships.

16   In some situations, withdrawing from college may be the best response. But there are going to be times in college when students—young or old— must simply determine, "I am going to persist." They should remember that no matter how hard their lives may be, there are many other people out there who are quietly having great difficulties also. I think of Dennis, a boy in my introductory psychology class who lived mostly on peanut butter and discount-store white bread for almost a semester in his freshman year. And I remember Estelle, who came to school because she needed a job to support her sons when her husband, who was dying of leukemia, would no longer be present. These are especially dramatic examples of the faith and hope that are sometimes necessary for us to persist.

"Be Positive."

A lot of people are their own worst   17 enemies. They regard themselves as unlikely to succeed in college and often feel that there have been no accomplishments in their lives. In my first year of college especially, I saw people get down on themselves all too quickly. There were two students in my developmental mathematics class who failed the first quiz and seemed to give up immediately. From that day on, they walked into the classroom carrying defeat on their shoulders the way other students carried textbooks under their arms. I'd look at them slouching in their seats, not even taking notes, and think, "What terrible things have gone on in their lives that they have quit already? They have so little faith in their ability to learn that they're not even trying." Both students hung on until about midsemester. When they disappeared for good, no one took much notice, for they had already disappeared in spirit after that first test.

18   They are not the only people in whom I have seen the poison of self-doubt do its ugly work. I have seen others with surrender in their eyes and have wanted to shake them by the shoulders and say, "You are not dead. Be proud and pleased that you have brought yourself here to college. Many people would not have gotten so far. Be someone. Breathe. Hope. Act." Such people should refuse to use self-doubts as an excuse for not trying. They should roll up their sleeves and get to work. They should start taking notes in class and trying to learn. They should get a tutor, go to the learning center, see a counselor. If they honestly and fully try and still can't handle a course, only then should they drop it. Above all, they should not lapse into being "zombie students"—ones who have given up in their heads but persist in hanging on for months, going through hollow motions of trying.

19   Nothing but a little time is lost through being positive and giving school your best shot. On the other hand, people who let self-doubts limit their efforts may lose the opportunity to test their abilities to the fullest.

"Grow."

20   I don't think that people really have much choice about whether to grow in their lives. To not be open to growth is to die a little each day. Grow or die—it's as simple as that.

21   I have a friend, Jackie, who, when she's not working, can almost always be found at home or at her mother's house. Jackie eats too much and watches TV too much. I sometimes think that when she swings open her apartment door in response to my knock, I'll be greeted by her familiar chubby body with an eight-inch-screen television set occupying the place where her head used to be.

22   Jackie seems quietly desperate. There is no growth or plan for growth in her life. I've said to her, "Go to school and study for a job you'll be excited about." She says, "It'll take me forever." Once Jackie said to me, "The favorite time of my life was when I was a teenager. I would lie on my bed listening to music and I would dream. I felt I had enormous power, and there seemed no way that life would stop me from realizing my biggest dreams. Now that power doesn't seem possible to me anymore."

23   I feel that Jackie must open some new windows in her life. If she does not, her spirit is going to die. There are many ways to open new windows, and college is one of them. For this reason, I think people who are already in school should stay long enough to give it a chance. No one should turn down lightly such an opportunity for growth.

"Enjoy."

24   I hope I'm not making the college experience sound too grim. It's true that there are some hard, cold realities in life, and I think people need to plan for those realities. But I also want to describe a very important fact—that college is often a wonderful experience.

There were some tough times when it would have been easy to just give up and quit, like the week when my son's babysitter broke her arm and my car's radiator blew up. If school had not been something I really enjoyed, I would not have made it.

25   To begin with, I realized soon after starting college that almost no one there knew me. That might seem like a depressing thought, but that's not how it felt. I knew that people at college had not made up their minds about what kind of person Jean Coleman was. I imagined myself as shy, clumsy, and average. But in this new environment, I was free to present myself in any way I chose. I decided from my first week in school that my college classmates and instructors were going to see the new, improved Jean. I projected° a confidence I didn't always feel. I sat near the front in every class. I participated, even took the lead, in discussions. Instead of slipping away after class, I made a point to chat with my teachers and invite other students to have coffee with me. Soon I realized that my "act" had worked. People regarded me as a confident, outgoing woman. I really liked this new image of myself as a successful college student.

26   Another of the pleasures of college was the excitement of walking into a class for the first time. At that point, the course was still just a name in a catalog. The possibilities for it seemed endless. Maybe the course would be a magic one sweeping me off my feet. Maybe the instructor would be really gifted in opening students' minds to new thoughts. Maybe through this course

I would discover potential in myself I never knew existed. I went into a new class ready to do everything I could— through my listening, participation, and preparation—to make it a success. And while some courses were more memorable than others, I rarely found one that didn't have some real rewards to offer me.

I even enjoyed the physical prep-   27 aration for a new class. I loved going to the bookstore and finding the textbooks I'd need. I liked to sit down with them, crack open their binding and smell their new-book scent. It was fun to leaf through a textbook and see what seemed like difficult, unfamiliar material, realizing that in a few weeks I'd have a better grasp of what I was seeing there. I made a habit of buying a new spiral-bound notebook for each of my classes, even if I had others that were only partially used. Writing the new course's name on the notebook cover and seeing those fresh, blank sheets waiting inside helped me feel organized and ready to tackle a new challenge. I was surprised how many other students I saw scribbling their class notes on anything handy. I always wondered how they organized them to review later.

Surely one of the best parts of   28 returning to school was the people I've met. Some of them became friends I hope I'll keep forever; others were passing acquaintances, but all of them have made my life richer. One of the best friends I made is a woman named Charlotte. She was my age, and she, like me, came back to school after her marriage broke up. I first met Charlotte in a basic accounting class, and she was scared to death. She was convinced that she could never keep up with the younger students and was sure she had made a big mistake returning to college. Since I often felt that way myself, Charlotte and I decided to become study partners. I'll never forget one day about three weeks into the term when I found her standing in the hallway after class, staring as if into space. "Charlotte?" I said, and she turned to me and broke into a silly grin. "Jean, I get it!" she exclaimed, giving me a quick hug. "I just realized I was sitting there in class keeping up as well as anyone else. I can do this!" Seeing Charlotte's growing confidence helped me believe in my own ability to succeed.

29   I found that I was looked to as an "older, wiser woman" by many of my classmates. And while I didn't pretend to have all of the answers, I enjoyed listening to their concerns and helping them think about solutions. My advice to them probably wasn't much different from what other adults might have said—take college seriously, don't throw away the opportunities you have, don't assume finding "the right person" is going to solve all the problems of life, and start planning for a career now. But somehow they seemed to find listening to such advice easier when it came from me, a fellow student.

30   Getting to know my instructors was a pleasure, as well. I remember how I used to think about my high-school teachers—that they existed only between nine and three o'clock and that their lives involved nothing but teaching us chemistry or social studies. But I got to know many of my college instructors as real people and even as friends. I came to think of my instructors as my partners, working together with me to achieve my goals. They weren't perfect or all-knowing—they were just people, with their own sets of problems and shortcomings. But almost all were people who really cared about helping me get where I wanted to go.

In Conclusion

31   Maybe I can put all I've said into a larger picture by describing briefly what my life is like now. I have many inner resources that I did not have when I was just divorced. I have a secure future with the accounting firm where I work. My son is doing OK in school. I have friends. I am successful and proud and happy. I have my fears and my loneliness and my problems and my pains, but essentially I know that I have made it. I have survived and done more than survive. I am tough, not fragile, and I can rebound if hard blows land. I feel passionately that all of us can control our own destinies.° I urge every beginning student to use well the chances that college provides. Students should plan for a realistic career, get themselves organized, learn to persist, be positive, and open themselves to growth. In such ways, they can help themselves find happiness and success in this dangerous but wonderful world of ours.

First Impressions

Freewrite for ten minutes on one of the following.

1. Did you enjoy reading this selection? Why or why not?

2. What careers most interest you? Which of those careers do you think would offer the best job prospects?

3. Do you know anyone who seems to you like a "zombie student"? Why do you think he or she behaves this way?

Vocabulary Check

_B_ 1. In the excerpt below, the word *peered* means
   A. twirled.
   B. looked.   If there was nobody to be seen, he must have
   C. joked.   looked in both directions.
   D. hid.

   "He opened up an imaginary door, stepped through, and peered around in both directions outside. There was nobody to be seen." (Paragraph 4)

_C_ 2. In the sentence below, the word *expanding* means
   A. closing.
   B. shrinking.   If people take courses just for the sake of learning,
   C. enlarging.   what will they be doing to their minds?
   D. confusing.

   "People should take some courses just for the sake of learning and for expanding their minds in different directions." (Paragraph 8)

_D_ 3. In the excerpt below, the word *dismayed* means
   A. satisfied.
   B. rude.   If they didn't fight back and they dropped out,
   C. excited.   they must have been stunned and discouraged
   D. discouraged.   by the unexpected low punch.

   "Life hit some of them with unexpected low punches and knocked them to the floor. Stunned and dismayed, they didn't fight back and eventually dropped out of school." (Paragraph 14)

_C_ 4. In the sentence below, the word *overwhelmed* means
  A. questioned.
  B. strengthened.
  C. defeated.
  D. unconcerned.

> If Nelson dropped out of college, he must have been defeated by his car troubles.

"Overwhelmed by his continuing car troubles, Nelson dropped out of school." (Paragraph 14)

Reading Check

Central Point and Main Ideas

The selection presents the author's five guidelines for survival and success in college and life. Each of the guidelines is signaled by a heading: "Be Realistic" (paragraphs 3–9), "Persist" (10–16), "Be Positive" (17–19), "Grow" (20–23), and "Enjoy" (24–30). Answers A, C, and D are too narrow.

_B_ 1. Which sentence best expresses the central point of the entire selection?
  A. All people experience great problems in the course of their lives, but they should not allow their problems to discourage them.
  B. Following certain guidelines will help you succeed in school and in life.
  C. Older adults may have a better attitude toward school than younger students.
  D. A number of common obstacles prevent people from succeeding in college.

See the first sentence in paragraph 3, the first sentence of paragraph 5, and the last two sentences of paragraph 8. Answer B covers only the last sentence of paragraph 5. Answer C covers only paragraph 7. Answer D covers only paragraph 6.

_A_ 2. Which sentence best expresses the main idea of paragraphs 3–8?
  A. Students should make sure that college prepares them for a career that they will enjoy and in which jobs are available.
  B. The author discovered in the *Occupational Outlook Handbook* which kinds of jobs are available now and which will be available in the future.
  C. The author's friend Sheila ended up with a job that had nothing to do with her college degree.
  D. The author is now working as an accountant and also toward becoming a certified public accountant.

Supporting Details

_A_ 3. Coleman feels that people who drop out of school
  A. often give up too quickly.
  B. never have a good reason.
  C. usually have a good reason.
  D. always have bigger problems than those who stay in school.

> See paragraph 23.

___D___ 4. The author
- A. took a straight liberal-arts curriculum.
- B. switched from being a French major to an accounting major.
- C. took accounting classes and ended up with a degree in art.
- D. took some general-interest classes but ended up with a degree in accounting.

See the first sentence in paragraph 6 and all of paragraph 8.

Inferences

___C___ 5. Coleman implies that successful people
- A. don't need to struggle in school.
- B. manage to avoid problems.
- C. welcome opportunities to grow.
- D. are unusually lucky.

See paragraphs 20, 23, and 25–27.

___B___ 6. From paragraph 25, we can conclude that in college the author
- A. became depressed.
- B. significantly gained self-confidence.
- C. had no self-doubts.
- D. met many of her fellow students from high school.

See the last two sentences of the paragraph. Answers A, C, and D are not supported.

___C___ 7. Coleman suggests that
- A. older college students are very lonely.
- B. older college students always have to work harder at their studies than younger students.
- C. younger students often welcome the company of older students.
- D. after a certain age, people should not return to college.

See paragraph 29. Answers A, B, and D are not supported.

The Writer's Craft

___A___ 8. The author's main purpose in writing "Learning Survival Skills" is to
- A. persuade readers to give themselves the best possible chance of success in college.
- B. inform readers about the best careers available to college graduates today.
- C. entertain readers with stories about things that can go wrong at college.
- D. inform readers about her own success in college.

Throughout the essay, Coleman uses phrases such as *People should* (paragraph 8), *We must* (10), *Grow or die* (20), and *I urge* (31). Clearly, she wants to persuade readers.

___D___ 9. What audience did Coleman seem to have in mind when she wrote this essay?
- A. Older adults who are considering returning to school
- B. Students who tend to be negative, unrealistic, and lazy
- C. Younger adults who are considering attending community college
- D. Anyone of any age who is just starting college

In paragraph 31, she says, "I urge every beginning student . . ." Her suggestions are valuable to anyone starting college. Also, the students she uses as examples are various ages.

___C___ 10. What does Coleman's conclusion do?
- A. It gives her a final opportunity to summarize her achievements.
- B. It presents a new idea to make readers think.
- C. It presents some final thoughts and recommendations.
- D. It restates the central point of her essay.

Sentences 1–9 and 12 present final thoughts.
Sentences 10 and 11 present recommendations.

Discussion Questions

1. What do you think Coleman means in paragraph 17 when she says, "A lot of people are their own worst enemies"? Have you ever observed anyone seemingly getting in the way of his or her own success? Have you ever done it yourself? Explain.

2. Coleman ends her introduction (paragraphs 1–2) by stating, "Here, then, are my secrets for survival in college and, really, for survival in life as well." She then makes five points: "Be Realistic," "Persist," "Be Positive," "Grow," and "Enjoy." Which of those points represents the biggest challenge for you right now? Why?

3. According to Coleman, students should plan for a career that both interests them and offers future job opportunities. What type of career interests you, and why? What degree would help you enter that field? Do you have any idea what the job prospects in that field might be?

4. Although the author encourages students to make practical career plans, she also writes, "People should take some courses just for the sake of learning and for expanding their minds in different directions." What are some courses you would like to take "just for the sake of learning"? What about them appeals to you?

Paragraph Assignments

1. As you read Coleman's selection, which of her "survival skills" seems of most personal value to you? Do you value that skill because you already possess it and know how helpful it's been to you? Or is it valuable because you *don't* possess it, and know that you need it? Write a paragraph about which one of Coleman's survival skills really stands out for you, explaining in detail exactly why. Your topic sentence can be something like this: "Of all the secrets for survival that Coleman describes, the one that speaks most directly to me is _____."

2. After presenting many of the "survival skills" needed in college, Coleman describes fellow students who neglected these skills and, as a result, eventually dropped out of college. It is estimated that nearly

50 percent of all people who begin college in the United States end up dropping out. Certainly, many of these dropouts may lack one or more of the survival skills Coleman discusses in her essay. But there are also many other reasons why nearly half the people who begin pursuing a college education never receive one.

Do some research on this topic, and then write a paragraph that presents some of the top reasons why many people never make it to their college graduation day. Google "why students drop out of college" or "why students don't finish college" to help you with your paragraph. Consider ending your paragraph, as Coleman does with her essay, with a word of encouragement or advice.

Essay Assignments

1. Coleman writes, "There are times for each of us when simple survival becomes a deadly serious matter. We must then learn to persist—to struggle through each day." What have been your most challenging struggles so far? Write a paper describing the challenges, what you had to do to deal with them, and how things worked out. You may also wish to comment on how you'd handle the challenges today if faced with them.

   As you work on the drafts for this paper, try to include the following:

   - Exact quotations of what you or other people said at the time (as Coleman does in paragraphs 22 and 28)

   - Descriptions of revealing behavior, actions, and physical characteristics (as Coleman does in paragraphs 21, 27, and 28)

   - Time transitions to clarify relationships between events (as Coleman does in paragraph 6).

2. Coleman categorizes college students in several ways, including students who give up when they hit an obstacle, students who take a negative attitude toward being in college, and students who have persistent, positive attitudes.

   Write an essay about three categories of students whom you have observed (at any stage of your education). Include plenty of details about just what makes those students fit into the category you are discussing. Those details might have to do with their physical appearance, their classroom behavior, their conversation, or other characteristics. Your thesis statement might be one such as the following: "Students seem to fall into three distinct categories: those who work hard, those who never work, and those who work just enough to get by."

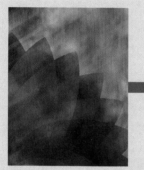

Unit Five

Examining Social Issues

33 Sleeping with Guns

Bruce Holbert

Preview

Bruce Holbert grew up around guns. He was expected to be interested in guns and, in addition, know how to handle them. However, in a split second one summer afternoon, as Holbert was inspecting a friend's gun, something went horribly wrong. That split second would haunt Holbert for the rest of his life.

Words to Watch

fedora (1): a felt hat
zealot (3): extremely enthusiastic fan
proficient (8): capable
fraud (8): fake, con
mythologized (9): considered heroic
vital (11): extremely important
component (11): part

1   The summer before my sophomore year in high school, I moved into my father's house. My father had remarried, and the only unoccupied bedroom in his house was the gun room. Against one wall was a gun case he had built in high school, and beside it were two empty refrigerators stocked with rifles and hundreds of rounds of ammunition. My bed's headboard resided against the other wall and, above it, a resigned-looking, marble-eyed, five-point mule deer's head with a fedora° on its antler rack.

2   The room had no windows, so the smell of gun oil filled my senses at least eight hours each day. It clung to my clothes like smoke, and like a smoker's cigarettes, it became my smell. No one in my high school noticed. We all smelled like something: motorheads of motor oil, farm kids of wheat chaff and cow dung, athletes like footballs and grass, dopers like the other kind of grass.

3   It did not appear to anyone— including me—that residing within my family's weapons cache might affect my life. Together, my three brothers own at least a dozen weapons and have yet to harm anyone with them. Despite their

guns (or, arguably, because of them), they are quite peaceable. As for me, I have three guns, one inherited and two gifts, and I'm hardly a zealot°. In fact I never had much interest in guns. Yet it is I who killed a man.

4   It was the second week in August, a Friday the 13th, in fact, in 1982. I was with a group of college roommates who were getting ready to go to the Omak Stampede and Suicide Race. Three of us piled into a red Vega parked outside a friend's house in Okanogan, Washington, me in the back seat. The driver, who worked with the county sheriff's department, offered me his service revolver to examine. I turned the weapon onto its side, pointed it toward the door. The barrel, however, slipped when I shifted my grip to pull the hammer back, to make certain the chamber was empty, and turned the gun toward the driver's seat. When I let the hammer fall, the cylinder must have rotated without my knowing. When I pulled the hammer back a second time, it fired a live round.

5   My friend, Doug, slumped in the driver's seat, dying, and another friend, who was sitting in the passenger seat, raced into the house for the phone.

6   The house sat beside one edge of a river valley, and I knew that between the orchard at the opposite side and the next town was 20 miles of rock and pine. I was a cross-country champion in high school. I could run through the woods and find my way to my cousins, who lived far into the mountains. I could easily disappear. But I remained where I was, mindful that even if I ran, I would escape nothing. So, when the sirens finally whirred and the colored lights tumbled over the yard and the doors of the cruisers opened and a police sergeant asked who was responsible, I raised my hand and patted my chest and was arrested.

7   Though the charges against me were eventually dropped, I have since been given diagnoses of a range of maladies, including post-traumatic stress disorder, depression, anxiety, and adult attention deficit disorders. The pharmacists fill the appropriate prescriptions, which temporarily salve my conscience, but serve neither my story nor the truth.

8   Where I grew up, masculinity involved schooling a mean dog to guard your truck or skipping the ignition switch to fire the points, and, of course, handling guns of all kinds. I was barely proficient° in any of these areas. I understood what was expected of me and responded as best I could, but did so with distance that would, I hoped, keep me from being a total fraud° in my own eyes.

9   Like many other young men, I mythologized° guns and the ideas of manhood associated with them.

10   The gun lobby likes to say guns don't kill people, people do. And they're right, of course. I killed my friend; no one else did; no mechanism did. But this oversimplifies matters (as does the gun control advocates' position that eliminating weapons will end violent crime).

11   My friend was killed by a man who misunderstood guns, who imagined that comfort with—and affection for—guns was a vital° component° of manhood. I did not recognize a gun for what it was: a machine constructed for a purpose, one in which I had no real interest. I treated a tool as an essential part of my identity, and the result is a dead man and a grieving family and a survivor numbed by guilt whose story lacks anything resembling a proper ending.

First Impressions

Freewrite for ten minutes on one of the following.

1. Did you enjoy reading this selection? Why or why not?

2. Holbert points out that he still owns three guns. Would you own guns after having an experience like Holbert's? Why or why not?

3. Why are guns considered by some to be "a vital component of manhood"? Do you agree with this idea? Why or why not?

Vocabulary Check

___D___ 1. In the excerpt below, the word *resided* means
   A. supported.
   B. was built sideways.
   C. blocked.
   D. occupied a space.

   If the headboard is against the wall, it occupies the space in front of the wall.

   "Against one wall was a gun case he had built in high school, and beside it were two empty refrigerators stocked with rifles and hundreds of rounds of ammunition. My bed's headboard resided against the other wall and, above it, a resigned-looking, marble-eyed, five-point mule deer's head with a fedora on its antler rack." (Paragraph 1)

___B___ 2. In the sentence below, the word *cache* means

    A. danger.

    B. collection.

    C. prize.

    D. money.

> In paragraph 1, he says his bedroom is the gun room with a gun case and two refrigerators containing guns. Therefore, he is residing in his family's weapons collection.

"It did not appear to anyone—including me—that residing within my family's weapons cache might affect my life." (Paragraph 3)

___C___ 3. In the sentence below, the word *maladies* means

    A. interests.

    B. remedies.

    C. diseases.

    D. punishments.

> The last part of the sentence gives four examples of diseases doctors have diagnosed.

"Though the charges against me were eventually dropped, I have since been given diagnoses of a range of maladies, including post-traumatic stress disorder, depression, anxiety, and adult attention deficit disorders." (Paragraph 7)

___A___ 4. In the sentence below, the word *salve* means

    A. soothe.

    B. erase.

    C. disturb.

    D. damage.

> Pharmacists fill prescriptions for medications that soothe pain and discomfort.

"The pharmacists fill the appropriate prescriptions, which temporarily salve my conscience, but serve neither my story nor the truth." (Paragraph 7)

Reading Check

Central Point and Main ideas

___C___ 1. Which sentence best expresses the central point of the entire selection?

The central point is summarized in paragraph 11. Answers A and B are not supported. Answer D is suggested in paragraph 10, but it is not the central point.

    A. Holbert realized too late, and with disastrous results, that he knew less about guns than he thought he did.

    B. Although Holbert remains upset about the gun accident, he supports and promotes the right to gun ownership.

    C. An accident with a gun when he was younger had a profound effect on Holbert and has made him reconsider his relationship with guns.

    D. Although there is always a chance of an accident, this fact should not affect the right to own guns since "guns don't kill people, people do."

_A_ 2. Which sentence best expresses the main idea of paragraph 3?

Answer B covers only sentence 3. Answer C is contradicted by sentence 5. Answer D covers only sentence 5.

    A. Holbert never imagined that guns would affect his life in the way they eventually did.

    B. Holbert's brothers all own guns, but none of them are violent men.

    C. The author enjoyed having guns in his life.

    D. The author has never had much interest in guns.

_C_ 3. Which sentence best expresses the main idea of paragraph 8?

    A. Growing up, the author learned how to train a dog, fix his truck, and handle guns.

    B. Certain things were expected of the author if he wanted to be considered an adult by others.

    C. The author was not particularly interested in or good at what were considered masculine traits where he grew up.

    D. The author often felt like a fraud as he was growing up.

Answer A is incorrect because the author says he was "barely proficient" in these things. Answer B is too general. Answer D is not supported.

Supporting Details

_D_ 4. When Holbert moved into his father's house, he had to live in

    A. the garage.

    B. the same room with his brothers.

    C. the guest room.

    D. the gun room.

See paragraph 1, sentence 2.

_C_ 5. After shooting his friend, Holbert suffered from

    A. nightmares and hallucinations.

    B. lack of appetite and violent outbursts.

    C. depression and anxiety.

    D. all of the above.

See paragraph 7, sentence 1.

Inferences

Answer B is suggested by the final words of the selection: ". . . a survivor numbed by guilt whose story lacks anything resembling a proper ending."

_B_ 6. We can infer from "Sleeping with Guns" that its author

    A. no longer supports gun ownership.

    B. may never be able to get over what happened.

    C. will eventually be able to forget what happened.

    D. is angry with his father.

_T_ 7. TRUE OR FALSE? The author implies that gun ownership and our attitude to guns are a much more complex issue than many of us realize.

See paragraph 10.

The Writer's Craft

_B_ 8. The pattern of organization used for this essay is
 A. time order.
 B. time order and cause-effect.
 C. listing order and cause-effect.
 D. comparison-contrast.

> Holbert presents the main elements of the selection— his relationship to guns while growing up, the shooting, and the long-term effects of the shooting— in time order. *Cause:* shooting his friend. *Effect:* the impact on the author's life.

_B_ 9. As the essay progresses, the author's tone grows increasingly
 A. angry.
 B. serious.
 C. alarmed.
 D. indifferent.

> The final paragraphs (7–11) become increasingly serious as Holbert describes the impact the shooting has had on his life.

_A_ 10. Holbert's main purpose for writing this essay is to
 A. persuade readers that guns are dangerous tools that need to be taken seriously.
 B. persuade readers to support stricter gun control laws.
 C. inform readers of how easily dangerous accidents can happen when one is not familiar with guns.
 D. entertain readers with a dramatic and personal story.

> Holbert hopes to persuade us of this point by showing the serious long-range effects the accident has had on his life.

Discussion Questions

1. In paragraph 4, Holbert provides a detailed description of how the shooting happened. Why do you think he writes about the incident in such detail?

2. Holbert ends his essay by saying that his story "lacks anything resembling a proper ending." What do you think he means by that?

3. Do you agree with the National Rifle Association that any U.S. citizen should be allowed to buy guns without a required background check? Why or why not?

4. Holbert explains that certain behaviors, like knowing about guns and training a dog to guard your truck, were associated with masculinity in the town he grew up in. Can you think of other behaviors that, fairly or unfairly, are considered "vital components" of masculinity? Are there also "vital components" of femininity? Are these ideas valid?

Paragraph Assignments

1. When writing about the shooting, Holbert describes it step by step, giving the incident an almost slow-motion feel. Can you think of some particularly horrible (or wonderful) moment in your life when time seemed to practically stand still? These are the kinds of moments that we can often remember in vivid detail for the rest of our lives. Write a paragraph that describes an event you remember that, like the shooting in Holbert's story, may have taken no more than a minute or two, but that has expanded in your memory to seem much longer. Be sure to include vivid and exact detail.

2. In his essay, Holbert points out that he actually lived in a room full of guns and ammunition when he was a boy. More often than not, young people have accidents with guns or use guns irresponsibly simply because the firearms are so easily accessible and the young person has not been taught how to handle them properly. Imagine that you have been chosen to write a paragraph persuading parents to be more responsible about gun ownership. What would you recommend they do to protect their children?

   Consider beginning your paragraph by presenting a real-life example of the consequences of irresponsible gun ownership by parents of a child or young person. (You can find numerous examples of these horror stories on the Internet.) Follow this example with specific recommendations. For example, instead of simply saying, "Parents should make sure guns are locked away" or "Children should be taught about guns," describe how and where guns should be secured, and how and what children should be taught.

Essay Assignments

1. The horrible memory of accidentally shooting his friend has, understandably, stayed with the author his entire life. But beyond just the haunting memory, Holbert's life is also disrupted by depression, anxiety, and other disorders associated with his lingering emotional response to the tragedy. Many of us have had something traumatic happen when we were younger that continues to affect us in one or more ways even years later.

   Write an essay that, like Holbert's story, describes an event that has affected you in a negative way. Begin by describing what happened. Use another paragraph to explain how the event continues to have an effect on your life. In your final paragraph, discuss what you have learned from the experience.

2. The debate over gun laws and gun ownership has gone on for decades in our country. Many people feel that there should be far stricter gun control laws. Others feel that restricting gun ownership goes against our Constitution and "the right to bear arms." As Holbert points out, there is merit to both sides of the debate, but some of the arguments oversimplify the issue.

How do you feel about the current gun laws in the United States? Do you think there should be more gun control, or do you think changing the laws would be unfair, even unconstitutional? Write an essay that presents your stance in your thesis statement, and then devote the body of your paper to three convincing arguments. Avoid generalizations ("Guns are dangerous") or oversimplifying statements ("Guns don't kill people, people do").

If you need some help with finding arguments, there are literally millions of pages and web sites on the Internet devoted to the gun control debate. In fact, simply typing "gun control debate" into a search engine will bring up millions of hits.

34 My Daughter Smokes

Alice Walker

Preview

Alice Walker is a famous novelist. She is also a mother. Like mothers everywhere, she would do nearly anything to protect her child from harm. How bitter, then, to see her daughter choose a habit that could end her life. From the starting point of her daughter's smoking, Walker branches into a broader discussion of tobacco, its role in society, and the way it has been corrupted by an ever larger and wealthier industry.

Words to Watch

consort (2): spouse
pungent (3): having a sharp, bitter taste
dapper (4): stylishly dressed
perennially (6): continually
ritual (12): activity done regularly
futility (16): uselessness
empathy (17): understanding
denatured (17): changed from its natural state
mono-cropping (17): growing of single crops apart from other crops
suppressed (18): kept down
cajole (20): gently urge

1   My daughter smokes. While she is doing her homework, her feet on the bench in front of her and her calculator clicking out answers to her algebra problems, I am looking at the half-empty package of Camels tossed carelessly close at hand. Camels. I pick them up, take them into the kitchen, where the light is better, and study them—they're filtered, for which I am grateful. My heart feels terrible. I want to weep. In fact, I do weep a little, standing there by the stove holding one of the instruments, so white, so precisely rolled, that could cause my daughter's death. When she smoked Marlboros and Players I hardened myself against feeling so bad; nobody I knew ever smoked these brands.

2   She doesn't know this, but it was Camels that my father, her grandfather,

industry, coupled with Hollywood movies in which both hero and heroine smoked like chimneys, won over completely people like my father, who were hopelessly addicted to cigarettes. He never looked as dapper° as Prince Albert, though; he continued to look like a poor, overweight, overworked colored man with too large a family; black, with a very white cigarette stuck in his mouth.

5   I do not remember when he started to cough. Perhaps it was unnoticeable at first. A little hacking in the morning as he lit his first cigarette upon getting out of bed. By the time I was my daughter's age, his breath was a wheeze, embarrassing to hear; he could not climb stairs without resting every third or fourth step. It was not unusual for him to cough for an hour.

smoked. But before he smoked "ready-mades"—when he was very young and very poor, with eyes like lanterns—he smoked Prince Albert tobacco in cigarettes he rolled himself. I remember the bright-red tobacco tin, with a picture of Queen Victoria's consort°, Prince Albert, dressed in a black frock coat and carrying a cane.

3   The tobacco was dark brown, pungent°, slightly bitter. I tasted it more than once as a child, and the discarded tins could be used for a number of things: to keep buttons and shoelaces in, to store seeds, and best of all, to hold worms for the rare times my father took us fishing.

4   By the late forties and early fifties, no one rolled his own anymore (and few women smoked) in my hometown, Eatonton, Georgia. The tobacco

6   It is hard to believe there was a time when people did not understand that cigarette smoking is an addiction. I wondered aloud once to my sister—who is perennially° trying to quit—whether our father realized this. I wondered how she, a smoker since high school, viewed her own habit.

7   It was our father who gave her her first cigarette, one day when she had taken water to him in the fields.

8   "I always wondered why he did that," she said, puzzled, and with some bitterness.

9   "What did he say?" I asked.

10   "That he didn't want me to go to anyone else for them," she said, "which never really crossed my mind."

11   So he was aware it was addictive, I thought, though as annoyed as she that he assumed she would be interested.

12   I began smoking in eleventh grade, also the year I drank numerous bottles of terrible sweet, very cheap wine. My friends and I, all boys for this venture, bought our supplies from a man who ran a segregated bar and liquor store on the outskirts of town. Over the entrance there was a large sign that said COLORED. We were not permitted to drink there, only to buy. I smoked Kools, because my sister did. By then I thought her toxic darkened lips and gums glamorous. However, my body simply would not tolerate smoke. After six months I had a chronic sore throat. I gave up smoking, gladly. Because it was a ritual° with my buddies—Murl, Leon, and "Dog" Farley—I continued to drink wine.

13   My father died from "the poor man's friend," pneumonia, one hard winter when his bronchitis and emphysema had left him low. I doubt he had much lung left at all, after coughing for so many years. He had so little breath that, during his last years, he was always leaning on something. I remembered once, at a family reunion, when my daughter was two, that my father picked her up for a minute—long enough for me to photograph them—but the effort was obvious. Near the very end of his life, and largely because he had no more lungs, he quit smoking. He gained a couple of pounds, but by then he was so emaciated no one noticed.

14   When I travel to Third World countries, I see many people like my father and daughter. There are large billboards directed at them both: the tough, "take-charge," or dapper older man, the glamorous, "worldly" young woman, both puffing away. In these poor countries, as in American ghettos and on reservations, money that should be spent for food goes instead to the tobacco companies; over time, people starve themselves of both food and air, effectively weakening and addicting their children, eventually eradicating themselves. I read in the newspaper and in my gardening magazine that cigarette butts are so toxic that if a baby swallows one, it is likely to die, and that the boiled water from a bunch of them makes an effective insecticide.

15   My daughter would like to quit, she says. We both know the statistics are against her; most people who try to quit smoking do not succeed.*

16   There is a deep hurt that I feel as a mother. Some days it is a feeling of futility°. I remember how carefully I ate when I was pregnant, how patiently I taught my daughter how to cross a street safely. For what, I sometimes wonder; so that she can wheeze through most of her life feeling half her strength, and then die of self-poisoning, as her grandfather did?

17   But, finally, one must feel empathy° for the tobacco plant itself. For thousands of years, it has been venerated by Native Americans as a sacred medicine. They have used it extensively—its juice, its leaves, its roots, its (holy) smoke—to heal wounds and cure diseases, and in ceremonies of prayer and peace. And though the plant as most of us know it has been poisoned by chemicals and

*Three months after reading this essay, my daughter stopped smoking.

denatured° by intensive mono-cropping° and is therefore hardly the plant it was, still, to some modern Indians it remains a plant of positive power. I learned this when my Native American friends, Bill Wahpepah and his family, visited with me for a few days, and the first thing he did was sow a few tobacco seeds in my garden.

18   Perhaps we can liberate tobacco from those who have captured and abused it, enslaving the plant on large plantations, keeping it from freedom and its kin, and forcing it to enslave the world. Its true nature suppressed°, no wonder it has become deadly. Maybe by sowing a few seeds of tobacco in our gardens and treating the plant with the reverence it deserves, we can redeem tobacco's soul and restore its self-respect.

19   Besides, how grim, if one is a smoker, to realize one is smoking a slave.

20   There is a slogan from a battered women's shelter that I especially like: "Peace on earth begins at home." I believe everything does. I think of a slogan for people trying to stop smoking: "Every home a smoke-free zone." Smoking is a form of self-battering that also batters those who must sit by, occasionally cajole° or complain, and helplessly watch. I realize now that as a child I sat by, through the years, and literally watched my father kill himself; surely one such victory in my family, for the rich white men who own the tobacco companies, is enough.

First Impressions

Freewrite for ten minutes on one of the following.

1. Did you enjoy reading this selection? Why or why not?

2. Have you ever been (or are you now) a smoker? Why did you begin smoking? If you still smoke, what are your reasons for continuing?

3. Do you know anyone whose health has obviously been harmed by smoking? What symptoms does he or she have? Does he or she still smoke? If so, why?

Vocabulary Check

_____A_____ 1. In the excerpt below, the word *emaciated* means
  A. thin.
  B. muscular.
  C. healthy.
  D. gray-haired.

> Paragraph 13 describes how feeble and ill Walker's father had become because he "had no more lungs." This suggests that he was thin.

"Near the very end of his life, and largely because he had no more lungs, he quit smoking. He gained a couple of pounds, but by then he was so emaciated no one noticed." (Paragraph 13)

_____C_____ 2. In the excerpt below, the word *eradicating* means
  A. curing.
  B. feeding.
  C. destroying.
  D. controlling.

> People who starve themselves of food and air are destroying themselves.

"In these poor countries . . . , money that should be spent for food goes instead to the tobacco companies; over time, people starve themselves of both food and air, effectively weakening and addicting their children, eventually eradicating themselves." (Paragraph 14)

_____A_____ 3. In the excerpt below, the word *venerated* means
  A. honored.
  B. ignored.
  C. ridiculed.
  D. forgotten.

> The word *sacred* suggests that *venerated* means "honored."

"For thousands of years, it has been venerated by Native Americans as a sacred medicine. They have used it extensively . . ." (Paragraph 17)

_____B_____ 4. In the sentence below, the word *redeem* means
  A. destroy.
  B. save from evil.
  C. treat with contempt.
  D. loosen.

> One way to restore tobacco's self-respect would be to save its soul from evil.

"Maybe by sowing a few seeds of tobacco in our gardens and treating the plant with the reverence it deserves, we can redeem tobacco's soul and restore its self-respect." (Paragraph 18)

Reading Check

Central Point and Main Ideas

B 1. Which sentence best expresses the central point of the entire selection?

Answer A covers only paragraph 15. Answer C covers only paragraph 17. Answer D is suggested only in paragraph 14.

  A. Most people who try to quit smoking are not successful.
  B. The pain Walker feels over her daughter's smoking leads her to think about all the harm done by the tobacco industry.
  C. Native Americans have used the tobacco plant for thousands of years as a sacred medicine and in ceremonies of prayer and peace.
  D. Tobacco ads that show healthy, attractive people are misleading.

A 2. Which sentence best expresses the main idea of paragraph 4?

Answer B is not supported. Answer C covers only sentence 1. Answer D covers only sentence 3.

  A. For Walker's father and others, the reality of smoking was very different from the images shown in ads and movies.
  B. Walker's father smoked because he wanted to look like Prince Albert.
  C. No one rolled his or her own cigarettes by the 1950s.
  D. Walker's father was poor, overweight, and overworked.

C 3. Which sentence best expresses the main idea of paragraph 5?
  A. Walker does not know when her father began to cough.
  B. When Walker was her daughter's age, she was embarrassed to hear her father wheezing.
  C. Walker's father's cough began quietly, but it grew to become a major problem.
  D. Walker's father had great difficulty climbing stairs.

Answer A covers only sentence 1. Answers B and D each cover only part of sentence 4.

Supporting Details

C 4. Walker is especially upset that her daughter smokes Camel cigarettes because
  A. she believes Camels to be especially bad for people's health.
  B. Camels are the brand that Walker herself smoked as a teenager.
  C. Walker's father, who died as a result of smoking, smoked Camels.
  D. they are filtered.   See the first sentence in paragraph 2.

D 5. When Walker's father picked up his granddaughter at a family reunion, he
  A. burned the child with his cigarette.
  B. put her down quickly so he could have another cigarette.
  C. warned her against smoking.
  D. was too weak to hold her for long.   See paragraph 13.

Inferences

___A___ 6. We can infer that Walker

Answer B is contradicted by paragraph 18. Answer C is not supported. Answer D is contradicted by paragraphs 17 and 18.

A. believes people who are poor, uneducated, and nonwhite have been especially victimized by the tobacco industry.

B. believes that the tobacco plant should be eliminated.

C. remains furious with her father about her daughter's decision to smoke.

D. believes Native Americans were wrong to honor the tobacco plant.

Item 7: ___B___ 7. We can assume that, for Walker, smoking as a teenager was

See paragraph 12. Answer A is not supported. Answer C is contradicted by the next-to-last sentence in paragraph 12. Answer D is contradicted by the last sentence in paragraph 12.

A. strictly forbidden by her parents.

B. an exciting experiment.

C. quickly habit-forming.

D. the end of her friendship with Murl, Leon, and "Dog" Farley.

___B___ 8. We can conclude that Walker's daughter

A. did not care that her mother was concerned about her smoking.

B. may have been helped to quit smoking by her mother's essay.

C. has no clear memories of her grandfather.

D. blamed her aunt for encouraging her to smoke.

See the footnote to paragraph 15. Answer A is contradicted by paragraph 15. Answers C and D are not supported.

The Writer's Craft

Item 9: In particular, paragraphs 1, 15, and 16 and the last sentence of the essay suggest the daughter as audience. But Walker also presents the story of her father and other details in a manner easily understood by anyone who smokes.

___D___ 9. What audience did Walker seem to have in mind when she wrote this essay?

A. Executives of the tobacco industry

B. Citizens of the Third World who are being targeted by tobacco advertising campaigns

C. Only her daughter, who Walker hoped would stop smoking after she read the essay

D. Her daughter plus anyone else who smokes

___B___ 10. What is Walker's tone in "My Daughter Smokes"?

A. Sad and hopeless

B. Serious and concerned

C. Complaining and sarcastic

D. Objective and unemotional

Examples of the serious tone include the description of what cigarettes did to her father (paragraphs 5 and 13) and the information about cigarette butts (last sentence of paragraph 14). Examples of the concerned tone include Walker's comments about people in the Third World (paragraph 14) and the passages about her daughter (paragraphs 1 and 16).

Discussion Questions

1. What would you do if you had a friend who was involved in self-destructive behavior, such as smoking, excessive drinking, or drug use? Would you ignore the behavior? Would you try to persuade the friend to stop the behavior? What would be the risks of either choice?

2. What is a bad habit of yours that you have tried to break? How successful were you? What made breaking that habit difficult?

3. Suppose that you had a sixteen-year-old son or daughter. What rules would you expect him or her to obey while living in your home? Would you, for example, have a curfew for your child? Would you allow him or her to smoke in your home? How would you respond if you learned that he or she was drinking, using drugs, or becoming sexually active?

4. It's clear that smoking is a health hazard. Study after study shows that smoking leads to a variety of diseases, including cancer, emphysema, and heart disease. It has also become clear that second-hand smoke—smoke that non-smokers breathe when they are around smokers—is dangerous as well. If you had the power to do so, would you make smoking illegal or put any legal restrictions on smoking? Or do you believe that smoking should continue to be an individual's right? Explain.

Paragraph Assignments

1. Write a paragraph in which you try to persuade a friend to quit smoking. In it, explain in detail three reasons you think he or she should quit. Use transitions such as *first of all, secondly, another*, and *finally* as you list the three reasons.

2. In her essay, Walker is critical of the glamorous, healthy image presented by cigarette advertisements. Write a paragraph in which you describe what you think an honest cigarette advertisement would look like. Who would appear in the ad? What would they be doing? What would they be saying?

   In preparation for this assignment, you might study two or three cigarette ads, using them as inspiration. Your topic sentence might be something like this: "A truly honest cigarette advertisement would not tempt anyone to smoke."

Essay Assignments

1. Think of three bad habits that you have. Perhaps you spend money impulsively, put things off until the last minute, eat too much junk food, speak before you think, or bite your nails. Write an essay explaining how you believe you acquired the habits, how you think they harm you, and how you could get rid of them. Here is a possible thesis statement for this essay: "There are several bad habits that I would love to break."

2. According to Walker, a viewer of movies from the 1940s and 1950s would get the idea that people could "smoke like chimneys" with no bad effects. What are some unrealistic images that today's movies and TV shows present? To answer that question, write an essay from the point of view of an alien from another planet. In order to learn more about the human race, you, the alien, are watching today's movies and TV shows. Write about at least three unrealistic—or just plain wrong—ideas that today's films and television teach you about human beings and society. Use specific examples from movies and TV shows to illustrate your points. Here are a few sample topic sentences for supporting paragraphs in this essay:

   - "Humans sustain themselves with bubbly drinks and messy food combinations."
   - "Humans play a wide variety of puzzling games."
   - "Young and mature humans speak somewhat different languages."

35 A Drunken Ride, a Tragic Aftermath

Theresa Conroy and Christine M. Johnson

Preview

It is a sequence of events that occurs all too often—high-school kids gather for a party that quickly turns drunken and raucous. The party spills out into the roadways, and an evening of alcohol-fueled celebration turns into a nightmare of twisted metal, mangled bodies, and anguished survivors. As this selection makes clear, the horror of such a night does not end with the funerals of those who died.

Words to Watch

carnage (19): massive slaughter
catharsis (62): refreshing release of emotional tension
fathom (64): understand
curtail (68): cut back on
vicariously (94): by imagining someone else's experience
adherence (95): sticking
subsidized (97): financed
peer-group (97): made up of people of a similar age, grade, etc.

1 When Tyson Baxter awoke after that drunken, tragic night—with a bloodied head, broken arm, and battered face—he knew that he had killed his friends.

2 "I knew everyone had died," Baxter, 18, recalled. "I knew it before anybody told me. Somehow, I knew."

3 Baxter was talking about the night of Friday, September 13, the night he and seven friends piled into his Chevrolet Blazer after a beer-drinking party. On Street Road in Upper Southampton, he lost control, rear-ended a car, and smashed into two telephone poles. The Blazer's cab top shattered, and the truck spun several times, ejecting all but one passenger.

4 Four young men were killed.

5 Tests would show that Baxter and the four youths who died were legally intoxicated.

6 Baxter says he thinks about his dead friends on many sleepless nights at the Abraxas Drug and Alcohol Rehabilitation Center near Pittsburgh, where, on December 20, he was sentenced to be held after being found delinquent on charges of vehicular homicide.

7　　"I drove them where they wanted to go, and I was responsible for their lives," Baxter said recently from the center, where he is undergoing psychological treatment. "I had the keys in my hand, and I blew it."

8　　The story of September 13 is a story about the kind of horrors that drinking and driving is spawning among high-school students almost everywhere . . . about parents who lost their children in a flash and have filled the emptiness with hatred . . . about a youth whose life is burdened with grief and guilt because he happened to be behind the wheel.

9　　It is a story that the Baxter family and the dead boys' parents agreed to tell in the hope that it would inspire high-school students to remain sober during this week of graduation festivities—a week that customarily includes a ritual night of drunkenness.

10　　It is a story of the times.

11　　The evening of September 13 began in high spirits as Baxter, behind the wheel of his gold Blazer, picked up seven high-school chums for a drinking party for William Tennent High School students and graduates at the home of a classmate. Using false identification, according to police, the boys purchased one six-pack of beer each from a Warminster Township bar.

12　　The unchaperoned party, attended by about fifty teenagers, ended about 10:30 p.m. when someone knocked over and broke a glass china cabinet. Baxter and his friends decided to head for a fast-food restaurant. As Baxter turned onto Street Road, he was trailed by a line of cars carrying other partygoers.

13　　Baxter recalled that several passengers were swaying and rocking the high-suspension vehicle. Police were unable to determine the vehicle's exact speed, but, on the basis of the accounts of witnesses, they estimated it at fifty-five miles per hour—ten miles per hour over the limit.

14　　"I thought I was in control," Baxter said. "I wasn't driving like a nut; I was just . . . driving. There was a bunch of noise, just a bunch of noise. The truck was really bouncing.

15　　"I remember passing two [cars]. That's the last I remember. I remember a big flash, and that's it."

16　　Killed in that flash were: Morris "Marty" Freedenberg, 16, who landed near a telephone pole about thirty feet from the truck, his face ripped from his skull; Robert Schweiss, 18, a Bucks County Community College student, whose internal organs were crushed when he hit the pavement about thirty feet from the truck; Brian Ball, 17, who landed near Schweiss, his six-foot-seven-inch frame stretched three inches when his spine was severed; and Christopher Avram, 17, a premedical student at Temple University, who landed near the curb about ten feet from the truck.

17　　Michael Serratore, 18, was thrown fifteen feet from the truck and landed on the lawn of the CHI Institute with his right leg shattered. Baxter, who sailed about ten feet after crashing through the windshield of the Blazer, lost consciousness after hitting the street near the center lane. About five yards away, Paul Gee, Jr., 18, lapsed into a coma from severe head injuries.

18   John Gahan, 17, the only passenger left in the Blazer, suffered a broken ankle.

19   Brett Walker, 17, one of several Tennent students who saw the carnage° after the accident, would recall later in a speech to fellow students: "I ran over [to the scene]. These were the kids I would go out with every weekend.

20   "My one friend [Freedenberg], I couldn't even tell it was him except for his eyes. He had real big, blue eyes. He was torn apart so bad. . . ."

21   Francis Schweiss was waiting up for his son, Robert, when he received a telephone call from his daughter, Lisa. She was already at Warminster General Hospital.

22   "She said Robbie and his friends were in a bad accident and Robbie was not here" at the hospital, Schweiss said. "I got in my car with my wife; we went to the scene of the accident."

23   There, police officers told Francis and Frances Schweiss that several boys had been killed and that the bodies, as well as survivors, had been taken to Warminster General Hospital.

24   "My head was frying by then," Francis Schweiss said. "I can't even describe it. I almost knew the worst was to be. I felt as though I were living a nightmare. I thought, 'I'll wake up. This just can't be.'"

25   In the emergency room, Francis Schweiss recalled, nurses and doctors were scrambling to aid the injured and identify the dead—a difficult task because some bodies were disfigured and because all the boys had been

carrying fake driver's licenses.

26   A police officer from Upper Southampton was trying to question friends of the dead and injured—many of whom were sobbing and screaming—in an attempt to match clothing with identities.

27   When the phone rang in the Freedenberg home, Robert S. and his wife, Bobbi, had just gone upstairs to bed; their son Robert Jr. was downstairs watching a movie on television.

28   Bobbi Freedenberg and her son picked up the receiver at the same time. It was from Warminster General. . . . There had been a bad accident. . . . The family should get to the hospital quickly.

29   Outside the morgue about twenty minutes later, a deputy county coroner told Rob Jr., 22, that his brother was dead and severely disfigured; Rob decided to spare his parents additional grief by identifying the body himself.

30   Freedenberg was led into a cinderblock room containing large drawers resembling filing cabinets. In one of the drawers was his brother, Marty, identifiable only by his new high-top sneakers.

31   "It was kind of like being taken through a nightmare," Rob Jr. said. "That's something I think about every night before I go to sleep. That's hell. . . . That whole night is what hell is all about for me."

32   As was his custom, Morris Ball started calling the parents of his son's friends after Brian missed his 11:00 p.m. curfew.

33   The first call was to the Baxters' house, where the Baxters' sixteen-year-old daughter, Amber, told him about the accident.

34   At the hospital, Morris Ball demanded that doctors and nurses take him to his son. The hospital staff had been unable to identify Brian—until Ball told them that his son wore size 14 shoes.

35   Brian Ball was in the morgue. Lower left drawer.

36   "He was six foot seven, but after the accident he measured six foot ten, because of what happened to him," Ball said. "He had a severed spinal cord at the neck. His buttocks were practically ripped off, but he was lying down and we couldn't see that. He was peaceful and asleep.

37   "He was my son and my baby. I just can't believe it sometimes. I still can't believe it. I still wait for him to come home."

38   Lynne Pancoast had just finished watching the 11:00 p.m. news and was curled up in her bed dozing with a book in her lap when the doorbell rang. She assumed that one of her sons had forgotten his key, and she went downstairs to let him in.

39   A police light was flashing through the window and reflecting against her living-room wall; Pancoast thought that there must be a fire in the neighborhood and that the police were evacuating homes.

40   Instead, police officers told her there had been a serious accident involving her son, Christopher Avram, and that she should go to the emergency room at Warminster General.

41   At the hospital she was taken to an empty room and told that her son was dead.

42   Patricia Baxter was asleep when a Warminster police officer came to the house and informed her that her son had been in an accident.

43   At the hospital, she could not immediately recognize her own son lying on a bed in the emergency room. His brown eyes were swollen shut, and his straight brown hair was matted with blood that had poured from a deep gash in his forehead.

44   While she was staring at his battered face, a police officer rushed into the room and pushed her onto the floor—protection against the hysterical father of a dead youth who was racing through the halls, proclaiming that he had a gun and shouting, "Where is she? I'm going to kill her. I'm going to kill him. I'm going to kill his mother."

45   The man, who did not have a gun,

46   Amid the commotion, Robert Baxter, a Lower Southampton highway patrol officer, arrived at the hospital and found his wife and son.

47   "When he came into the room, he kept going like this," Patricia Baxter said, holding up four fingers. At first, she said, she did not understand that her husband was signaling that four boys had been killed in the accident.

48   After Tyson regained consciousness, his father told him about the deaths.

49   "All I can remember is just tensing up and just saying something," Tyson Baxter said. "I can remember saying, 'I know.'

50   "I can remember going nuts."

51   In the days after the accident, as the dead were buried in services that Tyson Baxter was barred by the parents of the victims from attending, Baxter's parents waited for him to react to the tragedy and release his grief.

52   "In the hospital he was non-responsive," Patricia Baxter said. "He was home for a month, and he was nonresponsive.

53   "We never used to do this, but we would be upstairs and listen to see if Ty responded when his friends came to visit," she said. "But the boy would be silent. That's the grief that I felt. The other kids showed a reaction. My son didn't."

54   Baxter said, however, that he felt grief from the first, that he would cry in the quiet darkness of his hospital room and, later, alone in the darkness of his bedroom. During the day, he said, he blocked his emotions.

55   "It was just at night. I thought about it all the time. It's still like that."

56   At his parents' urging, Baxter returned to school on September 30.

57   "I don't remember a thing," he said of his return. "I just remember walking around. I didn't say anything to anybody. It didn't really sink in."

58   Lynne Pancoast, the mother of Chris Avram, thought it was wrong for Baxter to be in school, and wrong that her other son, Joel, a junior at William Tennent, had to walk through the school halls and pass the boy who "killed his brother."

59   Morris Ball said he was appalled that Baxter "went to a football game while my son lay buried in a grave."

60   Some William Tennent students said they were uncertain about how they should treat Baxter. Several said they went out of their way to treat him normally, others said they tried to avoid him, and others declined to be interviewed on the subject.

61   The tragedy unified the senior class, according to the school principal, Kenneth Kastle. He said that after the accident, many students who were friends of the victims joined the school's Students Against Driving Drunk chapter.

62   Matthew Weintraub, 17, a basketball player who witnessed the bloody accident scene, wrote to President Reagan and detailed the grief among the student body. He said, however, that he experienced a catharsis° after reading the letter at a student assembly and, as a result, did not mail it.

63   "And after we got over the initial

shock of the news, we felt as though we owed somebody something," Weintraub wrote. "It could have been us and maybe we could have stopped it, and now it's too late. . . .

64   "We took these impressions with us as we then visited our friends who had been lucky enough to live. One of them was responsible for the accident; he was the driver. He would forever hold the deaths of four young men on his conscience. Compared with our own feelings of guilt, [we] could not begin to fathom° this boy's emotions. He looked as if he had a heavy weight upon his head and it would remain there forever."

65   About three weeks after the accident, Bucks County Senator H. Craig Lewis launched a series of public forums to formulate bills targeting underage drinking. Proposals developed through the meetings include outlawing alcohol ads on radio and television, requiring police to notify parents of underage drinkers, and creating a tamperproof driver's license.

66   The parents of players on William Tennent's boys' basketball team, which lost Ball and Baxter because of the accident, formed the Caring Parents of William Tennent High School Students to help dissuade students from drinking.

67   Several William Tennent students, interviewed on the condition that their names not be published, said that, because of the accident, they would not drive after drinking during senior week, which will be held in Wildwood, New Jersey, after graduation June 13.

68   But they scoffed at the suggestion that they curtail° their drinking during the celebrations.

69   "We just walk [after driving to Wildwood]," said one youth. "Stagger is more like it."

70   "What else are we going to do, go out roller skating?" an eighteen-year-old student asked.

71   "You telling us we're not going to drink?" one boy asked. "We're going to drink very heavily. I want to come home retarded. That's senior week. I'm going to drink every day. Everybody's going to drink every day."

72   Tyson Baxter sat at the front table of the Bucks County courtroom on December 20, his arm in a sling, his head lowered and his eyes dry. He faced twenty counts of vehicular homicide, four counts of involuntary manslaughter, and two counts of driving under the influence of alcohol.

73   Patricia Ball said she told the closed hearing that "it was Tyson Baxter who killed our son. He used the car as a weapon. We know he killed our children as if it were a gun. He killed our son."

74   "I really could have felt justice [was served] if Tyson Baxter was the only one who died in that car," she said in an interview, "because he didn't take care of our boys."

75   Police officers testified before Bucks County President Judge Isaac S. Garb that tests revealed that the blood-alcohol levels of Baxter and the four dead boys were above the 0.10 percent limit used in Pennsylvania to establish intoxication.

76   Baxter's blood-alcohol level was 0.14 percent, Ball's 0.19 percent,

Schweiss's 0.11 percent, Avram's 0.12 percent, and Freedenberg's 0.38 percent. Baxter's level indicated that he had had eight or nine drinks—enough to cause abnormal bodily functions such as exaggerated gestures and to impair his mental faculties, according to the police report.

77 After the case was presented, Garb invited family members of the dead teens to speak.

78 In a nine-page statement, Bobbi Freedenberg urged Garb to render a decision that would "punish, rehabilitate, and deter others from this act."

79 The parents asked Garb to give Baxter the maximum sentence, to prohibit him from graduating, and to incarcerate him before Christmas day. (Although he will not attend formal ceremonies, Baxter will receive a diploma from William Tennent this week.)

80 After hearing from the parents, Garb called Baxter to the stand.

81 "I just said that all I could say was, 'I'm sorry; I know I'm totally responsible for what happened,'" Baxter recalled. "It wasn't long, but it was to the point."

82 Garb found Baxter delinquent and sentenced him to a stay at Abraxas Rehabilitation Center—for an unspecified period beginning December 23—and community service upon his return. Baxter's driver's license was suspended by the judge for an unspecified period, and he was placed under Garb's jurisdiction until age 21.

83 Baxter is one of fifty-two Pennsylvania youths found responsible for fatal drunken-driving accidents in the state in 1985.

84 Reflecting on the hearing, Morris Ball said there was no legal punishment that would have satisfied his longings.

85 "They can't bring my son back," he said, "and they can't kill Tyson Baxter."

86 Grief has forged friendships among the dead boys' parents, each of whom blames Tyson Baxter for their son's death. Every month they meet at each other's homes, but they seldom talk about the accident.

87 Several have joined support groups to help them deal with their losses. Some said they feel comfortable only with other parents whose children are dead.

88 Bobbi Freedenberg said her attitude had worsened with the passage of time. "It seems as if it just gets harder," she said. "It seems to get worse."

89 Freedenberg, Schweiss, and Pancoast said they talk publicly about their sons' deaths in hopes that the experience will help deter other teenagers from drunken driving.

90 Schweiss speaks each month to the Warminster Youth Aid Panel—a group of teenagers who, through drug use, alcohol abuse, or minor offenses, have run afoul of the law.

91 "When I talk to the teens, I bring a picture of Robbie and pass it along to everyone," Schweiss said, wiping the tears from his cheeks. "I say, 'He was with us last year.' I get emotional and I cry. . . .

92 "But I know that my son helps me. I firmly believe that every time I speak, he's right on my shoulder."

93 When Pancoast speaks to a group of area high-school students, she drapes

her son's football jersey over the podium and displays his graduation picture.

94   "Every time I speak to a group, I make them go through the whole thing vicariously°," Pancoast said. "It's helpful to get out and talk to kids. It sort of helps keep Chris alive. . . . When you talk, you don't think."

95   At Abraxas, Baxter attended high-school classes until Friday. He is one of three youths there who supervise fellow residents, who keep track of residents' whereabouts, attendance at programs, and adherence° to the center's rules and regulations.

96   Established in Pittsburgh, the Abraxas Foundation provides an alternative to imprisonment for offenders between sixteen and twenty-five years old whose drug and alcohol use has led them to commit crimes.

97   Licensed and partially subsidized° by the Pennsylvania Department of Health, the program includes work experience, high-school education, and prevocational training. Counselors conduct individual therapy sessions, and the residents engage in peer-group° confrontational therapy sessions.

98   Baxter said his personality had changed from an "egotistical, arrogant" teenager to someone who is "mellow" and mature.

99   "I don't have quite the chip on my shoulder. I don't really have a right to be cocky anymore," he said.

100   Baxter said not a day went by that he didn't remember his dead friends.

101   "I don't get sad. I just get thinking about them," he said. "Pictures pop into my mind. A tree or something reminds me of the time. . . . Sometimes I laugh. . . . Then I go to my room and reevaluate it like a nut," he said.

102   Baxter said his deepest longing was to stand beside the graves of his four friends.

103   More than anything, Baxter said, he wants to say good-bye.

104   "I just feel it's something I *have* to do, . . . just to talk," Baxter said, averting his eyes to hide welling tears. "Deep down I think I'll be hit with it when I see the graves. I know they're gone, but they're not gone."

First Impressions

Freewrite for ten minutes on one of the following.

1. Did you enjoy reading this selection? Why or why not?

2. If you were the parent of one of the boys who were killed, would you have responded to Tyson Baxter in the same way the parents in the story did? Or would you have behaved differently? Explain.

3. Do you know of alcohol-related accidents involving students? Did the accidents seem to have any effect on other students' attitudes toward drinking?

Vocabulary Check

___A___ 1. In the excerpt below, the word *spawning* means
  A. producing.
  B. preventing.
  C. protecting.
  D. predicting.

  Since we know the dreadful accident happened as a result of drinking and driving, this activity must have produced it.

  "The story of September 13 is a story about the kind of horrors that drinking and driving is spawning among high-school students almost everywhere . . ." (Paragraph 8)

___B___ 2. In the sentence below, the word *appalled* means
  A. relieved.
  B. horrified.
  C. pleased.
  D. aware.

  How would a person who had just lost his child react when he learned the person responsible for his loss was having fun at a game?

  "Morris Ball said he was appalled that Baxter 'went to a football game while my son lay buried in a grave.'" (Paragraph 59)

___C___ 3. In the sentence below, the word *deter* means
  A. punish.
  B. pay.
  C. prevent.
  D. hide.

  What might learning about a horrific accident and multiple deaths do to teenagers' plans to drive while drunk?

  "Freedenberg, Schweiss, and Pancoast said they talk publicly about their sons' deaths in hopes that the experience will help deter other teenagers from drunken driving." (Paragraph 89)

___B___ 4. In the excerpt below, the word *averting* means
  A. opening.
  B. turning away.
  C. asking.
  D. thinking of.

  If Baxter was hiding his tears, he must have turned his eyes away.

  "'I just feel it's something I *have* to do, . . . just to talk,' Baxter said, averting his eyes to hide welling tears." (Paragraph 104)

Reading Check

Central Point and Main Ideas

_A_ 1. Which sentence best expresses the central point of the entire selection?
   A. The experience of Tyson Baxter and his friends should serve as an example to teens of the dangers of drinking and driving.
   B. The parents of the boys killed in the accident have never forgiven the driver, Tyson Baxter.
   C. Drinking has become a routine part of life for many teenagers.
   D. Because of a high-school student's drunk-driving accident, a state senator began work on a bill targeting underage drinking.

   See paragraphs 8–10. The details that follow graphically illustrate what can happen when people drink and drive.

_A_ 2. Which sentence best expresses the main idea of paragraph 8?
   A. Many people are affected by the consequences of high-school students' drinking and driving.
   B. Parents who lose their children may be consumed with hatred.
   C. The driver of the automobile feels a great deal of grief and guilt.
   D. High-school students across the country are drinking and driving more.

   Answers B and C are too narrow; each applies to only part of the one-sentence paragraph. Answer D is not mentioned in the paragraph.

Supporting Details

_A_ 3. Which of the following was *not* a consequence of the accident?
   A. Students pledged not to drink during senior week at Wildwood, New Jersey.
   B. A senator held a series of public forums to think up ways to fight underage drinking.
   C. Many William Tennent students joined a Students Against Driving Drunk chapter.
   D. The parents of the boys who died began to meet every month.

See paragraphs 67–71. Note that the students pledged not to drive after drinking, but they still intended to drink.

_D_ 4. The task of identifying the bodies was made more difficult because
   A. the boys' friends were sobbing and screaming.
   B. the bodies were badly disfigured.
   C. the boys were carrying fake identification.
   D. of all of the above.

   See paragraphs 25–26.

Inferences

See paragraphs 73–74, 78–79, and 84–86, in which the parents place the entire blame on Baxter. Answers B and C are unsupported.

_A_ 5. From the comments made in court by the parents of the victims, we can infer that the parents
A. did not blame their own sons for their underage drinking.
B. believed Baxter had gotten false identification for their sons.
C. felt all of the victims that survived should be punished.
D. felt all of the above.

_C_ 6. We can infer from the statements made by seniors in paragraphs 67–71 that
A. many students at Baxter's high school had not heard of his accident.
B. graduation parties will be strictly chaperoned.
C. some students do not take the dangers of alcohol abuse seriously.
D. the drinking age is lower in Wildwood than in other places.
> Despite what happened, the students still intend to drink heavily during graduation week. Answers A, B, and D are not supported.

_B_ 7. We can assume that after being released from Abraxas, Tyson Baxter will
A. never drive a car again.
B. visit the graves of the four boys killed in the accident.
C. become a role model in the fight against drunk driving.
D. pretend that the accident never happened.
> See paragraphs 100–104. Answers A and C are unsupported; answer D is unsupported and unlikely.

The Writer's Craft

See paragraphs 1–2 and 98–104.

_B_ 8. The authors begin and end their essay with
A. remarks by the authors about the dangers of drunken driving.
B. quotations from Tyson Baxter.
C. quotations from the police who were first on the scene of the accident.
D. quotations from parents of the boys who died.

Starting with paragraph 11, the events are related in the order in which they happened, including the reactions of others involved.

_C_ 9. In general, this reading is organized according to which of the following patterns?
A. Listing order: a list of the measures people took after the accident to prevent drunk driving.
B. Cause-effect: explaining why so many teens get drunk during senior week.
C. Time order: the sequence of events that took place on September 13 and afterward.
D. Comparison-contrast: comparing and contrasting student attitudes toward drinking and driving before the accident and after the accident.

_C_ 10. The authors' primary purpose in this selection is to

    A. inform readers of ways that parents cope with the tragic deaths of their children.

    B. persuade readers that laws should be passed to make it more difficult for teenagers to purchase alcoholic beverages.

    C. persuade people in general, and particularly young people, not to drink and drive.

    D. entertain readers with a dramatic and horrifying true-crime story.

> See paragraphs 8–9. The authors have told this story, with the consent of the Baxters and the families of the victims, to serve as an object lesson for all of us.

Discussion Questions

1. The authors write in paragraph 14: "'I thought I was in control,' Baxter said. 'I wasn't driving like a nut; I was just . . . driving.'" What does this tell us about the effects of alcohol on drivers?

2. To what extent do you think Tyson Baxter was responsible for the accident? Do you feel his passengers also were at fault in any way? If so, to what extent were they also responsible? Is there anyone else that you think is partly to blame for the accident?

3. What do you think would be an appropriate punishment for Tyson Baxter? If you were the judge in his case, what sentence would you give him? Why?

4. Why do you think that, even after knowing what had happened to Tyson Baxter and his friends, some of his classmates would brag about their plans to "drink very heavily" during senior week? What, if anything, do you think could change those students' attitudes about drinking?

Paragraph Assignments

1. Tyson Baxter's friends might still be alive if he had not been drunk when he drove. But there is another way their deaths could have been avoided—they could have refused to get into his car. Such a refusal would not have been easy; after all, nobody likes to embarrass, anger, or offend a person who has offered him or her a ride. Pretend you are a guidance counselor who's been asked to write a short statement on this topic to be handed out to students a week before the prom. To help the students prepare for such a situation, write a paragraph in which you suggest one or more strategies you have used to turn down a ride with a driver who may be drunk.

2. While drunk drivers can be any age, a large percentage of them are young. Write a paragraph explaining what you think would be a truly

effective way of making young people understand the horrors of drunk driving. Keep in mind that the young are being cautioned all the time and that some of the warnings are so familiar that they probably have little impact. What approach would be so unusual, dramatic, or unexpected that it might really get young people's attention? Start your paragraph with a topic sentence such as the following: "Here is a way to truly convince the young of the horrors of drunk driving." Then, in the rest of your paragraph, develop your suggestion in great detail.

Essay Assignments

1. The parents of the boys who were killed in the accident were unable to forgive Tyson Baxter, feeling that it was entirely his fault that their sons were dead. In fact, one parent actually claimed that Baxter "used the car as a weapon." And most of the parents felt that Baxter should be imprisoned for life.

    Have you ever been too upset and angry to forgive someone for an action that person took, only to find forgiveness in your heart after time had passed? Write an essay about that experience. Take some time to recall exactly what took place. Use details and possibly even dialogue to make your essay vivid. When organizing your essay, devote the first paragraph of the body to describing the event and what happened. What was the person like who made you angry? What exactly did he or she do? Next, write a paragraph about how you felt at the time and why you thought you could never forgive this person. Finally, spend a paragraph explaining how and why you were finally able to find forgiveness. How do you feel about the person today, now that you're no longer angry? Are you in touch with him or her? What did you learn from this experience?

    In your conclusion, you might want to note how forgiveness has made you feel and how you will, hopefully, handle things differently the next time you're extremely upset with someone.

2. People have different views about how severely Tyson Baxter should be punished. Some believe that the intoxicated boys in his car share the blame for what happened. Others say that by offering to drive, Baxter assumed total responsibility for the accident. Write an essay about what you think would be an appropriate punishment for Tyson Baxter, and why. Your thesis statement should state the chosen punishment—for example:

    - The most appropriate punishment for Tyson Baxter would be life imprisonment.
    - For several reasons, Tyson Baxter should have received a one-year sentence to a minimum-security prison.

    Your supporting paragraphs should develop the various reasons why that punishment is appropriate.

36 Marijuana Today
Mark Bowden

Preview

The laws against marijuana use have been ineffective, expensive, and unevenly enforced. There is a strong case to be made, says former *Philadelphia Inquirer* columnist Mark Bowden, for legalizing pot. (In fact, since this essay was written, the states of Washington and Colorado have legalized the possession of small amounts of marijuana.) Whether people should actually smoke pot, though, is another question entirely.

Words to Watch

disabuse (10): correct
contrition (10): regret
revelry (12): celebration
leverage (16): influence
clarity (18): clearness

1 I knew when I saw my father sitting at the kitchen table that I was in trouble.

2 I was a teenager, returning home late from a night out with my friends. I was high. As we did most nights, my friends and I had been smoking pot. Nearly everyone I knew my age smoked pot.

3 My father was usually asleep long before I got home. I took a quick inventory of my state of mind and concluded that so long as my conversation with him was casual and brief, there was a chance he wouldn't notice that I was cockeyed stoned. One of the virtues of pot, or so I thought then, was this ability to play it straight. Fear was especially useful. It could straighten out your thinking in a hurry.

4 As was his style, he confronted me head-on.

5 "Mark, do you smoke?" he asked.

6 I could not lie to my father. Even to this day, I'm not sure why exactly; I hope it was because I respected him and knew he did not lie to me.

7 "Yes," I told him, and then braced myself.

8 He was furious, but not about my marijuana use. He had not even considered the possibility of an illicit drug. He was worried that I was smoking

cigarettes! I nearly swooned with relief.

9   I was not a cigarette smoker. They gave me a headache and left a god-awful taste in my mouth. They were addictive and caused cancer. No way. My father had been a heavy smoker in his youth, and he had quit cold turkey when the first of the surgeon general's warnings had come out. So he could not comprehend why one of his own sons would even consider flirting with the habit.

10   I did not disabuse° him. While I might not have been able to look my father in the eye and lie, I was expert at withholding the complete truth. I bore the cigarette scolding manfully, expressed agreement and contrition°, and gave the old man my word I would never smoke another cigarette. I have kept that promise.

11   It took me a little longer to stop smoking dope. Having raised five children of my own and entered upon grandfatherhood, I can report two things: (1) I think we ought to repeal laws against marijuana possession; (2) I no longer think smoking pot is a good idea.

12   Tomorrow, April 20, or 4/20, has become an unofficial national holiday for lovers of weed. There are supposedly 420 chemical elements in cannabis, or something like that. The reasons for 4/20 becoming the toker's special day are suitably confused, about as certain as most trains of thought under the influence. The revelry° both celebrates the substance and protests its illegality. I'm with them on the latter issue, not so much on the former.

13   Marijuana smoking is, if anything, more commonplace today than when I was a wannabe hippie 40 years ago. My sons, now grown, tell me that it was easier for them to get pot in high school in Chester County than it was to get beer. Generations of Americans have grown up getting high, long enough for everyone to know that all the old horror stories about its use are ridiculously exaggerated. No one I knew who smoked dope as a kid—and, as I said, just about everyone I knew did—turned into a heroin or cocaine addict.

14   I do know some folks who became alcoholics, and a number of them are no longer around. I believed then and I believe today that alcohol is a far greater public health and safety threat than marijuana. Tobacco, also legal, is an even greater curse.

15   Yet the war on weed rages on. Thirty-seven years after a special commission formed by Congress and President Richard Nixon concluded that punitive marijuana laws cause more social harm than the drug itself, nearly half of the drug arrests in this country are for pot. The numbers grow annually. More people were arrested for pot possession in America last year than ever before in our history, more than 800,000. In Pennsylvania, possession is a misdemeanor, and the possible prison sentence goes from 30 days to a year, depending on whether the amount is more or less than 30 grams. Although there are horrific exceptions, most of these offenders, unless they were involved in serious drug trafficking or some other illegal activity when

arrested, do not go to jail for simple possession. Still, what a tremendous waste of money and manpower! One of the strongest arguments against such misdemeanor drug laws is that they are completely ineffective.

16   More than that, the prohibition of marijuana gives police an undue amount of leverage° over average citizens. When something as widespread as pot possession is illegal, police can use it as an excuse to harass whole classes of otherwise law-abiding citizens. It should come as no surprise that the majority of those possession busts were young black and Latino men, even though surveys show that most of the marijuana users in this country are white.

17   I stopped smoking dope many years ago. I have always urged my children not to use it, just as I have counseled them to avoid using other drugs and getting drunk. The effects of pot use are more subtle than drunkenness, which leads many to conclude that marijuana is a less dangerous intoxicant than alcohol, but its very subtlety poses a unique threat. Because you can go to class high, go to work high, drive high, and otherwise function with apparent normality, it is easier to abuse marijuana constantly than alcohol, and that "normality" you feel isn't the truth. Marijuana doesn't make you out of control. It just makes you stupid. And while I haven't surveyed the most recent medical reports, I suspect the health effects of inhaling pot smoke are likely to be at least as harmful as the substance that so concerned my dad.

For me, as with most users, getting high was a symptom of boredom and rebellion. Once I grew up and found work that I loved, competitive work that demanded real effort and mental clarity°, I realized that the effects of getting high, the confusion and silliness, were a disadvantage. When I had children, the responsibility I felt for them weighed on me in a nice way, but also in a way that ruled out getting high. Weed began to induce less joy than worry. What if, feeling temporarily silly and indifferent, I failed my family in some way, large or small?   18

I know I am not alone in this. These are the kinds of decisions adults in our society make every day about their health, their responsibilities, and their happiness. Lots of people don't agree with me, including some of my friends. That may make them misguided, in my view, but it certainly shouldn't make them criminal.   19

First Impressions

Freewrite for ten minutes on one of the following.

1. Did you enjoy reading this selection? Why or why not?

2. In your opinion, should marijuana be legalized? Why or why not?

3. If marijuana were legalized, do you think its usage would increase, decrease, or stay about the same? Explain.

Vocabulary Check

_B_ 1. In the excerpt below, the word *illicit* means
   A. easily purchased.
   B. illegal.
   C. able to be smoked.
   D. expensive.

   Cigarettes are legal; Bowden's father was upset that his son was smoking a legal substance. As Bowden points out later in the selection, marijuana is illegal.

   "He was furious, but not about my marijuana use. He had not even considered the possibility of an illicit drug. He was worried that I was smoking cigarettes!" (Paragraph 8)

_D_ 2. In the sentence below, the word *punitive* means
   A. unenforceable.
   B. effective.
   C. relatively weak.
   D. intended to punish.

   What is the purpose of arresting someone?

   "Thirty-seven years after a special commission formed by Congress and President Richard Nixon concluded that punitive marijuana laws cause more social harm than the drug itself, nearly half of the drug arrests in this country are for pot." (Paragraph 15)

_C_ 3. In the excerpt below, the word *induce* means
   A. rule out.
   B. demonstrate.
   C. bring about.
   D. become an example of.

   What effect would accepting responsibility for children have on a tendency to worry about the consequences of one's behavior?

   "When I had children, the responsibility I felt for them weighed on me in a nice way, but also in a way that ruled out getting high. Weed began to induce less joy than worry." (Paragraph 18)

Reading Check

Central Point and Main Ideas

___D___ 1. Which sentence best expresses the central point of the entire selection?

Bowden states this central point in paragraph 11. Answer A covers only paragraph 17. Answer B covers only paragraph 15. Answer C covers only paragraph 14.

    A. Although the author smoked marijuana regularly as a teenager, he has always urged his children not to use it.

    B. The author believes that it is a waste of time and money to jail people for possessing marijuana.

    C. The author has come to believe that smoking marijuana is probably less harmful than consuming alcohol.

    D. Although the author no longer approves of smoking marijuana, he thinks laws against its possession ought to be repealed.

___C___ 2. The implied main idea of paragraphs 13–14 is that

    A. marijuana smoking is now more commonplace than when the author was young.

Answers A, B, and D are details that support answer C.

    B. generations of Americans have grown up smoking pot, proving that the old horror stories against its use are exaggerated.

    C. alcohol and tobacco are far greater health hazards than marijuana use, which is commonplace.

    D. none of the people whom the author smoked dope with as a kid turned into heroin or cocaine addicts.

___B___ 3. The implied main idea of paragraph 15 is that

    A. a special commission concluded that punitive marijuana laws cause more social harm than the drug itself.

Answers A, C, and D are details that support answer B.

    B. arresting people for marijuana possession is a waste of money and manpower and does nothing to reduce use of the drug.

    C. more Americans than ever are smoking pot, while the number of people arrested for pot possession continues to grow.

    D. even though hundreds of thousands of people every year are arrested for marijuana possession, most do not go to jail.

Supporting Details

___A___ 4. Which of the following statements was **not** true of the author's youth?

    A. He gave up smoking pot before he gave up smoking cigarettes.

    B. He often smoked pot with his friends.

    C. He successfully hid his pot smoking from his father.

    D. He agreed with his dad that smoking cigarettes was harmful.

See paragraphs 10–11.

___B___ 5. During the administration of President Nixon, a special commission concluded that

    A. nearly half of the drug arrests in the United States were for pot.

    B. punitive marijuana laws are more harmful to society than the drug itself.

    C. only people involved in serious drug trafficking should go to jail for possessing marijuana.

    D. punitive marijuana laws have little effect on people's behavior.

See the second sentence of paragraph 15.

Inferences

See paragraph 8. The author's father is furious that his son is smoking something legal. Answer A is contradicted in paragraph 6; answer D is contradicted in paragraph 9. Answer C is not supported.

___B___ 6. On the basis of paragraphs 1–10, we can infer that

    A. the author frequently lied to his father.

    B. the author's father would have been even more furious to learn that his son was smoking pot.

    C. the author's father considered smoking marijuana less harmful than smoking tobacco.

    D. the author did not believe the surgeon general's warnings about cigarettes.

___D___ 7. In paragraphs 17–19, the author suggests that

    A. although people can still function while high, they don't function nearly as well.

    B. there are negative health consequences to smoking marijuana.

    C. some of the author's friends still smoke marijuana.

    D. all of the above.

For answer A, see sentences 1–6 of paragraph 17. For answer B, see the last sentence of paragraph 17. For answer C, see the third sentence of paragraph 19.

The Writer's Craft

___C___ 8. The author begins his essay with

    A. shifting to the opposite.

    B. going from broad to narrow.

    C. a brief story.

    D. a series of questions.

Bowden tells a story about the time, when he was a teenager, that his father asked him if he smoked.

___D___ 9. In paragraphs 17–19. Bowden's tone is best described as

    A. self-pitying.

    B. sarcastic.

    C. angry.

    D. concerned.

In paragraph 17, Bowden expresses concern about the effects of marijuana—its subtlety, its potential for abuse, and the possibility that it is harmful to one's health. In paragraph 18, he states his concern that marijuana might lead to harming his family. In paragraph 19, he states his concern that possessing marijuana makes a person a criminal in the eyes of the police.

___B___ 10. The author's primary purpose in this selection is to
   A. inform readers that smoking marijuana is not nearly as dangerous as some people say it is.
   B. persuade readers that we should decriminalize marijuana possession.
   C. persuade readers that we need to pay more attention to alcohol abuse and less attention to marijuana abuse.
   D. entertain readers with examples of the silly things that pot smokers say and do.   See paragraphs 11 and 19. Answer A is one detail suggested in paragraphs 13 and 14. Answer C is an inference one might draw from paragraph 14, but it is not Bowden's primary purpose. Answer D is not supported.

Discussion Questions

1. Before reading this essay, were you in favor of the legalization of marijuana, or were you opposed to it? Did the essay change your thinking in any way?

2. One of the criticisms of marijuana is that it is a "gateway drug"—in other words, its use leads to later experiments with harder, more harmful drugs. Do you agree with the statement that using marijuana leads to other forms of drug abuse? Why or why not?

3. Bowden writes, "I believe today that alcohol is a far greater public health and safety threat than marijuana. Tobacco, also legal, is an even greater curse." Given the dangers posed by alcohol and tobacco, should these substances be made illegal? Why or why not?

4. The author confesses that for him, "getting high was a symptom of boredom and rebellion." Do you think this is the main reason young people smoke pot, or might there be other reasons? What are some other behaviors in which bored, rebellious youngsters engage?

Paragraph Assignments

1. Bowden begins his essay with the story of an encounter between him and his father, on a night when he came home stoned. Most people know the feeling of coming home, as teens or young adults, and finding an angry parent (or other family member) waiting to confront them about a problem. Write a paragraph about such an experience in your own life. Use dialogue to make your description of the encounter vividly alive.

2. Bowden writes that "when something as widespread as pot possession is illegal, police can use it as an excuse to harass whole classes of otherwise law-abiding citizens." When police do something like this, it is considered an abuse of the power they have. Technically, they have the legal right to arrest anyone for possession of marijuana, but targeting blacks and Latinos is unfair. Write a paragraph describing another abuse of power you have heard or read about. Who was in power? Who was abused? What was the final outcome? Conclude by suggesting ways such abuses might be prevented in the future.

Essay Assignments

1. Bowden clearly presents several ways he was concerned his life would be negatively affected if he continued to smoke pot: his job would suffer, his family might be in danger, and his health would deteriorate. Have you ever known, or do you know, someone who grew up but was never able to kick a habit of drugs or alcohol that started during his or her teen years? How is that person's addiction affecting his or her life? Write an essay about the person you know or have known. Present and detail three ways that addiction is hurting that individual's life. Consider such things as opportunities that may have been wasted, money spent on drugs/ alcohol, relationships harmed, health affected, legal problems, and so on.

2. Like marijuana, there are many things that are illegal in the United States—or parts of the United States— that some people feel should be legalized. These range from the right to keep chickens in your backyard, to being able to drink at 18, to allowing same-sex marriage. Similarly, there are quite a few things that are legal that some people feel should be *illegal*. Some examples include assault weapons, the death penalty, talking on cell phones while driving, and even high-caffeine energy drinks like Red Bull. Write an essay in which you argue that something that is illegal should be legal or vice versa. Your thesis should be similar to one of the following:

   - Even though _____ is illegal, it should be legal for three reasons.
   - Even though _____ is legal, it should be illegal for three reasons.

   The body of your essay, then, will present your three reasons.

37 Help Thy Neighbor and Go Straight to Prison

Nicholas D. Kristof

Preview

Does the punishment always fit the crime? Read this story about Edward Young, a hardworking father of four. When the justice system was through with him, Young was facing fifteen years in prison. You may find it hard to understand why he was accused of any crime at all.

Words to Watch

Dickensian (7): unfair (like a situation in the novels of Charles Dickens, who wrote about dreadful living conditions, injustice, and oppression)
mandatory (10): required
detains (11): puts in an institution
incarceration (12): imprisonment
monitoring (15): watching
caricature (24): exaggerated picture

1   If you want to understand all that is wrong with America's criminal justice system, take a look at the nightmare experienced by Edward Young.

2   Young, now 43, was convicted of several burglaries as a young man but then resolved that he would turn his life around. Released from prison in 1996, he married, worked six days a week, and raised four children in Hixson, Tennessee.

3   Then a neighbor died, and his widow, Neva Mumpower, asked Young to help sell her husband's belongings. He later found, mixed in among them, seven shotgun shells, and he put them aside so that his children wouldn't find them.

4   "He was trying to help me out," Mumpower told me. "My husband was a pack rat, and I was trying to clear things out."

5   Then Young became a suspect in burglaries at storage facilities and vehicles in the area, and the police

searched his home and found the forgotten shotgun shells as well as some stolen goods. The United States attorney in Chattanooga prosecuted Young under a federal law that bars ex-felons from possessing guns or ammunition. In this case, under the Armed Career Criminal Act, that meant a 15-year minimum sentence.

6   The United States attorney, William Killian, went after Young, even though none of Young's past crimes involved a gun, even though Young had no shotgun or other weapon to go with the seven shells, and even though, by all accounts, he had no idea that he was violating the law when he helped Mrs. Mumpower sell her husband's belongings.

7   In May, a federal judge, acknowledging that the case was Dickensian° but saying that he had no leeway under the law, sentenced Young to serve a minimum of 15 years in federal prison. It didn't matter that the local authorities eventually dismissed the burglary charges.

8   So the federal government, at a time when it is cutting education spending, is preparing to spend $415,000 over the next 15 years to imprison a man for innocently possessing seven shotgun shells while trying to help a widow in the neighborhood. And, under the law, there is no early release: Young will spend the full 15 years in prison.

9   This case captures what is wrong with our "justice" system: We have invested in mass incarceration in ways that are crushingly expensive, break up families, and are often simply cruel.

With less than 5 percent of the world's population, the United States has almost one-quarter of the world's prisoners.

10   This hasn't always been the case, but it is the result of policies such as mandatory° minimum sentences since the 1970s.

11   In 1978, the United States had 307,000 inmates in state and federal prisons. That soared to a peak of more than 1.6 million in 2009. Since then, the number of inmates has declined for three consecutive years to 1.57 million in 2012. The number of juveniles detained has also begun to drop since peaking in 2000, although the U.S. still detains° children at a rate five times that of the next highest country.

12   In short, there's some hope that this American experiment in mass incarceration° has been recognized as a

failure and will be gradually unwound. Among the leaders in moving away from the old policies are blue states and red states alike, including New York and Texas. But America still has twice as many prisoners today as under President Ronald Reagan.

13   Almost everyone seems to acknowledge that locking up vast numbers of nonviolent offenders is a waste of money. California devotes $179,400 to keep a juvenile in detention for a year, and spends less than $10,000 per student in its schools.

14   Granted, mass incarceration may have been one factor in reduced crime in the last couple of decades; there's mixed evidence. But, if so, the economic and social cost has been enormous— including the breakup of families and the increased risk that children of those families will become criminals a generation later.

15   There's also contrary evidence that incarceration, especially of young people, doesn't work well in preventing crime—especially for young people. One careful study of 35,000 young offenders by Anna Aizer and Joseph J. Doyle Jr. reached the startling conclusion that jailing juveniles leads them to be more likely to commit crimes as adults. Milder sentences, such as electronic monitoring° and home detention, were actually more effective at preventing adult crime.

16   Alternatives to incarceration are both cheaper and more efficient. Youth Villages has an excellent record of working with troubled youngsters and their families, and of keeping them

from committing crimes. So do some job-training and education programs. Mass incarceration has been particularly devastating for blacks and members of other minority groups, as well as for the poor generally. In this case, Edward Young is white.

17   Conservatives often argue that there is a link between family breakdown and cycles of poverty. They're right: Boys are more likely to get into trouble without a dad at home, and we have a major problem with the irresponsibility of young men who conceive babies but don't raise them.

18   We also have a serious problem with the irresponsibility of mass incarceration. When almost 1 percent of Americans are imprisoned (and a far higher percentage of men of color in low-income neighborhoods), our criminal justice system becomes a cause of family breakdown and contributes to the delinquency of a generation of children. And mass incarceration interacts with other government policies, such as the way the drug war is implemented, to have a disproportionate effect on African-Americans. Black men use marijuana at roughly the same rate as white men but are more than three times as likely to be arrested over it.

19   Young is particularly close to his children, ages 6 to 16. After back problems and rheumatoid arthritis left him disabled, he was a stay-at-home dad while his wife worked in a doctor's office. When the judge announced the sentence, the children all burst into tears.

20   "I can't believe my kids lose their daddy for the next 15 years," his wife, Stacy, told me. "He never tried to get a firearm in the 16 years I was with him. It's crazy. He's getting a longer sentence than people who've killed or raped."

21   Young's lawyer, Christopher Varner, of Chattanooga, is appealing the sentence and says he is shaken by the outcome. "It's shocking," he says. "That's not what we do in this country."

22   I asked Killian, the United States attorney, why on earth he would want to send a man to prison for 15 years for innocently possessing seven shotgun shells. "The case raised serious public safety concerns," Killian said.

23   Oh.

24   The classic caricature° of justice run amok is Inspector Javert in Victor Hugo's novel *Les Misérables*, pursuing Jean Valjean for stealing bread for hungry children. In that case, Valjean knew that he was breaking the law; Edward Young had no idea.

25   Some day, Americans will look back and wonder at how we as a society could be much more willing to invest in prisons than in schools. They will be astonished that we sent a man to federal prison for 15 years for trying to help a widow.

First Impressions

Freewrite for ten minutes on one of the following.

1. Did you enjoy reading this selection? Why or why not?

2. Kristof states that there are too many people in prison in the United States. Do you agree? Why or why not?

3. The author writes, "Boys are more likely to get in trouble without a dad at home." Why might this be true?

Vocabulary Check

_D_ 1. In the sentence below, the word *leeway* means
   A. information.
   B. preference.
   C. highway.
   D. flexibility.

   If the judge thinks the case is unfair but gives Young a long prison sentence anyway, the law must not give the judge any flexibility.

   "In May, a federal judge, acknowledging that the case was Dickensian but saying that he had no leeway under the law, sentenced Young to serve a minimum of 15 years in federal prison." (Paragraph 7)

_B_ 2. In the excerpt below, the word *devastating* means
    A. effective.
    B. destructive.   A system that causes family breakdown and
    C. useful.   contributes to delinquency is destructive.
    D. random.

"Mass incarceration has been particularly devastating for blacks and members of other minority groups, as well as for the poor generally. . . . When almost 1 percent of Americans are imprisoned (and a far higher percentage of men of color in low-income neighborhoods), our criminal justice system becomes a cause of family breakdown and contributes to the delinquency of a generation of children." (Paragraphs 16–18)

_C_ 3. In the excerpt below, the word *disproportionate* means
    A. healthy.
    B. appropriate.   If black men are three times as likely to be
    C. unequal.   arrested as white men for the same offense,
    D. related.   the policies have an unequal effect.

"And mass incarceration interacts with other government policies, such as the way the drug war is implemented, to have a disproportionate effect on African-Americans. Black men use marijuana at roughly the same rate as white men but are more than three times as likely to be arrested over it." (Paragraph 18)

_A_ 4. In the sentence below, the words *run amok* mean
    A. out of control.
    B. in real life.   If the police inspector spends his life pursuing a man
                  who stole a loaf of bread to feed starving children, he
    C. applied quickly. is a caricature of a justice system that is out of control.
    D. well deserved.

"The classic caricature of justice run amok is Inspector Javert in Victor Hugo's novel *Les Misérables*, pursuing Jean Valjean for stealing bread for hungry children." (Paragraph 24)

Reading Check

Central Point and Main Ideas

Answer B is not supported—according to the government, Young did commit a crime. Answers C and D cover only paragraph 13.

_A_ 1. Which sentence best expresses the central point of the entire selection?
    A. Edward Young's experience is a prime example of what is wrong with the United States's justice system.
    B. Edward Young's prison sentence was unfair since he did not commit a crime.
    C. Placing so many nonviolent criminals in prisons is a waste of money.
    D. Americans are willing to spend more money on prisons than on schools.

Answer A
is an inference one
might draw, but it is
not the main idea.
Answer B covers only
the last sentence of
paragraph 12. Answer
D is not supported—
the passage says only that there is *some* hope that mass incarceration will *gradually* wind down.

___C___ 2. Which sentence best expresses the main idea of paragraphs 11 and 12?
  A. There are too many Americans in prisons.
  B. Since Reagan was president, the number of prisoners has doubled.
  C. Although most Americans agree that prison is not the answer, rates of imprisonment continue to be high.
  D. There is hope that in the near future, there will be fewer and fewer people sent to prison.

___C___ 3. Which sentence best expresses the main idea of paragraph 15?
  A. Milder sentences and home detention are effective methods for preventing crime.
  B. Young people who are imprisoned are more likely to commit crimes as adults.
  C. Prison sentences for young people are not as effective in preventing crime as milder sentences are.
  D. A study of young offenders proved that prison time only leads to more crime.   Answer A covers only the last sentence. Answer B covers only sentence 2. Answer D is not supported.

___A___ 4. Which sentence best expresses the main idea of paragraph 18?
  A. Mass imprisonment creates family breakdown, and it unfairly targets black men.
  B. Mass imprisonment affects mostly people in low-income neighborhoods.
  C. Blacks and whites commit the same crimes, but black people are arrested more often.
  D. The problems with our justice system are similar to the problems with our war on drugs.   Answer B covers only part of sentence 2. Answer C is suggested only in sentence 4. Answer D is not supported.

Supporting Details

___D___ 5. Young was prosecuted under a federal law that bars ex-felons from possessing
  A. stolen goods.
  B. burglar tools.   See paragraph 5, sentence 2.
  C. guns or knives.
  D. guns or ammunition.

___D___ 6. Although the United States has only 5 percent of the world's population, it has almost _____ percent of the world's prisoners.
  A. 7
  B. 10   See paragraph 9, the last sentence.
  C. 15
  D. 25

Inferences

_C_ 7. We can infer that
A. the author was in prison when he was younger.
B. the author personally knew Edward Young.
C. the author is disgusted by the current state of the United States justice system.
D. the author plans to interview Edward Young for his next column.

> In particular, see paragraph 1 and paragraphs 23–25.
> Answers A, B, and D are not supported.

The Writer's Craft

_C_ 8. The author's main purpose for writing this essay was to

Kristof clearly has an opinion on the problems in the justice system. However, his straightforward manner of presentation and his use of facts and statistics show that his primary purpose is to inform the reader.

A. entertain readers with amazing and startling facts and figures about the justice system.
B. persuade readers to become involved in the movement for reform of our prison system.
C. inform readers about the serious problems with our justice system, using Young's case as an example.
D. persuade readers that Young was innocent and should be released from prison.

_C_ 9. In paragraph 9, the author places quotation marks around the word *justice* to indicate

His use of quotation marks conveys the same meaning as if he had written "our so-called justice system."

A. how important that word is.
B. that he's quoting someone else.
C. that he doesn't believe there is any justice in the justice system.
D. that he's referring to a national system.

_B_ 10. Paragraph 22 is followed by a single word: "Oh." What is the author's specific tone here? (Reread paragraphs 24 and 25 to get a better idea.)
A. Curious
B. Sarcastic
C. Surprised
D. Angry

> Paragraphs 24 and 25 show how ridiculous he finds Killian's explanation. His simple "Oh" sets the same sarcastic tone as saying, "Yes, of course. That's obvious."

Discussion Questions

1. What do you think of the fifteen-year sentence that Edward Young received? How did you feel when you read about what he did and, ultimately, the punishment he received? Explain.

2. Why do you think the United States attorney claimed that what Young had done "raised serious public safety concerns"? Do you agree? Why or why not?

3. The author points out, "Black men use marijuana at roughly the same rate as white men but are more than three times as likely to be arrested over it." What reasons might account for this difference?

4. Do you believe Young's situation is an unusual case—or not so unusual? Do you know of any other case in which someone received an unfair sentence?

Paragraph Assignments

1. Clearly, the punishment Young received did not fit the crime. In fact, many would argue that Young committed no crime at all. Have you ever been punished unfairly or been accused of doing something you didn't do? Write a paragraph describing what happened, how you felt about it, and what you learned from the experience.

2. Imagine that you are an appeals judge who has been appointed to review this case. What would be your decision regarding Edward Young as well as the prosecuting attorney, William Killian? Write an opinion explaining the thinking behind your decision and recommending appropriate action.

Essay Assignments

1. Kristof points out that incarceration does not necessarily cut down on crime and, in fact, often leads to more crime when young people are jailed. More and more Americans are coming to realize that we need alternatives to prison. Obviously, criminals need to be punished in some way(s), but prison time is astoundingly costly and often ineffectual.

   What do you think would be fair, effective, and low-cost punishment? Write an essay in which you suggest three different alternatives to prison sentences. Be as creative as you want, but try to be realistic (for example, don't send prisoners into outer space or ship them to a desert island).

You might consider organizing your essay by describing three different punishments, based on the severity of the crime. For example, think of appropriate punishments for shoplifting, then armed robbery, and finally, murder or rape. For each, describe the punishment, and then explain why you feel it would be effective.

2. In this essay, the author uses one remarkably unfair case to help prove his point that our criminal justice system could use some reform. There are, of course, many more examples of cases in which the sentence does not fit the crime. Write an essay that, like this selection, argues that the United States's criminal justice system is broken. In your supporting paragraphs, present three cases to help prove your point. You can research cases by Googling phrases such as "unfair prison sentences" or "when the punishment doesn't fit the crime."

   Remember that you can also use examples of clearly guilty individuals who barely received any punishment at all to help argue your point. As Kristof notes, there are a disproportionate number of low-income and African-American men in our prisons. There are, then, probably quite a few wealthy white men who may have received lighter sentences or no prison time at all for their crimes.

38 What Causes Hearing Loss
Jane E. Brody

Preview

Most of us assume that older people become hard of hearing because they're, well, *old*. Their ears are simply wearing out, right? Actually, new evidence is showing that age has nothing to do with hearing loss. In fact, it's fairly likely that you (regardless of your age) have done something today that may affect your ability to hear many years from now.

Words to Watch

blithely (3): casually, without any concern
proprietors (6): owners
retrofitted (6): modified, newly equipped
auditory (8): hearing
chronic (9): repeated
cumulative (11): growing over time
aficionados (11): enthusiastic fans
otolaryngology (13): the study of ear, nose, and throat
lethal (14): deadly

1   Noise, not age, is the leading cause of hearing loss. Unless you take steps now to protect to your ears, sooner or later many of you—and your children—will have difficulty understanding even ordinary speech.

2   Tens of millions of Americans, including 12 percent to 15 percent of school-age children, already have permanent hearing loss caused by the everyday noise that we take for granted as a fact of life.

3   "The sad truth is that many of us are responsible for our own hearing loss," writes Katherine Bouton in her new book, *Shouting Won't Help: Why I—and 50 Million Other Americans—Can't Hear You.* The cause, she explains, is "the noise we blithely° subject ourselves to day after day."

4   While there are myriad regulations to protect people who work in noisy environments, there are relatively few governing repeated exposure to noise outside the workplace: portable music devices, rock concerts, hair dryers, sirens,

lawn mowers, leaf blowers, vacuum cleaners, car alarms, and countless other sources.

5 We live in a noisy world, and every year it seems to get noisier. Ms. Bouton notes that the noise level inside Allen Fieldhouse at the University of Kansas often exceeds that of a chain saw.

6 After poor service, noise is the second leading complaint about restaurants. Proprietors° believe that people spend more on food and drink in bustling eateries, and many have created new venues or retrofitted° old ones to maximize sound levels.

7 When I'm told about a new restaurant, my first question is, "Is it noisy?" My friends and I will never return to one in which the racket makes it impossible to converse with tablemates. Perhaps the young diners the restauranteurs covet "talk" by texting.

8 The ears are fragile instruments. When sound waves enter the ear, they cause the eardrum to vibrate. The vibrations are transmitted to the cochlea, in the inner ear, where fluid carries them to neatly organized rows of hair cells. These in turn stimulate auditory° nerve fibers, each attuned to a different frequency. These impulses travel via the auditory nerve to the brain, where they are interpreted as, say, words, music, or an approaching vehicle.

9 Damage to this delicate apparatus results from both volume and length of exposure to sound. Very loud noises, or chronic° exposure to sound even when it is not particularly loud, can wreak havoc on hair cells, causing them to become disarranged and to degenerate.

10 We are born with a fixed number of hair cells; once they are dead, they cannot be replaced, and auditory sensitivity is permanently lost. Usually, sensitivity to high-frequency sounds is first to go, followed by an inability to hear the frequencies of speech.

11 Furthermore, the effects of noise exposure are cumulative°, as Robert V. Harrison, an auditory specialist at the University of Toronto, noted recently in *The International Journal of Pediatrics*. Although we start out with a redundancy of hair cells, with repeated noisy insults, enough are destroyed to impair hearing. Thus, damage to hair cells incurred early in life, as has happened to many rock musicians and rock concert aficionados°, can show up in midlife as difficulty understanding speech.

12 Sound volume is measured in decibels (dB), and the level at which

noise can cause permanent hearing loss begins at about 85 dB, typical of a hair dryer, food processor, or kitchen blender.

13   Dr. Michael D. Seidman, the director of otolaryngology° at Henry Ford West Bloomfield Hospital in Michigan, told me to use ear plugs when I dry my hair or mow my lawn with a gas-powered mower, and to cover my ears when an emergency vehicle passes with siren blasting. Ear protection is a must for people who shoot guns as well as those who ride motorcycles or use snow blowers, leaf blowers, hand or pneumatic drills, or chain saws.

14   But even noisier than many of these is the maximum output of some portable music players, which can exceed occupational safety levels and produce sound levels in the ear on a par with that of a jet taking off. If you listen to music with earbuds or headphones at levels that block out normal discourse, you are in effect dealing lethal° blows to the hair cells in your ears, Dr. Seidman said.

15   A national study in 2006 by the American Speech-Language-Hearing Association found that among users of portable music devices, 35 percent of adults and up to 59 percent of teenagers reported listening at loud volumes.

16   Dr. Harrison urges purchasers of such "personal entertainment devices" to read and heed the warnings and practical advice on package inserts. Too often people turn up the volume to overcome surrounding noise. A better plan is to set a maximum volume while in a quiet environment and never go above that.

17   In general, if other people can hear what you're listening to, the volume is turned up too high. Many times I've had to change my seat on the subway or bus because the rider next to me was using a music player as if it were a boombox.

18   Some portable listening devices come with the ability to set a maximum volume, which may be worth the added cost to parents concerned about protecting their children's ears.

19   At a given volume level, earbuds deliver higher noise levels than over-the-ear headphones. If earbuds are used, Dr. Harrison suggests selecting ones that fit loosely and never inserting them tightly into the ear canal. Alternatively, when you are alone and not at risk of missing important environmental cues, like an approaching vehicle, consider using noise-canceling over-the-ear headphones that block out background noise and enable you to listen at a lower volume.

20   Even toys meant for young children can generate ear-damaging levels of noise. The American Speech-Language-Hearing Association lists, as potential hazards, cap guns, talking dolls, vehicles with horns and sirens, walkie-talkies, rubber squeaky toys, musical instruments, and toys with cranks. According to the association, some toy sirens and squeaky rubber toys can emit sounds of 90 dB, as loud as a lawn mower.

21   It suggests that parents with normal hearing test new toys before giving them to a child. "If the toy sounds loud, don't buy it," is the recommendation. For noisy toys already bought, consider removing the batteries or taping over the speaker.

First Impressions

Freewrite for ten minutes on one of the following.

1. Did you enjoy reading this selection? Why or why not?

2. Do you engage in some of the activities that can lead to hearing loss? After reading this selection, what steps might you take to counteract these effects?

3. The author states, "We live in a noisy world." What makes our world so noisy? What can we do about it?

Vocabulary Check

_A_ 1. In the excerpt below, the word *myriad* means
   A. many.
   B. strange.
   C. new.
   D. obvious.

   The antonym few suggests that myriad means "many."

   "While there are myriad regulations to protect people who work in noisy environments, there are relatively few governing repeated exposure to noise outside the workplace ..." (Paragraph 4)

_C_ 2. In the excerpt below, the word *bustling* means
   A. shiny and new.
   B. open until late.
   C. noisy and active.
   D. unhealthy and fattening.

   If restaurants are designed to maximize sound level, the owners must believe people will spend more in a noisy and active restaurant.

   "After poor service, noise is the second leading complaint about restaurants. Proprietors believe that people spend more on food and drink in bustling eateries, and many have created new venues or retrofitted old ones to maximize sound level." (Paragraph 6)

_B_ 3. In the sentence below, the words *wreak havoc* mean
   A. sneak up.
   B. have a destructive effect.
   C. settle calmly.
   D. have a strengthening effect.

   If the sounds cause the hair cells to degenerate, those sounds have a destructive effect.

   "Very loud noises, or chronic exposure to sound even when it is not particularly loud, can wreak havoc on hair cells, causing them to become disarranged and to degenerate." (Paragraph 9)

___A___ 4. In the sentence below, the word *redundancy* means

A. large surplus.

B. small supply.

C. great variety.

D. complete lack.

> The sentence implies that the loss of a few cells would not harm our hearing, but the loss of "enough" does impair hearing. Therefore, there must be a surplus of cells when we start out.

"Although we start out with a redundancy of hair cells, with repeated noisy insults, enough are destroyed to impair hearing." (Paragraph 11)

Reading Check

Central Point and Main Ideas

Answer A covers only paragraphs 8–9. Answer B states only what is *not* the cause of hearing loss (old age), but the selection concentrates on what *is* the cause (noise), as stated in answer C. Answer D covers only paragraphs 13–21.

___C___ 1. Which sentence best expresses the central point of the entire selection?

A. Our hearing mechanism is very delicate and can be damaged easily.

B. Old age has often been blamed, inaccurately, for hearing loss.

C. Repeated exposure to common noises, not aging, is what damages our hearing.

D. Toys, portable listening devices, and even blow dryers are only a few of the everyday items that can damage hearing.

Answer A covers only paragraph 5. Answer B covers only paragraph 4. Answer C covers only paragraph 3.

___D___ 2. The implied main idea of paragraphs 3–5 is that

A. we live in a noisy world that continues to get noisier.

B. there are very few, if any, laws that protect our hearing outside the workplace.

C. we are each personally responsible for our own hearing loss.

D. everyday noises can damage hearing, and we need to stay informed if we want to protect our hearing.

Answer A covers only paragraph 15. Answer C is too broad. Answer D is suggested only by paragraphs 15 and 18.

___B___ 3. The main idea of paragraphs 14–18 is that

A. most people listen to portable music devices too loudly.

B. listening to portable music devices too loudly can damage hearing.

C. portable listening devices are dangerous.

D. teens and children are most likely to be affected by hearing loss from portable music devices.

Supporting Details

For answer A, see paragraph 8. For answer B, see paragraph 9. For answer C, see paragraph 10.

___D___ 4. The hair cells in our ears

A. help carry sound waves to the brain.

B. can be destroyed by repeated exposure to noise.

C. cannot be replaced once they are gone.

D. all of the above.

___C___ 5. Hair dryers, food processors, and blenders all emit ____ decibels, the
level of noise that can cause permanent hearing damage.
A. 25
B. 50
C. 85
See paragraph 12.
D. 100

Inferences

___B___ 6. We can infer that the author of this selection
A. has suffered permanent hearing loss due to everyday noise.
B. is careful about exposing her ears to loud everyday noise.
C. feels that portable music devices should be banned.
D. dislikes restaurants, rock concerts, and riding the subway.

See paragraph 7.

___A___ 7. Paragraphs 6 and 7 suggest that

The facts that noise
is the second leading
complaint and that
the author won't go
to a noisy restaurant
suggest statement A.

A. restaurant owners who think that diners like a loud restaurant are
mistaken.
B. only older people are upset by noise in restaurants.
C. texting instead of actually talking is becoming more common at
restaurants.
D. maximizing sound in restaurants is important for attracting customers.

The Writer's Craft

___C___ 8. Which of the following statements best describes the author's purpose?
A. To persuade the American public to demand safety regulations on
everyday noise

The author presents
objective information
about noise and
hearing loss in a
straightforward
manner.

B. To persuade older people to consider past habits that may have
caused hearing loss
C. To inform readers about everyday noise that can create permanent
hearing damage
D. To entertain readers with vivid descriptions of the noises they are
forced to listen to on a daily basis

___C___ 9. Brody supports her central point mainly by providing
A. reasons why young people should not listen to loud music.
B. personal experiences she has had with permanent hearing damage.
C. examples of damaging everyday noises and how they affect hearing.
D. statistics proving which everyday noises are the most harmful.

Brody gives examples of damaging everyday
noises in paragraphs 4–6 and 12–20. She explains
how they affect hearing in paragraphs 8–11.

___B___ 10. For what kind of audience did Brody probably write this selection?
  A. Concerned parents of young children
  B. A general audience of young and older adults
  C. Older people who have suffered hearing loss and are looking for answers
  D. Medical professionals

The second sentence in paragraph 1 suggests a general audience. In addition, the examples Brody gives are noise sources that young and older adults are likely to be exposed to. Also, in paragraphs 18 and 21, she gives advice to parents.

Discussion Questions

1. What is the loudest sound you've ever been exposed to? Where were you when you heard it? What did it sound like? Do you think it may have affected your hearing?

2. Do you prefer to eat in a quiet restaurant or a noisy one? Why? Are there any situations in which you might not mind some noise?

3. After reading this selection, do you plan to change anything to lessen the impact of the noise you're exposed to? If so, which piece of Brody's advice would you be most likely to follow?

4. In her essay, Brody points out that we take our hearing for granted, even though our hearing apparatus is astoundingly complex and fragile. What other things about our bodies do we take for granted? Have you ever suffered an injury or illness that made you more aware of your body's limits? Explain.

Paragraph Assignments

1. Brody talks about never returning to noisy restaurants and having to get up and move away from people whose music is turned up too loudly in their headphones. Have you ever had to get away from (or complain about) someone or something that was too loud or irritating? Perhaps it was an audience member talking in a movie theater or an all-night party in your apartment building or even a coughing and sniffling classmate during an exam. Write a paragraph about that experience. Describe the noise/sound problem and what you did about it.

2. As Jane Brody points out, our world is a noisy place. Most of us have gotten so used to the noise that we hardly even notice it anymore. For this assignment, take some time to listen to the world around you. Make a list of all the everyday noises that you are subjected to on a regular basis. Then write a paragraph that describes the noises you hear, starting in the morning and ending at night. Be as creative as you can be.

Essay Assignments

1. What are the *best* sounds you've ever heard? Think of all the wonderful things you've heard in your life, and write an essay about the top three. Take some time to consider what constitutes a "best sound" for you. It could be a voice, a song, ocean waves from a memorable vacation, certain words from someone important to you, the engine of your car starting when you thought you were stranded in the middle of nowhere, or even the sound of silence after a long and noisy day.

   Your thesis statement can be as simple as this: "There are three sounds I've heard in my life that were so wonderful that I'll never forget them."

2. As Brody points out, noise is an ever-increasing problem in our culture. In fact, excess noise can be so destructive and disturbing that it is often referred to as "noise pollution." What are some other common examples of noise pollution? What else, other than hearing, does noise pollution negatively affect? Finally, what can we do to counteract this increasing problem?

   Write an essay that attempts to answer these three questions. You can research this topic by typing "dangers of noise pollution" or "how noise pollution is hurting us" or "how to stop noise pollution" into Google or another search engine. Your thesis statement for this essay could be something like "Noise pollution is a real problem that needs some real solutions" or "Everyday noise has reached alarming and destructive levels, and it's time to do something about it." Then devote one paragraph in the body of your paper to each question.

39 The Bitter Truth about Sugar
Emily Carlin

Preview

The fact that America is getting fatter is beyond dispute. Since the early 1980s, we have been growing steadily heavier; more than 75 percent of adults and one-third of our children are now overweight—if not obese. Many serious illnesses are linked to being overweight, and the rates of those diseases are skyrocketing. What in the world has happened to us in the last few decades? This selection identifies a major culprit and explains how it has been quietly added to our food supply in shocking quantities.

Words to Watch

ostracism (3): exclusion

endocrinologist (12): a doctor who specializes in treating disorders of the endocrine system, such as diabetes. The endocrine system is a collection of glands that secrete hormones directly into the bloodstream.

triglycerides (18): a type of fat found in the blood

hankering (25): craving

diminished (25): gotten smaller

scoffed at (41): made fun of

subsidies (45): money paid by the government to support certain businesses

perimeter (49): border

abhorrent (50): distasteful

calibrated (50): adjusted

unprecedentedly (51): never before known or experienced

explicit (56): fully and clearly expressed

1   You hear it all the time. Americans are slobs. *Fat* slobs.

2   We have no self-control, no will power. We know if we ate less and exercised more, we could be lean and healthy, but it's just too hard to do that. We're eating ourselves into all kinds of awful diseases and early graves because we're undisciplined and lazy and we just don't care.

3   We know that being obese makes us targets of bullying and social ostracism° as children and costs us workplace promotions as adults. And still, we keep choosing to be fat.

4   We're puzzled, it's true, that our

ancestors didn't suffer from obesity and diabetes at anything close to the rate we do. It's odd that small children—even newborn babies—are fatter than ever. Even our pets are heavier than they were a generation ago. Still, everyone says that being fat and unhealthy is our personal responsibility. It's our fault alone that we've gotten to this point, and we should hang our heads in shame.

5   Right?

6   Most people—overweight ones included—would say "Yes." They'll tell you in a second that obese individuals are at fault because they eat too much and don't exercise enough. Through the poor choices they've made in diet and lifestyle, they've "chosen" to be this way.

7   They're wrong.

8   Personal choice is only part of a larger puzzle. We American consumers are unwitting participants in a huge and deadly experiment run by the corporate food industry. We are rats released in the clean, well-lighted laboratory of the modern-day supermarket, where we fill our shopping carts with a thousand varieties of attractively packaged, deceptively labeled poison. As the food processing industry grows ever richer, and our government passively looks on, we are testing how much sugar the human body can absorb before it is irreversibly damaged.

Let's Talk about Sugar

9   We've always known that too much sugar isn't good for us. Sweet desserts make us fat; sugary drinks rot our teeth.

10   But the truth about the sugar in our foods today is much more complicated—and deadlier—than a matter of a few extra pounds and some cavities.

11   To start, we need to define what we mean by "sugar." For the purposes of this discussion, we'll talk primarily about *fructose*, the super-sweet molecule that is part of all caloric sweeteners. Fructose aliases include cane sugar, beet sugar, organic turbinado sugar, high fructose corn syrup (HFCS), honey, maple syrup, agave syrup, molasses, or any of the other *forty-plus names for sugar* that show up on food labels.

12   Why focus on fructose? In the words of Robert Lustig, M.D., a pediatric endocrinologist° and author of the 2012 book *Fat Chance: Beating the Odds Against Sugar, Processed Food, Obesity, and Disease*, fructose is "the Voldemort of the dietary hit list," the nutritional equivalent of the lethal super-villain in the Harry Potter series.

13   Here's a simplified overview of some of the ways fructose affects our bodies:

14   Unlike other nutrients, which are broken down and used by various parts of the body (such as the pancreas, the digestive tract, the muscles, and the brain), fructose goes straight to the liver. When we consume a large amount of fructose, as we usually do, the liver is overwhelmed. Unable to gradually process all that fructose, it turns it into liver fat.

15   A fatty liver, in turn:

16   ● Is at risk for developing cirrhosis (a potentially fatal disease usually

associated with alcoholism), liver scarring, and even liver cancer.

17   ● Causes insulin resistance. Insulin is the hormone that regulates the amount of sugar in the blood. When the cells in a person's body become insulin resistant, they stop responding normally to this important hormone. The result is Type 2 diabetes—the kind that used to be called "adult onset" diabetes, but which is now epidemic among children. People with Type 2 diabetes have abnormally high blood sugar. Their condition can lead to heart attacks, strokes, blindness, kidney failure, and poor circulation, resulting in amputation.

18   ● Releases fats into the bloodstream as triglycerides°, which are associated with "bad cholesterol" and increased risk of heart disease.

19   And there's more. When we eat naturally occurring sugar—say, in the form of a banana—that sugar contains not only fructose, but also the less-sweet molecule of *glucose*. Once in our bodies, glucose has two important functions. First, it stimulates the production of insulin, the hormone that regulates our blood sugar and fat storage. Second, it triggers the production of another hormone called *leptin*. Leptin tells our brains that we're no longer hungry and should stop eating. In short, insulin and leptin are essential for normal fat storage and appetite control.

20   Fructose, on the other hand, does neither of these things. You already know that fructose contributes to insulin resistance. But it has another insidious effect: it actually *blocks* leptin from reaching the brain. Without leptin, the brain never gets the message, "Stop eating." We never feel satisfied. We just keep eating.

21   So the problem with fructose is not only that it provides what are commonly called "empty calories": it *actively damages our health*. It contributes to diabetes, obesity, and heart disease. It interferes with our brain's ability to know when we're full. It is no exaggeration to say that it is toxic.

Our Hard-Wired Sweet Tooth

22   Now, none of this would be a problem if we didn't love sugar so much. But we do. We're hard-wired for it.

23   Initially, our taste for sugar was a blessing, not a curse. Sweetness was nature's way of telling our ancestors that a food was safe to eat. In nature, there are no sweet foods that are poisonous.

24   In addition, we craved sugar because we needed the extra fat it quickly provided. Our ancestors had to work hard for every bite they consumed. Whether they were hunters or harvesters, they expended a lot of energy just staying alive. For a brief time every year when fruit was in season, they gorged themselves on it. Those sweet calories gave their bodies the extra fat needed to survive demanding life stages like puberty, pregnancy, and nursing.

25   Unfortunately for us, our hankering° for sweets hasn't diminished° since our ancestors' day—even though our

activity levels certainly have. And now, sugary foods are available 24/7, not only during a brief harvest season. In fact, to say that sugar-packed foods are "available" to us is a little like saying oxygen is "available." We're practically swimming in the stuff.

26   In the average supermarket, about 80 percent of the packaged foods available to consumers include added sugar. And the worst part is that so much of it is hidden.

27   The manufacturers of those foods get very indignant at the idea of "hidden sugars." "The labels are right there," they say. "All the shoppers have to do is read them."

The Tangled Web of Nutritional Labels

28   But reading nutritional labels is easier said than done. Let's look at one such label. This is from Kellogg's Honey Smacks cereal. (It used to be called "Sugar Smacks." Kellogg's P.R. people apparently decided that "honey" sounded healthier than "sugar.")

29   One of the first things you might notice about the Honey Smacks nutritional label is that while it lists the percentage provided of the recommended daily value (RDV) of fat, sodium, cholesterol, potassium, and carbohydrates, it does not list an RDV for sugar. That's because the Food and Drug Administration (FDA) has not set any such value. Despite all the evidence that excessive consumption of sugar significantly contributes to widespread, chronic disease among Americans, the FDA consistently submits to

pressure from food industry lobbyists and declines to set a recommended maximum daily level.

30   The American Heart Association (AHA), however, has been bolder. It recommends that adult women consume no more than 5 teaspoons of added sugar a day (about 20 grams); adult men 9 teaspoons (about 36 grams), and children 3 teaspoons (about 12 grams). In contrast, surveys have shown that the average American consumes 22.2 teaspoons (almost 90 grams) of added sugar a day. More than half that sugar is in the form of sodas and other beverages.

31   Secondly, you'll notice that while "sugar" is listed as the first ingredient in Honey Smacks—meaning that the cereal contains more sugar than any other ingredient—the ingredients also

include "dextrose" and "honey." Those two ingredients are sugar in slightly different forms.

32   Third, you will see that in every ¾-cup serving of Honey Smacks (and most kids consume much more than that amount in a sitting), there are 15 grams of sugar—that's more than 3½ teaspoons of sugar per serving. This already exceeds the AHA's maximum daily sugar allowance for children, and we haven't even left the breakfast table yet. (By comparison, a Krispy Kreme glazed donut contains less than that— 10 grams of sugar.)

33   Now, Honey Smacks is an easy target of criticism. It is consistently ranked as one of the unhealthiest cereals on the market. By weight, Honey Smacks is *more than 55 percent sugar.* But many other foods that are widely considered "good for you" are equally surprising, once you look beyond the attractive packaging.

34   Take yogurt, for instance. Yogurt is generally thought of as "health food." And before the processed-food industry got hold of it, it was. A six-ounce Greek yogurt with no added sweeteners contains 16 grams of sugar. That sugar is lactose, the sugar that occurs naturally in milk. Unless you're lactose-intolerant, lactose is no problem. But compare that serving of Greek yogurt to a six-ounce serving of Yoplait, a yogurt brand very popular with children. The Yoplait contains 27 grams of sugar—that's 11 grams, or 2.75 teaspoons, more than the Greek yogurt.

35   Nowhere on the Yoplait label does it explain that there is any difference between the 16 grams of naturally occurring sugar and 11 grams of added sugar. Food labels don't have to provide that information. When the FDA has requested such labeling, the food processors have responded that revealing the amount of "added sugar" would be the same thing as giving away their recipes, and their competitors could copy their formulas. Again, the FDA gave in to the food industry and backed off implementing requirements for sugar. So the only way you and I can figure out how much added sugar is in a processed food is to do the kind of supermarket detective work described above—hardly something most American consumers have the time or the know-how to accomplish.

36   And so, when a well-meaning dad gives a child a container of Yoplait, believing it to be a wholesome snack, he is giving her a serving of yogurt *plus as much sugar as is in eight ounces of Coca-Cola.*

The Sugar-Industrial Complex

37   In the face of all this—as the rates of obesity, diabetes, heart disease, hypertension, and other diet-related health problems reach devastating levels in the U.S. and beyond, and the evidence piles ever higher that the sugar in our diet is largely to blame— you might reasonably ask, "What are we going to do about this?"

38   And if you do, the processed-food industry will confidently answer, "Not a darn thing."

39   There *was* one remarkable attempt to tackle the question from the inside. In

the spring of 1999, a secret meeting was held in Minneapolis, at the headquarters of the Pillsbury Company. The attendees included top executives from industry giants Nestlé, Kraft, Nabisco, General Mills, Procter & Gamble, Coca-Cola, and Mars. The meeting and its aftermath are described in a 2013 Pulitzer Prize-winning book, *Salt Sugar Fat: How the Food Giants Hooked Us*, by journalist Michael Moss.

40 At the meeting, two top Pillsbury executives laid out the facts: how Americans were growing ever fatter and unhealthier; how advertising aimed at children encouraged exactly the opposite of good eating habits; and how the ever-growing availability of convenient, cheap, super-sized processed foods packed with sugar, salt, and fat were contributing to this state of affairs. The executives even compared their industry's role in damaging Americans' health with the role of the tobacco industry. These executives made it plain: We're harming children's health, they told the assembled giant food companies. We're doing it knowingly. We need to be more responsible. Let's talk about working together, as an industry, to make processed foods healthier.

41 They were shot down, instantly. The head of General Mills led the charge. He scoffed at° the idea that the industry shared any part of the blame for America's health crisis. We just give shoppers what they want, he said. It's up to them to choose whether or not to buy it.

42 And so business went on as usual. Only for the food industry, "business as usual" becomes more sophisticated with each passing year. It takes advantage of every technological breakthrough to better understand not only what consumers want, but also how to make them want *more* of it. Companies use brain scans that reveal that a hefty dose of sugar makes our brains light up exactly the way that cocaine does. They've discovered that the sweeter they make their breakfast cereals, the sweeter kids want their cereals to be. Like lab animals, children are easily trained to crave ever-higher amounts of sugar. In fact, there is a whole host of evidence that suggests that sugar is actually addictive, just like alcohol (which is derived from fermented sugar).

43 And knowing all this, the food industry is loading its products ever more heavily with sugar. It does this for the most understandable of reasons. It's making tons of money. And much of that profit is connected to its use of high fructose corn syrup (HFCS).

44 It does all this not only without interference from our government, but with its enthusiastic cooperation. It is estimated that members of Congress spend five hours of each day meeting with professional lobbyists—people whose job it is to persuade lawmakers to favor their cause. Many of the mostly successful and highly paid lobbyists are employed by the food industry. As a result of their work, our government permits absurd, health-damaging

actions such as allowing food stamps to be used to purchase sodas and classifying HFCS as "safe."

The Sweet Success of High Fructose Corn Syrup

45   In recent years, HFCS has become the sweetener of choice for the food industry. While sugar derived from sugar cane has become increasingly expensive, due in part to hurricanes in the Caribbean that damaged the cane crop, the cost of corn has plummeted, thanks to government subsidies° to farmers. As a result, the food industry has turned enthusiastically to cheap HFCS, which is now the most commonly used sweetener in the United States. And "most commonly used" hardly does it justice—it's *everywhere*.

46   HFCS is like a gift from heaven for the industry. It's 75 percent sweeter than cane sugar. Not only is it cheap, and not only does it sweeten food, but it causes baked goods to turn an appetizing color *and* increases the shelf life of processed foods. (In order to make foods last a long time, food processors not only add HFCS but also routinely strip their products of fiber, further increasing their health-damaging qualities. But that's an appalling subject for another day). The average American eats *42 pounds* of HFCS a year.

47   Because it is so cheap, and because the food processors understand so well consumers' insatiable hunger for (and possibly even addiction to) sweets, HFCS is turning up in the most unlikely places. You'd expect heavy doses of sweeteners in candies, cookies, and other dessert-like foods, but a quick label-reading supermarket tour reveals HFCS's presence in barbecue sauce, baby's crackers, ketchup, lemonade, dog food, stuffing mix, juice boxes, frozen entrées, salad dressings, hamburger buns, macaroni and cheese, frozen pizza . . . the list goes on and on. And the name? *High Fructose* Corn Syrup? That should give you a clue about its effects on our bodies. It is to diabetes and obesity what fertilizer is to a garden.

Where Do We Go From Here?

So here are a few final thoughts.   48

1. Yes, it would be beneficial for   49 people with obesity-related health problems to exercise more and eat less. Particularly, it would benefit them to concentrate their shopping on the perimeter° of the supermarket, where the roughly 20 percent of the supermarket's foods that are unprocessed (fresh fruits, vegetables, meats, fish) reside. In addition, it would benefit us all to learn to cook from-scratch meals that utilize whole grains and unprocessed fruits and vegetables.

2. The kind of changes needed to   50 bring about #1 will require time, effort, and education. We've been raised in a culture that values convenience above all things. Many of us don't know how to cook. The idea of giving up our Lunchables and Velveeta Shells & Cheese, our Coca-Cola and Froot Loops is abhorrent°. And why wouldn't it be? We've grown up watching nearly

5,000 food ads a year, each scientifically calibrated° to appeal to our youthful appetites.

51   But think about this. If a foreign enemy were sneaking a substance into our food that caused skyrocketing rates of diabetes, heart disease, obesity, and hypertension, creating an unprecedentedly° huge public health crisis that would tax our medical system to its utmost and had the potential to cripple our economy, would we expect our government to do something in response?

52   Why does the American food industry get a free pass when it is— quite openly—doing the same thing?

53   Government regulation of dangerous substances is not a new thing. Our government has played a role in regulating the distribution of two other toxic substances: alcohol and tobacco. It has acknowledged that depending upon "personal responsibility" is not an adequate response for substances that can inflict such serious social damage.

54   It is time for the government to step up to the plate in a similar way regarding sugar. It should take a variety of steps, including the following:

55 • Limit the amount of sugar added to processed foods.

56 • Require explicit°, easily understood labeling on processed foods, showing their natural *and* added sugar content.

57 • Impose sugar taxes to raise the costs of highly sweetened foods.

58 • Ban advertisements of sugary foods aimed at children.

59 • Ban the use of HFCS.

60   The idea that we've "chosen" to become a sick, obese society is a cynical lie, happily promoted by the processed-food industry. "Freedom of choice" and "personal responsibility" are meaningless concepts when our food environment has been dramatically manipulated—some might say *poisoned*—and the government has turned a blind eye. For the sake of generations to come, we must educate ourselves about the sugar-coated toxins in our foods—and demand action.

First Impressions

Freewrite for ten minutes on one of the following.

1. Did you enjoy reading this selection? Why or why not?

2. Did any of the facts or statistics in this selection surprise you? Which ones?

3. Will you make any changes in your own shopping and eating habits after reading this essay? Why or why not?

Vocabulary Check

_____A_____ 1. In the excerpt below, the word *insidious* means

    A. harmful.

    B. unreal.

    C. positive.

    D. calming.

> If fructose actually stops the brain from getting an important message, what kind of effect does it have?

"You already know that fructose contributes to insulin resistance. But it has another insidious effect: it actually *blocks* leptin from reaching the brain. Without leptin, the brain never gets the message, 'Stop eating.'" (Paragraph 20)

_____B_____ 2. In the excerpt below, the word *implementing* means

    A. preventing.

    B. putting into effect.

    C. advertising.

    D. explaining.

> If the FDA "gave in" to the food industry, what did it *not* do to its proposed requirements for warning labels?

"When the FDA has requested such labeling, the food processors have responded that . . . their competitors could copy their formulas. Again, the FDA gave in to the food industry and backed off implementing requirements for sugar." (Paragraph 35)

_____D_____ 3. In the sentence below, the word *insatiable* means

    A. irregular.

    B. decreasing.

    C. easily satisfied.

    D. unable to be satisfied.

> If people are addicted to a substance, their hunger for it will not be satisfied.

"Because it is so cheap, and because the food processors understand so well consumers' insatiable hunger for (and possibly even addiction to) sweets, HFCS is turning up in the most unlikely places." (Paragraph 47)

Reading Check

Central Point and Main Ideas

_____C_____ 1. Which sentence best expresses the central point of the entire selection?

Answers A, B, and D are each too narrow. Answer A covers only paragraphs 6–8. Answer B covers only paragraphs 46–47. Answer D covers only paragraph 44.

    A. Many Americans are overweight because they eat too much and don't exercise enough, but these are not the only reasons.

    B. Although high fructose corn syrup is found in many foods, consuming large amounts of it is harmful to one's health.

    C. The food processing industry is harming our health by getting us addicted to foods that contain too much added sugar.

    D. Because of the influence of professional lobbyists, our government has done little to regulate the food processing industry.

___A___ 2. The main idea of paragraph 45 is found in its
  A. first sentence.
  B. second sentence.
  C. third sentence.
  D. last sentence.

> The first sentence indicates that HFCS is the most popular sweetener used by the food industry. The other sentences in the paragraph support this statement.

Supporting Details

___C___ 3. Brain scans reveal that a large dose of sugar has the same effect on the brain as
  A. a glass of wine.
  B. smoking a cigarette.
  C. cocaine.
  D. a cup of coffee.

> See paragraph 42.

___B___ 4. Which of the following is **not** a reason that the food industry adds HFCS to foods?
  A. It is both cheaper and sweeter than cane sugar.
  B. It is more easily digested than cane sugar.
  C. It makes baked goods look more appetizing.
  D. It increases the shelf life of processed foods.

> See paragraphs 45–46.

Inferences

___B___ 5. The implied main idea of paragraphs 22–27 is that

> Answer A covers only paragraph 24. Answer C covers only paragraph 25. Answer D covers only paragraph 26.

  A. our ancestors needed to consume sugary foods to survive demanding life stages like puberty, pregnancy, and nursing, but we don't.
  B. manufacturers of processed foods are taking advantage of our hard-wired craving for sugar by adding sugar to packaged foods.
  C. although our craving for sweets hasn't diminished, we don't need to consume them as much as we used to.
  D. most of the packaged foods available to consumers include added sugar.

___B___ 6. The fact that there are forty-plus names for fructose that show up on food labels suggests that

> Paragraphs 28–36 illustrate how difficult it is for consumers to know how much sugar they are consuming. Answer A is contradicted by the last part of paragraph 35. Answer C is contradicted by paragraph 29.

  A. most American consumers have become very knowledgeable about different types of sugar.
  B. it can be difficult for American consumers to know just how much sugar they are consuming.
  C. the U.S. government strictly regulates the amount of each type of sugar that processed foods contain.
  D. all of the above.

___A___ 7. The selection suggests that

Answer A is
suggested in
paragraph 19.
Answers B and C
are not supported.

A. it's healthier to eat bananas and other naturally sweet fruits than processed foods containing high fructose corn syrup.
B. everyone should gradually reduce their consumption of sugary foods to zero.
C. people who consume high fructose corn syrup will definitely develop Type 2 diabetes.
D. all of the above.

The Writer's Craft

The idea
that Americans
are overweight
because they're lazy
(paragraphs 1–6) is
contradicted by the
facts about the food
industry's practices.

___B___ 8. Which of the following best describes how the writer introduces this selection?

A. She makes a broad statement that narrows down to a specific point.
B. She introduces an idea that is the opposite of the point of the selection.
C. She asks a series of challenging questions.
D. She provides an anecdote that illustrates her central point.

___D___ 9. Carlin supports her central point with

For answer A, see
paragraphs 14–21.
For answer B, see
paragraphs 22–25.
For answer C, see
paragraphs 37–47.

A. facts about the effects of sugar on the human body.
B. reasons that people crave sugar in the foods they eat.
C. details revealing the food industry's plan to keep Americans addicted to sugar.
D. all of the above.

___C___ 10. Which of the following statements best describes the writer's purpose?

A. To inform overweight people that being overweight is not entirely their fault
B. To entertain readers with outrageous examples of the many ways that food manufacturers sneak sugar into processed foods
C. To persuade readers to push the government to regulate how much added sugar goes into processed foods and to ban the use of HFCS
D. To criticize American consumers for not taking the time to learn just how much added sugar goes into processed foods

For the selection's persuasive purpose, see paragraphs 51–60
and, especially, the last sentence of paragraph 60.

Discussion Questions

1. Do you have any idea how much sugar you consume on an average day? Do you suspect the amount is higher than is good for you? What are some ways you would be willing to lower your sugar intake?

2. According to the head of General Mills, the processed-food industry bears no responsibility for damaging Americans' health because it is "simply giving shoppers what they want." Do you agree with his opinion? Why or why not? Cite evidence from the selection to support your response.

3. The author makes several suggestions to consumers—including encouraging them to shop the perimeter of supermarkets and to learn to cook from-scratch meals using natural ingredients. Do you think the people you know would be willing to change their shopping and eating habits in response to these recommendations? Would you? Why or why not?

4. Given the power of the food industry, do you think it's likely that the government will ever regulate sugar in the same way it regulates tobacco and alcohol? What steps would have to be taken to make such regulation occur? Would you be willing to take part in such an effort? Explain.

Paragraph Assignments

1. How did your family eat as you were growing up? Were there lots of fast food and processed foods? Were soda and fruit punch in the refrigerator? Or did you eat fresh vegetables, whole grains, and fresh fruit? Write a paragraph in which you describe your family's diet. Then add whether this is a diet you want to stick with in your own life, or if there are changes you'd like to make.

2. At the end of her essay, Carlin concludes that not only has our food environment been dangerously manipulated, but the government has refused to deal with this crisis. She also explains that many government officials are persuaded to ignore the problem by highly paid lobbyists who work for the food industry. Essentially, then, the government has put money and politics ahead of the best interests of American citizens.

   Can you think of another instance or issue where the government has refused to do the right thing? Write a paragraph about this situation. Your paragraph can focus on either something that the federal government has ignored or something disregarded by your local or state government.

Essay Assignments

1. Today, the majority of Americans are overweight, and one in three is obese (weighing 20 percent more than normal body weight standards). Although hidden and unhealthy sugar in the foods we eat clearly adds to our nation's weight problem, it is obviously not entirely to blame. Carlin points out other factors that can lead to weight gain: too much food, too little exercise, and unwillingness or inability to cook—things that "require time, effort, and education."

   Think about your own health. Whether or not you're overweight, what are three things you could change or work on in your life to improve your health and/or weight? Then write an essay that presents your three ideas for improving your health/weight. Your thesis could be something similar to this: "My health would definitely be better if I paid more attention to three specific areas of my life."

2. Carlin writes, "We've been raised in a culture that values convenience above all things." Most Americans do seem to prefer doing everything as quickly and painlessly as possible. Some might argue that conveniences such as drive-through restaurants or microwave ovens or instant foods are beneficial because they free up time for more important things. On the other hand, others might argue that our reliance on convenience makes us lazy.

   Write an essay that supports one of the following thesis statements:

   - Increasing our dependence on modern conveniences may be harmful at times.

     or

   - Modern conveniences are good things that benefit us.

   In the body of your essay, present three examples of modern conveniences that help support your thesis. In each paragraph, describe how these conveniences are either beneficial or detrimental to society.

40 Young and Isolated
Jennifer M. Silva

Preview

Is the so-called American Dream dying? For young working-class men and women, the dream already appears to be dead. There was a time when education and hard work naturally translated to a bright future. But for many of today's young people, there seems to be no hope for any kind of decent future at all.

Words to Watch

embody (5): represent
deindustrialization (5): removal or reduction of industry
venture (11): project, undertaking
milquetoast (11): someone who can be easily controlled
rendered (13): made
empathy (15): understanding
solidarity (18): unity

1 In a working-class neighborhood in Lowell, Mass., in early 2009, I sat across the table from Diana, then 24, in the kitchen of her mother's house. Diana had planned to graduate from college, marry, buy a home in the suburbs, and have kids, a dog and a cat by the time she was 30. But she had recently dropped out of a nearby private university after two years of study and with nearly $80,000 in student loans. Now she worked at Dunkin' Donuts.

2 "With college," she explained, "I would have had to wait five years to get a degree, and once I get that, who knows if I will be working and if I would find something I wanted to do. I don't want to be a cop or anything. I don't know what to do with it. My manager says some people are born to make coffee, and I guess I was born to make coffee."

3 Young working-class men and women like Diana are trying to figure out what it means to be an adult in a world of disappearing jobs, soaring education costs, and shrinking social support networks. Today, only 20 percent of men and women between 18 and 29 are married. They live at home longer, spend more years in college,

change jobs more frequently, and start families later.

4   For more affluent young adults, this may look a lot like freedom. But for the hundred-some working-class 20- and 30-somethings I interviewed between 2008 and 2010 in Lowell and Richmond, Va., at gas stations, fast-food chains, community colleges, and temp agencies, the view is very different.

5   Lowell and Richmond embody° many of the structural forces, like deindustrialization° and declining blue-collar jobs, that frame working-class young people's attempts to come of age in America today. The economic hardships of these men and women, both white and black, have been well documented. But often overlooked are what the sociologists Richard Sennett and Jonathan Cobb in 1972 called their "hidden injuries"—the difficult-to-

measure social costs borne by working-class youths as they struggle to forge stable and meaningful adult lives.

6   These are people bouncing from one temporary job to the next; dropping out of college because they can't figure out financial aid forms or fulfill their major requirements; relying on credit cards for medical emergencies; and avoiding romantic commitments because they can take care of only themselves. Increasingly disconnected from institutions of work, family, and community, they grow up by learning that counting on others will only hurt them in the end. Adulthood is not simply being delayed but dramatically reimagined along lines of trust, dignity, and connection and obligation to others.

7   Take Jay, for example. He was expelled from college for failing several

classes after his mother suffered a severe mental breakdown. He worked for a year, then went before the college administration and petitioned to be reinstated. He described it as a humiliating experience: "It's their jobs to hear all these sob stories, you know, I understand that, but they just had this attitude, like you know what I mean, 'Oh, your mom had a breakdown and you couldn't turn to anyone?'"

8   Jay got back in and graduated (after a total of seven years of college). But when I talked to him, he was still working food-service and coffee-shop jobs at 28, baffled about how to turn his communications major into a professional job. He felt as if he was sold fake goods: "The world is at my fingertips, you can rule the world, be whatever you want, all this stuff. When I was 15, 16, I would not have envisioned the life I am living now. Whatever I imagined, I figured I would wear a suit every day, that I would own things. I don't own anything."

9   I heard many people express feeling betrayed by the major institutions in their lives, whether colleges, the health care system, employers, or the government.

10   Christopher, who was 25, stated simply, "Well, I have this problem of being tricked." He explained: "Like, I will get a phone call that says, you won a free supply of magazines. And they will start coming to my house. Then all of a sudden I am getting calls from bill collectors for the subscriptions to *Maxim* and *ESPN*. It's a runaround: I can't figure out who to call. Now I don't

even pick up the phone, like I almost didn't pick up when you called me." He described isolation as the only safe path; by depending on no one, Christopher protected himself from trickery and betrayal.

11   These fears seep into the romantic sphere, where commitment becomes yet another risky venture°. Kelly, a 28-year-old line cook, spent 10 years battling depression and living off and on in her car. She finally had a job and an apartment of her own. But now she was worried about risking that hard-earned sense of security by letting someone else into her life. "I like the idea of being with someone," she said, "but I have a hard time imagining trusting anybody with all of my personal stuff." She said she would "rather be alone and fierce than be in a relationship and be milquetoast°."

12   Men often face a different challenge: the impossibility of living up to the male provider role. Brandon, who worked the night shift at a clothing store, described what he thought it would be like to be in a relationship with him: "No woman wants to sit on the couch all the time and watch TV and eat at Burger King. I can only take care of myself."

13   It is not that these men and women don't value family. Douglas, then 25, talked about loss: "Trust is gone. The way people used to love is gone." Rather, the insecurities and uncertainties of their daily lives have rendered° commitment a luxury they can't afford.

14   But these young men and women don't want your pity—and they don't expect a handout. They are quick to

blame themselves for the milestones they have not achieved. Julian, an Army vet from Richmond who was unemployed, divorced, and living with his mother at 28, dismissed the notion that his lack of success was anyone's fault but his own: "At the end of the day, looking in the mirror, I know where all my shortcomings come from. From the things that I either did not do or I did and I just happened to fail at them." Kelly echoed that: "No one else is going to fix me but me."

15   This self-sufficiency, while highly prized in our culture, has a dark side: it leaves little empathy° to spare for those who cannot survive on their own.

16   Wanda, a young woman with big dreams of going to college, expressed virulent anger toward her parents, a tow-truck driver and a secretary, for not being able to pay her tuition: "I feel like it's their fault that they don't have nothing." Rather than build connections with those who struggled alongside her, Wanda severed relationships and willed herself not to be "weak-minded" like her parents: "If my mentality were different, then most definitely I would just be stuck like them."

17   Working-class youths come to believe that if they have to make it on their own, then everyone else should, too. Powerless to achieve external markers of adulthood like marriage or a steady job, they instead measure their progress by cutting ties, turning inward, and numbing themselves emotionally.

18   We don't want to go back to the 1950s, when economic stability and social solidarity° came at the cost of exclusion for many Americans. But nor can we afford the social costs of going forward on our present path of isolation. The social and economic decline of the American working class will only be exacerbated as its youngest members make a virtue out of self-blame, distrust, and disconnection. In order to tell a different kind of coming-of-age story, we need to provide these young men and women with the skills and support to navigate the road to adulthood. Our future depends on it.

First Impressions

Freewrite for ten minutes on one of the following.

1. Did you enjoy reading this selection? Why or why not?

2. Are you, or is someone you know, currently dealing with student loans? How long do you think it will take to pay these loans back?

3. Let's say you'd like to reach out to one of the people described in "Young and Isolated." What suggestions would you make to _____ (*fill in the person's name*) that might help him or her feel less alone and powerless?

Vocabulary Check

_____A_____ 1. In the excerpt below, the word *affluent* means
   A. wealthy.
   B. lazy.
   C. intelligent.
   D. spoiled.

> People who are working (usually for minimum wage) at gas stations and fast-food chains are the opposite of wealthy.

"Today, only 20 percent of men and women between 18 and 29 are married. They live at home longer, spend more years in college, change jobs more frequently, and start families later.

"For more affluent young adults, this may look a lot like freedom. But for the hundred-some working-class 20- and 30-somethings I interviewed between 2008 and 2010 in Lowell and Richmond, Va., at gas stations, fast-food chains, community colleges, and temp agencies, the view is very different." (Paragraphs 3–4)

_____C_____ 2. In the sentence below, the word *forge* means
   A. imagine.
   B. decide on.
   C. build.
   D. copy.

> The youths would want to build stable and meaningful lives. The entire selection is about their difficulty in building a meaningful life.

"But often overlooked are what the sociologists Richard Sennett and Jonathan Cobb in 1972 called their 'hidden injuries'—the difficult-to-measure social costs borne by working-class youths as they struggle to forge stable and meaningful adult lives." (Paragraph 5)

_____D_____ 3. In the sentence below, the word *virulent* means
   A. amused.
   B. vague.
   C. sick.
   D. strong.

> Wanda's statement blaming her parents shows that her anger is strong.

"Wanda, a young woman with big dreams of going to college, expressed virulent anger toward her parents, a tow-truck driver and a secretary, for not being able to pay her tuition: 'I feel like it's their fault that they don't have nothing.'" (Paragraph 16)

_____A_____ 4. In the excerpt below, the word *exacerbated* means

A. made worse.

B. improved.

C. prevented.

D. explained.

> Young people's self-blame, distrust, and disconnection would make the social and economic decline worse.

"But nor can we afford the social costs of going forward.... The social and economic decline of the American working class will only be exacerbated as its youngest members make a virtue out of self-blame, distrust, and disconnection." (Paragraph 18)

Reading Check

Central Point and Main Ideas

_____D_____ 1. Which sentence best expresses the central point of the entire selection?

Answer A covers only paragraph 14. Answer B covers only paragraph 5. Answer C covers only paragraph 3. Answer D is supported by the entire selection and emphasized in the concluding paragraph.

A. Today's working-class young people often blame themselves for not being more successful.

B. A shortage of blue-collar jobs is making it difficult for many young people to live on their own.

C. Because working-class young people are having such a hard time finding good jobs, they are putting off getting married and starting families.

D. Our society needs to help young working-class men and women who are struggling to build meaningful lives.

_____B_____ 2. The implied main idea of paragraphs 5–6 is that

Answer A covers only part of paragraph 5. Answer C is not supported. Answer D covers only part of paragraph 6.

A. Lowell and Richmond are two communities that have been hard hit by deindustrialization and a lack of blue-collar jobs.

B. because so many young people today are struggling economically, they are becoming less able to lead traditional adult lives.

C. there have been many studies done on the economic problems of today's working-class youths.

D. many young people today take temp jobs, drop out of college, use credit cards to pay for medical emergencies, and avoid commitments.

Supporting Details

_____D_____ 3. The author presents which of the following as an example of a structural force that shapes people's lives?

A. The fact that many young people are putting off marriage

B. A decline in the willingness to trust others

C. A refusal to accept personal responsibility for mistakes

D. A decline in the number of blue-collar jobs   See paragraph 5.

___D___ 4. According to the author, many of today's working-class young people
  A. blame the government for their problems.
  B. don't value family the way earlier generations did.
  C. still believe that their situations will improve over time.
  D. blame only themselves for their problems.   See paragraph 14.

Inferences

___C___ 5. The reading suggests that today's working-class young people

None of the young people interviewed say anything about social forces. They directly or indirectly blame themselves.

  A. recognize that their lives are being shaped by forces beyond their control.
  B. find a sense of freedom in putting off marriage.
  C. don't realize that social forces beyond their control are making life more difficult for them.
  D. are willing to help out those less fortunate than they are.

___C___ 6. Paragraphs 7 and 8 suggest that Jay

He feels as if he was sold fake goods. His hard work to complete college got him nowhere, and he has nothing.

  A. would not be working food-service if he hadn't been expelled from college.
  B. should not have gone back to college.
  C. feels bitter and frustrated about his life so far.
  D. believes that his life will improve sometime soon.

___B___ 7. We can infer from paragraphs 14–17 that today's working-class young people
  A. will eventually succeed if they try hard enough.
  B. aren't succeeding, no matter how hard they try.
  C. aren't as mentally strong as their parents' generation.
  D. refuse to look honestly at their own shortcomings.
          They feel powerless to achieve the "external markers of adulthood."
  Answer A is not supported. Answer C is contradicted by paragraph 16.
          Answer D is contradicted by paragraph 14.

The Writer's Craft

___B___ 8. Which method of introduction does the author use in this selection?
  A. Going from the broad to the narrow
  B. Telling a brief story
  C. Shifting to the opposite
  D. Asking a series of questions
          In paragraphs 1–2, Silva tells the story of Diana.

Silva summarizes the cause and effect in paragraph 18, sentence 3. Social and economic decline in the working class causes self-blame, distrust, and isolation in young men and women.
In turn, this emotional numbing will cause the social and economic decline to get worse.

_____B_____ 9. In general, this essay is organized according to which of the following patterns?

  A. Listing order: a list of the reasons why many working-class young people are struggling in our culture

  B. Cause-effect: explaining why many working-class young people are having difficulty building meaningful lives

  C. Comparison-contrast: comparing and contrasting working-class young people with more affluent young people who have more opportunities

  D. Time order: following a sequence of events in the lives of several young adults

_____D_____ 10. The tone of the last paragraph of the selection is

  A. detached.

  B. matter-of-fact.

  C. frightened.

  D. concerned.

Words such as *Our future depends on it* show a tone of concern.

Discussion Questions

1. Overall, the author presents a rather grim picture of the lives of today's working-class young people. Do you think her picture is accurate? Have you or has anyone you know had similar struggles?

2. In the selection, a young man named Christopher describes isolation as "the only safe path." Another young person, Kelly, says that she would "rather be alone and fierce than be in a relationship and be milquetoast." Might there be any negative consequences to becoming isolated? If so, what might they be?

3. How do you think today's world is different from the world of your parents? Was it in some ways easier for them than it has been for you? Or do you think that, for the most part, their world was harder? Explain.

4. According to the author, many working-class young people believe that "if they have to make it on their own, then everyone else should, too." Do you agree that it's up to the individual to make it on his or her own? Or are there things that society can do to help? Explain.

Paragraph Assignments

1. A number of young people interviewed in this essay point out that the lives they're living are far from the lives they thought they'd be living as adults. Think about your own life. Is the life you're living now similar to or different from what you had envisioned when you were younger? Is it better or worse than what you had imagined? Do you think it might eventually become the life you thought you'd be leading? Write a paragraph in which you explore these questions.

2. Consider Christopher's story in paragraph 10. He claims that he keeps getting "tricked," and that the only way to avoid this trickery is to isolate himself and depend on no one. Do you agree that if one feels as though he is constantly being taken advantage of, his best option is to shut himself off from everyone and everything? How might Christopher handle this situation differently? Write a paragraph that either explains why Christopher's approach is best or presents an alternative way of dealing with the problem.

Essay Assignments

1. Silva points out that the experiences of more affluent young adults are quite different from the experiences of young people who come from working-class backgrounds. Young people whose families have more money often have more opportunities, more financial support, and a safety net in place if plans should fall through. These advantages shape both their lives and the way they think about their lives. Young people from a working-class background, as we learn in this essay, rarely have the same benefits.

   Think of two people you've known who come from different backgrounds, and write an essay comparing and contrasting three different aspects of their lives. You might consider such things as their day-to-day lives, their surroundings, their relationships with friends and family, and the ways they think of themselves and their futures. Use specific details to make your comparison/contrast more vivid. You might also want to use dialogue from conversations that you've had with these two friends.

2. In the selection, the author suggests that society as a whole bears responsibility for helping working-class youth overcome the challenges they face. In your opinion, should government play a role in helping individuals overcome the obstacles they are facing, or should responsibility rest with the individual? Write an essay supporting your position.

   Your thesis might be similar to one of these:

   - Government should play a leading role in helping young people overcome economic hardships.

   or

   - Whatever life brings, it is primarily up to the individual to look after himself or herself.

   You may find it helpful to research this topic by Googling "role of government and individuals."

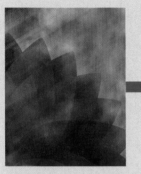

Unit Six

Writing a Research Paper with Sources

41 The Research Paper

Research: In a Nutshell

For some papers that you write, you can develop your point simply by drawing upon your personal knowledge and experience. For other papers, you will want to support your point by using outside sources as well. Most often, those outside sources will be in the form of books and articles.

The best source for books will be a school or local library or an online book site such as Amazon or Barnes and Noble. (At both sites, you can often order an inexpensive used copy of a given book title.) The best source for articles, as pointed out on page 28, is simply going online and using the search engine Google (www.google.com). For example, if you Googled the general topic of "inequality in America," you would find *more than 22 million articles*! Just looking at several of those articles could help you begin to think about how to narrow down and limit the topic. As you will see in the model paper that follows, one student decided to focus his paper on the causes and effects of financial inequality in America today.

Two Cautions about Using Outside Sources

1   As mentioned on page 28, never for a moment believe that "If it's on the Internet, it must be true." Technology today allows anyone to publish anything at any time. For any given article that you find, you must clearly identify its author or source. Moreover, that author or source should be a *knowledgeable, qualified, and reliable authority* for the data presented. Look at the credentials cited, and use your common sense to make sure you are getting legitimate examples, solid facts and/or statistics, and expert opinion.

2   When you are writing your paper, you must take care not to *plagiarize*—that is, to use another author's words and ideas as your own. If you cite another author's words, enclose those words in quotation marks and indicate the source. If you cite another author's ideas, indicate the source. The model paper that follows will show you how to document another person's or source's words or ideas. By using citations, you demonstrate that your work has been carefully researched. See the "Guide to Documentation" on pages 445–446.

A Model Research Paper with Sources

Double-space; leave 1″ margin on all four sides

Martinez 1

Joseph Martinez

Dr. Williams

English 101

26 November 2014

The Problem of Inequality

Title (centered)

    Imagine that you are at the starting line of a race. There are one hundred racers, and you hope you have a shot at winning. But when the starting gun is fired, only one runner is allowed to move forward. In fact, he is allowed to run nearly to the finish line before most runners can even start. What's more, none of the officials say anything about it! Unfortunately, it appears such inequality has become the norm in America today. The financial difference between the super-rich 1 percent of Americans and the 99 percent of the rest of us has made it difficult for many to move forward at all. They remain at the starting line.

    To begin with, let's take a look at how far apart the 1 percent is from the 99 percent. The "1 percent" is the percentage of people in the United States who earn the most money and have the most assets. "Assets" are the possessions that make up someone's wealth, like property, investments, and so on. In 2012, it was estimated that 1.2 million Americans (roughly 1 percent of wage earners) earned an average household income of $717,000 a year, while the average household income of the other 99 percent was around $51,000. (Dunn)

In-text citation

    The greatest inequality is seen in the top 1/10th of the 1 percent. The 400 richest individuals in this group control more wealth in America than the bottom half of all earners in our country (150 million people) combined (Reich xiii). Many of these multi-billionaires earn many thousands of times a day what the average American worker earns in a year; in fact, the average CEO's salary is 380 times the salary of the average worker (Wealth). To put things into perspective, consider financial tycoon John Paulson. In 2010, he made $2.4 million *an hour*! It would take someone earning $50,000 a year for 47 years to earn what Mr. Paulson earned

Martinez 2

in one hour (Hayes 142). Another example is the Walton family of Wal-Mart fame. The six heirs to the Wal-Mart fortune are worth as much as the bottom 41 percent of American households put together (Kristof).

When so much of the wealth in our country is in the pockets of so few people, the middle class (most Americans) suffers and begins to shrink. People don't have as much money as they used to have, so they take out loans and mortgages and go into debt. And when there's too much debt and wealth imbalance, eventually the national economy crashes. This is what happened during the "Great Recession" of 2008. The only economic collapse that was worse in the history of our country was the Great Depression of the 1930s, and in both periods the crashes were preceded by 1 percent of Americans controlling most of the national wealth (*Inequality for All*).

Recovery from the Great Recession of 2008 has been slow to nonexistent, mainly because the divide between the very wealthy and the rest of us has remained so huge. It has been estimated that America now has more wealth inequality than any other industrialized and democratic country (Hayes 60). On the wealth inequality worldwide scale, the United States ranks below Iran and just above Mexico (Domhoff).

The gap between the 1 percent and the 99 percent has widened over the past thirty to forty years for a number of reasons. For one thing, the richest people in the United States pay the *least* amount of tax. Today, the wealthy pay less than half of what they paid in taxes in the 1950s. In addition, taxes on corporations dropped from about 30 percent in the 1950s to 10 percent by 2011 (Nahigyan). Many politicians believed that lowering taxes on the rich would encourage the wealthy to reinvest their money in the economy, thereby increasing employment and opportunities. It was claimed that in this way, money would "trickle down" from the rich to the middle class. But in fact the wealthiest people in our country are not investing in new companies that create jobs—they're investing in investments on Wall Street and in big banks. In other words, their money is staying in their own pockets and their own accounts. The only thing tax cuts for the wealthy have done is to make the rich richer. As former Secretary of Labor Robert Reich explains, "Trickle-down economics is a cruel joke. . . . The rich don't create jobs. Jobs are created when the vast majority of Americans buy enough to make companies add capacity and hire more workers" (Reich 93–94).

Meanwhile, as the rich have gotten richer, most Americans have gotten poorer. Today's minimum wage, at $7.24 an hour, has actually declined in value by more than 12 percent in the past 40 years (Mishel, 279–80). That means living in or near poverty for millions of Americans. In 2010, it was estimated that over 46 million Americans lived in poverty—the most in 52 years (Smith 70). Furthermore, with the majority of wealth in the hands of only an extremely small number of Americans, businesses suffer because fewer and fewer people have money to spend. This lack of spending, in turn, results in layoffs, lowered wages, fewer benefits, and higher job insecurity. When people spend money and the middle class is strong, the result is a healthy economy. But today, because of the inequality between the very wealthy few and the weak middle class, the United States's economy is doing poorly.

Actually, a broken economy due to wealth inequality makes it harder for many Americans to move ahead at all. Because the people with the bulk of the wealth in our country are paying very little tax on it, there is much less money for the federal government to spend. This means that funding for all types of public programs has been reduced. In particular, funding for education has been cut, and college tuitions have skyrocketed. Today, nearly 75 percent of students entering the nation's top universities come from the country's richest families, while only 3 percent come from the poorest families (Mishel 158). And since education is one of the main keys to opportunity and moving ahead, the greatest chances for moving ahead are overwhelmingly awarded to the children of wealthy parents.

Today, children of poor parents have a far smaller chance of being better off than their own parents than did young people in past generations. A child born into wealth is seven times more likely to be successful than a child born into the bottom percentage of earners (Hayes 61). "Starting at the bottom of the earnings ladder is more of a handicap in the United States than in other countries," social scientist Julia Isaacs pointed out in 2012 (Smith 71). Although 70 percent of Americans still believe in the dream of working from rags to riches—the hard facts are proving otherwise (Stiglitz 21). The opportunity to achieve the American Dream depends far more on the economic status one is born into than on one's desire and will to achieve.

There are still those who "blame" the poor (or even the middle class) for their plight. In 2011, for example, presidential candidate Herman Cain voiced what many conservatives believe when he said: "Don't blame Wall Street, don't blame the big banks. If you don't have a job and you're not rich, blame yourself! It is not a person's fault because they succeeded; it is a person's fault if they failed" (Bingham). What Cain and others do not acknowledge is the ever-dwindling opportunity for success amid joblessness, unfair pay, a shrinking middle class, and a weak economy. The poor have not "failed." Most have not even had the chance to *try*, much less fail. While some continue to believe that poor people deserve to be in the position they're in because they are lazy and "take advantage" of government assistance, the fact remains that nearly half the households receiving assistance include at least one working adult (Johnson). And because of the low minimum wage, many poor people work two jobs and still find it a struggle to make ends meet.

Why don't our officials do something about this inequality? It doesn't seem to make sense. "The problem is Wall Street's excessive power," writes Reich. "[It] is the most powerful industry in America with the closest ties to the federal government . . . routinely bankrolling congressional kingpins" (59). The fact is that money buys campaign donations, lobbyists, favors, and more. Many political decisions that affect the 99 percent—like continuing the outrageous tax breaks for the wealthy—are strongly influenced by the 1 percent. It probably doesn't help that nearly half of the members of Congress are millionaires themselves. Many of them are clearly out of touch with the population they are supposedly representing.

So what can be done? Many people fear that America is in real danger of becoming a plutocracy, a society that is governed by its wealthiest members. According to Joseph Stiglitz, a Nobel Prize winner in economics, the first and most obvious steps are to be aware of what is really happening in our country and to stop listening to the 1 percent. It is extremely important that we realize that there *are* alternatives to the direction in which our country is headed. "The 1 percent has worked hard to convince the rest that an alternative world is not possible; that doing anything the 1 percent doesn't want will inevitably harm the 99 percent," Stiglitz writes (287). The next step is taking action by speaking out, joining others in protest against the unfair (some would argue illegal) advantages of the 1 percent. No one, of course, is claiming that there should be no super-wealthy in the United States or that wealth is to be condemned. Wealth is absolutely necessary in a healthy economy and in a nation that encourages self-motivation, hard work, and free enterprise. However, 1 percent of the population should absolutely *not* control over 40 percent of our nation's wealth (Jilani).

"The great arc of American history reveals an unmistakable pattern," writes Reich. "Whenever privilege and power conspire to pull us backward, we eventually rally and move forward" (137). Protest has changed the course of our history from the American Revolution to the civil rights movement and beyond. Wealth inequality is an injustice that does far more harm than just giving a small percentage of people some special advantages in the race for a better life. It keeps a large percentage of people forever stuck at the starting line. The time to rally and move forward is upon us.

Sources, listed in
alphabetical order
and double-spaced

Works Cited

Bingham, Amy. "Herman Cain Tells Occupy Wall Street Protestors to 'Blame
　　Yourself.'" *ABC News.* ABC News Internet Ventures, 5 Oct. 2011.
　　Web. 15 Nov. 2014.

Domhoff, William G. "Wealth, Income, and Power." *Who Rules America?*
　　University of California at Santa Cruz, Feb. 2013. Web. 15 Nov. 2014.

Dunn, Alan. "Average America vs. the One Percent." *Forbes.* Forbes Incorporated,
　　21 Mar. 2012. Web. 15 Nov. 2014.

Hayes, Christopher. *Twilight of the Elites: America after Meritocracy.* New York:
　　Random House, 2012. Print.

Inequality for All. Dir. Jacob Kornbluth. Anchor Bay Entertainment, 2013. Film.

Jilani, Zaid. "How Unequal We Are." *Think Progress*, n.p. 3 Oct. 2011.
　　Web. 14 Nov. 2014.

Johnson, Melody. "Hannity Omits the 'Food Stamp' Facts." *Media Matters for
　　America*, n.p. 18 Sept. 2012. Web. 14 Nov. 2014.

Kristof, Nicholas. "It's Now the Canadian Dream." *The New York Times*,
　　n.p. 14 May 2014. Web. 14 Nov. 2014.

Mishel, Lawrence, Josh Bivens, Elise Gould, and Heidi Shierholz. *The State of
　　Working America*. Ithaca, New York: Cornell University Press, 2012. Print.

Nahigyan, Pierce. "8 Facts about American Inequality." *Nation of Change*,
　　n.p. 21 Jan. 2014. Web. 14 Nov. 2014.

Reich, Robert B. *Beyond Outrage*. New York: Random House, 2012. Print.

Smith, Hedrick. *Who Stole the American Dream?* New York: Random House,
　　2013. Print.

Stiglitz, Joseph E. *The Price of Inequality*. New York: W.W. Norton & Company,
　　2012. Print.

"Wealth Inequality in America." *New Economy Coalition*, n.p. n.d. Web.
　　14 Nov. 2014.

42 Formatting and Documentation

If asked to do so by your instructor, you can use the Modern Language Association (MLA) formatting and documentation style. This is the style Joseph used for his research paper.

General Formatting Guidelines

When you put together a formal research paper, there is a specific format that you should follow. Unless your instructor indicates that you should use alternative formatting, the following guidelines apply:

- To begin with, use good quality 8½ inch × 11-inch paper when printing out your research paper.

- Make sure the margins on each page are set to 1 inch on all sides. The only exception to the 1-inch margin is the author's last name/page number in the upper right-hand corner of each page ("Martinez 1" on the student paper example). Your last name and the page number should be set ½ inch from the top of every page of your paper, including your Works Cited page.

- Double-space your entire paper, including the Works Cited page.

The first page of your paper will differ from the rest of your paper in these ways:

- In the upper left-hand corner, you will list your name, the name of your instructor, the name of your course, and the date you are turning your paper in. Note that the date is written like this: 26 November 2014. As before, double-space these lines.

- After the date, skip a line, and center the title of your paper on the page. Do not use all capital letters, italics, quotation marks, or boldface in your title. Also, do not underline the title or put a period at the end of it.

- Double-space again between your title and the first line of your paper. Remember to indent the first line of each paragraph.

In-text Citations

Whenever you quote someone or present information that is not widely known, like statistics, new ideas, and facts, you must credit the source of that information. An in-text citation is simply an easy way for the reader to refer to your Works Cited page to see the source you've used. Typically, you will present two types of in-text citations:

- When you have used information from **printed material** (a book or magazine, as opposed to a Web site), you will place the author or editor's last name and the page number where the information was found inside parentheses following the information.

  For example, in the student essay, the second sentence of the third paragraph contains an in-text citation for a book. The author or editor's last name is Reich, and the information was found on page xiii. Now look at the Works Cited page: Robert Reich is the author of the book titled *Beyond Outrage*.

  Note: If you have already given the author or editor's last name in this particular reference, cite only the page number. See the example in the third paragraph on page 4 of Joseph Martinez's paper.

- When you have used information from a **Web site**, you will simply put the author's last name inside parentheses with no page number, since there are typically no numbered pages on Web sites. If the information you use is from an online source that shows no author, put the first word of the title of the article/story inside the parentheses instead.

  For example, look at the in-text citation for "Dunn" at the end of the second paragraph in Joseph Martinez's paper. Referring to the Works Cited page, you can see that Alan Dunn is the author of an article titled "Average America vs. the One Percent" at the Web site for *Forbes* magazine. Then, in the middle of the third paragraph, you will see "Wealth" as an in-text citation. Here, no author's name is given on the New Economy Coalition's Web site, so the first word of the article is used instead.

Remember to put your in-text citations at the very end of the sentence that contains the cited material. Also, put the period outside the parentheses.

A Guide to Documentation

Citing Sources

When exactly should you cite a source? As previously mentioned, any time you present quoted material, or facts and statistics that are not well known, you should cite your source. However, sometimes the definition of what is "not well known" can get a little confusing. For example, think about the Civil War. It is widely known that many thousands of soldiers died. You would not need to back that fact up with a cited source. However, if you wrote, "It is estimated that 620,000 soldiers died in the Civil War," you would need to cite your source. Perhaps a Civil War buff might know that specific statistic, but in general, most people would not.

But what about a fact like "General Robert E. Lee was initially reluctant to lead the Confederate Army"? That's a fairly well-known fact, but there are certainly many people who might be surprised to read that. Should you cite your source or not?

Your best bet is to use a citation whenever you present information that is new and/or surprising to *you*, or when you're unsure whether or not you should cite a source. You may risk having a few more citations than you need, but that's better than risking plagiarism. Still, you want to use common sense and not cite a source for everything in your paper. For example, you may have forgotten that the Civil War lasted from 1861 to 1865, but that is not a new or widely unknown fact. And remember that the whole point of using research in your paper is to back up *your* ideas and point of view. The last thing you want to do is just string together pages of statistics and other people's ideas.

The Works Cited Page

The Works Cited page is the final page of your paper, and it provides all the information needed to verify your sources. There are very specific guidelines when it comes to formatting your Works Cited list, and some students find the details a bit overwhelming and tedious. However, once you've worked through the first few entries, you'll get the general hang of it.

General Guidelines

- Center "Works Cited" at the top of a new page. Even if there is nearly a full page left at the end of your paper, do not begin the Works Cited list on that page.

- Determine whether you are citing a book or a Web site, and follow the specific guidelines (on the next two pages) for each entry.

- Arrange your entries in alphabetical order. As discussed, you will use either the author's last name or, if there is no author listed, the first word of the title of the article/story you have cited.

  Note: Use the first *main* word of the title. If the title begins with an article (*the, an, a*), do not list it by that word. For example, an article titled "The Case for a Higher Minimum Wage" would be alphabetically listed by the word "Case." This is also the word you would use for your in-text citation.

- Double-space everything on the page. Do not add extra spaces between entries. If an entry takes more than one line, indent the second line one-half inch by spacing or by hitting the "tab" key on your keyboard.

Specific Entry Guidelines

Web Site Entries

For an example, look at the first entry on the Works Cited page of Joseph's paper:

> Bingham, Amy. "Herman Cain Tells Occupy Wall Street Protestors to 'Blame
>
> Yourself.'" *ABC News.* ABC News Internet Ventures, 5 Oct. 2011.
>
> Web. 15 Nov. 2014.

In this case, the source is a story from the Web site for *ABC News*. The format for most Web site sources is as follows:

- Type the author's last name first, then a comma, and then the first name. Follow this with a period.

- Next, type the title of the article/story, followed by a period, and put quotation marks before the title and after the period.

- This will be followed by the name of the Web site. Type this in italics, followed by a period.

- Next, provide the name of the publisher. Often, you can find the publishing information near the bottom of the home page of a Web site. Type the publisher's name, and follow it with a comma.

- The date the story/article was written follows the comma. Place a period after the date. Remember that the date is written like this: 15 Nov. 2014. Note that in the Works Cited section, you will abbreviate the month.

- Next, indicate that this source is from the Internet by typing "Web" followed by a period.

- Finally, add the date that you accessed this story on the Web site. Because Web sites change and are updated so frequently, it's important to indicate when you visited the site.

Of course, sometimes not all of the information required is available. If no author is listed, simply begin with the title of the article/story. Sometimes there is no publishing information available, and other times no date is given for when the article was written. In these cases, you will put "n.p." for "no publisher" and "n.d." for "no date." In the final entry of Joseph's Works Cited page, for example, there is no listed author. Additionally, there is neither a publisher nor a date:

> "Wealth Inequality in America." *New Economy Coalition*, n.p. n.d. Web. 14
>
> Nov. 2014.

Book Entries

Book entries tend to be a little less involved than Web site entries because books don't change. The fourth entry on the Works Cited page of Joseph's paper is for a book:

> Hayes, Christopher. *Twilight of the Elites: America after Meritocracy*. New
>
> York: Random House, 2012. Print.

The format for books is as follows:

- Type the author's last name, then a comma, then the first name. Follow this with a period.

- Next, type the title of the book in italics, followed by a period. (Note that if the title ends in punctuation, as in the book by Hedrick Smith later on the page, there is no need for a period.)

- Provide the name of the city where the book was published, followed by a colon.

- Next, give the name of the publisher, followed by a comma, and then the copyright date, followed by a period. Typically, you can find all this information on the copyright page, a page at the very beginning of the book.

- Finally, simply add the word "Print" followed by a period. This is to clearly differentiate your source from a Web source.

If there is more than one author, list the authors in the order in which their names are shown on the book. (Note that the names of the additional authors are typed exactly as they appear on the book, first name before last name.) For example:

> Mishel, Lawrence, Josh Bivens, Elise Gould, and Heidi Shierholz. *The State of*
>
> *Working America*. Ithaca, New York: Cornell University Press, 2012. Print.

If there is an editor rather than an author, simply place a comma and "ed." after the editor's name. For example:

> Pringle, Peter, ed. *A Place at the Table*. New York: Public Affairs, 2013. Print.

As you might expect, there are different guidelines when writing a Works Cited entry for a periodical, an interview, or even a text message. If you need more help with your Works Cited page, there are various Web sites such as the *Purdue Online Writing Lab* that detail the format of nearly every kind of Works Cited entry imaginable.

Additional Writing Assignments

Note: Each of the following fifteen assignments asks students to read two essays from the book and then to write a paper based on both. The assignments are listed in the order in which the first essay in each pair appears in the book.

1 The Scholarship Jacket

A *narrative* is simply a story told in the order in which the events occurred. A first-person narrative like "The Scholarship Jacket" (page 41) has special power, because the writer can tell not only what happened, but also how he or she felt about it. Write a first-person narrative about a memorable event in your life. As Marta Salinas does, use rich sensory details (how things looked, sounded, smelled, tasted, felt) as well as your own emotional responses to make the reader experience the event as you did. Before beginning your paper, read "Shame" (page 207), another example of a vividly detailed first-person narrative.

2 A Small Victory

As shown by the response to Steve Lopez's original column, "A Small Victory" (page 59) evoked strong emotions from the people who read it. Lopez had carefully chosen details to make his readers see Mrs. Knight as he did: a small, frail woman, elderly and dignified, being victimized by a large, faceless bureaucracy.

Write a description of a person who evokes a similarly strong emotional response from you. Your first task will be to state your central point, using a sentence that puts into sharp, tight focus just what the rest of your paper will explain. Your central point might be like one of these:

- My grandmother, although soft-spoken, is the strongest and most determined person I've ever known.

- The man who runs the convenience store in our neighborhood seems as if he carries a grudge against the whole world.

In your paper, provide plentiful details to show your reader just what you mean. As Lopez does, include bits of dialogue, so that your reader can hear your subject in his or her own words.

Before you write, be sure to read "All the Good Things" (page 199), paying special attention to the brief, but sharply drawn, description of Mark Eklund. Notice how the carefully chosen details make clear why Mark was so special to his teacher.

3   Migrant Child to College Woman

In "Migrant Child to College Woman" (page 79), the reader learns of the process Maria Cardenas went through in her transformation from a frightened, barely literate girl to a courageous, successful adult. The essay "Rowing the Bus" (page 235) describes the steps involved in another person's transformation: in this case, from a victim of bullying to a defender of the bullied. Write a paper in which you describe a significant, gradual change that you have gone through (or someone you know has gone through). Use transitional words like *first, next, after that,* and *finally* to emphasize that this change was a process, rather than something that happened in one single step.

4   He Was First

As "He Was First" (page 93) demonstrates, many baseball fans were shocked at first to see black and white athletes playing on the same field. But just a few years later, the children of those fans thought nothing of seeing African American athletes participating in professional sports. This is just one example of how parents' and children's attitudes towards racial issues can differ. How do your racial attitudes differ from the attitudes held by your parents? Are you, for example, more likely to have friends of different races than they are? Do you feel differently about interracial dating and marriage than they do? Write a paper that states how you and your parents differ in your attitudes about race, and give examples illustrating those differences.

(Alternatively, you could write about how you and your parents differ on another important social issue, such as capital punishment, gun control, abortion, women's rights, or gay rights.)

Read the essay "Marijuana Today" (page 387) for some insight into how people of different generations—or the same person at two stages of life—can have very different reactions to a social issue.

5   Responsibility

In his essay (page 141), author Scott Peck provides what is, in a sense, a lengthy definition of the word *responsibility*. He describes what responsibility is, gives vivid examples of irresponsible behavior, and suggests the negative consequences of living without a sense of personal responsibility. Write a paper in which you define another desirable human trait, such as courage, kindness, maturity, wisdom, patience, compassion, perseverance, or tolerance. As Peck does, give your reader clear examples of how people behave when they possess that trait, as well as how they behave when they do not. Before writing, read "Love" (page 267) to see how another writer defines a quality we are all familiar with.

6 The Bystander Effect

In "The Bystander Effect" (page 177), the author relates several well-publicized incidents to make her point that bystanders are reluctant to get involved, even when someone's life seems to be in danger.

Look through recent editions of your local newspaper to find two or three stories in which people act in surprising ways. (Those surprising actions may be either positive or negative.) Write a paper in which you explain what happened in each incident and why you found the people's actions surprising. Then provide your best theory about why the people involved acted as they did. Your theories will be based not only on the facts in the newspaper story, but also on your own observations of human nature.

In "Responsibility" (page 141), psychiatrist Scott Peck illustrates his belief that rather than take responsibility for their own lives, people often act in self-destructive ways. His essay may give you some evidence for your theories.

7 All the Good Things

Write a paper in which you expand on what Sister Helen's students did in "All the Good Things" (page 199). Choose a person whom you like and admire, and select three "good things" about that person. In your paper, state what those "good things" are, and describe in detail how you have seen those things demonstrated in the person's life. Whenever possible, give examples of the "good things" in action. Before writing, read Alex Haley's essay, "Thank You" (page 149) to see how one writer made his readers understand why he valued certain people highly.

8 Shame

In "Shame" (page 207), Dick Gregory relates an incident in which an insensitive teacher humiliated him. Almost everyone has a teacher who stands out in his or her memory, because the teacher was either exceptionally good or remarkably bad. Drawing upon your own experience as a student, write a paper based on one of the following two central points:

- "Everyone should be lucky enough to have a teacher like _____."
- "No one should be forced to learn from a teacher like _____."

In your paper, provide at least three reasons why this teacher was the best or worst you ever had. Support each of those reasons with examples that vividly illustrate the points you are making.

For an example of an experienced, effective teacher, read "The Fist, the Clay, and the Rock" (page 277), paying special attention to the character of Mr. Gery.

9   Adult Children at Home

After reading "Adult Children at Home" (page 217), write a paper in which you suggest at least three guidelines, based on your own experience and observations, for healthy parent-child relationships. Include specific examples of common parent-child conflict, and show how your guidelines would help in such circumstances. Reading "Dealing with Feelings" (page 167) before you begin to write will help you think of ways that parents and children can avoid or resolve painful situations.

10   The Rudeness Epidemic

In "The Rudeness Epidemic" (page 245), Gary Wooten protests the "epidemic" of rudeness he says is sweeping the country. What is another "epidemic" you would like to put a stop to? Perhaps it involves something relatively harmless: clothing that's in bad taste, TV "comedies" that aren't funny, or professional athletes who are overpaid. Or maybe it's something more serious: our nonstop attention to smartphones or the Internet, the widespread politicizing of the news as opposed to straight reporting, the use of commercials to distort the truth about candidates or products, or the tendency of lawmakers to act on behalf of special interests rather than a majority of the American people. Write a paper in which you, like Wooten, criticize your epidemic of choice. Your paper may be either humorous or serious. Feel free to use invented or actual scenarios, as Wooten does, to drive your point home.

Steve Lopez's "A Small Victory" (page 59) will provide you with a serious critique of what the author could have called "an epidemic of bureaucratic stupidity."

11   The Professor Is a Dropout

A catalyst is defined as "an agent that provokes or speeds significant change or action." Although Guadalupe Quintanilla, in "The Professor Is a Dropout" (page 319), was terrified of going back to school, her concern for her children acted as the catalyst that pushed her into action. Write a paper about a catalyst that has pushed you into making some positive change in your life. That catalyst might have been a flash of insight, a remark you heard, something you read, an incident in which you participated or which you learned about second-hand, or any other force that provoked you to action. Explain in detail what the catalyst was and exactly what change you made because of it. You will find an example of a catalyst in "A Door Swings Open" (page 133), in which the author discusses an experience that motivated her to look at life in a new way.

12   The Medium Is the Medium

"The Medium Is the Medium" (page 335) argues that the Internet is producing a generation of short-attention-span students who lack the ability to engage in deep thought. What is another negative effect you think the Internet has on young people? (Or instead of the Internet, you may choose another powerful influence on today's young people, such as advertising, TV, video games, movies, music videos, or popular music.) Write a paper in which you state your concern. Your central point might be something like this: "I am concerned that video games influence young people to become isolated and potentially violent." The rest of your paper will state your reasons and present arguments in support of those reasons. For another essay that presents a writer's arguments against a substance that is part of our everyday lives and that is more harmful than most people realize, read "The Bitter Truth about Sugar" (page 412).

13   Learning Survival Skills

"Learning Survival Skills" (page 343) shares a number of secrets which are valuable for succeeding in school. Write a paper in which you provide secrets of success in another field. You might consider offering tips on how to succeed in the workplace (in general, or within a specific occupation), on an athletic team, in a romantic relationship, in a friendship, or as a neighbor. To see another example of an essay based on a series of suggestions, read "Adult Children at Home" (page 217).

14   My Daughter Smokes

In "My Daughter Smokes" (page 365), Alice Walker describes influences that may cause people to adopt one unhealthy habit: smoking. Write a paper about an unhealthy habit that you find hard to resist. It might, for example, be smoking or drinking, overeating, choosing the wrong foods, not getting enough sleep, or not exercising. In your paper, state what the tempting habit is, several influences that make you want to indulge in that habit, and what you think the consequences of that habit have been for you. The essay "Soft Addictions" (page 187), which discusses three apparently harmless habits that can become all-consuming, may provide some useful insights.

15   A Drunken Ride, a Tragic Aftermath

As "A Drunken Ride, a Tragic Aftermath" (page 374) shows, a single event can have widespread consequences. In this case, an accident has had far-reaching effects on individuals, families, a school, and a town. Write a paper in which you show the connection between a single event—a cause—and its effects. That cause and its effects may have affected just you or a larger community. Before writing, read "A Change of Attitude" (page 285), which describes a specific incident in the author's life and its life-altering effects, to see another example of a cause-effect essay.

Acknowledgments

Text Credits

Barkin, Dorothy. "The Bystander Effect." Reprinted by permission.

Barry, Dave. "The Ugly Truth about Beauty." Originally published as "Beauty and the Beast." From the *Miami Herald*, February 1, 1998. Copyright © 1998 by Dave Barry. Reprinted by permission.

Bashard, Tim. "Soft Addictions." Reprinted by permission.

Berry, Grant. "A Change of Attitude." Reprinted by permission.

Black, Roxanne. "A Door Swings Open." Originally published as "In the Beginning." From *Unexpected Blessings* by Roxanne Black, copyright © 2008 by Roxanne Black. Used by permission of Avery Publishing, an imprint of Penguin Group (USA) Inc.

Bowden, Mark. "Marijuana Today." Reprinted by permission of the author.

Broderick, Bill. "Life Over Death." Reprinted by permission.

Brody, Jane E. "What Causes Hearing Loss." From the *New York Times*, March 26, 2013, © 2013 the *New York Times*. All rights reserved.

Brooks, David. "The Medium Is the Medium." From the *New York Times*, July 9, 2010, © 2010 the *New York Times*. All rights reserved.

Cardenas, Maria. "Migrant Child to College Woman." Reprinted by permission.

Carlin, Emily. "The Bitter Truth about Sugar." Reprinted by permission.

Coleman, Jean. "Learning Survival Skills." Reprinted by permission.

Conroy, Theresa, and Christine M. Johnson. "A Drunken Ride, a Tragic Aftermath." From the *Philadelphia Inquirer*, June 8, 1986. Reprinted by permission of the authors.

Gregory, Dick. "Shame." From *Nigger: An Autobiography*, copyright © 1964 by Dick Gregory Enterprises, Inc. Used by permission of Dutton, a division of Penguin Putnam Inc.

Haley, Alex. "Thank You." Originally published in *Parade* Magazine, November 21, 1982. Copyright © 1982 by Alex Haley.

Hill, Miriam. "Abusive Relationships among the Young." Reprinted by permission.

Hoffman, Gail. "The Blind Vet." Reprinted by permission.

Holbert, Bruce. "Sleeping with Guns." From the *New York Times*, April 28, 2013, © 2013 the *New York Times*. All rights reserved.

Holland, Donald. "The Fist, the Clay, and the Rock." Reprinted by permission.

Johnson, Beth. "Joe Davis: A Cool Man." Reprinted by permission.

Johnson, Beth. "The Professor Is a Dropout." Reprinted by permission.

Kellmayer, John. "He Was First." Reprinted by permission.

Kristof, Nicholas D. "Help Thy Neighbor and Go Straight to Prison." From the *New York Times*, August 11, 2013, © 2013 the *New York Times*. All rights reserved.

Langan, Paul. "Reading to Survive." Reprinted by permission.

Photo Credits

Unit One

Chapter 1, p. 32 © Image Source/SuperStock; Chapter 2, p. 42 © Hal Taylor; Chapter 3, p. 52 courtesy Bill Broderick; Chapter 4, p. 60 © Brian Eichhorn/Shutterstock; Chapter 5, p. 70 courtesy Beth Johnson; Chapter 6, pp. 80 and 87, courtesy Beth Johnson; Chapter 7, p. 94 © AP Photo; Chapter 8, p. 107 © Jack Young-People/Alamy.

Unit Two

Chapter 9, p. 118 © Tyler Olson/Shutterstock; Chapter 10, p. 126 © Rick Smolan/Against All Odds Productions; p. 130 © Jim McHugh, *People Weekly*; Chapter 11, p. 134 © Hal Taylor; Chapter 12, p. 142 © UK Stock Images Ltd./Alamy; Chapter 13, p. 150 © Bettmann/CORBIS; Chapter 14, p. 160 © Avril O'Reilly/Alamy; Chapter 15, p. 168 © Monkey Business Images/Shutterstock; Chapter 16, p. 178 © Andrew Butterton/Alamy; Chapter 17, p. 188 © Monkey Business-Fotolia.com.

Unit Three

Chapter 18, p. 200 © age fotostock/SuperStock; Chapter 19, p. 208 © Corbis Bridge/Alamy; Chapter 20, p. 218 © Kablonk/SuperStock; Chapter 21, p. 226 © Martyn Vickery/Alamy; Chapter 22, p. 236 © Weston Colton/Ruberball/Corbis; Chapter 23, p. 246 © Elena Elisseeva/Alamy; Chapter 24, p. 256 courtesy The Press News Group; Chapter 25, p. 268 © Blend Images/Alamy.

Unit Four

Chapter 26, p. 278 © Stephen Rees/Shutterstock; Chapter 27, p. 286 © Larry Marcus; Chapter 28, p. 297 © Peter Casolino/Alamy; Chapter 29, pp. 306, 313 courtesy Ryan Klootwyk; Chapter 30, pp. 320, 323, 325, 327 courtesy Guadalupe Quintanilla; Chapter 31, p. 336 © Blend Images/Alamy; Chapter 32, p. 344 © Flirt/SuperStock.

Unit Five

Chapter 33, p. 358 © Mike Kemp/In Pictures—Corbis; Chapter 34, p. 366 © CORBIS/SuperStock; Chapter 35, p. 376 © Gunter Marx/AC/Alamy; Chapter 36, p. 389 © Vince Bevan/Alamy; Chapter 37, p. 396 © Album/Prisma/Album/SuperStock; Chapter 38, p. 405 © Kzenon-Fotolia.com; Chapter 39, p. 415 © FDA/Alamy; Chapter 40, p. 426 © Frances Roberts/Alamy.

Index